The Wisconsin Garden Guide

Books by Jerry Minnich

The Wisconsin Garden Guide *(Madison, WI, 1975, 1982)*
The Earthworm Book *(Emmaus, PA, 1977)*
No Time for House Plants *(Norman, OK 1979)*
The Rodale Guide to Composting *(with Marjorie Hunt, Emmaus, PA, 1979)*
Gardening for Maximum Nutrition *(Emmaus, PA 1983)*
The Wisconsin Almanac *(general editor, Madison, WI, 1989)*
Wisconsin With Kids *(with Kristin Visser, Madison, WI, 1991)*
Eating Well in Wisconsin *(Madison, WI, 1993)*

The Wisconsin Garden Guide

Jerry Minnich

PRAIRIE OAK PRESS
Madison, Wisconsin

Third edition, second printing, 1996
Copyright © 1995 by Jerry Minnich
Originally published in 1975 as *A Wisconsin Garden Guide* by Wisconsin House Book Publishers
Second edition published in 1982 by Stanton & Lee Publishers, Inc.
Reissued in 1989 by Heartland Press, an imprint of NorthWord Press, Inc.

Prairie Oak Press
821 Prospect Place
Madison, Wisconsin 53703

Cover photograph by Brent Nicastro
Typeset by KC Graphics, Inc., Madison, Wisconsin
Printed in the United States of America by BookCrafters, Chelsea, Michigan

Library of Congress Cataloging-in-Publication Data

Minnich, Jerry.
     The Wisconsin garden guide / Jerry Minnich. -- 3rd ed.
          p.   cm.
     Includes bibliographical references (p.   ) and index.
     ISBN 1-879483-24-6 : $18.95
     1. Gardening--Wisconsin.   I. Title.
SB453.2.W6M56 1995   95-2342
635'.09775--dc20   CIP

In memory of my father,
Samuel Foelker Minnich
1908–1995

Contents

Tables

Maps

Preface to the Third Edition

The Wisconsin Garden Guide and I have now been together for twenty years. It has been a most pleasant association, one that I hope will continue for as long as this book finds a useful place on the shelves and in the tool sheds of Wisconsin gardeners.

The first edition was published in 1975. I initially proposed the book in 1973 to Mark E. Lefebvre, who was then head of Wisconsin House Book Publishers, in Madison. Mark thought the idea of offering a complete gardening handbook to citizens of this northern state was a good idea. I had been living in Madison since 1965, and had some idea of the challenges facing gardeners here. Not only were there tricks to handling the northern climate, but many of the plant varieties suggested in general garden books and magazines could not be trusted here. The clincher came in mid-March, 1973, when I read in one book that peas should be planted on George Washington's Birthday. Looking outside at fifteen inches of snow on the ground, and laughing bitterly, I decided that Wisconsin definitely needed its own gardening book.

The first edition of the *Wisconsin Garden Guide* went through four printings in the years from 1975 to 1979. I revised the book substantially in 1982, and a new publisher, Stanton & Lee, brought out a second edition in a new and larger format—the one with the bright orange carrots on the front. That edition went through two printings, including one published by NorthWord Press, of Minocqua, Wisconsin, and then the book was allowed to go out of print for several years. Now, in 1995, it returns under the imprint of Prairie Oak Press to celebrate its twentieth anniversary.

Many people ask me where I trained as a horticulturist, where I received my degree. The truth is, I have no degree in horticulture, no credentials to hang on the wall. My gardening experience extends back to my father's World War II Victory Garden, in Allentown, Pennsylvania, in which my major job was to drop bugs into a jar of kerosene. But my first real gardening knowledge came after I joined the staff of *Organic Gardening* magazine, a Rodale Press Publication, in the 1950s. With book learning in the extensive Rodale library, and practical experience at the Rodale Experimental Farm plots, I gradually learned gardening on the job. I spent ten years with the Rodale organization, before moving to Wisconsin, and I have kept in touch with the Rodales for most of the time since then, contributing to the *Complete Book of Compost*, the *Encyclopedia of Organic Gardening*, the *Rodale Encyclopedia of Indoor Gardening*, and other books.

I am still no gardening expert, and have never claimed to be. There are thousands of Wisconsin gardeners who are more talented in the field than I. What I have done, rather, is bring together the experience, advice, findings, recommendations, and wisdom of many others —horticulturists, entomologists, botanists, soil scientists, county agents, other garden writers, readers of previous editions of this book, and many backyard gardeners just like myself, all of whom contribute regularly to the common store of garden knowledge. If I have made it easier for Wisconsin gardeners to share the knowledge of others, and indeed of each other, then my purpose in writing this book will have been served.

This new edition contains hundreds of changes, and yet previous readers might not notice many of these changes immediately. That's because the basic format of the book has remained the same. In gardening, most things don't change from year to year, or from decade to decade (which, incidentally, is one of the reasons why gardening is so satisfying a hobby).

We still make a compost heap in the same way as we always did, we still plant peas in April instead of on George Washington's Birthday, and it's still hard to get lettuce to head up in Wisconsin. Certainly there are new varieties to consider, new hybrids to try, new books to read, and new wrinkles in technique here and there. I have tried to account for these as best I can. But basically, the essential processes of growing plants remain in balance and continue to follow nature's rules.

Together, as always, we all will become better gardeners by studying those rules.

Jerry Minnich
Madison, Wisconsin
March, 1995

It All Begins in the Soil

Half of our misery and weakness derives from the fact that we have broken with the soil and that we have allowed the roots that bound us to the earth to rot. We have become detached from the earth, we have abandoned her. And a man who abandons nature has begun to abandon himself.

—Pierre Van Paasen
That Day Alone (1941)

1 What is this soil, this good earth that Van Paassen accuses us of abandoning?

Go to a poet and he will fill your imagination with pictures of the soil as the giver of life: Mother Earth, the patient, forgiving, and generous bearer of us all. Choosing a favorite poetic passage about the earth is as difficult as choosing the most perfect flower in the world. But who can resist John Milton's tribute?

> Sweet is the breath of morn, her rising sweet,
> With charm of earliest birds; pleasant the sun
> When first on this delightful land he spreads
> His orient beams, on herb, tree, fruit, and flower,
> Glist'ring with dew; fragrant the fertile earth
> After soft showers; and sweet the coming on
> Of grateful ev'ning mild, then silent night
> With this her solemn bird, and this fair moon,
> And these the gems of heaven, her starry train.
>
> *Paradise Lost*, 4:641-649

Go to a Wisconsin geologist and you will get quite a different picture. He will talk of residual soils and transported soils, and bowldery sand, and glacial gravel, and stratified clay. He will tell you how modern alluvium was laid down by rivers, how peat bogs were formed by a hundred centuries of vegetable accumulation, and how great valleys were formed by the land's erosion. His eyes will brighten when he tells you about the great continental glacier of 20,000 years ago, and how it drastically altered the face of three fourths of Wisconsin's landmass. He would love to show you the mesas and buttes at Camp Douglas, and he would have no trouble giving you the history of your own garden soil no matter where in Wisconsin you live. Geologists are interesting people. They can instill in us a respect for the land by giving us its history.

Go to a soil scientist and she will tell her own story of soil. She will speak of silt loams, red clays. and green sands. She will discuss soil texture and water-holding capacities. She will bring out profile charts and point to A_1 horizons and A_2 horizons. She will bring out multicolored soil maps, and she will be able to tell you more about your soil than you ever knew, even though she has never seen it. She will slap a label on your garden soil, because soil scientists are compelled to attach labels. You might find that you have a Bergland deep black topsoil over bluish gray clay over red clay, if you live near Superior. Or, if you happen to be in Janesville, you might find yourself living on a Carlisle muck.

There are hundreds of different soil types in Wisconsin, and the soil scientists haven't made it any easier for us poor amateurs by deciding, somewhere along the line, to give soil types (or series) the names of the places where they were first discovered. Thus, you might have a Dubuque soil if you live in Menomonie, or a Kewanee soil if you live in Whitefish Bay. Wisconsin soil scientists seem to have one aim in life — to survey and classify every cubic foot of the state's soil above bedrock. These dedicated people are integral to the success of Wisconsin agriculture, and they can be quite a bit of help to us home gardeners, too.

Ask a farmer about the soil and he will most likely speak of productivity. For him, the soil is a way to make a living. And, sad to say, many farmers today see the soil as little more than that. Whereas farming was, not too long ago, a way of life for a large segment of America, it has gradually and surely followed a clear trend: fewer and larger farms, more crop specialization, intense emphasis on yield rather than quality, increasing dependence on chemicals for land and crop management, and a widening separation of the farmer from the land that supports him. This trend has led us from traditional farming to modern agribusiness and corporate enterprise. Respect for the soil is lost, here, in deference to the greater respect for profits. The soil becomes little more than a convenient substance to hold plants upright. It is mined of its natural productivity, and crops are virtually spoon-fed the minerals they need for growth. Vegetable varieties are chosen not for taste or nutritional quality, but for their easy handling by the harvesting machines, for their uniform size, for their attractive color, shipping qualities, shelf life, yield per acre, and for any other purpose that might add to corporate profits. Certainly there are many farmers in Wisconsin who still hold a proper respect for the soil, and there are still family farms in nearly every part of the state. But the economic pressures brought on by modern agribusiness have made family farming difficult for most and impossible for many, all to the ultimate detriment of the soil. Every year there are fewer family farms, the farms that remain are larger, and their owners are more distant from the land itself.

What has this trend done to the soil? Here in the United States we have lost an estimated 50 to 60 percent of our topsoil in less than 200 years of farming. Indeed, most farms west of the Middle Atlantic states are barely more than 100 years old. Then we look at the farmers of China, who have lived from the soil for more than *4,000 years*, by returning all organic wastes to the soil. The American record speaks for itself, and the trend is obvious for all to see. What will we leave to our grandchildren?

Talk to organic farmers and you will get a different story. They are the ones who are holding on to—or recapturing—traditional respect for the land. Organic farmers are ecologists. They see the soil as a vital part of a larger life community. They study its character and needs. And they feed the soil, not the plants. They know that a healthy soil will produce healthy plants, and that a sick soil can be mined for only so long before its patience wears thin. In an effort to keep a natural balance on their farms at all times, they encourage insect-eating birds, pollinating honeybees, and soil-enriching earthworms. They return all plant wastes to the land because they know they cannot keep taking from the soil without replacing the things they take.

Perhaps the difference between an agribusiness farmer and an organic farmer is that one thinks of being the owner of the land, while the other thinks of being a visitor there. And the organic farmer is right. We are all visitors on the land, for the land was here long before we came, and it will be here long after we are gone. The land, the soil, has been a mighty gracious host, too, since it has sustained each of us for all our lives. We, as guests, must remember our manners if we want the land to treat our grandchildren in the same hospitable manner.

In This Soil

The soil in your garden is, indeed, part of a vital life community—an ecosystem, if you will—and it is teeming with life. In your garden soil are countless billions of microorganisms. Some cause plant troubles, but most are friendly creatures, working ceaselessly to break down plant and animal residues and to liberate nutrients for all your garden plants. A single gram of garden soil contains more than a billion bacteria, a veritable soil-conditioning army. Millions of actinomycetes help in the decomposition process and make minerals available to growing plants. The familiar odor of freshly turned soil in the spring is caused by the products of these actinomycetes. Fungi of many kinds also break down organic matter and improve soil texture. Millions of algae, when exposed to sunlight, form chlorophyll and change carbon dioxide from the air into organic matter for the soil. Other living microorganisms, including protozoa and yeast, also aid in soil conditioning and in making nutrients available to plants. During the long Wisconsin winter, these creatures are slow to move. But in spring they begin to stir into action, and by midsummer they are in a frenzy of activity.

In your garden soil, there are (I hope) thousands of earthworms, burrowing, tunneling, aerating the soil, creating water passages, eating the very earth as they go, and leaving behind their castings, which are far richer than the soil from which they are made. Earthworms are held in such high regard by organic gardeners and farmers that many either buy or raise them for introduction into the soil.

There are also thousands of insects in your soil in both summer and winter. Some are good for the garden and some are bad; but in the end, all leave their bodies to be claimed by the good earth and digested by microorganisms, thus further enriching the soil.

All these creatures call the dark, moist earth their home, and together they work in relative harmony, living from the products of plant life and, in turn, enabling plants to live and flourish.

Organic matter. Despite their staggering numbers, all the microorganisms and the earthworms and the insects form an infinitesimal percentage of the total soil body. In fact, all the living creatures and all the once-living creatures. including both plant and animal life, account for perhaps no more than *1 or 2 percent* of the soil in the average garden. These once-living things constitute, in the soil, its *organic matter*. With ample organic matter, the soil can carry on the never-ending processes of decay and rebirth that make it a vital life community. Without organic matter, the soil will be lifeless and barren, incapable of supporting any significant plant life.

But what is in the other 98 or 99 percent of the soil body? This consists of air (perhaps 25 percent), minerals (49 percent), and water (25 percent). The proportions vary, of course, according to the soil, and often they vary dramatically. But an average productive garden or farm soil might have these percentages.

Air. Soil cannot support life without air. A lack of sufficient air will inhibit or stop the important work of microorganisms; it will cause plant roots to suffocate and die; it will cause the soil to become hard, dense, and compact; it will prevent the oxidation of mineral matter, making it unavailable to plants; and it will destroy the vital chemical balance of the soil. You can insure adequate soil aeration, however, by the introduction of organic matter, the addition of rock powders, proper cultivation, and proper planning for soil drainage. More about all these later.

Minerals. The mineral content of your soil, which accounts for about half the total volume, comes from the age-old crust of the earth itself. When this land we call Wisconsin was very young, it was covered by barren rock and water. Through eons of time, the upper layers of rock were upheaved. broken, crushed, and ground, through the effects of underground disturbances and atmospheric weathering, and particularly by the alternate freezing and thaw-ing of water and the advance of the great ice sheets. Soon after the first crude plant life appeared, its deposited remains combined with smaller mineral particles, and with water and air, to form soil. Thus did both soil and plant life multiply together, each encouraging the other, until the Wisconsin landscape was changed from a barren and desolate wasteland to a world of green and living things.

Mineral matter is a necessary ingredient of soil, since plants need many different mineral elements to carry on their life processes. The most important are phosphorus and potassium, which, along with nitrogen, comprise most standard chemical fertilizers. But many other essential mineral elements are needed in smaller amounts: aluminum, calcium, iron, magne-sium, manganese, sulphur, titanium, and others. When minerals are needed in very small amounts, they are called *trace minerals* or *trace elements.*

Water. No one needs to be told of the impor-tance of water to a garden. Suffice it to say that water acts as the transportation system of the soil's life community, carrying every molecule of every nutrient from the soil to the plant roots, and from the roots to the stem, leaves, and fruit. Water enables bacteria and other microorgan-isms to liberate mineral elements for plant use. Without sufficient water, element transportation comes to a screeching halt, and life processes of every kind come to an end. More will be said later about ways to provide ample water for opti-mum soil and plant health.

What Kind of Soil is That?

You can take perfectly good care of your own garden soil without learning the hundreds of specialized terms used by geologists, soil sci-entists, and agronomists. But there are a few terms that you should know, since we do run into them fairly often in receiving, and giving, soil-care advice.

Soil profile. A side view of your garden soil, beginning with the bedrock below and running all the way up to the surface, is called a *profile.*

Soil profiles are comprised of layers (called *hori-zons*) which include the topsoil, various layers of subsoil, parent materials, and eventually bedrock.

Texture. This refers to the proportional amounts of the various-sized particles that make up your soil. Gravel, of course is very large. Sand is smaller but still coarse in soil terms. Silt particles are still smaller (from 8/100,000 inch to 2/1,000 inch), while clay particles are the smallest recognized. You can get some idea of the composition of any soil by rubbing a bit of it between your thumb and index finger. Sand will feel gritty. Silt will feel floury. And clay will feel sticky.

Structure. In good garden soils, the indi-vidual particles of sand, clay, and silt naturally group together into larger units called *granules* or *aggregates*. This process is necessary to a good garden soil, since it promotes aeration and water drainage. And the success of your soil in forming these aggregates is called its *structure* or *crumb structure*. Sandy soils have poor struc-ture, since the sand is too coarse to form aggre-gates, while a heavy clay will become compact and dense when wet, inhibiting good plant growth.

Porosity. This term refers to the pore spaces in your soil. i.e., all the space not occu-pied by soil itself. The pores may be filled with either air or water and should occupy from 40 to 60 percent of a good soil's total volume. Good soil structure will encourage good porosity. A heavy clay, with poor structure, will not allow enough room for pore spaces. A light, sandy soil may have good porosity, but its light character will make it unable to hold water, filling most of the pores with air. The excess air will cause soil nitrogen to be released too quickly, and a nitrogen shortage will result. Gardeners should work for a good medium loam with good struc-ture and porosity.

pH. This symbol is used in discussing the soil's acid or alkaline nature. The midpoint on the pH scale is 7. A soil with pH of 7 is neutral —neither acid nor alkaline. Numbers above 7 indicate an alkaline soil: those under 7, an acid soil. Since all plants express a preference for soil in a certain range of the pH scale, it is important that you test your soil's pH and, if necessary, correct the soil to bring it within the proper range. Full directions for managing soil pH are given later in this chapter.

Soil groups. Soils are grouped according to their textures. The *sand group* includes soils with less than 20 percent of silt and clay. Those in the *clay group* have less than 20 percent sand. The *loam group* includes soils of a happy medium, containing good proportions of sand, silt, and clay. These are best for general gardening.

It must be said here that the definitions, especially regarding percentages, are far from rigid. Some scientists try to establish mathematical relationships in order to classify, while others pay scant attention to the percentages. Francis D. Hole and Gerhard B. Lee, in their booklet *Introduction to the Soils of Wisconsin*, identify a loam as containing about 20 percent clay. 40 percent silt, and 40 percent sand.

Actual soils. naturally, do not fall into these neat categories. Therefore, we break down the three major groups into subgroups. Sandy soils may be, in order of coarseness, gravelly sands. coarse sands, medium sands, fine sands, or loamy sands. Loams may be coarse sandy loams, medium sandy loams, fine sandy loams, silty loams, or clay loams. Clay soils can be stony clays, gravelly clays, sandy clays, silty clays, or pure clays.

Soil series. Soil groups are further divided into soil series. The series is named, as mentioned before, for the name of a place where it was first found and identified. For instance, the series *Hixton sandy loam* was named after the village of Hixton, in Jackson County, where it was first studied.

Soil classification. Soils are also herded into broader groups called *classifications*. *Podzol* is one important classification, referring to a soil where once forests or heaths stood, making the soil quite acid over the years. Often, the soil structure is poor and the soil is low in organic matter. It tends to erode easily, and aeration is often insufficient. About one fifth of the soil in the United States is podzolic; the percentage in Wisconsin is higher, covering most of the northern half of the state and dipping southward in the eastern half, through Manitowoc County. Any area that supports natural coniferous (cone-bearing) forest is apt to offer podzolic soil.

Alluvial soils are named for alluvium, the fine-particle clay carried from uplands by streams and rivers and redeposited in bottomlands. A great alluvial valley has been created by the Mississippi River, which has affected the soils of western Wisconsin (although far less than it has affected southern states). There are also large areas of alluvial soils surrounding many Wisconsin waterways. Some of the world's great agricultural lands are alluvial, and some of Wisconsin's best gardening soil is, too. It is apt to be moderately well-drained silt loam, rich in nutrients and ready for planting with little or no structural repair.

Peat and *muck* are related terms, often used loosely, although mucks are usually said to contain less than 50 percent of organic matter, while peats contain more than 50 percent. Both, however, refer to wet, spongy, acid soils. composed mainly of decayed vegetable matter and very high in organic content. Their water-retaining capacities are extraordinarily high, particularly peats, which can hold up to 13 times their dry weight in water. Sphagnum moss, which is the principal ingredient of Wisconsin's peat bogs, is always in demand among florists, creating a nice little industry for many people in the bog-rich central counties of the state.

Raw sphagnum peat is rich in total nitrogen content, but this nitrogen is not in a form available to plants. So poor is this soil in available nitrogen, in fact, that some of the most common wild plants in bogs are the insectivorous species. These plants—including the pitcher plant, the sundews, and the bladderworts—find no nitrogen in the soil, and so they get their nourishment from the insects that they trap and devour! Peat is equally low in mineral elements, too, and so it does not, by itself, make good garden soil. Properly treated, muck soils can make one of the best-producing vegetable soils of any in America. But, except for cranberry production, peat bogs are better utilized to gather materials to add to more nourishing soils. Peat moss is extremely valuable in breaking up heavy clay soils and in adding good texture and structure to sandy soils.

In Wisconsin, most of the peat bogs are located in the northern and eastern parts of the state, although there are some impressive old bogs in the Kettle Moraine district of Waukesha and Walworth counties, and others in Jefferson and Columbia counties. These bogs are very old and very deep. It has been estimated that it takes nature from 100 to 800 years to lay down a single foot of peat moss, and many Wisconsin bogs are more than 50 feet deep.

Prairie soils are much like podzols, except that they were formed without the contribution of trees. The organic content of these soils is high, the granular structure is good, and their general fertility is high. Prairie soils make up some of the best agricultural lands in the nation. Most of Iowa's soil is prairie, about three fourths of Illinois, and a portion of Minnesota's.

Wisconsin is on the northeastern boundary of the great American prairie, and so its prairie area is largely confined to the southwestern part of the state. Draw a triangle on a state map. with the three points being at Racine, Grant, and Polk counties, and you will have fairly well encompassed Wisconsin's prairie area. Gardeners in this region are fortunate, in that nature has provided them with the best of materials to work with.

There are many, many other classifications of soils—chernozem, laterite, tundra, planosol, and rendzina, to name just a few—but we have neither the space nor the need to go into them here. Soil science is a highly developed field of inquiry that could turn into a consuming interest if you are so inclined. But the home gardener should be able to make intelligent decisions with only scant knowledge of these matters. After all, it is your own soil that holds the keenest interest, and you need not study the soils of the world to get to know your own backyard.

The Soils of Wisconsin

Wisconsin has a wide variety of soils, the result of the great glacier (which missed about a fourth of the state, called the Driftless Area) and the

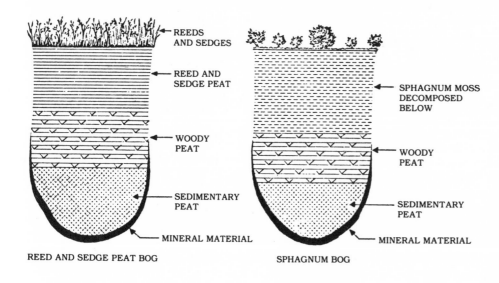

REED AND SEDGE PEAT BOG — REEDS AND SEDGES / REED AND SEDGE PEAT / WOODY PEAT / SEDIMENTARY PEAT / MINERAL MATERIAL

SPHAGNUM BOG — SPHAGNUM MOSS DECOMPOSED BELOW / WOODY PEAT / SEDIMENTARY PEAT / MINERAL MATERIAL

This illustration, prepared by the United States Department of Agriculture, shows a typical profile of a peat formed mainly from sedges and reeds; another composed chiefly from sphagnum moss.

influence of the Mississippi River and Lakes Superior and Michigan. Other influences have been the intrusion of the great prairie into Wisconsin's southwest and the extensive stands of pine and hardwood forests throughout the north.

In the center of the state is a large region of light, sandy soils, bounded roughly by Portage and Wisconsin Dells on the south, Stevens Point and Wisconsin Rapids on the north, Waupaca and Berlin on the east, and Black River Falls and Sparta on the west. A similar section is found in the northeastern part of the state, beginning around Shawano and running northeastward through Marinette County. Still a third sandy area is located in the northwest, beginning in Burnett County and running northeastward through Douglas and Bayfield counties (but excluding the Superior area). A fourth area, including parts of Forest, Langlade, Lincoln, Oneida, and Vilas counties, is not wholly sandy but has some sandy areas in among loams.

A fairly extensive region of fine sandy loam northwest of Black River Falls runs across Jackson, Eau Claire, Chippewa, and Dunn counties and includes the southern part of Barron County. Soils in the rest of the state usually run to silt loams, except for red clay areas, one running along the shore of Lake Michigan, beginning at Milwaukee and going northward, and another running along Lake Superior.

The map showing major soil regions (map 1) should give you some idea of the kind of soil—that is common in your area. You can get far more detailed information by taking advantage of some of the useful publications offered by the University of Wisconsin Geological and Natural History Survey. Most of these are somewhat technical and detailed, providing information not really essential for the home gardener's needs. But you might find some of the publications to be very interesting, particularly if you want to dig deeper into the study of soils. There are. for instance, soil surveys of nearly all Wisconsin counties, most available for a few dollars each. There are also soil maps, including a beautiful multicolored wall map, 46 by 36 inches, of the entire state which pinpoints 190 different soil groups. These publications, and more, can be seen by visiting your local public library or the office of your county Extension agent or by writing for a complete list of publications to the University of Wisconsin Geological and Natural History Survey, 3817 Mineral Point Rd., Madison, Wisconsin 53705. A comprehensive and handsome book on the subject. *Soils of Wisconsin*, by Francis D. Hole, is available from the University of Wisconsin Press, 114 North Murray St., Madison, Wisconsin 53715.

But How About Your Soil?

Let's get to *your* soil. What is it like? How does it rate in terms of structure, porosity, organic content, and supplies of all the essential and trace mineral elements? Are you working with sand, clay, or an ideal garden loam? Are earthworms in plentiful supply? Are conditions right for your army of microorganisms?

If you have been working with your soil for some time, you probably know the answers to these questions. You may have become intimately acquainted with your soil over the years, learning its needs and capabilities as you would those of a dear friend. But if you are going to work a garden plot for the first time, you must spend some time in analyzing your soil. Even if you have been gardening in one spot for some years, you might not be happy with the results you have been getting. If this is the case, the first place to look for answers is in the soil—where it all begins.

Soil type. You can easily determine your soil type by checking a detailed soil map or by calling your county Extension horticultural or agricultural agent. If you find that your soil type is not well suited to gardening, do not despair. Samuel Ogden, a Vermont gardener with more than 40 years of experience, worked a large plot on a soil called Stony Berkshire, which he described as "just about the worst soil classifi-

MAP 1

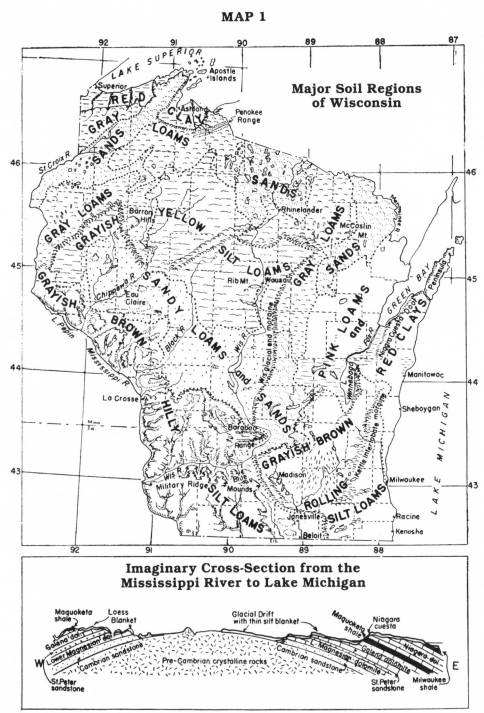

Major Soil Regions
of Wisconsin

Imaginary Cross-Section from the
Mississippi River to Lake Michigan

The Soil Survey Division, Wisconsin Geological and Natural History Survey

cation that there is in the United States." Yet, Ogden achieved tremendous results with vegetables of all kinds by following standard organic practices and his good common sense. In speaking of soil types and classifications in his book *Step-by-Step to Organic Vegetable Growing*, Ogden says:

> I came to the conclusion that there is very little, if any, relationship between the nature of the soil and the kind of parent rock which lies beneath the surface, and I returned to my previously held conviction, which came as the result of practical experience, that the most important aspect of a soil is its physical or mechanical condition. In other words, the important factors are not the derivation of the soil, or its classification, but rather its texture, its depth, its content of air and moisture, the presence or lack thereof of rocks and stones, etc.

I tend to follow Ogden's common sense, here. Much of the advice of experts is geared to the farmer or the commercial grower, and the experts tend to forget that the home gardener can afford to treat his soil in ways that the large-scale grower would find unfeasible or uneconomic. Especially if you have only one likely spot for your garden, then, do not be discouraged in discovering that your soil type is not the best for growing things.

Structure, texture, and drainage. If at all possible, try to observe your prospective garden soil after a heavy rain. If, after a few hours, the soil has not absorbed the rain, then you might well have a drainage problem. The soil might be too heavy, loaded with clay and lacking in porosity. Or, you might find that the topsoil is shallow, overlying a dense hardpan or rock bed. You can deal with a clay topsoil; but a shallow topsoil over rock or hardpan requires a job scarcely worth the undertaking. Dig a hole two feet deep in several parts of your garden to get an informal soil profile for yourself, and to get some idea of soil texture and structure at different levels. Look at it, feel it, crumble some in your hands. Look for earthworms and evidence of root growth.

If you want a better idea of the soil structure, try the bottle test. Fill a quart or pint bottle one-fourth full of a representative soil sample. (Try to get a straight cylinder of soil for an accurate sample.) Fill the rest of the bottle with water and shake vigorously until a homogenous mixture is obtained, and then put the bottle on a shelf for half a day. The sand will sink quickly to the bottom, the silt will settle on top of the sand, and the fine clay particles will slowly filter down to form a top layer. By measuring with a ruler, you can get a rough idea of the proportions of these various materials in your soil.

Of course, you might find yourself to have the opposite problem—too much drainage, or, a lack of water-holding capacity. I remember visiting Richard Higby's Adams County place some years ago, my first visit to a Wisconsin "sand county" farm. There had been a terrific rainstorm the night before, Three inches had fallen, and the rain had not subsided until an hour before I pulled into the front yard. I was there to observe a composting demonstration that Mr. Higby had organized, and I had expected to be walking in mire up to my ankles. Much to my surprise, the ground was scarcely damp. The rain had been absorbed as quickly as it had fallen, drawn deeply underground where growing plants cannot reach, carrying valuable nutrients with it. Fortunately, you can deal with a soil of this nature. It takes some substantial initial effort, but it is a job well worth the doing.

Another factor affecting drainage is the garden's position on the lay of the land. Lowlands will tend to receive the water runoff and drainage from higher lands and will thus drain more slowly. Fine clay particles are gradually carried downhill where they might improve sandy soils. If you find that your soil is heavy, a higher spot on the hill might afford advantages. Conversely, a lowland sand will have a better chance at water retention than one at a higher elevation. Again, look at the soil, dig into it, touch it, feel it. Get to know your soil.

Table 1. Weeds as Indicators of Soil Type

The weeds growing on your land are not an infallible guide to soil type, but they do provide some clues. The following soils will provide good environments for the weeds listed opposite.

WET LAND	Ferns, horsetail, sedge, rush, cattail, buttercup, pennywort. *The surface may be dry but these weeds are a sure indication that the land is wet below. There may be a drainage problem.*
SOUR LAND (ACID)	Sorrel, dock, wild strawberry, bramble. *The soil should be limed.*
POOR, DRY SOIL	Devil's paintbrush, spurge. *Manures and sludge are needed.*
TIGHT, COMPRESSED SOIL	Knotwood. *Break up surface, work in sand, manure, compost, and peat moss.*
DEEP CLAY	Self-heal, wild onion. *Needs compost and sand.*
LIMESTONE	Chicory, Teasel. *Check pH.*

What's growing now? Another quick indicator of a soil's potential is its present performance. Is the area rampant with weed growth? Is there a healthy stand of quack grass? If so, you can be fairly sure that the soil is capable of growing other plants of your own choosing. If, on the other hand, weed growth is sparse and there are large bare areas, you can suspect that something is wrong with this soil. It might be a problem easily corrected, such as a lack of minerals or of organic matter. But, on the other hand, the problem might go deeper, involving basic structural flaws. Investigate.

Soil testing. Your soil should be tested if you have never tested it before, or if you have not had it tested within the past couple of years, or if you are having problems and are unsure of the reasons for those problems. If you know your soil intimately, have been following a comprehensive feeding and conditioning program, and have been satisfied with year-end results, there might be no need to test. I suspect that few gardeners fall into this last category, however, and so a professional soil test is recommended. The information it provides can be both interesting and valuable.

In Wisconsin, we are fortunate to have one of the best soil-testing programs of any state in the nation, run by the University of Wisconsin. You may have your soil tested for pH (acidity-alkalinity), organic matter content, phosphorus, potassium, and soluble salts, for a fee of only a few dollars. For another few dollars, you can have a physical analysis made, telling you the percentage of sand, silt, and clay (which will be more accurate, doubtless, than your home "bottle test"). And, for a little more, you may have the same soil tested for calcium, magnesium, manganese, boron, and zinc. Not only will the University test for all these characteristics, but you will be sent specific fertilizing recommendations made especially for the crops or plants you specify, whether they be rhubarb, lawn grass, spinach, chrysanthemums, or your favorite dogwood tree.

Getting a soil test is fairly simple. Write or call your county Extension agent and say that you want to have a soil test made. Ask for a copy of Circular A2166, *Sampling Lawn and Garden Soils for Soil Testing*, as many plastic-lined soil sample bags as you will need (one for each sample—you will want to test different areas of the garden), and an information sheet which you must fill in and return with each soil sample. Or, if you prefer, you may obtain the informational circular and sample bags directly from the UW Soil and Plant Analysis Laboratory, 5711 Mineral Point Rd., Madison, WI 53705; phone 608 262-4364, or from the UW Soil and Forage Analysis Laboratory, 8396 Yellowstone Dr., Marshfield, WI 54449; phone 715 387-2523. Ask for the current fee and send a check or pay it to your local Extension office. After you have taken the samples, you may, if you choose, send them back directly to the laboratory at Madison or Marshfield. But it is better to work with your county agent, who will be happy to forward them for you. In fact, it will pay you to get on a first-name basis with the agent, since the day will come when you will want expert advice on one point or another.

The last word about soil testing is one of caution. Remember that the test results will be only as good as the samples you take, and that your samples might not necessarily be representative of your general garden soil (although you can swing the odds heavily in accuracy's favor by taking samples at different locations in the garden). Some successful gardeners, in fact, have little or no faith at all in the tests. Prominent among these is Leonard Wickenden, author of the book *Gardening with Nature*, who makes the interesting observation that, whereas soil samples are taken at a depth of only six or eight inches, the roots of common garden plants might reach down six or eight *feet* into the soil to draw up nutrients. Those deep-lying nutrients will not show up on your soil test. He also makes the point that testing procedures vary from laboratory to laboratory, and so do results. I have more faith in the tests than Mr. Wickenden, but it is important to remember that the test results should be regarded as helpful, rather than sacred.

Correcting Basic Flaws

Improving a sandy soil. A representative "light sandy" soil might contain 70 percent sand, 20 percent silt, and 10 percent clay. You can work with a soil like this, but you will get better results by changing these percentages. And if the percentage of sand is significantly higher than 70 percent, it is essential that you correct it.

The answer to a sandy soil is the addition of organic matter. Some experts advise the addition of heavy clay, but this is difficult and often produces unsatisfactory results. The clay is difficult to break apart and incorporate with the sand. It adheres to itself, and you are likely to be left with the same old sandy soil, sprinkled with clay lumps. Organic matter, on the other hand, is lighter in consistency and mixes in more readily.

If you have the money, of course, you can have several truckloads of rich topsoil brought in and spread to a depth of from four to six inches or more. This is the quickest way to cure a sandy soil, but it is horribly expensive. And if you do choose this course, be absolutely certain of the quality of that topsoil. It will probably be good. having been scraped off the site of a new building project—but not every dark-colored soil is good garden soil. If you intend to invest this kind of money in topsoil, insist on a soil test before buying.

More likely, you will want to take on the enrichment project yourself. And for this you will need all the organic materials you can possibly find and haul back to your garden. Gardeners in Dane County, for instance, can pick up the aquatic weeds that are harvested from the Madison lakes. Milwaukee area gardeners should have little trouble coming upon spent hops from the breweries. Canning factories offer abundant organic matter, rich in minerals. Those in forested regions can bring home bushels and bushels of well-rotted leaf mold (which is likely to be very acid, and should be neutralized with ground limestone). Spoiled hay can be picked up from many farmers, often for nothing, sometimes for a dollar a bale. Remember that anything once living can be used to enrich a sandy soil. Chapter 2 includes a representative list of organic materials (page 30) that will give you some ideas to pursue. Look over the possibilities in your area and begin to investigate. Call the city or county parks department and ask what happens to the leaves that they collect in fall. They may dump them in huge heaps in a forgotten corner of the county. And if they do. you will find beautiful, brown, crumbly leaf mold on the insides of those heaps. Is there a sawmill nearby? Sweep up baskets full of sawdust, which makes an excellent conditioner for sandy soils.

You can incorporate these organic materials into the soil in two ways. The first is by building a compost heap (for which directions are given in the next chapter) or beginning the practice of *sheet composting.* In traditional composting, you build the heap, wait months for it to decay and mature, then dig it into the soil in the fall or early spring, before planting. In sheet composting, you spread the raw materials directly over the soil, till or dig them under, and let the composting process take place right in your soil. The advantage of sheet composting is that it takes far less work; the disadvantage is that it will take that part of your garden plot out of production for a year.

The second way to add organic matter to the soil is through *green manuring.* Here, a cover crop is grown for the sole purpose of being plowed or tilled under. The process is not difficult, and the results are very good. You can add literally tons of organic matter in this way without the burden of hauling it to your land. Annual or winter rye grass is a good cover crop, and winter wheat is especially popular in Wisconsin. Among legumes (which will help fix nitrogen in the soil) are hairy vetch, crimson (red) clover, alfalfa, cowpeas, and lespedeza. But the easiest to sow and quickest-growing cover crop is buckwsheat. Its probing roots bring up minerals from deep in the subsoil, and it grows so vigorously that it crowds out even the most agressive weeds. Just broadcase seed on tilled soil at 2 pounds per 1,000 square feet.

Whichever method you choose—composting, sheet composting, or green manuring—you must add all the organic matter you possibly can to correct a sandy soil in the shortest possible time.

The proper treatment for sandy and clay soils is essentially the same — the incorporation of plenty of organic matter.

If you are planting trees, shrubs, perennials, or foundation plants in a sandy soil, you might not want to wait for the time it takes to turn your entire soil body into an ideal structure. You might wish to spot-treat the soil in these cases. Dig the planting hole about twice as large as recommended for any plant. Fill the hole with four parts good topsoil, one part rotted manure, and one part peat moss. Add a little sand from your own soil. This mixture will give nearly any plant a good start and should serve its needs until the surrounding soil has been corrected. (Note: Allow for the pH preference of any plant variety by the addition of necessary limestone.)

When growing anything in sandy soil, remember also to apply a mulch. The water in sandy soils evaporates quickly, and a good mulch will retard that evaporation, preserving precious moisture. The mulch will also break down slowly at the soil surface and can be tilled under after each growing season, adding still more organic matter. Further information about cover crops, green manuring, and mulching is given later.

Victory over clay. Far more difficult than building up sandy soil is the process of breaking down a heavy clay. Your soil may be in a natural clay region, or you may have purchased a new home where the builder has stripped the topsoil, leveled out the lot with clay subsoil from the basement excavation, and spread an inch or so of topsoil over it, just enough to support a scraggly lawn. Whichever way you got your clay, you are stuck with it. In more ways than one. Even if you buy good topsoil to spread, you might well have a drainage problem that will keep your soil waterlogged and unproductive.

The treatment for a clay soil is essentially the same as for a sandy soil. You must incorporate all the organic matter you can, and you can do it by composting, sheet composting, or green manuring. The difference is that, in attacking clay, you should also incorporate quantities of builder's sand.

No one has to tell you that clay is sticky. It sticks to your garden tools, it sticks to your children's shoes. it sticks to your dog—and it sticks to itself. And because it sticks to itself, it tends to resist homogenization when other materials are introduced to the soil. Peat is an especially good material to add, because of its light and porous character. But any organic material is better than none, and you should spend a great deal of time during the first two years to incorporate that material. The rewards later will more than repay your early efforts.

Some gardeners report victory over clay with *strip composting.* This is a form of sheet composting in which the entire garden plot is divided into strips, perhaps three feet wide, running the entire length of the plot. Alternate strips are used for sheet composting. All collected organic matter is put into these strips and tilled under periodically—perhaps once a month during the growing season. The final tilling is done in the fall, and the land is left in rough condition so that some heaving will take place during winter's freezes and thaws. The following year, the composted strips are used for planting and the alternate strips are used for composting. In this way, you can plant half of your garden space each year, while building up the soil at the same time. Only when your soil reaches what you consider to be optimum condition will you begin to use the entire plot for annual plantings.

If your soil has a severe drainage problem, it must be solved before you can expect to have a productive garden of any kind. And if the drainage problem lies in the subsoil, rather than just the topsoil, all the foregoing suggestions still will not lead to a satisfactory garden soil. After all your work, rainwater will be absorbed into the renovated topsoil, but will be held on the subsoil like water in a basin. Your soil will remain cold, sour, and unfit for any of the flowers and vegetables you want to grow.

The breaking up of a clay subsoil or hardpan might require extraordinary measures, including subsoiling, trenching, or the laying of drainage tiles. *Subsoiling* is done with a special plow—a subsoiler—which breaks up the subsoil but does not bring it up to the surface. If you have a hardpan horizon in your soil profile, this might do the trick, for a hardpan is nothing more than a layer of subsoil whose pores have been filled in with fine clay particles, eventually forming a cementlike substance, impervious to water. The subsoil under the hardpan might be perfectly good and well drained. but the water never gets past the hardpan. A subsoiler can break up the hardpan in a matter of hours.

Trenching is a method of exchanging the top foot of soil (or the depth of one spade blade) with the foot of soil beneath it. This is a long and back-breaking job, since it is done by hand, row by row, but it might be the answer when you are presented with good topsoil over heavy clay. By placing the topsoil in the bottom position you can improve the clay more easily on the top, and in the end you will have twice as much good topsoil and far better drainage. I have read of trenching often but I have never known anyone who has actually done it. Personally I hesitate to recommend this laborious procedure to anyone, but I present it here as another method you might wish to investigate.

Drainage tiles might also be the answer to inadequate subsurface drainage. These tiles are actually ceramic tubes that come in lengths of from two to eight feet. A common diameter is four inches. The tiles are laid two feet or more underground and are slanted downhill and toward a natural drainage area or dry well. As with the other procedures, drainage tiling is a major operation involving some expense. You might find however that this procedure will give your soil the drainage it needs to become productive.

Before you undertake any of these extraordinary measures, I recommend strongly that you ask your county agent to make a personal asessment of the problem and to give you a recommendation. A severe drainage problem requires the personal attention of an expert, and your county agent has the needed expertise in this area. Quite likely your drainage problem will be one that has been shared by some of your neighbors, and your county agent will be able to tell you how others have solved the problem in your area.

Fertilizer—What Kind? How Much?

In coming to the subject of fertilizer, we run into the first of two great controversies. Will it be chemical—or organic? (The second great controversy, met later on in this book, concerns insect control methods.)

My personal gardening approach is unabashedly organic, and I will make no apologies for that because I think it is right. On the other hand, I do not believe that chemical fertilizers are an insidious plot hatched by sinister forces out to destroy us. Chemical fertilizers are, I believe, simply unnecessary in the home garden. They become harmful only if applied to excess or if the gardener comes to depend on them to the neglect of his soil. I have personally known hundreds of gardeners who get gratifying-to-tremendous results year after year using no chemical fertilizer at all.

Chemical fertilization is scarcely a hundred years old. Gardening itself is thousands of years old. The use of chemicals began with the great nineteenth-century chemist Justus von Liebig, who discovered that certain mineral elements are necessary to the growth of plants. Virtually singlehanded, von Liebig overthrew the then-held theory that plants ate humus, and the age of scientific agriculture was born. The distinguished and talented Englishman Sir Albert Howard, who ironically was born in the same year that von Liebig died (1873), led the counterattack against the chemical theory of soil treatment and crop fertilization some years later, and became the father of the organic movement. Howard's 30 years of agricultural research in India led him to doubt the wisdom of von Liebig's "fractionalized" approach to agriculture, which he saw as potentially or actually harmful to soil, plants, and humans. Howard died in 1947, but his work had by then been brought to popular attention in America by the writings of J. I. Rodale.

Rodale, a New York accountant in his early years, became so interested in Howard's work that in the 1930s he moved to a rundown farm near Emmaus, Pennsylvania, and proceeded to build it into a lush and productive showplace, using Howard's organic method (which he refined and improved upon over the years). Rodale founded a magazine, then called *Organic Farming and Gardening*, in 1942, and subsidized it personally for many years. Today, *Rodale's Organic Gardening* claims more than a million subscribers, many of whom were drawn to organic methods during the environmental movement that began in the 1960s. Rodale died in 1971, and the magazine was then run by his son, Robert Rodale, who tragically was killed in a traffic accident in Moscow, in 1990, as he was working with Russian officials to bring organic methods to that country.

The chemical side. Chemical fertilizers are generally formed by the addition of chemicals to natural ground rock bases. These fertilizers are soluble and immediately available to plants, as opposed to natural rock powders and the minerals found in all organic matter that become available more slowly, as they are liberated in the soil through the actions of microorganisms. The scientific application of chemical fertilizers will give plants a quick "shot in the arm," and will improve production on a soil that lacks those mineral elements supplied by the fertilizers. Chemical fertilizers give quick results.

Most chemical fertilizers contain three elements—nitrogen (N), phosphate (P_2O_5), and potash (K_2O). In grower's language, these elements are referred to as N, P, and K. On the fertilizer bag, the percentages of each are given in N-P-K order. A 5-10-5 fertilizer for instance, will contain 5 percent nitrogen, 10 percent phosphate. and 5 percent potash. The common chemical form of nitrogen is ammonium sulfate. Phosphate is usually supplied through superphosphate. And potash often comes in the form of muriate of potash. Trace mineral

J. I. Rodale — founder of the organic movement in America.

supplements and lime are also supplied through the chemical treatment of natural rock powders.

Most government and university agricultural and horticultural experts are adherents of the chemical school of fertilization, although the cleavage between the two schools has been softened considerably in recent years. The benefits of organic matter have become known to the establishment scientists, and many organic gardeners have come to believe that a little straight chemical application for special situations will not bring the end of the world. The fire in the organic movement—which was once a true crusade—was dampened with the deaths of the Rodales.

The organic side. Organic adherents claim that chemicals are not only unnecessary but harmful. Chemicals, they say, destroy soil texture; they inhibit or retard the growth of soil life, including earthworms and microorganisms; they alter the vitamin and protein content of certain crops; they make certain crops more vulnerable to disease by destroying the plants' natural biological controls; and they prevent plants from absorbing some needed minerals. Despite their short-term effects, they say, chemicals will eventually lead to poor yields and inferior crops because of their deleterious effects on the soil. Last, organic gardeners and farmers swear that organically grown vegetables taste far better than their chemical counterparts.

Organic soil feeding, on the other hand, is shown to be patterned after nature's own methods, which certainly have an impressive track record. Soil test results, since they are usually prepared by government or university agencies, are accompanied by fertilizer recommendations in chemical terms. But the organic gardener will substitute compost, animal manures, green manure, or other forms of natural fertilizers for the recommended chemicals.

Further, organic gardeners and farmers place far more emphasis on year-round soil building and feeding. They do not apply fertilizers just when a soil test indicates that a certain mineral is needed for a certain crop, but they carry on a continual program of feeding the soil, returning wastes, composting, mulching, and green manuring, so that the soil will be built into a peak of health and efficiency, capable of supporting lush growth and production of any common garden plant or farm crop. Again, we get back to the difference in philosophy between *feeding the plant* and *feeding the soil*, which distinguishes the approaches of these two schools.

Nitrogen supplies. Nitrogen is the nutrient most directly responsible for the healthy growth and dark green color of plants above the ground. Insufficient nitrogen will result in weak and stunted plant growth and a pale or yellow color in the foliage.

Nitrogen is supplied to plants from decaying organic matter through a complex chemical process that takes place in the soil. In brief, the protein from organic matter is broken down into its component amino acids from which ammonium compounds are formed. Certain bacteria then break down these compounds into nitrites, and different bacteria turn the nitrites into nitrates. It is only in the form of nitrates that plant roots can absorb nitrogen.

If your soil is now nitrogen-rich, you can keep it that way by annual applications of compost or manure. If, however, a soil test shows a serious lack, you can add large amounts in a hurry by growing *legume green manure crops*.

A green manure crop is one grown solely for the purpose of being turned under for soil enrichment, as I have said before. Legumes are members of the plant family *Leguminosae*, and include peas, beans, clover, cowpeas, hairy vetch, and alfalfa as more familiar members of the family. The unique feature of legumes is their ability to draw huge amounts of nitrogen from the air, which is then stored in little lumps called *nodules*, which adhere to the roots of the plant. When the legumes are cut in fall, the nitrogen remains in the soil to aid next year's plantings. Further, the leafy parts of the plant, when plowed or tilled under, add other minerals and organic matter to the soil. It has been estimated that a single planting of a legume green manure crop will add as much nitrogen to one acre of soil as ten tons of manure, or 2,820 pounds of a 5-10-5 fertilizer.

In Wisconsin's climate. the best kinds of legume green manure crops are alfalfa and the clovers. Table 2 shows the results of legume tests carried out by researchers in Ames, Iowa.

You can see that Madrid sweetclover has done the best, by far, as a nitrogen-adding green manure legume. The sweetclover weevil, *Sitonia cylindricollis*, has caused many Wisconsin farmers to turn to other legumes less susceptible to the weevil; but the home gardener should not be bothered by this insect unless it is already in the area.

Growing legumes for green manure is not difficult. The soil should be prepared as for any other crop, and the seed should be planted as directed when the soil warms up in the spring. Be sure that the soil is well supplied with phosphate and potassium for best results. (The incorporation of well-rotted manure or compost before planting will take care of this.) In addition, you should inoculate your seed with a *bacterial inoculant* for food nitrogen fixation. The inoculant is inexpensive and easy to use. It will appear as a dark brown or black powder, but actually it contains billions of beneficial bacteria that will enter the root hairs and form nodules on them. The nitrogen will be stored in these nodules, to the ultimate benefit of next year's plantings.

Since legumes are very deep-rooted plants, their nitrogen-giving benefits will extend way down to the subsoil, far beyond any that can be produced by spoon-feeding chemical forms of nitrogen. Last, remember that beans and peas are legumes, too, and will add significant amounts of nitrogen to the soil. Plant these crops in different parts of the garden each year, to help insure adequate nitrogen supplies for your entire garden plot. Also keep in mind that an early harvest of peas can be followed by another quick-growing vegetable crop in the same season—and the second crop will benefit from the nitrogen left in the soil by the peas.

Phosphorus. This mineral element is important for good root growth, for brighter color in all garden flowers, and for general plant health. Without sufficient phosphorus, the maturation of fruit (including that of vegetable plants) will be delayed, plants will be stunted, and the foliage may have a purplish tinge.

Many organic materials have substantial phosphorus content, but the best source naturally available is *phosphate rock*, which is actually about 30 percent pure phosphate—the other 70 percent being comprised of other minerals that are also beneficial to soil and plants. Again, a continuing program of organic soil feeding will add phosphorus—as well as other nutrients—to the soil throughout the year so that you should rarely have to worry about adding any single nutrient for any specific planting.

Potassium. This element is essential to plant growth, particularly in building strong stems, in aiding the plant to resist disease, in forming good fruit, and in reducing the moisture requirement of plants. If your plants are stunted in growth, if the fruit is small, and if the leaves turn brown, there is a chance of potassium deficiency.

Potassium, like all other plant nutrients, can be supplied through a general organic feeding program, using plenty of compost and manure. When large amounts are needed to correct a deficiency, however, it is best to turn to potash rock or to one of the other natural fertilizers high in potassium—granite dust, basalt rock, or greensand. Plant residues will also add potash to the soil, since much of the potash brought up by the plant roots is stored in the stems of the plant.

Calcium. This mineral element is important as a vital factor in chemical reactions of both soil and plants. It helps to neutralize toxic acids that might develop in plants, and it is important in preventing magnesium toxicity. Calcium is the principal element of limestone, and so it is inexorably a part of keeping the soil in the proper pH range. For more information on lime, see the section on acidity-alkalinity that follows.

Trace elements. The many so-called trace elements—including boron, cobalt, copper, iron,

Table 2. Legume Production and Nitrogen Yield

Legume	Tons per Acre of Roots Plus Tops	Total Nitrogen Pounds per Acre
Madrid sweetclover	2.57	141
Grimm alfalfa	1.48	87
Southern common alfalfa	1.51	82
Ladino clover	1.30	74
Huban annual sweetclover	1.24	54
Medium red clover	.83	48

Source: Fribourg and Johnson, *Agronomy Journal* 47:73-76.

magnesium, manganese, molybdenum, and zinc—are vital to plants, but are needed in only very small amounts. A general organic soil-feeding program should be adequate insurance for the good supply of all these elements, without any further thought about them. But if you have been gardening chemically, or if you are working a plot that has been overworked in the past, shortages of any of them can cause problems. In this case, you should apply a mixture of rock powders, limestone, leaf mold (since trees bring up minerals from deep within the earth), and, if possible, some form of seaweed fertilizer. The idea is to get materials from outside your immediate area, since your own soil is already deficient in the minerals you are trying to introduce, and compost from plants grown in that soil will be similarly deficient.

Acidity, alkalinity, and pH. The pH scale, which runs from 0 to 14, is used to indicate your soil's degree of acidity or alkalinity. The neutral point of the scale is 7. Soils that test out higher than 7 are alkaline; those that test out lower than 7 are acid.

Most garden plants—vegetables, fruits, and ornamentals—like a slightly acid soil, perhaps in the pH range of 6.5 to 7.2. There are significant exceptions, however, most involving bush and cane berries. Among those plants that like a more acid soil (5.0 to 6.5) are blackberries, blueberries, and raspberries, as well as marigolds, gardenias, and pink lady's slippers. Many other plants like a soil only slightly less acid, while some plants prefer a soil just slightly on the alkaline side. These include alyssum, iris, phlox, asparagus, beans, beets, cabbage, cantaloupes, cauliflower, celery, cucumbers, lettuce, onions, peas, rhubarb, and squash. When cultivating instructions are given for specific plants in later chapters, the pH preference of the plants will be mentioned if it falls to the outside of the 6.5 to 7.2 range. Virtually no plant likes a soil pH below 4.3 or above 7.4, however.

The soils of Wisconsin vary widely along the pH scale, although most are favorable for general plant growth. The northern counties tend to have a neutral or slightly alkaline soil, although the surface may be acid. Many of the north-central soils are substantially acid in nature, requiring correction before good garden crops can be produced. The entire eastern third of the state has predominantly neutral soil, as do the counties on the Minnesota and Iowa borders. Finally, many soils of the southwest tend to be mixed, running from the neutral range to fairly acid.

The best way to ascertain your soil's pH value is to have it tested. The test is a simple and inexpensive one. (See page 10 for instructions.) You can also make a pH test yourself, using one of the little kits that many garden centers and catalogs offer. In fact, you can tell immediately whether your soil is acid, alkaline, or neutral by exposing it to a piece of litmus paper. If the paper turns pink, the soil is acid. If it turns blue, it is alkaline. If it does not change color at all, the soil is neutral. You can also use the litmus paper to test the water you

Table 3.
Pounds of Ground Limestone Needed to Raise pH in Seven Inches of Soil Depth

SOIL TYPE & AREA	pH 3.5 to 4.5	pH 4.5 to 5.5	pH 5.5 to 6.5
Sand & loamy sand:			
one acre	8,000.0	1,000.0	1,200.0
100 sq. ft.	1.8	2.3	2.8
Sandy loam:			
one acre		1,600.0	2,600.0
100 sq. ft.		3.7	6.0
Loam:			
one acre		2,400.0	3,400.0
100 sq. ft.		5.5	7.8
Silt loam:			
one acre		3,000.0	4,000.0
100 sq. ft.		6.9	9.2
Clay loam:			
one acre		3,800.0	4,600.0
100 sq. ft.		8.8	10.6
Muck:			
one acre	5,800.0	7,600.0	8,600.0
100 sq. ft.	13.3	17.7	19.7

(Based on USDA agricultural tonnage figure recommendations.)

might use for your garden. This is only a very general test, however.

Correcting the soil's pH. As nearly every gardener knows, the way to correct an overly acid soil is through the addition of lime. I believe that natural ground limestone is best, since there is no danger of poisoning the soil's life forms when the natural product is used. Limestone adds calcium to the soil, as well, thus serving double duty. (Note: If you want to add calcium to the soil without raising its pH, which is an unusual but conceivable situation. gypsum is the product generally recommended. Organic gardeners generally avoid it, since gypsum is a hydrated calcium sulfate, but it is difficult to find a substitute other than the lavish introduction of plant residues, which carry calcium in their leaves.)

The recommended amounts of lime to apply are given on the manufacturer's bag, or will be supplied with the return of your soil test. The recommended application will depend on your soil texture, but a normal application on loam, to move the pH up one full point, is 75 pounds of limestone per 1,000 square feet of soil—more in heavy soils, less in sandy soils.

Last, do not add lime to your soil each year as a routine matter. I do not know where the practice of annual and automatic liming got started, but I do know that plants are far more susceptible to an overly alkaline soil than to one that is acid—and that it is much more difficult to bring down the pH into the neutral range than to raise it from an acid condition.

If the soil is too alkaline, it can be brought down into the neutral range by the incorporation of organic matter with healthy helpings of peat moss, which is a naturally acid substance. Powdered sulfur is often recommended for this purpose, but the advantages of organic matter go far beyond the correction of pH, while the addition of sulfur provides few additional benefits.

The last word on pH is this: Do not take it too seriously. Do not get yourself in the position where you are trying to treat little patches of the garden differently because a pH of 6.5 is recommended for one crop and 7.0 for another. Nearly any garden plant will do well in the 6.5 to 7.2 range, no matter what the experts recommend. If, in your flower borders, you wish to incorporate peat to take down the pH for certain large plantings, fine. And if you want to do the same for your permanent berry patches, that's good. But if you try to put too fine a point on this pH business, you will soon find yourself tearing out your hair and cursing the day you ever heard of pH. A healthy soil, fed organically, seems to receive nearly all plants with equal grace. If, after a soil test, you want to correct the pH in a new garden plot, this is a wise thing to do. But after that, don't give it much thought. You will have better things to do.

Composing and Mulching

One aker well compast is worth akers three.
—Thomas Tusser (1557)

2 The heart of the organic method of gardening and farming is compost. It is the keystone, the core, the pivotal activity of the natural method. To many organic gardeners, the compost heap is a chief source of pride. On a chilly autumn day, they will make a special trip behind the tool shed just to watch it steam. They will spend more time in investigating better composting methods than in looking for income tax deductions. And no wonder. Compost produces terrific results.

The subject of compost has received considerable attention not only from scientists but from poets. I will borrow a poem by Walt Whitman that gives full praises to compost (while saying something less laudatory about mankind):

Behold this compost! behold it well!
Perhaps every mite has once formed part
   of a sick person—yet behold!
The grass of spring covers the prairies,
The bean bursts noiselessly through the
   mould in the garden.
The delicate spear of the onion pierces
   upward,
The apple-buds cluster together on the
   apple-branches,
The resurrection of the wheat appears
   with pale visage out of its graves,
What chemistry!

That the winds are really not infectious,
That all is clean forever and forever,
That the cool drink from the well tastes
   so good,
That blackberries are so flavorous and
   juicy.
That the fruits of the apple-orchard
   and the orange-orchard, that melons,
   grapes, peaches, plums, will none of
   them poison me,
That when I recline on the grass I do not
   catch any disease,
Now I am terrified at the Earth, it is that
   calm and patient,
It grows such sweet things out of such
   corruptions.
It turns harmless and stainless on its
   axis, with such endless successions
   of diseas'd corpses.
It distills such exquisite winds out of such
   infused fetor.
It gives such divine materials to men,
   and accepts such leavings from
   them at last.

Compost! Wonderful stuff, indeed. But just what is it?

There are various definitions in different dictionaries, textbooks, and agricultural bulletins, not all of which agree. My own definition of compost would be: *a mixture of different organic materials, air, and water, with the possible addition of soil and/or mineral products, which together have advanced so far in the process of decomposition as to be a valuable addition to soil for growing plants.*

That's quite a mouthful, but I do believe it is as short a definition as accuracy will allow. First, compost is a mixture—just as *fruit compote* is a mixture (both from the Latin *compositus*). Decomposed leaves alone are not compost, but they are *leaf mold*. Composted manure is not compost, but it is composted manure.

Second, compost is not compost until it has been composted! A pile of lawn clippings and garden refuse is not compost, and it will not be, until it is "finished"—sufficiently decomposed to be of immediate value in the soil to growing plants. The decomposition process requires both air and water, and so they are essential ingredients. On the other hand, both soil and mineral products (such as limestone) are valuable additions—but it is possible to make compost without them.

Composting is an essential part of nature's wheel of life, the never-ending process that brings new life from death. On the land, plant life springs from the soil, is fed by the sun and the rain, and, in death, returns to the soil to be composted and reborn. The marigold you grow today might contain a molecule (or one of Whitman's "mites") that has been the part of a thousand plants before, and traveled through the bellies of a hundred animals and birds. It may have ridden halfway around the world on the wind or the water. It may have formed part of a single cell of a small animal, or stayed for a hundred years in the trunk of a stately oak. It has died and been reborn countless times. So does nature conserve and recycle its resources and so does compost play a vital role in this recycling process.

Composting is, then, an integral part of the wheel of life. It is nature's way of reducing raw organic materials (leaves, dead plants and animals, animal manure, etc.), mainly through the actions of soil organisms, to a crumbly brown humus that then becomes a vital part of the soil itself. All organic matter occurring naturally in the soil has gotten there by this composting process which has been going on ever since the first crude plant life appeared and died on the face of the earth.

From raw plant wastes to rich, dark compost. Whether done in fourteen days or fourteen months, composting is the keystone of the organic method.

When you compost your kitchen wastes, you simply emulate nature's own methods. Of course, you have learned how to make certain refinements to help along and speed the process and you use that compost where it will do your garden plants the most good. In this way you work in harmony with nature while achieving your own gardening ends in a most scientific and efficient way.

What Compost Does

Compost is a fertilizer. It contains nitrogen, phosphorous, potassium, calcium, the essential trace minerals—all the chemical nutrients that plants need for healthy growth. How much of these nutrients it contains depends of course on the ingredients that go into it. You can help determine its chemical composition by the materials you select.

Compost is a soil conditioner. It will lighten a heavy clay, add substance to a light sand, add porosity where it is lacking, improve water-holding capacity, aid soil structure, and enhance the physical environment for the growth of all plants.

Compost increases the population of the soil's life forms. It encourages the rapid multiplication of microorganisms and earthworms, both of which are vitally important to healthy plant growth.

Compost is a chemical catalyst for the release of mineral nutrients. The acids it forms during decomposition cause chemical changes that release those minerals so that plant roots can absorb and use them in the plant's natural growth processes. Other organisms that are encouraged by compost emit disease-resisting antibiotics to protect growing plants, while still others are able to fix nitrogen for plant absorption.

Last, many gardeners and farmers who have worked with compost for many years are convinced that it has some powers that we have not yet identified. This feeling comes about when composters look at the results of their efforts—the trees laden with sweet fruit, the vines heavy with robust vegetables, the large and brilliantly colored blossoms of their flowering plants, the rarity of disease and insect attack, and the vastly superior quality of everything they grow. It is a quality that they swear cannot be duplicated by any combination of chemical applications, and so they can attribute it only to some benefits imparted by compost, known to nature but unknown to humans. This is not to imply that any mystical powers are involved, but merely to acknowledge that we have not yet learned all there is to know about the earth.

George Washington Carver, who was himself an agricultural chemical wizard, advised, "Make your own fertilizer on the farm. Buy as little as possible. A year-round compost pile is absolutely essential and can be had with little labor and practically no cash outlay." Dr. Carver had plenty of experience with both compost and chemical fertilizers. He died in 1943 before the advocates of agribusiness had convinced most farmers that composting was old-fashioned, impractical, and inefficient.

How to Use Compost

Compost will help all growing plants. You will screen it to use as a potting soil and to start seedlings and grow house plants. You will till it into the vegetable garden and the flower beds. You will side-dress your peonies with compost, and you will make a "tea" of it to feed your roses in midsummer. You will spoon-feed it to your baby McIntosh apple tree, and you will rake it into the lawn in the spring. Your landscape plantings will gobble up tons of compost as the years go by, and you will be glad they did. You will use compost for everything you grow, after you have learned of its versatility and seen the results of its use. Compost is the nearest thing to a garden panacea that you are ever likely to see.

In the vegetable garden. Use all the compost you can in the vegetable garden. In the fall, spread a 2-to-3-inch layer and till it in, along with the last of the plant wastes. When planting in spring, incorporate plenty of well-rotted compost with every seedling you transplant, and mix in plenty in the furrows where you plant seeds. During the growing season, apply compost as a top-dressing, hoeing it shallowly into the soil. It is virtually impossible to use too much compost, as you can see for yourself by sinking a tomato seedling into a well-advanced compost heap. The production of that plant will make your eyes pop.

In the flower garden. The liberal use of compost will give you larger and healthier plants of all kinds, with larger and more brilliant blooms. When planting spring-flowering bulbs in the fall, work plenty of fully matured compost directly under and around each bulb. When sowing annuals in the spring, treat the seedbed with compost just as you would for vegetable sowings. When perennials have come up in the spring, work generous amounts of compost into the beds after loosening the top several inches of soil. During the growing season, all flowers will benefit from feedings of "compost tea." Just fill a bucket one-third full of compost and fill the rest of the bucket with water. Stir well and let this stand for a day. Then stir again and pour the tea around your perennials and annuals. The good nutrients will soak down into the soil and feed the plant roots without disturbing them. You can use the same compost for several applications of tea, and afterward you can work the remaining solid material into the soil for general enrichment purposes.

For the lawn. Compost will help you to establish a permanent and healthy lawn that will last a lifetime. The use of compost in building new lawns and renovating sick lawns is explained in Chapter 8, beginning on page 235. For regular lawn feeding, compost should be screened as fine as possible and scattered lightly over the lawn at regular intervals. In the spring, a major feeding may be made, using a spike-tooth aerator. The holes that the aerator makes will catch screened compost and send it down to the roots, while rains will envelop surface compost and carry nutrients down slowly, thus providing nourishment throughout the season.

Mulch window boxes with finished, sifted compost. The soil in the box will hold moisture longer, and each rainfall will wash nutrients down to hungry plant roots.

For trees and shrubs. No tree or shrub should be planted without incorporating a bushel or more of compost into the planting hole. The compost, mixed with topsoil, leaf mold, peat moss, limestone, and sand (or any combination of these, depending on soil requirements) will give a permanent planting a great send-off and will help it to become well established in short order by providing an ideal root environment. Compost should also be used to keep tree and shrub roots well supplied with nutrients during the growing season. Again, full directions are given later on, in the chapter devoted to trees and shrubs.

For seedlings and house plants. You can use your very best compost, well screened, as a potting soil for house plants and for starting seeds in the early spring. You should use your most mature compost for this purpose, to avoid any chance of burning the tender young seedlings during their crucial first days.

Compost, then, is your all-around soil conditioner/fertilizer, more valuable than any commercial products you might buy. And you can make it yourself, right at home, for practically nothing or absolutely nothing. There is no greater bargain in the world.

How to Make Compost

When you think about it, the term "making compost" is an arrogant one. We don't really *make* compost—we merely try to create the conditions that will encourage Nature to make the compost herself. We are not following a dress pattern, here, or building a table—we are working with the very process of life itself. Neither are we working with a magic formula that will produce results with no understanding or effort on our part. I venture these thoughts not to air my personal philosophy, but because I think it can help us to work toward better compost and better gardens.

Some years ago, an interesting article appeared in the *Wall Street Journal*. The writer, Ralph E. Winter (an Ohioan who, the article tells us, was brought up on a Wisconsin dairy farm), was telling of his garden troubles and failures, including an unresponsive compost heap. He writes:

That brings up the compost pile. It was supposed to solve the soil problem by providing virtually free fertilizer along with humus to condition the soil. We dutifully piled up the grass clippings all the previous summer and in the fall added a large mound of leaves. We even drove around the community and picked up leaves the neighbors had bagged. We stirred it all together and left it to "compost" over winter.

Well, something went wrong because when spring came we still had a pile of leaves, some wet and some dry but still perfectly sound leaves, instead of the expected decayed mulch. We dug it into the garden anyway rather than wait another year to see if the magical composting process would work.

Apparently, Mr. Winter received some bad advice, or, at best, incomplete advice on making compost. He followed bad directions with little understanding of the life processes he was dealing with, and then he sat back and waited for the "magical composting process" to perform for him. Just from his short description, I can count three major mistakes that he made:

1. He *"dutifully piled up the grass clippings all the previous summer."* Instead, he should have been adding the clippings to a properly constructed heap all summer long, and he should have included topsoil and at least some manure, which would have introduced essential microorganisms to the mixture.

2. *". . . and in the fall added a huge mound of leaves."* Leaves are perhaps the most difficult of all organic materials to compost (unless you choose to compost bones). They should be shredded, first, and in no case should they make up the bulk of any compost heap, unless you have all the time in the world.

3. *"We stirred it all together and left it to 'compost' over winter."* Winter is the worst time for

composting, because the cold temperatures inhibit the actions of the microorganisms that break down organic materials. The compost heap should have been working away all summer long.

In short, Mr. Winter did everything wrong, and then he counted on the "magic" of composting to produce humus for his garden. I think that no gardener will make mistakes like these if he approaches composting with a realistic attitude—and that attitude is, as I have said, one of *encouraging life processes*. A compost heap must have water, because water is essential to all life. It must have air because the essential microorganisms cannot live without air. It must have soil from the garden because soil contains the microorganisms that will multiply rapidly throughout the heap, eagerly attacking the other materials and breaking them down into humus. The compost heap must be large enough to allow for its heating up, too—four by six feet is the smallest generally recommended—because a heap that is too small will lose too much heat from surface contact with the air. All these factors—the basics of compost making—are vitally important in creating the composting life environment. Think about your composting project in these terms, and you will get better compost.

Six Composting Methods

The Indore method. There are quite a few ways to let nature make compost for you—under the ground, above the ground, in bins, boxes, bags, and garbage cans, in strips, in sheets, in trenches, in 14 months or in 14 days, indoors or outdoors. But they all stem from the famous Indore method developed by Sir Albert Howard during his agricultural research in India. This is the basic method of composting, and the one that is still used most widely today. Here is how to do it.

Select a good spot for the heap. The area should be fairly level, at least four by six feet, preferably larger: six by ten would be ideal for optimum heat conservation. Most people choose a spot at the back of the garden, perhaps hidden by a small fence or a low hedge. But remember that a compost heap does not have to be unattractive, and it certainly shouldn't give off any offensive odors or attract rodents—not if it is built right. Most people want to contain the heap by constructing some sort of walls on three sides of the designated area (leaving the fourth side open for working room). These walls can be made of cinder blocks, wooden posts and boards, or some other permanent construction—or, if you do not want a permanent bin, you can use walls of sod or of posts and wire fencing (which can be rolled up and moved after the heap is finished), or an arrangement of boards that can be removed easily, perhaps built upon the concept of the Lincoln Logs we used to play with as kids. Or, you can have no walls at all—but in this case, you should have plenty of room to work in, because the heap will tend to spread out as you add materials to it.

After you have selected the site. dig away the topsoil (12 to 18 inches) from the area and pile it to one side. You will use this to stimulate the heap from time to time, and you will be improving the subsoil that you have exposed.

Next, put a layer of brush over the area, perhaps a foot deep, to form a good base that will provide drainage. Now you are ready to begin to "sandwich" the layers of organic materials. (And the only reason for sandwiching layers is to be able to measure amounts of the different materials with some degree of accuracy.) Over the brush, put down a six-inch layer of green matter—weeds, grass clippings, plant wastes, leaves, etc. If you can shred these materials—with a compost shredder or by attacking a pile of them with your rotary lawn mower—they will decay much faster. (The microorganisms will have more surface area to work on.) After that, put down a two-inch layer of manure, followed by a sprinkling of topsoil mixed with powdered limestone. Repeat these layers—green matter, manure, topsoil/limestone—until the heap reaches about five feet in height. After that, keep the heap watered so that it is damp but not soggy, and wait for about six weeks. Then it will be time to turn it so that the

A compost bin can be quite attractive, if a little thought is put into it.

Wire fencing makes a good portable compost bin.

A split log compost bin allows air to enter for more efficient composting.

materials on the outer edges of the heap get a chance to go into the inside, where all the action is. Turning the heap sounds like a back-breaking job, and if your back is weak, perhaps it is. But you need do it only twice a year at most, and a heap of the size I have just described can be turned in half an hour. If you shovel your own snow in winter, then turning the heap will present no problem. If not, then I suggest that you hire a husky boy for the job. Indore tradition specifies that you turn the heap a second time, in another six weeks, although some veteran gardeners have expressed doubts about the necessity of the second turning. Neverthe-

less, after three months, the heap should be finished and ready for use.

When compost is finished. How can you tell when the compost is finished? If it is crumbly, dark brown, and has the characteristic earthlike odor, it is finished. But if the materials are still easily recognizable, it is not. You can check the progress of your heap by plunging your hand into it and feeling the temperature. If it is "working" properly. the heap will be very hot inside—uncomfortable to the touch—because of the intense bacterial action. The heating process should begin during the first few days. After a number of days of heating the heap will cool down slowly, and when it seems quite cool inside the major composting action will be finished in that part of the heap.

Compost problems. If you detect a musty odor in the heap, like the one you get when you leave a sack of potatoes in the basement too long, this indicates that mold is forming because of a lack of air. Tear apart the heap, add some spoiled hay or straw to loosen it up, and put it back in the bin. On the other hand,

If the heap does nothing at all, it is usually a sign of a lack of nitrogen materials, or of microorganisms. Manure and topsoil are the remedies here. There are bacterial activators on the market, but they have never been proven more effective than topsoil, which has all the activators your heap can use.

The three-month estimate for finished compost is based on following directions for building the traditional Indore heap. The amount of

Keep the heap watered, making sure that it is always damp but never soggy. Bacteria cannot work without moisture.

Powdered limestone is a valuable addition to the heap.

if you detect an ammonia smell, it means that you are losing nitrogen through the formation of free ammonia. The problem may be too much fresh manure or too much lime. Cut down on these, tear apart the heap, add spoiled hay or straw and more green matter, and return the materials to the bin.

time it takes for your heap to complete its composting process will depend on several factors, including the weather (longer, if it is cool), the size of the heap (longer, if it is small), and the particle size of the green matter you use (shorter, if you shred all materials).

The Fourteen-Day method. When I worked as an editor for *Organic Gardening and Farming* magazine back in the 1950s, we ran experiments at the Rodale Organic Experimental Farm in Emmaus, Pennsylvania, to see in just how little time we could make finished compost. Scientists at the University of California had cut the minimum time to 14 days, just by shredding all materials and turning the heap every two or three days. We followed the California recommendations and, after adding a few wrinkles of our own, got to the point where we could produce finished compost in *10 days*. Now you

The Indore method specifies that the heap be built in layers, so that measurement of materials is reasonably accurate. Here, a layer of green matter is being added.

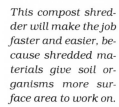

This compost shredder will make the job faster and easier, because shredded materials give soil organisms more surface area to work on.

may have absolutely no desire to set any world records for composting—and neither did we, for that matter. But the lesson to be learned in such experimenting is just what factors are responsible for encouraging the composting process. Shredding of materials, of course, is the major factor. Another important one is the use of sufficient manure, which contains plenty of nitrogen and produces heat within the heap in the shortest possible time. The third factor of importance is moisture. Microorganisms cannot work in a bone-dry environment, nor in a constantly soggy one. Keep the heap *damp*, and provide good drainage. Aeration never presented a problem in our experiments, but it is

When compost is crumbly, dark brown, and has that characteristic earth-like odor, you know it is finished and ready for use.

doubtless a fourth important factor that you should consider carefully.

The anaerobic method. Anaerobic composting (composting without air) is a method that has led to some systems of municipal composting, the large-scale composting of urban wastes. The advantage of anaerobic composting is that it presents no problems with odor, which might be particularly important if you work with fresh manure on a small city lot. You can compost manure by piling it on the ground (not on grass or sod, which might discourage earthworms from coming up), soaking the manure heap with water, covering it with black plastic (to shut out the sun), sealing the edges with soil and rocks, and forgetting about it for a couple of months. When you lift the plastic, you should have crumbly. sweet-smelling, composted manure, the kind that you buy in bags at garden centers and seed stores.

Other gardeners have reported success with anaerobic composting in dark-colored leaf bags or in garbage cans. Still, the method is not a very widespread one, and much research remains to be done in the area.

The earthworm method. Still another composting method lets the earthworms do the work for you. Build wooden pits of any size, but probably no more than two feet high. Mix the materials in about the same proportions as recommended for the Indore method, and fill the pits to within a few inches of the top. Then moisten the mixture thoroughly and add earthworms. The more earthworms you add, the faster will be the composting process. About 500 would be the absolute minimum for a pit three feet square. Then, put a lid on the box, since earthworms prefer to work in the dark, but do not make it too tight fitting. After that, let the earthworms go to work. At the end of a few months, you will have beautiful, crumbly compost, and about four times as many earthworms as you started with. Put about half of the earthworms into the garden (or let the kids sell some of them for fishworms), and start out again with more raw material.

Strip composting and sheet composting. Both of these methods were discussed briefly in Chapter 1 (page 12). Sheet composting is simply the process of spreading the raw materials over the soil and tilling them into the earth, thus allowing the composting process to take place right in the soil instead of in a heap or bin. The advantage of sheet composting is that there is very little work involved, and more of the material's nitrogen will be preserved (since some of a heap's nitrogen is inevitably vaporized and lost). The disadvantage is that you cannot plant anything in the garden during the month or two that the materials are working. The heat generated by the composting process would burn plants, especially if fresh manure is used.

Strip composting is identical to sheet composting, except that you divide the garden plot into wide strips, perhaps five feet each, and apply the compost materials to every other strip—or even every third strip—while you plant the other strips as usual. In the next growing season, you plant the strips you had composted the previous year, and compost the strips that you had planted the previous year. In this way, you take only part of your garden out of production each year, while enriching the remaining part for future years. Both strip and sheet composting are excellent methods of improving the soil for plants, but only if you are fortunate enough to have the garden space to spare.

Great Materials for Composting

By now you may be asking yourself, "Just where does he think I am going to get all this manure? How will I find enough green matter to build this glorious heap?" Perhaps the only material you really have in abundance is leaves, and you get those only once a year, in a whirl of autumn color.

Well, the gathering of composting materials can be a problem, but it is one you can solve. Begin in and around your own home, of course, with plant wastes, kitchen scraps, grass clippings, and any other organic materials you might come across. Then, if you need more, go out and scavenge. Need manure? Many farmers wouldn't part with their manure under threat of death, but the operators of riding stables would, and so will many dairy farmers who keep large herds and till relatively little land. Is there a livestock feeding lot nearby? You can probably get all the manure you can use there. Or perhaps you have a farmer friend or relative. You probably can sweet-talk a friend out of enough manure to service your compost heap for a year. Investigate.

Then, for green matter and other materials, use your imagination and all the resources of your community. Get out the yellow pages and let your fingers do the walking. Call meat-packing houses, mills, breweries, dairies, vegetable-processing plants, etc. Call the city parks department to ask for lawn clippings and last year's leaves. Live near the water? Aquatic plants are always in abundance—often a nuisance in the water, where they clog up boat propellers, but a blessing in the compost heap. With a little effort and a little ingenuity, you will find all the materials you want—and you might have some pleasant adventures along the way. I certainly have.

Here are 14 materials that are great for composting. Most are fairly common, while others are harder to get but well worth going after. All are highly recommended for building the dark brown humus that makes plants grow.

Alfalfa hay. NPK (nitrogen-phosphorus-potash percentages) 2.45-0.50-2.10. A good source of both nitrogen and potash, alfalfa hay is available from many farmers in late August or September—or you might be able to buy a couple of bales of last year's crop at any time during the year, if the farmer has a surplus.

Bloodmeal is not only a good source of nitrogen, but an effective rabbit repellent, as well.

Bat guano. NPK 6.00-9.00-0.00. Here is a manure not available to everyone, but a great source of nitrogen and phosphorus, if you can get it. Large numbers of bats often roost in farmers' barns and in deserted outbuildings. Collect the guano during the day, when the bats will be sleeping high in the rafters. (It is best to keep out of their way during the evening feeding flight.)

Blood meal. NPK 15.00-1.30-0.70. A terrific nitrogen source, and also an effective rabbit repellent when sprinkled around the vegetable garden. Call meat-packing houses to ask about blood meal. You can buy it by the pound in garden centers, but the price is apt to be high.

Bone meal. NPK 4.00-21.00-0.20. One of the richest sources of phosphorus available; most composters will have to buy it at the garden center. but some lucky ones can pick it up at bone mills.

Brewer's grains (wet). NPK 0.90-0.50-0.05. The golden hops that make Wisconsin's beer sparkle can make your compost heap absolutely glow! Brewers discard mounds of hops after they have been "spent," and will likely let you have all you can haul away.

Cattle manure (fresh). NPK 0.29-0.17-0.10. Manure is the greatest activator for your compost heap; it is very important for fast heating. Get some any way you can, but get some! (If the farmer is a real friend he will lend his old Ford pickup truck to you for hauling it home.)

Duck manure (fresh). NPK 1.12-1.44-0.49. My waterfowling friends tell me that you can scrape copious amounts of wild duck manure off the ice of ponds in the early spring. But you will be luckier if you know a farmer who raises domestic ducks.

Horse manure (fresh). NPK 0.44-0.17-0.35. Find out on which days the stable hands clean out the stalls—and then get there before they do. One hour's volunteer effort will reward you with hundreds of pounds of the stuff—enough to last for months and months.

Kitchen scraps. The food scraps you discard end up either in Wisconsin's waters, where they pollute, or in dumps or landfill sites. Why not put them into your garden, where they will do some good? Kitchen wastes can attract both domestic and wild animals (usually rodents), however, and you should be careful to bury them about a foot deep into the heap and cover with soil. In sheet or strip composting, just trench them into the earth as you apply them.

Oak leaves. NPK 0.65-0.13-0.52. Any kind of leaves are great, especially as a source of trace minerals, and oak leaves are given just as an example. But remember that they're tough and should be shredded before going into the heap.

Rabbit manure. NPK 2.4-1.4-0.6. Of all the manures, rabbit manure is the highest in nitrogen. It is so high, in fact, that it should be used in limited quantities and mixed with other materials until it has composted thoroughly. Some rabbit raisers put earthworm boxes beneath wire rabbit cages to catch the droppings. The earthworms quickly compost the material into a rich and safe fertilizer/soil conditioner.

Swine manure. NPK 0.60-0.41-0.13. You'll learn a new respect for the much-maligned sow, when you learn that her manure is more valuable than that of any other large farm animal. Use it wisely!

Tobacco leaves. NPK 4.00-0.50-6.00. Residents of Wisconsin's tobacco-growing region should investigate the possibilities of picking up spoiled leaves from growers in the late summer and early fall. Shredding is essential for these giant leaves (and the stems, too), but the rewards in nutrients are well worth the effort expended.

Wood ashes. NPK 0.00-1.50-7.00. Potash is the big reward here. Save all the ashes from your fireplace, and urge your noncomposting neighbors to do the same. A single winter should produce a 20-gallon pail full of them if you use your fireplace a couple of times a week. And with the price of commercial fertilizers, saving your ashes is like getting a deposit back on your fireplace wood! (Don't use coal ashes.)

(Note: The NPK percentages given above for all manures assume that they are fresh. thus containing plenty of moisture. Dried manure contains up to four times the percentage of nutrients, pound for pound.)

Making leaf mold. Those who have a surplus of leaves—too many to use in other composting systems—will do well to make a leaf mold bin. You can use a circle made from old snow fence or wire fencing—anything that is open, letting in lots of air. Just fill the enclosure with shredded leaves and tamp them down as tightly as you can. Put the enclosure in an out-of-the-way place because it will take several years for the leaves to break down into mold. Shredding will reduce the time greatly.

There are two other ingredients you should have on hand when you use leaves for making leaf mold or compost. One is manure—fresh, if available but the commercial bagged kinds are okay too. The second is ground limestone. The manure is needed for its nitrogen content, which will enable the microorganisms to attack

Twenty great organic soil builders. TOP ROW: (l. to r.) wood ashes, basic slag, leaves, sawdust, blood meal. SECOND ROW: raw phosphate, greensand, bone meal, peat moss, cottonseed meal. THIRD ROW: seaweed, dried manure, tankage, peanut shells, leaf mold. FOURTH ROW: wood chips, manure, cocoa bean shells, compost, grass clippings.

Table 4. Nutrient Content of Representative Wisconsin Leaf Varieties

Tree	Calcium	Magne-sium	Potassium	Phos-phorus	Nitrogen	Ash	pH
Balsam fir	1.12	0.16	0.12	0.09	1.25	3.08	5.50
Red maple	1.29	0.40	0.40	0.09	0.52	10.97	4.70
Sugar maple	1.81	0.24	0.75	0.11	0.67	11.85	4.30
American beech	0.99	0.22	0.65	0.10	0.67	7.37	5.08
White ash	2.37	0.27	0.54	0.15	0.63	10.26	6.80
White oak	1.36	0.24	0.52	0.13	0.65	5.71	4.40
E. hemlock	0.68	0.14	0.27	0.07	1.05	--	5.50

Courtesy *Organic Gardening*

the leaves and break them down. (You can substitute other high-nitrogen materials such as blood meal or cottonseed meal, but manure is readily available and it adds other nutrients, too.) The other ingredient, limestone, is used to counteract the acid nature of most leaves. A good heaping handful of limestone with every wheelbarrow full of leaves should do the trick.

Finally, how do you shred leaves? Those lucky folk with a compost shredder will laugh at this question although the rest of us will continue to wonder. The best means I have come across is the use of an ordinary rotary mower. Simply heap the leaves next to a broad wall—a barn or garage will do fine. Then gradually dip the running mower into the leaves, avoiding stalls, and blow the shredded leaves against the side of the building. You can reduce a giant pile of leaves in short order by using this method. You may also use a bagger or a mulching mower.

Secrets of Mulching

The practice of mulching, like composting, is taken straight from nature's textbook. In the wild, all living soil is covered, either by growing plants or by the plant wastes of years gone by. The forest is covered constantly with a deep leaf mulch, and the prairie fields are never bare, summer or winter. Nature's mulch is her one giant step toward composting, for when any dead plant materials touch the ground, they come into contact with soil microorganisms and become intimately involved in the process of composting and soil formation. Noting the success of Mother Nature in forest and field, we do our best to emulate her in our gardens.

A mulch is simply any material—organic or inorganic—placed on top of the soil to benefit growing plants. Most mulches are organic, such as hay and sawdust. but others are inorganic, including plastic sheets and rocks.

The benefits of mulches cannot be counted on two hands, so valuable are they to garden success, especially here in Wisconsin's cold climate. But here are the major rewards, any one of which should be sufficient to send you on your way to gather up mulch materials for every part of the garden:

1. Mulches conserve moisture, protecting your plants against drought by slowing down evaporation. This is important for all plants, but especially so for the shallow-rooted ones such as blueberries. It is also essential for vegetable plantings in areas where watering is difficult or impossible.

2. Mulches increase soil aeration by keeping the surface soil loose and preventing soil crusting.

3. Mulches check weeds, saving you hours of work and grumbling.

4. Mulches improve soil texture and fertility, and they encourage soil microorganisms and earthworms. Organic mulches break down slowly from the bottom up and can actually be

regarded as a slow form of sheet composting. In the fall, many organic mulches can be plowed under for further soil enrichment.

5. Mulches moderate soil temperature. They reduce the possibility of root crops freezing in the late fall, and they protect young plants against late spring freezes, thus extending the growing season for many plants. During the summer, they also protect heat-sensitive crops (such as peas) from too much sun.

6. Mulches offer protection to small and tender plants from heavy winds, rain, and hail. A hay mulch can quickly be pulled up around young plants when bad weather threatens.

7. Mulches prevent the rotting and discoloration of those crops that ripen naturally on the ground, such as tomatoes, strawberries, cucumbers, and squash. They form a clean bed for these crops.

8. Mulches prevent root damage to perennials from winter heaving. The small feeder roots of perennials—especially the shallow-rooted ones—are often damaged by the heaving of the ground during alternate freezes and thaws, particularly during late fall and early spring. A heavy mulch helps to keep the soil temperature steady, thus preventing soil heaving and reducing root damage.

9. During heavy rains, mulches prevent mud from splashing on low-growing flowers, on sidewalks, on the siding of the house, on anything else that you would rather keep clean.

10. Mulches reduce the need for cultivation, sometimes eliminating it completely. Cultivating with a hoe kills weeds and keeps the soil loose and porous. A mulch does the same thing.

Materials for Mulching

A wide variety of materials are suitable for mulching, although some are more suitable than others. Here is a rundown of some of the more popular ones:

Buckwheat hulls. This is a very nice-looking mulch, effective against weeds and easy to handle, although a little light and subject to blowing for the first few days. Buckwheat hulls let water pass through easily, which is a big point in their favor. This is a mulch you will have to buy at the garden center unless you have access to a processing plant.

Cocoa bean hulls and shells. Both are attractive and effective mulches, suitable for your showy flower beds. For the first week, they will make your garden smell like one giant chocolate bar, which always delights the children. These must be purchased at the garden center, and the price is apt to be high enough for you to rake them up and store them in the autumn instead of tilling them under.

Fibercloth. This is a relatively new product made from wood waste, and a real advance over the black plastic which it largely replaces. Designed specifically as a garden mulch, fibercloth lets in water but prevents seeds from germinating. It costs more than plastic, but is reusable. It comes in rolls, like linoleum.

Horsehair mats. Many people who install new carpeting throw out the old carpeting—including those old horsehair mats. Collect these whenever possible, because they make a great mulch. They are virtually earth-colored, too, making them suitable for use in the perennial beds. They will turn darker after a few rains, blending in nicely with the soil around them. and they will last for several years.

Lawn clippings. Here is an effective mulch that you can apply all season long. Clippings are effective against weeds, easy to handle, and they stay put. They do tend to heat up and decompose quickly, though, especially if they are very moist and the day is hot. Keep newly trimmed grass away from tender plant stems.

Leaves. Unshredded leaves tend to mat down like thousands of little ink blotters, excluding both air and moisture from reaching the soil. It is best to shred them and mix them with other materials, perhaps hay or sawdust.

Paper and plastic. Both are sold commercially, in rolls. They are effective against weeds, but awfully unsightly, easily torn and blown away, and, in my opinion, ecologically offensive. They offer nothing for the soil after their use as a mulch has expired. Some gardeners have used several sheets of newspaper as mulch.

This is okay, if you want a garden full of newspapers, but never use newsprint with colored inks, such as the Sunday comics. These inks may cause small amounts of lead to be absorbed by plants. Plastic sheeting also contains polychlorinated biphenyls—PCBs—but these pose no threat unless they are burned, in which case the harmful PCBs are released into the air.

Peat moss. This is a good-looking material—rich, dark brown, and neat—that will really dress up flower beds. But weeds tend to grow up through peat, unless the peat is applied fairly heavily; and after it becomes dry it tends to shed water with all the facility of wax paper.

Pine needles. These are a good mulch for acid-loving plants such as berries, and, of course, young pine plantings.

Sawdust and wood chips. Both are effective mulches, although some experts believe there is some danger of sawdust robbing the soil of nitrogen. Sawdust is recommended for

Spoiled hay is of little use to the farmer — but it is far and away the favorite mulch for the vegetable garden.

berries, especially, while the chips are rather attractive when used with landscape plantings. They turn darker with age.

Spoiled hay. This is the most popular mulch for the vegetable garden. Buy or beg bales from a farmer. To place the mulch, cut the baling twine and just peel off six to eight-inch slabs to place between the vegetable rows. The hay slabs go down fast, almost like putting carpet tile in your garden. Hay is effective against weeds, lets rain pass through easily, and keeps the soil moist and cool during summer. At the end of the season, just pick up the intact slabs and store them for next year. Any loose hay can be tilled under in the fall, used for winter protection of perennials, trees, and shrubs, or added to the compost heap.

Stones and rocks. If you have access to large, flat stones, try them as a mulch, especially on banks and steep slopes where they will help to prevent erosion most effectively. As a discourager of weeds, stones are obviously unbeatable, and they trap the sun's heat during the day, keeping the surrounding soil warmer on cold spring nights. There are disadvantages, however; stones are heavy to work with, and they do harbor some destructive insects.

Weeds. There is nothing wrong with using weeds for mulch, except that they are unattractive and capable of depositing unwanted seeds in the garden if they are added when the seeds are mature. For larger plantings of potatoes, squash, etc., however, they can be quite useful—although most gardeners prefer to relegate weeds to the compost heap.

Wheat straw. This is nearly as effective as spoiled hay, and you can often get it free from farmers. A possible disadvantage is that it is likely to be full of wheat seeds, which will sprout lovely green shoots throughout your garden. The sprouting wheat won't affect your growing crops, but weedophobes might be bothered by the extra plant growth.

Other materials. There are dozens of other materials you can use, including cornstalks and cobs, rotted pinewood, wastes from vegetable-processing plants, tree bark and sawmill scraps, leather tannery wastes, and other natural products and industrial wastes. If it isn't toxic and if it does the job, use it. Again, walk the yellow pages to find all the free and low-cost mulch materials you can use in every corner of your garden.

When to apply mulch. For annual flowers and vegetables, apply a spring mulch after the soil has warmed up fully and the seedlings and transplants are well established. If you apply mulch too early, the soil will not receive the full warming effects of the sun, and plant growth will be slowed. This is crucial here in Wisconsin, where spring is slow enough as it is.

Your prize landscape plants can be protected over the winter by the application of a heavy autumn mulch, preferably made after the soil has frozen. Remove the mulch after the last average spring frost date.

For your perennials, adopt the same policy. After the weather turns warm in the spring, remove the winter mulch and stack it near the beds. Cultivate lightly and then replace the mulch.

For all plants, the mulch should be applied after you have fertilized and incorporated any supplemental organic matter to the soil, just as a matter of convenience. This is true for both spring and fall mulch applications. If you apply more fertilizer during the season, the mulch can be pushed aside quite easily for the purpose, then replaced.

How much mulch? The amount of mulch you apply depends on how much is needed to do the job. You should apply enough so that the weeds do not grow through. In the case of hay, it might be eight inches or more—but only one inch of sawdust should do the same job. For materials such as cocoa bean shells, buckwheat hulls, pine needles, and lawn clippings, from two to three inches should be about right. As you experiment, you will quickly learn the right amounts of different mulches to use for all garden purposes.

The Ruth Stout no-work method. In 1955, Ruth Stout, an inveterate Connecticut gardener, published a book called *How to Have a Green*

Thumb without an Aching Back. The book created a sensation in the gardening world because it advocated a deep, year-round hay mulch all over the garden. With the continuous mulch, Ruth Stout had eliminated all plowing, tilling, cultivating, composting, and several other time-honored gardening chores. Each spring, she simply pushed aside the mulch, dropped in the seeds or new plants, and returned to the back porch to watch another season of spectacular results.

Well, actually there is more to the method than that, and if you are interested in Miss Stout's revolutionary approach, I refer you to her books, which are certainly among the most delightful, entertaining, and informative in all garden literature. Ruth Stout died in 1980 at the age of 96. She gardened actively until she was 95. She was a fascinating, warm, and delightful person, both in her books and in person. And her system worked, at least for her. I have never been brave enough to adopt it, myself, but I do recommend that you look into her no-work system, especially if age or physical infirmity limits your activities.

Growing Your Own Mulch

If you need 30 or more bales of hay for a good-size garden, your pocketbook might not be able to stand the strain, not to mention your back in transporting the bales from the farm to your garden. That is why some gardeners are now planting their own hay crops. Anyone with an unused half-acre can plant it to a grass or legume crop and in a short time can begin to harvest and dry home-grown mulch. Of course, the hay may also be used as a livestock feed or can be plowed under as a green manure crop to upgrade the soil on which it is grown. Even if you cut and remove it, the soil will be vastly improved in its organic matter content, because the root systems are generally equal in volume to the top growth. If you harvest a ton of hay from a plot, in other words, you'll know that you have also added a ton of green organic matter to the soil of that plot.

Timothy, fescue, and other volunteer grasses are the least expensive, but clover and alfalfa make the best hay, especially if you plan to use any of it for feed. A half-acre of alfalfa will require about 20 pounds of seed. Add the

Mulch, mulch, and more mulch was the key to success for Ruth Stout, shown here working in her Connecticut garden.

cost of any manure you plan to add to the soil, and you can pretty well figure your costs.

Any soil that now supports good stands of thistles and tall-growing grasses will support good stands of hay. The soil pH for alfalfa should be between 6.5 and 6.9, and the seed should be double or triple inoculated for best results. Planting times vary, so it is best to check with your county Extension agent.

The small plot may be prepared with a garden tiller, but larger areas should be plowed and disked. The seed may be broadcast by hand or planted with a mechanical drill. If broadcast (or spread with a lawn seeder), the patch should be harrowed lightly to cover the seed.

Small plantings are easily cut with a mower attachment on a power cultivator or tractor. If you are really sentimental (and in top physical shape), you might wish to harvest with a scythe. Scything, however, is largely a lost art, and the gardener who tries it once might never want to attempt it again.

The hay is usually cut before seed heads form (in the case of grasses) or before the flowers fade and die (in the case of alfalfa and other legumes). Just like Wisconsin farmers, you should be able to get up to three crops a year from a single plot.

After hay is cut, it is swept with a hayfork into long and narrow windrows, where it is left to dry. After it has dried sufficiently, it can be piled into haystacks or baled. How can you tell whether hay is dry enough to store? Take a one-quart ice cream container lined with wax or plastic, place a cut sample of the hay in it, and add one-half teaspoon of dry table salt. Seal the container and shake it for two or three minutes. If, after this, the salt is dry, then the hay is safe for storage. Hay that is not sufficiently cured before it is stacked or baled will quickly rot. If stored in a barn or shed, it may easily self-combust and burn the whole place down.

A good way for the home gardener to move hay from place to place (lacking the proper machinery) is to get an old living-room-size rug, sandwich two wood strips at the edge of the rug to hold it firm, and run ropes from the wood strips to the car bumper. The rug will hold plenty of hay and you can simply pull it from the field to the place you choose to store it. This is infinitely simpler than making 40 trips with a garden cart.

What to Do About the Weather

At Christmas I no more desire a rose
Than wish a snow in May's new-fangled mirth;
But like of each thing that in season grows.
　　　　　—Shakespeare
　　　　　　Love's Labour's Lost
　　　　　　(1594-95)

3 Shakespeare apparently didn't foresee the age of the FTD florist truck which can bring a rose at any old time—but he and his contemporaries must have kept a better sense of the natural order of things. In contrast we have learned just enough to make ourselves dissatisfied with the weather, particularly in the early Wisconsin spring when we feel we just can't take any more snow and freezing temperatures.

In Shakespeare's time we would have learned to resign ourselves to the coming and going of the seasons. Now we fight. And the tools with which we fight are growing more numerous all the time.

If ever a way is found to make the weather perfect the year around, we Wisconsin gardeners would be a sorry lot. We love to complain about the weather. Some of us find it a handy scapegoat for many or our garden failures. Others hold up our harsh northern climate as a badge of courage, making our garden triumphs that much more satisfying. Most of us, though, usually just grumble or smile contentedly, depending on the weather of the day, and then we do the best we can.

In early April, when the books say we should be putting in our peas, we laugh bitterly as we grab our snow shovels, hopefully for the last time that season. Then scarcely a month later, an early heat wave wilts our peas and sends our spinach bolting to seed. And no sooner do we pick the spinach when a cold and rainy week rots our lima beans cold in the ground, right where we planted them the week before.

At this point, I cannot help but share my favorite gardener's prayer, this one taken from the delightful little book *The Gardener's Year,* written by Karel Capek and published originally in Czech in 1929. The first English translation appeared two years later, and the University of Wisconsin Press published an American edition in 1984.

O Lord, grant that in some way it may rain every day, say from about midnight until three o'clock in the morning, but, you see, it must be gentle and warm so that it can soak in; grant that at the same time it would not rain on campion, alyssum, helianthemum, lavender, and the others which you in your infinite wisdom know are drought-loving plants—I will write their names on a bit of paper if you like—and grant that the sun may shine the whole day long, but not everywhere (not, for instance, on spiraea, or on gentian, plantain lily, and rhododendron), and not too much; that there may be plenty of dew and little wind, enough worms, no plant-lice and snails, no mildew, and that once a week thin liquid manure and guano may fall from heaven. Amen.

As you can see, a gardener's concerns are both universal and timeless.

Grumble as we may, though, we Wisconsin gardeners are more fortunate than many. Weather changes can come quickly, but not nearly so quickly as in the northern plain states to the west. Our growing season is short, but still long enough for us to grow almost all the vegetable crops we want (especially if we choose the right varieties) and enough different ornamental plants to afford ourselves an infinite variety of foliage and bloom for most of the year. And, perhaps most important, Wisconsin is blessed with one of the most favorable rainfall climates in the world, according to a fact-packed booklet called *Wisconsin Weather.*

In this chapter, we will not go into the volumes of climatological statistics for the state. For such statistics, as well as for much general and helpful information about Wisconsin's climate, I refer you to the aforementioned booklet, *Wisconsin Weather*, which is available from your county Extension agent. Instead, we will concentrate on the ways that weather affects your garden and ways in which you can work within Wisconsin's climate to grow better gardens.

The growing season. The time between the last killing frost in spring and the first killing frost in autumn is the active growing season. That time, in Wisconsin, ranges from about 182 days down in Kenosha County in the extreme southeast, to 112 days up in Bayfield County, where the last spring frost can be expected on May 28, while the first frost of autumn comes around September 17, only 16 weeks later.

Sixteen weeks seems an unmercifully short season, but most garden annuals—both flowers and vegetables—can be grown successfully in that time. When it comes to trees, shrubs, and perennials, varieties must be chosen with more care, since they must be winter hardy. But even gardeners in Wisconsin's coldest corners can stretch the season by the use of cold frames and hotbeds, by wise mulching methods, and by intelligent soil management. In Wisconsin,

we do everything we can to start plants earlier in the spring, and to nurse along crops well into the fall. By applying season-stretching methods, we can form, for our own gardens, a microclimate nearly equivalent to the natural climate of any garden several hundred miles to the south.

Choosing Varieties for Wisconsin

When buying seeds and plants, be sure to choose those varieties that will do well in Wisconsin's climate. You can play it safe by picking up the annual lists of recommended vegetable, fruit, and flower varieties from your county agent's office. These have been tested by state and university experts and have passed all tests. You can plant them with assurance. If you are adventurous, however, you will go beyond the official recommendations and try some varieties that have not been officially tested, but which sound interesting to you.

In selecting annuals, you can afford to be adventurous. Just remember that buying non-recommended varieties is a gamble—and you should gamble only as much as you can afford to lose. Perhaps the best plan is to keep the bulk of your garden space to the recommended varieties and devote a smaller portion to experimental varieties. When choosing new permanent plantings, of course, the stakes are much higher. Few things are more discouraging than investing heavily in an attractive shrub or tree, nursing it along for three or four years. falling in love with it, only to have it winter-killed when it is approaching maturity.

If you choose varieties from the seed catalogs, look for the clues to northern hardiness. The first clue is the location of the seedsman or nursery. Generally, stock purchased from northern and local growers can be assumed to be fully hardy for our area. Local nurseries, in fact, would be foolish to sell you any other kind. However, the misconception is still common among northern gardeners that southern-grown stock is untrustworthy, that it will be tender and more susceptible to winter-kill than the same plant raised in a northern climate.

This belief is effectively put to rest by Laurence Manning, head of the nationally known Kelsey Nursery Service for many years, in his book *The How and Why of Better Gardening*:

"Now most nurseries, north and south alike, do not collect their own seed at all but buy it from seedsmen: hence the location of the nursery has nothing to do with the inherited hardiness of the plants grown there. Moreover, the named varieties of plants most commonly grown in nurseries never grow from seed, but only from grafts or cuttings and are identical in every respect, including hardiness, no matter where grown.

"How could such an erroneous idea get started? Probably because in early days most southern-grown roses and fruit trees died their first winter in the north. Northern gardeners damned southern stock, but the true villain was the calendar with its arbitrary divisions of the year. A woody plant is not safe until it has hardened off, no matter what the calendar says. The northerners wanted their shipments in October—the proper time for northern-grown plants—and southern nurserymen obliged. But in the south many plants do not harden off in October—It may be as late as early December—and unripened wood dies in the first freeze.

"As soon as the facts began to be known, scrupulous southern nurserymen refused early shipments. Sales were more difficult, for plants arrived north in December, rather late for planting; they usually had to be stored carefully over the winter and not planted until spring. Incidentally, well-managed storage proved so safe and such an advantage for early spring shipments, that fall digging and winter storage are practiced more every year, both north and south, for such plants as can safely be handled that way. (Deciduous trees and shrubs can; evergreens usually cannot)."

Southern-grown trees and shrubs, then, can be shipped north safely in early spring but not in autumn, unless you are willing to handle them in uncomfortably cold weather.

Look for other clues in the catalog, too. Look for the terms "winter hardy in the north,"

"extremely hardy," or "survived in winter trials at such-and-such below zero."

Hardiness, of course, refers to a plant's ability to withstand cold winters without being killed. A plant's hardiness depends on its parentage, i.e., in what climate its predecessors originated. Modern plant-breeding methods have attempted to encourage hardiness in trees, shrubs, and perennials, but their success has been limited. Unless you have a greenhouse, then, better take Shakespeare's advice. Don't look for roses at Christmas—or even for peas in May, for that matter.

In the catalogs, you will also see references to "half-hardy" plants. These are plants which are hardy under normal conditions, but which might be killed or severely injured by climatic abnormalities such as a prolonged cold snap out of season or an abnormal period of alternate freezing and thawing.

Protecting half-hardy plants. You can offer your half-hardy plants special protection, increasing greatly their chances for survival. Remember that these are plants teetering on the edge of their natural climates, and that you can do things to make them feel more at home. Here are the rules, as set down by Mr. Manning:

1. Plant half-hardy plants on a hill, where frosts will not settle. A north slope is better, since spring growth will be delayed until after late frosts have passed.

2. Ensure good drainage to encourage autumn ripening or "hardening off" of woody stems.

3. Protect plants from strong winds that might draw too much moisture from them. Wrap tree trunks with paper tape made for the purpose. Try to plant the half-hardies south of a windbreak—shrubs, trees, a hill, a building—anything that will break up sweeping fall and winter winds.

4. Mulch the plants after the ground has frozen. Soil moisture will be conserved and ground heaving will be minimized.

5. Keep plants well pruned to prevent wind damage.

6. Plant half-hardies in spring (not fall), so that they will have a full growing season to become accustomed to their new environment and prepare for the winter.

7. Avoid pruning, watering, and feeding in late summer, to encourage hardening off and prevent new soft growth just before freezing temperatures set in. (In the case of evergreens, though, water heavily in the late autumn, since the roots must supply moisture to plants throughout the winter.)

8. For half-hardy perennial flowers, simply mulch heavily after the ground has frozen. The tops of perennials die back after the plant has bloomed, and the sap then retreats to the roots to await another spring. It is the roots that must be protected until warm weather returns. The mulch should be removed as soon as the sun

This sturdy, young tomato plant can be transplanted into the open as soon as all danger of frost has passed. But it still will not make any significant growth until the temperature gets into the 60s.

begins to warm the ground, usually in May, sometimes earlier in the southern reaches of the state.

In growing annual flowers and vegetables, you need not be concerned about winter hardiness, since the plants will be expected to complete their growing cycle during a single growing season. Here, you should watch instead for the stated number of days to maturity. You can calculate your own growing season by checking the frost maps on pages 57-59. The spring map gives the average frost date for your locality (meaning that there is a 50 percent chance that frost will occur after that date) and an alternate date after which there is only a 10 percent chance of frost. The fall map gives similar percentages for chances of frost occurring before the dates indicated.

When calculating your growing season, remember that seeds do not germinate and plants do not grow when the temperature is below 40°, and that growth is slow among hot-weather plants until the thermometer gets into the 60s. An especially cold spring, even without frost, can retard plant development, and so can a long dry spell in summer. To be on the safe side, you should add about 20 percent to whatever figure the seed company gives as the days to maturity.

If you can find no clue to hardiness in the catalog or on the seed pack, check the lists of recommended varieties that are available from your county agent. If you still cannot find the plants you are interested in, do not hesitate to call your agent. He may not have the answer right at hand, since he would have to have a veritable computer for a brain to memorize the characteristics of hundreds of thousands of plants, but he can find out and call you back. (Suggestion: Make your plant selections in January and February and call your agent at that time; the demands on his time are enormous during the spring.)

Soil temperature. Plants respond to soil temperature just as they do to air temperature—sometimes even more. Seeds will be retarded in germinating in a cold soil, and so will plant growth after those seeds have germinated. Soil temperature depends on air temperature, of course, but there are other factors. Heavy clay soils, for instance, warm up much more slowly in spring than sandy soils do. The number of hours of sunlight a soil receives has a great effect on its warming up, too, so that the soil temperature will be different in different parts of your garden. During the first really warm days of spring, mulches should be pulled aside so that the soil can receive the full warming effects of the sun.

Mulches are your best regulator of soil temperature. In general, they tend to keep soil temperatures in a moderate range, warming them in cold weather and keeping them cool in very hot weather. This is important not only for the physical protection of plants, but also as a conserver of water and an encourager of soil microorganisms. These microorganisms, which help to deliver plant nutrients, operate most efficiently in a moderate temperature—not below 41° and not above 130°, according to T. Bedfore Franklin, author of *Climates in Miniature* . Luxuriant growth of all plants depends on the delivery of nitrogen to the plant roots, and the soil bacteria will not deliver nitrogen efficiently when the soil is too cold. Again, remember that the "days to maturity" cited on the seed packet might be calculated for an ideal climate where the soil warms up early in the spring. Don't put full trust in these claims.

Before planting seeds directly into the garden, be sure to check the seed packets for any instructions pertaining to soil temperature. Some annuals, such as asters and lettuce, should be planted after danger of frost is past but while the soil is still cool. Others, including most flowers and vegetables, should be planted only after the soil has warmed up. And "warmed up" means warmed to at least 65° at the depth to which the seeds will be planted.

Several factors, aside from air temperature and sunlight, affect soil temperature. Remember that a light, sandy soil will warm up more quickly in the spring than a heavy clay, and that the soil on a southern slope will warm up faster than soil on a northern slope, where the sun's rays are less direct. Shade from large trees or buildings will keep soil cooler in the spring and summer—but since the sun shifts in the sky as the season progresses, the shaded areas will shift also. And remember, too, that the length of the summer days increases as you go northward. Wisconsin's northern residents can take solace in this gift of Old Sol, which compensates for the slightly lower summer temperatures. In fact, the compensation is ample, since the size of fruits and vegetables often depends more on the duration of daily sunlight than on the temperatures. Cabbages grow larger in Bayfield than in Kenosha. (The difference in average August temperatures between Bayfield and Kenosha counties, incidentally, is a scant four degrees, despite their being in opposite corners of the state.)

Air temperature. Late spring and early fall frosts are banes of the Wisconsin gardener. Who has not been tempted to plant after a week of unseasonably warm April weather, only to remember the killing frosts of Aprils (and Mays, for that matter) of years past? Nevertheless, if the ground is sufficiently warm before the normal planting time, you can get an early start if you take proper precautions. Keep on hand an ample supply or hot caps, cloches, plastic milk jugs, or other homemade or store-bought seedling protectors.

If your new plants are tender ones, keep your eye on the thermometer and on the weather reports, and cover all emerged seedlings if a heavy frost is predicted. You can cover them with a light, but thick, covering of hay or straw to ward off frost damage, by using the individual plant covers just mentioned, or by erecting simple structures of old storm windows supported by walls constructed of bales of hay. If your garden is small enough, you can get away with tricks like these. But if you are growing a half-acre or so, you would be foolish to plant before the recommended time.

Cool-weather gardening tips. It is an ill wind that blows no good at all, and Wisconsin's brisk spring winds do blow some good things our way. The same cool climate that rules out mangoes and cowpeas makes it possible for us to grow the country's most luscious and flavorful peas, crisp garden lettuce, and tangy strawberries, not to mention firm and tasty potatoes, rutabagas, and other root crops. These plants do best in cool weather. You may have noticed for yourself that strawberries lose a great deal of their taste when they ripen in unseasonably hot weather. And peas grow little when the temperature rises above 72°. Hot-weather crops stop growing when the temperature drops below 50° or rises above 110°. Most plants need the lowest temperature for germination, a moderate level for leafy growth, and the highest temperature for blossoming and fruiting. Wisconsin's spring and summer climate certainly fills this bill. Take, for example, the growing of cucumbers in Dane County. In May, when seeds are germinating, the average temperature is a cool 58°. In June, when the main leafy growth takes place, it has warmed up to an average of 68°. And in July, when the first serious blossoming and fruiting is taking place, the temperature is at a year's high of 73°. The same principle holds true in all parts of Wisconsin, for all hot-weather annual vegetables.

In view of the above rule, it is not difficult to see why second plantings of vegetables made in July and August often do not do as well as initial spring plantings. Here, the order is reversed, the temperatures becoming progressively cooler as the plant germinates, leafs, and sets fruit. Still, second plantings produce enough for us to keep on making them year after year, and more will be said about them in another chapter.

A plant's resistance to cold is enhanced by ample supplies of the trace elements copper, zinc, aluminum, and molybdenum. These can be added to the soil by compost, but not by ordinary chemical fertilizers, giving just one more reason why compost is so vitally important to gardening success in Wisconsin!

Sunlight and plants. The effect of light on garden plants is a fascinating study in itself, worth your investigation. We won't have time to plunge deeply into the subject here, but some of the major principles should be set forth because they are important to gardening success.

Not only is light necessary for the plant's formation of carbon, hydrogen, and oxygen into plant tissue (photosynthesis), but it acts as a time clock for every plant, dictating its behavior to a large measure. In growing garden plants, this is important to remember. Many wild flower enthusiasts have made enough annual springtime trips to nearby woods to be able to anticipate the blooming of certain species, on certain days, at certain spots. These are native plants, almost fully predictable in their habits. Garden plants, often originating hundreds of miles away where light conditions are quite different, are something else again. Nevertheless, by close observation and some careful note taking, you can learn to predict the behavior of all your garden plants.

Dahlias and chrysanthemums are southern plants, which might come as a surprise to some people who think of them as fall bloomers. Because they are southern plants, their time clocks specify that blooming must take place when there is a certain amount of sunlight each day. Here in the North, the summer days are much longer than those in the South. In effect, the sun tells the chrysanthemum and the dahlia not to bloom until they receive a precise amount of daylight—and this does not happen until late summer or autumn, when the days have begun to shorten. Commercial growers of potted plants can force chrysanthemums in pots at any time of the year, by regulating the amount of light they receive. I suppose we could force-bloom in our gardens, too, although it would require an awful lot of careful attention. I just can't picture myself throwing huge black bags over my dahlias at a certain time every afternoon.

Some plants like full sun, some like partial shade, and others like fairly heavy shade or at least they will tolerate it. You should check the light requirements for every plant you choose. and plant accordingly. Use your shade trees to best advantage. Spring-flowering perennials, especially roses, do well when planted just under the southern reaches of a shade tree. The plant will receive full sun in the spring, encouraging blooming; then in midsummer when the sun is higher in the sky, the fully leafed branches of the tree will offer good protection. But heat-loving plants, such as moss roses and marigolds, and most vegetables, should get full sun all day long.

You can make your own observations of the effect of light on garden plants if you will take the time to be observant. Moss roses (portulaca) open at a definite time in the morning and close at a definite time in the afternoon, provided that the sun is shining. Some of your flowering plants that seem to be growing at unattractive angles may be reacting to the shade of a nearby tree, shrub, or building. By all means, keep a garden diary and record these observations. You will want to refer back to them at some date when you contemplate changes in your garden arrangement.

The effect of frost on plants. Different garden plants have widely differing tolerances to frost. Bell peppers may cave in to temperatures just a few degrees below 32, while Brussels sprouts in autumn aren't worth a hill of beans until they have been touched by a heavy frost or two. Here is some fascinating information presented by L. T. Pierce, Weather Bureau State Climatologist at Columbus, Ohio:

"In general, plants are injured by freezing whenever irreversible protoplasmic changes take place within the plant tissues. The temperature at which damage occurs varies with the kind of plant as well as with its stage of development.

"The appearance of frost in the form of ice crystals on the surfaces of leaves is popularly taken as visual indication of plant injury, although in the case of freeze resistant varieties this is certainly not the case. On the other hand, low temperature damage can take place without

Table 4-A. Freezing Temperature and Injury to Plants

Severity	Temperature Limits	Type of Damage
Light	28–32°	Little or no damage to most plants. Heavy damage to tender plants and semi-hardy plants in low lands.
Moderate	24–28°	Some damage to most plants. Heavy damage to fruit blossoms, tender and semi-hardy plants, particularly in low spots.
Severe	Less than 24°	Heavy damage to most plants not in a dormant condition.

Table 4-B. Temperature Danger Points for Certain Fruits

Fruit	Buds closed	In blossom	Setting fruit
		Stage of Plants	
Apple	25–27	28–29	28–30
Peach	20–29	25–30	27–30
Cherry	22–29	28–30	28–30
Plum	25–30	28–31	28–31
Grape	30	31	31

any deposit of hoar frost whatsoever. This is the case when there is insufficient moisture in the air to condense at 32° F—the dewpoint of that air is below freezing. "Frosts" occurring under such conditions are often called "black frosts;" and it becomes obvious that the accumulation of feathery frost crystals is not a true indicator of the extent of plant injury. It is the low temperature which causes plant injury—not the frost deposit. The extent of injury sustained is determined, not only by the lowest temperature reached, but also by the duration of freezing temperatures, the rate of temperature change, the kind and condition of plants, and very likely by several other factors. This explains why the Weather Bureau some 10 years ago ceased to record the occurrences of frost, and started keeping a detailed record of the last 32°, 28°, 24°, 20°, and 16° temperatures in spring and the first such occurrences in fall."

Getting the Jump on Spring

If you want to put out large, robust tomato plants during late May or early June (when all danger of frost is past), there are two ways you can do it. Either you can purchase large, robust plants at the local nursery or garden center—in which case you will pay dearly and have little choice of varieties—or you can grow your own plants from seed, starting them in the house, transferring them to a cold frame in April, and setting them out at the usual time. In this way, you can have your choice of many varieties—and you can build a cold frame for about the same price you might pay for a couple dozen robust tomato plants.

Cold frames and hotbeds (a hotbed is simply a cold frame with the addition of a heating device) can push back the spring, enabling you to start many plants earlier than you otherwise could, thus increasing your production for the season. But cold frames and hotbeds have other uses, too. Cold frames can be used to grow salad greens right up to Thanksgiving. You can use them for propagating cuttings of perennials during the summer. You can, in fact, use the cold frame or hotbed for any purpose requiring the regulation of air and soil temperatures and protection of small plants against frost in both spring and fall.

Cold frames and hotbeds can expand your gardening opportunities not only by lengthening the growing season for ordinary plants, but by enabling you to experiment with exotic varieties that would otherwise be difficult or impossible to grow here in Wisconsin. Your local plant supplier, if she is typical, can afford to offer only a relatively small selection of annual flowers and vegetables, those that she knows she won't be stuck with after "setting-out" time is past. But, if you are capable of starting your own plants from seeds, a whole new world of horticultural exploration is opened up for you. You can order seeds from any of dozens of specialty houses, and your cold frame or hotbed will enable you to start them successfully for transplanting when the weather turns warm. The cold frame or hotbed will, further, offer protection and breathing space for plants that arrive from mail-order nurseries too early for planting.

Directions for starting seeds in cold frames and hotbeds are given later on, in Chapter 4. Here we will concentrate on various ways of building cold frames and hotbeds.

Building the cold frame. The best site for a cold frame is the one that receives the most sun—in other words, a southern or southwestern exposure unshaded by large trees or buildings. Even on cold, raw days, the sun can heat a cold frame to 30° or more above the outside air temperature.

The size and actual construction of the cold frame will vary according to your needs, the space available, and the materials you happen to have on hand. Many gardeners use waste lumber and old storm sashes for construction materials, while others prefer a more finished-looking job and are willing to pay for it. The choice is yours.

Whatever your actual construction decisions, however, there are certain basic rules that you should follow:

1. If possible, use two-inch-thick lumber for all frames to provide good protection from swiftly changing temperatures.

2. If you use old storm sashes for lids, let their size determine the size of the frame.

3. The entire frame should be sunk two inches or more into the ground. It can be any length you choose, but the front of the frame should extend from six to ten inches above the ground (an eight- to twelve-inch board, in other words) and the back of the frame should be about six inches higher to allow for a back-to-front slope. The slope should be to the south, of course, to catch the maximum rays of the sun.

4. The depth of the frame can be any size you wish, although you will find it difficult to work within the frame if its depth is longer than your reach. And, if the depth is especially short, the difference in height between the back and the front boards can be less, while still retaining a proper slope of the lid.

5. Anchor the frame to the ground by driving two-by-four-inch stakes in all four corners, at least 18 inches into the ground. Nail the planks of the frame securely to the stakes, and be sure to firm up the soil on all sides to prevent drafts. If you must affix one plank on top of another to gain the proper height, be sure that the fit is tight; use a wood filler if necessary.

6. The lid, which can be either a storm sash or a simple wood frame with a tightly anchored transparent plastic cover, should be hinged in the back, and provisions should be made for propping it open at various levels. (A notched stake is commonly used; dropping the lid to a lower notch will lower the lid.)

Soil for the bed. Since the cold frame will be crucial in growing many young seedlings, you should take care in establishing a good soil bed for it. Before putting together the frame, dig down at least ten inches and loosen the soil. If it is heavy, add sand and well-rotted compost to loosen It up and improve drainage. If the soil is far from ideal, remove the top eight inches and replace it with a mixture of 50 percent good garden loam, 25 percent sand, and 25 percent well-rotted leaf mold or compost. Do not add new compost or manure. Soil that is too rich in nitrogen will stimulate growth too quickly and result in spindly and unhealthy plant.

Making a hotbed. There are two ways to make a cold frame into a hotbed. The first is the old traditional way: Dig out two feet of soil from the bed, then fill it with 18 inches of fresh horse or chicken manure that has been thoroughly soaked and packed down firmly. Cover the manure with six inches of bedding soil. The manure will produce plenty of heat, even in the dead of winter, and will last for several weeks. This is the organic method.

The second method is strictly artificial: Arrange electric heating cables about five inches below the soil surface (or according to manufacturer's directions) and plug into the nearest outlet. This is the inorganic way. And if there is any point where I tip my hat and part company with the old organic way, this is it. The electric method produces a more even and controlled heat, is infinitely easier to set up, and will last for as long as your local power plant survives. Nevertheless, if you do not have access to power in the area of your hotbed, or if you are more of a purist than I, the manure-heated bed works just fine—and it has the added benefit of producing composted manure all the while it is heating up the bed.

Controlling moisture, heat, and light. Cold frames form special microenvironments, very different from the outside environment when their lids are closed. Mother Nature will watch over your garden plants outside, but you must be responsible for the environment within your frame.

Moisture control is especially important when you are germinating seeds in a cold frame or hotbed. Very young seedlings are especially susceptible to damping-off, a fungus attack that causes them to wilt and die very quickly, often killing off entire flats. The fungus lives very near the soil surface and attacks the plant at the soil line. If you would prevent damping-off, you must prevent the conditions that enable the fungus to thrive and grow—and those conditions are (1) high humidity in both air and soil, and (2) lack of aeration.

Be sure to allow your germinating seeds at least some air movement by cracking the lid of the frame just a fraction of an inch whenever possible. If the weather is very cold, then let the air in just during the warmest part of the day. If you find a great deal of condensation on the glass in the morning, be sure to give the plants air as soon as temperatures permit. Last, avoid the most common (and fatal) error in germinating seeds—overwatering. The surface of the seedling soil should be dry, or very nearly dry, although there should be sufficient moisture under the surface. As an extra precaution, you might want to buy some vermiculite and spread a very thin layer of it over the top of the seedling bed. The seedlings will push up through it easily, and it will not support the killing fungus. Last, avoid overcrowding of young seedlings, because this, too, can encourage damping-off.

After your seedlings have established themselves into strong and healthy young plants, your problem might be the opposite—too little moisture. It is not difficult to forget about the moisture requirements of the cold frame, especially if you are preoccupied with chores out in the garden. Make it a habit to check into the cold frame every day. Do not overwater at any time, but avoid excessive dryness, too. Always give tepid water to plants in the cold frame—never cold water from the hose. It is a good idea to keep a large sprinkling can filled and standing ready by the cold frame all during the growing season, so that the water inside will approximate the air temperature.

Heat control is also important. You should keep an outdoor thermometer in the cold frame at all times and watch it carefully, at least for the first year. Young seedlings should never be exposed to temperatures above 80° or below 50°. If frost is predicted, cover the frame with blankets and bank up leaves around the frame to act as insulation. And during the day, remember that the sun—even when the air temperature is cool—can heat up the cold frame very quickly. Watch the thermometer and give the frame a little more air if it hits 70°. After you have worked with a cold frame for a year, you will not have to keep such a close check on its environment, since you will have learned to judge fairly well what is happening inside by what is happening outside.

When your young plants are about two weeks away from transplanting into the open garden, you should begin the hardening-off process, which is simply a way of allowing them to become exposed to the outside environment slowly. Open the frame a little more each day, and cut back a little on the water during this time. (But protect against frost, no matter what.) By the time you are ready to transplant your seedlings, the frame should have been wide open for two or three days, and any transplanting shock should be absolutely minimized.

If you use electric cables to heat a hotbed, your control of temperature is obviously much finer. You will be able to plant earlier, and you will not have to worry so much about early morning frosts. Still, you must pay careful attention to moisture requirements—which can be very tricky if you cannot open the frame because of very cold weather. It would be best to begin with a cold frame, and then add heat after you have worked with it for a year or two.

Light is the third important factor, and the rules here are simple and few (unless you get into the forcing of blooms, which is another matter entirely). Germinating seeds should have very little light. You can lay blankets over the frame lid until the seeds have germinated. After that, they should be exposed to light gradually. A couple of layers of cheesecloth will filter direct sun very effectively. As the plants grow the layers can be removed, one by one, until the plants are able to take direct sunlight. Again, the object is to expose young plants to the outside environment gradually, to prevent shock.

Other ways to challenge spring. The cold frame is by far your best ally in getting the jump on spring. But there are other ways of getting the best of an early start, too:

1. Take advantage of the lay of the land when choosing a spot for your vegetable garden. Remember that a gradual slope to the south is the best possible site, since it will warm up most quickly in the spring. A southeast or southwest slope is nearly as good, and an east-facing slope is not bad. In any case, avoid planting early vegetables in a ground pocket or between two slopes, since these are frost collectors in both spring and fall.

2. Keep a winter mulch on your vegetable garden and on your flower beds and borders. The mulch—applied in the fall after the ground has frozen—will prevent the frost line from going so deeply into the soil and will allow the soil to warm up more quickly in spring. Remove the mulch during the first warm days of spring.

3. If your soil is heavy, with a high percentage of clay, keep working to loosen it up and lighten it by incorporating plenty of compost and sand. Lighter soils warm up more quickly in the spring, and they provide better drainage, too.

4. Change the color of your soil. Old-time gardeners in northern Wisconsin used to sprinkle coal dust over the snow in April, because they knew that the black dust helped to melt the snow and warm the earth by absorbing the sun's heat. You can use the same principle to improve soil color—not with coal dust, but with composted leaves, manure, or other organic materials. The many benefits of organic matter were listed in the preceding chapter. In this case, the key material in organic matter is its *lignin* content, for it is the lignins—woody material—that cause organic matter to be dark. Further, lignins are slow to decompose and will help to condition and darken your soil for many years after their application. All organic matter contains some lignins, but leaves are especially rich, which is why leaf mold is so dark. Forest humus is composed of 48 percent lignins, and is perhaps the best material of all for the purpose.

A short-term answer to warming the soil is in the use of black plastic. I don't recommend plastic as a permanent mulch, but it can be laid along the rows in early spring and weighted down with rocks or boards, and will cause the soil to warm up quickly. Plants can be set in the soil by punching holes in the plastic at appropriate intervals along the row, and the plastic will retain the day's heat through the night. After the soil has warmed up thoroughly, the plastic mulch may be replaced by straw or hay.

5. Start seeds as early as possible indoors and tend them with care. In April, you can transfer them to the cold frame where you can harden them off gradually until planting time. The earlier you start, the bigger your plants will be at planting time.

6. Plant cool-weather crops, such as peas and lettuce, as early as possible in your area. These can take a couple of light frosts without damage. You can lessen the effect of any frost, also, by sprinkling your young plants with cold water on the morning of the frost, before the sun has hit them. The water will dissipate the frost quickly.

7. Be prepared with hot caps, cloches, and other plant protectors for your early-planted vegetables. When frost threatens, cap the young plants in the early evening, before dark. Remove the caps the next day, when the sun has reached the garden patch.

Some gardeners will not want to go to the extra effort necessary to get plants into the open ground as early as possible—and some maintain that later plantings will catch up sooner or later, anyway. I am somewhat sympathetic to this view—but on the other hand, I still can feel a sense of pride and accomplishment (or perhaps that good old American sense of competition) in getting in crops earlier than the recommended dates and having them thrive. The neighborhood garden hero is still the one who holds up the first ripe tomato.

Extending the Summer

Just as cold frames and hotbeds can push back the spring, they can extend the summer into fall, giving you salad greens right up to Thanksgiving and beyond. The usual crops grown for harvest in the cold frame are lettuce and endive, but you might wish to experiment with

Bales of hay and some old storm sashes can be used to protect tomato plants from early frosts. After the season is over, the same structure can be used to store root crops over the winter. In spring, use the hay for mulching.

carrots, radishes, and other vegetables as well. Just remember that any crops planted for this purpose must be low growing and should be tolerant to cool weather. In other words, bush beans and eggplant are out.

Check the seed packets of the vegetables you want to grow and note the days to maturity. Then, figuring backward in time, plant in order to harvest in early November. A 40-day leaf lettuce, for instance, should be planted about September 22 to be harvested about November 1. But you will probably want to begin several weeks sooner, making plantings every week or two, in order to have a continuous supply of greens throughout the fall. Remember, though, that lettuce does not germinate well in hot weather. Protect very young plants against direct sunlight when the weather is hot.

Along about November, when the first light snows have powdered the Wisconsin landscape, the fresh greens from the cold frame become an increasing source of pride. You might find yourself throwing dinner parties just to show off your fresh salads. You will want to do everything you can to ward off frost and keep the greens coming for just another week. Again, throw blankets over the lid and bank up the frame with leaves on very cold nights. Go out in the morning and check the plants. If they have been frostbitten, sprinkle them gently with cold water. Generally, they will revive nicely—until that fateful morning when we will at last have to admit that Shakespeare had a point: at Christmas we should no more desire fresh endive than wish a snow in May's new-fangled mirth. Winter will be upon us.

When all Danger of Frost is Past

The frost maps on pages 57 and 59 will enable you to find the average last frost date for spring and the average first frost date for fall, for your locality. The difference in days between these two dates, of course, is your average growing season.

Table 5. Chances of Spring and Fall Frost Occurrences

Table 5a.

ASHLAND
Location: four miles west of Ashland, near Chequamegon Bay in northwestern Wisconsin
Last average spring frost: May 30
First average fall frost: September 16
Growing season: 109 days

Chances of Frost Occurring after Date in Spring

Temperature	20%	40%	60%	80%
32° or below	June 9	June 2	May 27	May 20
28° or below	May 29	May 22	May 16	May 9
24° or below	May 21	May 14	May 7	Apr. 30
20° or below	May 3	Apr. 25	Apr. 19	Apr. 11
16° or below	Apr. 21	Apr. 13	Apr. 7	Mar. 30

Chances of Frost Occurring before Date in Fall

Temperature	20%	40%	60%	80%
32° or below	Sept. 6	Sept. 13	Sept. 20	Sept. 27
28° or below	Sept. 17	Sept. 25	Oct. 1	Oct. 9
24° or below	Sept. 29	Oct. 7	Oct. 14	Oct. 21
20° or below	Oct. 14	Oct. 22	Oct. 28	Nov. 5
16° or below	Oct. 26	Nov. 3	Nov. 9	Nov. 17

Table 5b.

HANCOCK
Location: two miles south of Hancock in western Waushara County in central Wisconsin
Last average spring frost: May 17
First average fall frost: September 30
Growing season: 135 days

Chances of Frost Occurring after Date in Spring

Temperature	20%	40%	60%	80%
32° or below	May 27	May 20	May 14	May 7
28° or below	May 16	May 9	May 2	Apr. 26
24° or below	May 6	Apr. 29	Apr. 22	Apr. 15
20° or below	Apr. 26	Apr. 18	Apr. 11	Apr. 3
16° or below	Apr. 13	Apr. 6	Mar. 31	Mar. 23

Chances of Frost Occurring before Date in Fall

Temperature	20%	40%	60%	80%
32° or below	Sept. 19	Sept. 26	Oct. 3	Oct. 10
28° or below	Sept. 26	Oct. 4	Oct. 10	Oct. 18
24° or below	Oct. 9	Oct. 16	Oct. 23	Oct. 31
20° or below	Oct. 20	Oct. 28	Nov. 3	Nov. 10
16° or below	Oct. 26	Nov. 3	Nov. 9	Nov. 17

Table 5c.

MARSHFIELD
Location: two miles southeast of Marshfield in Wood County on the central Wisconsin plains
Last average spring frost: May 17
First average fall frost: September 27
Growing season: 133 days

Chances of Frost Occurring after Date in Spring

Temperature	20%	40%	60%	80%
32° or below	May 27	May 20	May 14	May 7
28° or below	May 13	May 6	Apr. 30	Apr. 23
24° or below	May 1	Apr. 23	Apr. 17	Apr. 9
20° or below	Apr. 19	Apr. 12	Apr. 5	Mar. 28
16° or below	Apr. 8	Apr. 1	Mar. 25	Mar. 18

Chances of Frost Occurring before Date in Fall

Temperature	20%	40%	60%	80%
32° or below	Sept. 17	Sept. 24	Sept. 30	Oct. 7
28° or below	Sept. 25	Oct. 2	Oct. 9	Oct. 17
24° or below	Oct. 7	Oct. 15	Oct. 22	Oct. 29
20° or below	Oct. 20	Oct. 27	Nov. 3	Nov. 10
16° or below	Oct. 30	Nov. 7	Nov. 13	Nov. 21

Table 5d.

SPOONER

Location: two miles southeast of Spooner in Washburn County in northwestern Wisconsin
Last average spring frost: May 24
First average fall frost: September 20
Growing season: 120 days

Chances of Frost Occurring after Date in Spring

Temperature	20%	40%	60%	80%
32° or below	June 3	May 27	May 21	May 14
28° or below	May 20	May 13	May 7	Apr. 30
24° or below	May 11	May 3	Apr. 27	Apr. 20
20° or below	Apr. 29	Apr. 21	Apr. 14	Apr. 7
16° or below	Apr. 18	Apr. 11	Apr. 4	Mar. 28

Chances of Frost Occurring before Date in Fall

Temperature	20%	40%	60%	80%
32° or below	Sept. 10	Sept. 17	Sept. 24	Oct. 1
28° or below	Sept. 19	Sept. 27	Oct. 4	Oct. 11
24° or below	Oct. 1	Oct. 9	Oct. 15	Oct. 23
20° or below	Oct. 12	Oct. 19	Oct. 26	Nov. 2
16° or below	Oct. 25	Nov. 2	Nov. 8	Nov. 16

Table 5e.

STURGEON BAY

Location: two miles north of Sturgeon Bay on the Door Peninsula between Green Bay and Lake Michigan, in northeastern Wisconsin
Last average spring frost: May 17
First average fall frost: October 2
Growing season: 137 days

Chances of Frost Occurring after Date in Spring

Temperature	20%	40%	60%	80%
32° or below	May 27	May 20	May 14	May 8
28° or below	May 10	May 3	Apr. 27	Apr. 20
24° or below	Apr. 27	Apr. 20	Apr. 13	Apr. 6
20° or below	Apr. 15	Apr. 8	Apr. 1	Mar. 24
16° or below	Apr. 5	Mar. 29	Mar. 23	Mar. 15

Chances of Frost Occurring before Date in Fall

Temperature	20%	40%	60%	80%
32° or below	Sept. 22	Sept. 29	Oct. 5	Oct. 12
28° or below	Oct. 8	Oct. 15	Oct. 22	Oct. 29
24° or below	Oct. 22	Oct. 30	Nov. 5	Nov. 13
20° or below	Nov. 3	Nov. 11	Nov. 17	Nov. 25
16° or below	Nov. 14	Nov. 21	Nov. 28	Dec. 5

Source: *Climate at the University of Wisconsin Experimental Farms*, Research Report 17, Experiment Station, College of Agriculture, University of Wisconsin, U.S. Department of Commerce, Weather Bureau, Cooperating; December 1964.

In addition, the maps report data for several dozen scattered points of observation where long-term records have been kept. For each of these points of observation, there is given both the average date and a "10 percent validity" date. This latter date is the one at which there is only 10 percent chance of frost occurring, meaning that gardeners there can plant with a 90 percent assurance of safety from frost.

As an example, take the one point of observation in Lafayette County, in the southwest corner of the state. On the spring map, the average last frost there occurs on May 4. But the 10 percent validity date is May 23. There is only a 10 percent chance of frost occurring that late in the spring.

On the fall maps, the same information is given, except that we are now talking about the chances of frost occurring before the dates given. Again, taking Lafayette County, the first average frost occurs on September 30, and there is only a 10 percent chance that frost will occur as early as September 21.

The maps are very helpful to gardeners in all areas of the state. But you might wish to calculate your odds a little more closely. You might, for instance, be planting peas. You know that they can stand a nightly low of 32°, which is an official frost, but you wouldn't like to see the temperature go down as low as 28°, and certainly not to 24° or below.

How do you calculate your odds? For complete information, I suggest that you ask your county agent to get for you a copy of a booklet called *Climate at the University of Wisconsin Experimental Farms*, prepared by the College of Agriculture in cooperation with the United States Weather Bureau. This booklet contains a wealth of climatological data for the nine experimental farms of the University of Wisconsin, spread throughout the state: Ashland, Spooner. Marshfield, Lancaster, Hancock, Sturgeon Bay, Valders, Arlington, and Madison (Charmany). You will find (for each year of recording) monthly mean temperatures, highest and lowest temperatures for each month,

precipitation totals and chances of precipitation. and much additional information, mostly in table form.

From that booklet, I will borrow Table 5 (a to e) of critical temperatures, which gives the percentage chances of freezes occurring before the official average dates.

Using these tables, you can find, for instance, that in Spooner, where the average last frost occurs on May 24, there is still a 20 percent chance of a freeze occurring up until June 3, and a 40 percent chance of the temperature dipping to 24° or below on May 3.

To calculate the odds of frosts of varying severity occurring near your area, both spring and fall, consult the tables for the location nearest to your own.

When it Rains—and When it Doesn't

Despite Wisconsin's favorable rainfall patterns, gardeners are not averse to grumbling when the rain does not fall exactly when they want it to, as gently as they would like it to, and in just the right amounts. Our springs are sometimes oddly dry. We carry buckets of water out to the young tomato plants, where the garden hose cannot reach, and we feel that the zucchini seeds must certainly have become desiccated in their parched little hills.

Then, in July, we go through a week or two when it seems to be raining all the time. The garden is a sea of mire, and we don't see how anything can escape either drowning or rot. We begin to chant Karel Capek's "gardener's prayer."

Still, we always seem to make it through the season—and so, usually, do our garden plants. And we have to admit that the weather hasn't been all that bad, after all.

There are things you can do to protect your plants against both dryness and prolonged rains, so that even mini-droughts and rainy weeks will have minimal effects on your flowers and vegetables.

Fighting drought. For the small backyard garden, the garden hose offers surefire drought

MAP 2

Map Series Showing
Climatic Influences on Soils
and Crops in Wisconsin
1. Spring Frost (1925-1949)

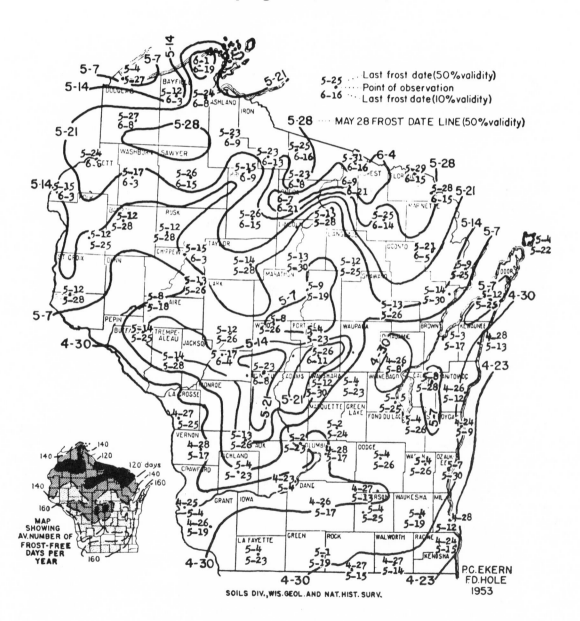

5-25 ···· Last frost date(50%validity)
······· Point of observation
6-16 ···· Last frost date(I0%validity)

5-28 ···· MAY 28 FROST DATE LINE(50%validity)

P.G.EKERN
F.D.HOLE
1953

SOILS DIV.,WIS.GEOL.AND NAT.HIST.SURV.

MAP
SHOWING
AV.NUMBER OF
FROST-FREE
DAYS PER
YEAR

protection—if it is used properly. Remember, though, that plants have built-in mechanisms to combat drought. They undergo definite physical and chemical changes in every cell, enabling them to survive fairly long periods of dryness. If you use the hose capriciously, watering once or twice and then neglecting the chore after that, you may be doing more harm than good, for you will have sent the plants back into their defenseless posture, meaning that continuing drought will hurt them more than if you had not watered at all. A tomato plant is like an expensive daughter—once she has been given the good things of life, she will continue to expect them in the future.

You should be aware, too, of the cost of watering your backyard garden with the hose. The USDA estimates that about 2,700 gallons of water are used in thoroughly watering a 60-by-70-foot garden plot. This comes out to about 64 gallons per 100 square feet. You know the cost of water, whether you buy yours from the city or maintain your own well. How much more simple, timesaving, and economical to adopt good mulching practices to conserve the water that your soil does receive!

Allies in drought. Your very best allies in drought are a good soil, a good mulch, and deep fertilizing.

The texture of your soil is vitally important to its water-holding capacity. The coarser the soil, the less is its ability to hold water. A sandy soil will hold only about .75 inch of water per foot; a fine sandy loam will hold 1.25 inches; and a silt loam, clay loam, or clay will hold from 2.5 to 3.0 inches per foot. If you live in one of Wisconsin's sand counties, then, you will do well to begin the soil-building program outlined In Chapter 1 (page 11), in order to build your soil's texture to the point where it will hold enough water to fight drought during the growing season.

And if you seem blessed with good garden loam, dig down two or three feet in the garden to see how your subsoil looks. You might find almost pure sand down there, meaning that many of your plant roots will be growing in sand, where the water drains quite rapidly. Your contractor, in building your home, might have blessed you with gravel fill under your topsoil. If so, you will have to ensure your garden plants of the water they need, because they will not be able to bring it up from deep within the subsoil.

In a drought, the soil dries from the top down. A week of drought might dry out about two inches of soil—less each week, after that. And here is where your second ally comes in. A good mulch will reduce surface evaporation greatly, thus helping to conserve the moisture that your soil receives from normal rainfalls. An eight- to ten-inch hay mulch is my choice for the vegetable garden, while buckwheat hulls or cocoa bean shells (three inches) look nice on the flower beds. All three are effective, in that they allow rainwater to pass through them easily, while still keeping the soil cool and preventing moisture escape.

Your third ally against drought is deep fertilizing. When drought strikes and the soil begins to dry out at the upper levels, plant roots begin to seek water at deeper levels. This means that they will draw their nutrients from those deeper levels, too, since nutrients are transported through the roots and to the plant system by water. If the soil is deficient in nutrients at those deeper levels, the plant will suffer accordingly. When a plant suffers during drought, it is not always because it cannot get water—it is because the water it receives contains very few nutrients. The answer is to carry on a year-round system of deep fertilization, including plenty of compost spaded or tilled as deeply into the soil as you can manage. Such a program will increase the soil's water-holding capacity, while providing a source of deep-lying, slow-releasing nutrients. You will be building up a veritable bank account of nutrients that your garden plants can call upon in time of need.

Too much rain. A problem less often encountered is that of too much rain, resulting in rot and strangulation of plants because of oxygen lack.

MAP 3

Map Series Showing
Climatic Influences on Soils
and Crops in Wisconsin
2. Fall Frost (1925-1949)

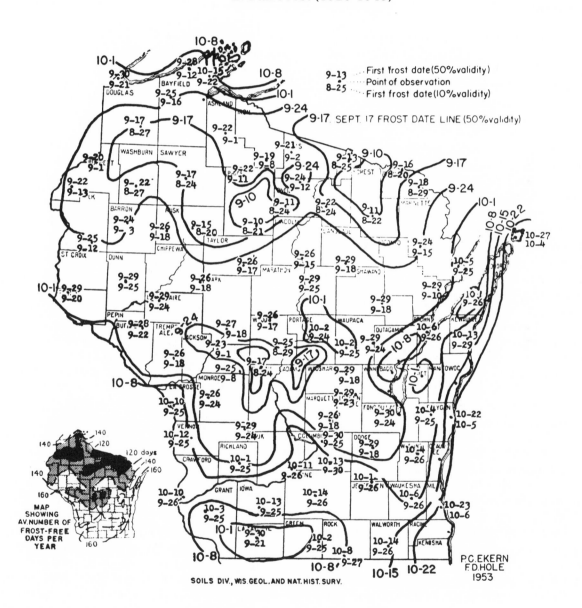

SOILS DIV., WIS. GEOL. AND NAT. HIST. SURV.

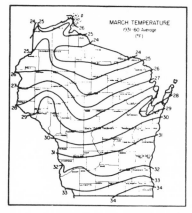

MAP 4
MARCH TEMPERATURE
1931-60 Average
(°F)

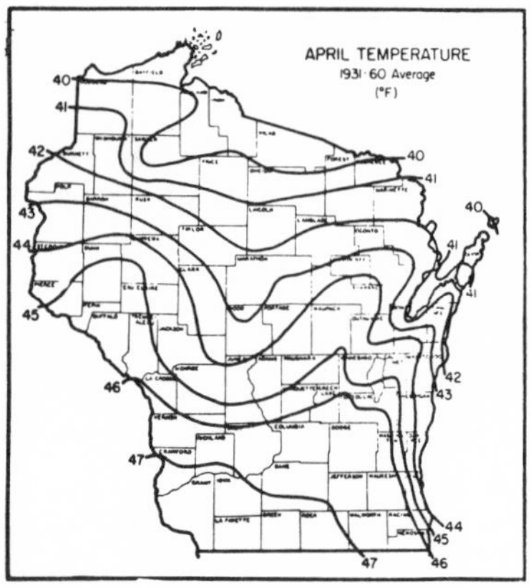

MAP 5
APRIL TEMPERATURE
1931-60 Average
(°F)

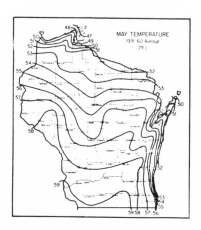

MAP 6
MAY TEMPERATURE
1931-60 Average
(°F)

MAP 7
JUNE TEMPERATURE
1931-60 Average
(°F)

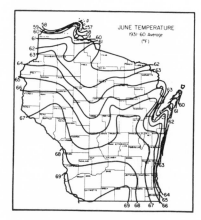

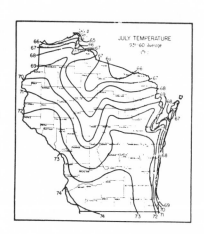

MAP 8
JULY TEMPERATURE
1931-60 Average
(°F)

MAP 9
AUGUST TEMPERATURE
1931-60 Average
(°F)

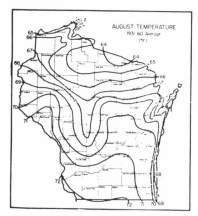

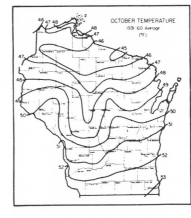

MAP 10
SEPTEMBER TEMPERATURE
1931-60 Average
(°F)

MAP 11
OCTOBER TEMPERATURE
1931-60 Average
(°F)

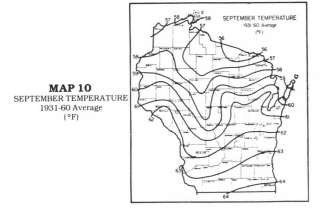

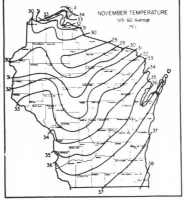

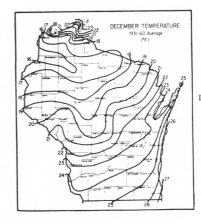

MAP 12
NOVEMBER TEMPERATURE
1931-60 Average
(°F)

MAP 13
DECEMBER TEMPERATURE
1931-60 Average
(°F)

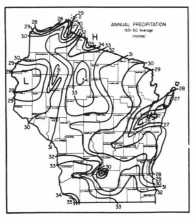

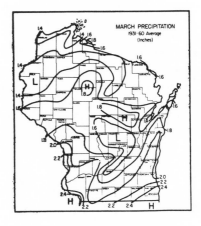

MAP 14
ANNUAL PRECIPITATION
1931-60 Average
(Inches)

MAP 15
MARCH PRECIPITATION
1931-60 Average
(Inches)

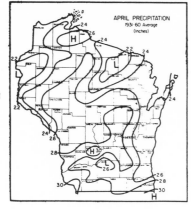

MAP 16
APRIL PRECIPITATION
1931-60 Average
(Inches)

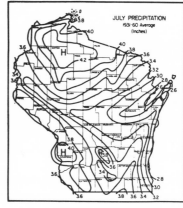

MAP 17
MAY PRECIPITATION
1931-60 Average
(Inches)

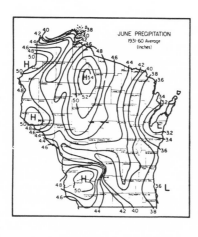

MAP 18
JUNE PRECIPITATION
1931-60 Average
(Inches)

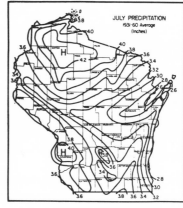

MAP 19
JULY PRECIPITATION
1931-60 Average
(Inches)

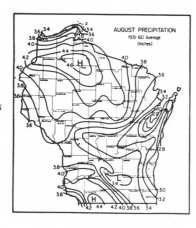

MAP 20
AUGUST PRECIPITATION
1931-60 Average
(Inches)

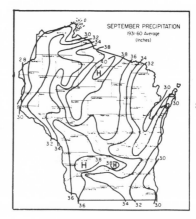

MAP 21
SEPTEMBER PRECIPITATION
1931-60 Average
(Inches)

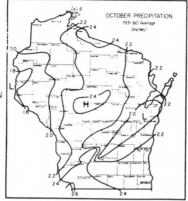

MAP 22
OCTOBER PRECIPITATION
1931-60 Average
(Inches)

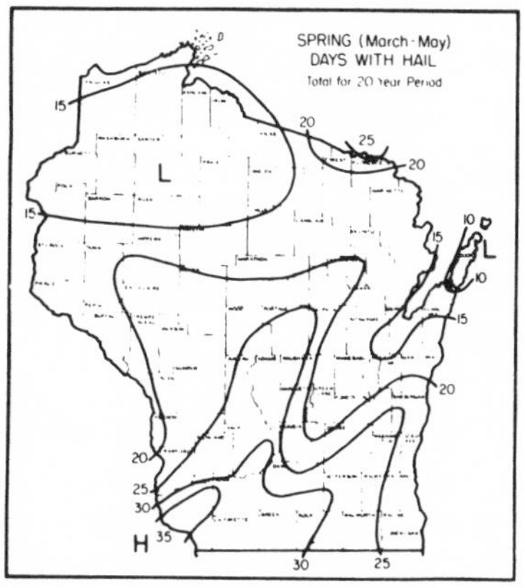

MAP 23
SPRING (March-May)
DAYS WITH HAIL
Total for 20 Year Period

MAP 24
SUMMER (June-August)
DAYS WITH HAIL
Total for 20 Year Period

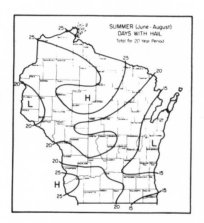

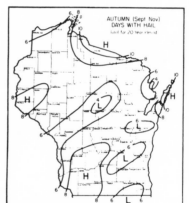

MAP 25
AUTUMN (Sept.-Nov.)
DAYS WITH HAIL
Total for 20 Year Period

MAP 26
ANNUAL
DAYS WITH HAIL
Total for 20 Year Period

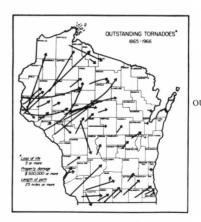

MAP 27
OUTSTANDING TORNADOES*
1865-1966

If your garden soil is still swimming in water more than a few hours after a heavy rain, look for the answer in the soil's texture, or, more often, in the subsoil. You may have a hardpan subsoil, which is impervious to water, thus preventing proper drainage. This is often a difficult and serious problem, sometimes requiring drastic steps for correction. Those steps are discussed in Chapter 1 (page 13).

Weather aids. The maps on the following pages, prepared by government and university agencies, will provide you with a wealth of useful data in greatly concentrated form. Aside from the frost maps, which we have already discussed, you will find maps giving average temperatures, rainfall, frost depths, snowfalls, hailstorms, and even tornadoes, for different months of the year and in different parts of the state. You will want to refer to one or more of these maps when planning many of your garden operations throughout the year.

Phenology for Gardeners

Gardeners who have an avid interest in the weather—and there are many who do—are also attracted to the science of *phenology*, the study of natural periodic events in the life cycle of plants and their relationship to each other.

Phenology fans know that corn may be safely planted when oak leaves become the size of a mouse's ear and that peas, beets, and lettuce may be planted when the first leaves appear on the common lilac. When the crocus blooms it is time to uncover the peonies, and when the lilac blooms it is time to plant corn and beans.

Phenology is folk wisdom based on science—or science based on folk wisdom. In any case, it is a happy and compatible meeting of the two. It is an ancient study, dating back to several centuries before Christ. when the Chinese had a phenological calendar.

An old New England saying holds that spring advances at the rate of 100 miles a week. In 1918, the American scientist A. D. Hopkins developed his "bioclimatic law," which states that the advance of spring is delayed by four days for each degree of latitude north, for every

400 feet of elevation upward, and for every five degrees of longitude eastward from the Rocky Mountains. That works out, incidentally, to about 100 miles a week. And studies in the 1960s showed that leaf and blossom dates for the Persian lilac advanced 14 miles a day. That's 98 miles a week.

In his book *Making the Weather Work for You* (Garden Way), James J. Rahn says, "The growth and development of plants is strongly related to environmental conditions and represents the sum total of all the effects of air and soil temperatures, sunshine, precipitation, humidity, wind, dew, frost, etc. Thus, for example, comparing the time of the first bloom of a certain variety of lilac with the time of the first bloom the previous year, indicates whether the current spring is as advanced as the past year's. At the same time, comparing the dates of first bloom of similar plants at two or more locations during the same season gives a good idea of the differences in climate between those areas. In practice, differences in phenological events are usually most strongly influenced by air temperature and sunshine, with moisture conditions playing a lesser role."

Phenologists have found that some plants react more dependably to weather conditions than others. The most dependable plants are used for comparison and are called indicator plants. If you want to begin to look for and record phenological signs, here are the recommended plants to use:

Vernal witch hazel (*Hamamelis vernalis*)
Forsythia (*Forsythia intermedia*)
Purple lilac (*Syringa vulgaris*)
Shrubby cinquefoil (*Potentiall fruficosa*)
Glossy abelia (*Abelia grandiflora*)
Spiraea (*Spiraea bumalda*)
Witch hazel (*Hamamelis virginiana*)

Almost everybody has some common purple lilac or forsythia around, so, if you have a notebook and pencil, you, too, can become a genuine phenologist.

Phenology works because the same climatic conditions that affect one plant will soon affect another, as well as affecting other natural phenomena, such as the hatches of insects. Montana farmers, for instance, found that by making their first cutting of alfalfa within 10 days following the blooming of the lilac, they usually complete their harvest before the alfalfa weevil eggs become a problem. The lilac bloom, the ripening of alfalfa, and the weevil egg hatch are all ultimately affected by the same weather and climatic conditions. By observing one, you get a good clue to the others.

All the phenological tips in old almanacs don't hold true today, because not only has climate changed slightly, but the new varieties of crops are often more tolerant than the old ones. We have to catch up to our grandfathers in folk wisdom by developing new phenological data that will be reliable for our time and our place here in Wisconsin.

If you want to become a phenologist, just choose your indicator plants and then begin to keep careful records. Note the first flowering of crops, the first appearance of insects, the first heading of broccoli, the first picking of beans, and everything else that's important to you. After a few years, you can begin to note the proper relationships and you will have some valuable data upon which to base your gardening procedures.

Even better, get some friends and relatives in different areas to do the same, then compare notes. Consider forming your own local phenological club.

Finally, in considering the weather, I would like to offer a little piece of advice for that inevitable Saturday in early May, the one you had reserved to till the garden because the weather had been so beautiful all that week. You arise at half past seven, only to find outside your bedroom window what we charitably call "onion snow," this time mixed with both sleet and rain. At that time, it is perhaps best to take advice not from Shakespeare. who promised us newfangled mirth in May, but from Jonathan Swift, who, more than two centuries ago, said—

" 'Tis very warm weather when one's in bed."

66

"If we can grow at least a part of our food to feed our family, then we can reaffirm our own sense of independence. . . ."

Vegetable Growing—Bounty for the Table

Let first the onion flourish there,
Rose among roots, the maiden-fair
Wine-scented and poetic soul
Of the capacious salad bowl.
—Robert Louis Stevenson
To a Gardener (1887)

4 From the first tender asparagus tip of April until the last crisp carrot is dug in November, no gardening activity yields so much sheer satisfaction as vegetable growing. Flowers are beautiful to look at and to smell. Vegetables are beautiful to look at—and to eat!

If you have ever grown your own vegetables, you already know that there is absolutely no comparison between your homegrown varieties and those you buy at the supermarket. Peas are sweeter and more tender. Beets and potatoes are more solid. and they have *real taste*. Green beans are plump, flavorful, and plentiful. Onions are—well, winescented and poetic, actually. And tomatoes! To compare your first ripe, red tomato of the season to those pale and plastic imitations you have been buying at the supermarket is to know the whole reason for vegetable gardening.

But there are other rewards besides taste. Your homegrown vegetables are apt to be more nutritious. Processed vegetables inevitably lose some vitamins in the canning or freezing process. Even "fresh" vegetables from the grocery produce bins have lost a good portion of their vitamin C in transit from distant farms. Commercially grown vegetables are chosen for their profitability—but your own vegetables are chosen and grown for taste and nutrition.

In your own vegetable garden, you can grow varieties that you rarely see in the supermarket: Oriental cabbages—arugula—European white eggplant—elephant garlic—Swiss chard—burpless cucumbers—ground-cherries—Serrano peppers—vegetable spaghetti—radicchio—tomatillos—Dutch corn salad and other interesting salad greens. Your options are limited only by your imagination, your daring, and the Wisconsin climate.

A vegetable garden can save your money, too. Your savings will be greatest if you are cost-conscious when planning your garden. If, on the other hand, you choose to spend hundreds of dollars on chemical fertilizers, unnecessary pesticides, and every garden gadget that you see in the garden center, then you might not come out ahead at all. To me, one of the challenges of gardening is to keep the cost low by using available materials and by going along with nature as closely as possible.

Last, I believe that the very act of growing one's own vegetables satisfies something deep within us—a desire for self-sufficiency in a world where we have been made increasingly dependent on the services of people we have never even met. If we can grow at least a part of our food to feed our family, then we can reaffirm our own sense of independence, in full spirit if not in full actuality. For many of us, then, vegetable growing has a certain spiritual quality, one that every farmer has certainly felt at some time. And I think that quality makes better people of us.

Choosing the Site

If you are a city gardener, you may have only one available site for your vegetable garden—probably at the rear of the backyard. If it is an ideal spot—sunny, protected, and level—well and good. If not, then you must do anything within reason to bring it within specifications. You cannot, however, hope to grow a vegetable garden under a huge oak tree, or on the shady side of a garage. Sunlight is a most important consideration here, since you have little control over it (unless, of course, you choose to rip up the oak tree or knock down the garage).

If, on the other hand, you are fortunate enough to have a choice of garden sites, either on your own land or on a borrowed or rented plot, then your options might come into play.

Sunlight. A vegetable garden should be in a spot where it can receive full sun all day long. If obstacles make full sun impossible, the vegetable crops can still do well with sun for most of the day. But production will be decreased as the amount of sunlight is decreased. (Remember, if you are choosing a plot in winter, that the summer sun is much higher in the sky, thus shortening shadows from large trees and buildings.)

Soil. Next to sunlight, soil is the most important consideration. Look for well-drained soil of good texture, soil that is now perhaps supporting a healthy crop of weeds. Its nutrient content need not be high since you can correct that in a season or two, but texture and drainage are far more difficult to handle. Review Chapter 1 on soils, before exercising a choice of garden sites.

Trees. Large trees should not be too near the vegetable garden. A good rule of thumb is to keep the garden ten feet away from beneath the outermost reaches of any tree's branches. The problem is not only shade, but the competition of the tree's roots for your garden nutrients. In a battle like that, your garden plants will probably lose.

If you must use an area that is shaded for part of the day, use it for those vegetables that can stand partial shade—broccoli, lettuce, cauliflower, kale, Swiss chard, spinach, or some other large-leaf plants. Do not use it for potatoes, carrots. onions, or other root crops that have a relatively small leaf area and yet must produce large amounts of energy for root development.

Slope. A moderate slope in any direction will not hurt the garden's performance. In fact, a southern slope will help it, since the rays of the sun will be more direct. But plants can do well even with a northern slope if it is not too severe. All vegetable rows should be at right angles to the slope to prevent soil runoff, erosion, and nutrient loss. If there is no slope, however, then it is better to run the rows north and south, since the sun's rays will be distributed more equally in passing from east to west.

Proximity to house. The vegetable garden should, if at all possible, be fairly close to the house. Not only will you be able to reach it with the garden hose when necessary, but you will be encouraged to spend odd moments in weeding, mulching, tying, and staking—those ten-minute jobs that you would not bother to undertake if you had to walk or drive some distance to the garden. In addition, your garden will be less susceptible to ravaging by raccoons, rabbits, neighboring dogs, and other marauders.

Size. The size of the vegetable garden should be determined by the space available, the family's need, and the gardener's desire and ability to maintain it properly. A 20-by-30-foot plot (600 square feet) is a nice size for a family of four, capable of providing many vegetables for the table from June through September, and quite a few for canning and freezing, too.

A 20-by-50-foot plot (1,000 square feet) is even better, since it will provide copious amounts of a larger variety of vegetables and enough for canning and freezing to last through the winter. The larger family, of course, will require a larger garden—but no vegetable garden should be undertaken unless the family has the desire to keep it free of weeds, stake and tie up those plants that need support, carry and place mulching materials, occasionally pick insects, and do the other chores that will encourage good results. The enthusiasm of spring too often gives way to disinterest and neglect in the heat of July.

If garden space is limited, be sure to include as many vegetables as you can, even if you have to limit your selection to a couple of tomato plants in large tubs on the patio and cucumbers trained to climb a trellis on the side of the garage.

Which Vegetables? Which Varieties?

Many so-called ideal vegetable garden plans are followed blindly by gardeners. But it would be foolish to plant a row of kale when nobody in the family cares a hoot for kale. And it would be equally foolish not to plant a double portion of acorn squash if your family really likes acorn squash. So, the first rule is a common sense rule: *Plant the vegetables you like.*

As for specific varieties, be guided by those that appear attractive to you, those that are recommended for Wisconsin's climate. and those that have been bred to be resistant to disease. In addition, if you plan to fill your freezer by the end of the year, choose varieties that are especially recommended for freezing. All these qualities are indicated in the listing of vegetables, beginning on page 99.

If your garden is a small one, you will also want to choose varieties that take up less space than others: (bantam corn, pole beans instead of bush beans, etc.) and vegetables that yield the most for the space that they take. Here are some of the more common garden vegetables, with the expected yield given for each *per 100 feet of row:*

HEAVY YIELDERS

Cabbage (late)	175 lbs.
Carrots (late)	100 lbs.
Cauliflower	45 heads
Cucumbers	150 lbs.
Rutabaga	150 lbs.
Tomatoes	200 lbs.

MEDIUM YIELDERS

Beets	100 lbs.
Cabbage (early)	100 lbs.
Carrots (early)	100 lbs.
Eggplant	125 fruits
Onions	75-100 lbs.
Parsnips	100 lbs.
Radishes	1,200 radishes
Sweet potatoes	100 lbs.
Turnips	100 lbs.

LIGHT YIELDERS

Asparagus	12-24 lbs.
Broccoli	50 lbs.
Bush beans	50 lbs.
Corn	100 ears
Lettuce (head or leaf)	50 lbs.
Lima beans	60-75 lbs.
Peas	40 lbs.
Potatoes	75 lbs.
Soybeans	50 lbs.
Spinach	50 lbs.
Squash	100 fruits

Another factor that you must take into consideration, in addition to the yield per row-foot, is the distance between rows. I have placed squash in the "light-yielder" category because it takes up so much room between rows (six to eight feet), while onions are counted as medium yielders because, although they yield only 75 to 100 pounds per 100 feet of row, their rows are only 15 to 18 inches apart. (The recommended distances between rows for 39 common garden vegetables are given in the Planting Guide on pages 76-81).

Succession planting. By early or mid-July, the early spring crops—leaf lettuce, spinach, radishes, and peas—will have been harvested. In addition, early cabbages and cauliflower will be harvested during July, and the early beans may then be playing themselves out, as well.

All of this midseason harvesting will leave some gaping holes around the garden, with several months of good growing weather ahead. But they may be filled with *succession crops,* which will enable you to get maximum use out of every inch of your garden. Calculate carefully the days to frost in your area, and you will be able to harvest succession crops in plenty of time for fresh use and winter storage.

Among the best candidates for succession planting are carrots, Chinese cabbage, beets, chard, cucumbers, kohlrabi, broccoli, cauflower, beans, Brussels sprouts, potatoes, leaf lettuce, and winter radishes. Of these, beets and leaf lettuce can be tricky, since either can be sent bolting to seed in a spell of unusually hot weather. More often, however, bolting is a result not so much of hot weather, but of day length. Early-planted radishes, for example, will bolt in July, but will not bolt if planted in late August because they then mature when the days are growing shorter.

In spring planting, seeds are germinated in cool soil and crops come to maturity in warm weather. In midsummer planting, the order is reversed: the seeds germinate in warm soil and the crops mature in the cooler weather of September and early October. Chinese cabbage and winter radishes take this reverse order quite well; in fact, they should not be planted in spring. For the other crops, however, you must practice a few tricks to make life easier for them.

Sow all seeds more thickly (perhaps half again as many) and a little more deeply than you would in spring. Better, germinate seeds indoors and plant them as they begin to sprout.

When you plant, soak the bottom of the furrow thoroughly with water, then water again after the seeds have been covered. Supply plenty of water until the plants are well established.

Succession planting can increase your garden yield by fully a third. Here, the soil is being prepared in early July for a row of carrots, in the same space where spinach has just been harvested.

A good mulch will keep the soil cool and moist and it can be pulled back as the plants emerge from the ground.

Part of the midsummer planting game, of course, involves an element of luck. Often, we beat the odds and enjoy moderate autumn weather well past the date of the "average" first frost. Still, you must consider the possibility of an early frost. Choose the earliest-bearing varieties you can get and give them plenty of compost and water for quick development.

Carrots will not be injured by a few hard frosts in autumn. Although they will not grow when the temperatures dip into the 40s and 30s, they will hold on—and if you then experience a few weeks of Indian summer they will pick right up again. You can prolong the growing period by mulching heavily as cold weather approaches, protecting the ground from frost that settles in during the night. Give carrots plenty of water with extra potash fertilizer (wood ashes are good) for extra-quick development.

Chinese cabbage (also called bok-choy or celery cabbage) is well suited to August planting, since it matures best in the cool weather of early autumn. In fact, it can take temperatures into the 20s with no apparent harm. Give Chinese cabbage lots of water and nourishment for quick and tender growth.

Beets can be sent bolting in very hot weather, so you will definitely be gambling in using them as a succession crop. But try it anyway, since the odds are that cooler weather will take over just as they are beginning their push to maturity. The Spring Red variety is slower to bolt than most, so it is a good bet for July or August planting. Again, supply plenty of water and potash for quick and tender growth. You can keep beets in the ground until just before the first really hard frost, 25°, or below.

Chard, or Swiss chard, is a good midsummer green, often used as a hot-weather substitute for spinach, and it is very slow to bolt. You should have no trouble with it if you supply plenty of water and nitrogen. The leaves may be harvested as soon as they are large enough to make the picking worthwhile, and the plant will keep coming back even after it has been cut. For a good, dependable source of greens all during September, and, in most areas, into October, nothing could be easier than chard.

For cucumbers, choose the earliest-bearing variety you can find. (Try Victory, for slicing; Spartan Dawn for pickling.) Plant them in early July and pray for a late frost. One thing you will not have to worry about is the cucumber beetle, whose invasion will long since have taken place.

Kohlrabi is a very quick-growing vegetable that matures well in the cool days of early autumn. It grows equally well in hot or cool weather, and the tender above-ground bulbs or "knobs" should be picked while they are still the size of a golf ball. All in all, kohlrabi is a good bet for midsummer planting.

Most leaf lettuce should mature in 40 to 45 days, and by the time it gets mature enough to bolt, the weather will probably have turned cool. Plant it about seven weeks before the first average autumn frost. If you have a cold frame, you can grow leaf lettuce right up to Thanksgiving.

Winter radishes are designed for planting in mid-summer and harvesting in the fall. Also called Chinese radishes, they are larger than their spring-planted counterparts but are equally crisp and flavorful. Recommended varieties include Round Black Spanish, New White Chinese, China Rose Winter, China Rose, and China White. All are suitable for Wisconsin and should be planted about two months before the first average frost.

Intercropping. In addition to succession planting, you can plant some vegetables in between the rows of others, harvesting the quick growers while the others are just beginning to make good progress. O. B. Combs and John A. Schoenemann, professors of horticulture at the University of Wisconsin-Madison, give some good examples in their popular booklet *The Vegetable Garden* (available from your county Extension agent):

"Early radish and spinach, for example, may be planted in the same row before late beet, late carrot, Chinese cabbage, cucumber or tomato. When you grow tomatoes this way, the plants are often set in the row before the early crop is all harvested. Cucumbers, if transplanted or seeded in hills, may be planted in the same way.

"Early, quick-growing crops like radish and spinach, as well as early beet, carrot, pea and leaf lettuce also may be planted between rows of cucumber, pumpkin, squash, tomato or late planted sweet corn. Likewise, head lettuce plants may be set between plants of early cabbage, early cauliflower, or tomato or ahead of late cabbage plants."

The main thing to remember when practicing succession planting and intercropping is to keep your soil well supplied with nutrients.

After harvesting an early crop, return all plant wastes to the compost heap and then dig in some well-rotted compost before planting the succession crop. A few applications of compost tea during the growing season will do no harm either. And, after the last crop in autumn has been harvested, dig in some half-finished compost and let it finish its job over the winter and into the following spring.

Companion planting. This is the planting together of vegetables, herbs, and flowers that appear to like each other, perhaps provide a service for each other, or at least seem to thrive in each other's presence.

The basis for companionship may exist in light relationships—one plant providing a filtered light suitable for another plant. Or, a deep-rooted plant may break up soil that can

Marigolds are good companions for many garden vegetables, because their strong aroma repels some harmful garden insects.

better feed a shallow-rooted plant. There are slow and fast growers that can live happily side by side, as explained earlier in discussing inter-cropping. Or, one plant can offer support for another, such as corn supporting pole beans. Certain flowers and herbs also seem to emit odors that repel some harmful insects. The Herb Society of America tells us that mint drives away the white cabbage butterfly, thus making cabbage and mint good companions. We know that borage attracts bees, so it is a good com-panion for cucumbers, squash, and other crops that depend on insect-aided pollination.

Or, if we wish to believe the startling research that Peter Tompkins and Christopher Bird report in their equally startling book, *The Secret Life of Plants*, plants may even like each other for purely emotional, intellectual, or social reasons. I am not prepared to explain the work-ings of companion planting—but I do know that a garden is an ecosystem, where every plant has a certain effect upon every other plant, however slight, and I know just as well that the horti-cultural experts have not even begun to sort out these interrelationships.

As our old Vermont friend Sam Ogden said, "There are mysteries that keep turning up in the garden, and of this I'm certain, that I've never solved any of them."

So, companion planting is presented here as a mystery, an avenue that you might wish to explore. It is probably the last remaining avenue that hasn't already been staked out by the experts, and so you might wish to have some fun with your own experiments.

Table 6, then, is a list of common garden vegetables, their companions and their antag-onists, as gathered from a variety of sources and observations, including reports that have come to me from gardeners in several parts of Wisconsin.

Charting the Garden

After you have determined the size of your gar-den and which vegetables you want to plant, and after you have taken into consideration the benefits of succession planting, intercropping,

and companion planting, you will want to draw up a vegetable chart to plan out your entire garden. This is great fun for one of those cold days in mid-March, when the winter has really gotten the best of you. Use quarter-inch graph paper, if you have it, or any ruled paper that you can block off into equal squares. Let each square represent one foot of garden space. That way, a standard 8½-by 11-inch sheet of quar-ter-inch graph paper will represent a garden 34 by 44 feet.

Then, use the Planting Guide (Table 7) to help you to devise your own garden scheme. The guide will give you the approximate earliest planting dates, number of seeds or plants to a foot of row, planting depth, distance between rows, distance between plants in the row, the amount to plant to feed one person, and the number of days to harvest—all you need to know to draw up a workable plan.

Nearly every book on vegetable gardening gives one or more "ideal" plans, and I do not like these very much because they are so filled with vegetables my family doesn't like—and they lack many of the vegetables we do like—that by the time I have made substitutions, I have so dis-turbed the general plan that I tear it up and start from scratch. Nevertheless, I will borrow one here to present to you (Table 8) so that you can see how it works. This particular plan is for a moderate-size garden, 20 by 50 feet, and it comes from Combs and Schoenemann's *The Vegetable Garden*. It is the best that I could present as an example, not only because it makes eminent sense, but also because all the vegetables were selected to suit the Wis-consin climate.

Starting Seeds Indoors

There are several good reasons for starting your own seedlings indoors, rather than buying sets at the garden center at transplanting time. The most obvious advantage is cost: Your home-started seedlings will save you 80 percent or more, when compared with the cost of buying seedlings commercially. Another advantage is the far greater variety of plants offered by seed packets. The garden centers necessarily limit their seedling varieties to the most popular, which, although generally dependable, offer little room for experimentation. You cannot buy seedlings of the coveted white European eggplant, or Serrano chili peppers, or most of the new Oriental vegetables that offer excitement in gardening. To try something new, you often must start it from seed.

Another reason for starting your own seedlings is an intensely personal one. The sense of satisfaction in harvesting a bushel of beefsteak tomatoes in August is just that much greater, knowing that you started those seeds on a snowy day the previous March, nursed them along until transplanting time in June, and have now come nearly full cycle with your plants. You won't have to share your satisfaction with the commercial grower, who did part of your work for you (although you might owe a debt of gratitude to the plant breeder who produced the seed).

Last, the cultivated ability to grow your own plants from seed is just one more skill that makes you a complete gardener. And if you take one further step—the saving of your own seeds—then you will have at least some assurance that, if the situation should ever require, you could feed yourself and your family with no help from the outside, just as your ancestors once did. You will have—in a psychological sense, at least—severed your dependence upon the supermarket and taken a little more control of your own life.

The seeds to start indoors are those of long-term crops that take well to transplanting—broccoli, cabbage, cauliflower, celeriac, celery, eggplant, endive, head lettuce, muskmelon, okra, some onions, parsley, peppers, pumpkins, tomatoes, and watermelon. Of course, you may also start many flowering annuals at the same time.

The starting medium. Begin preparations for spring seed starting during the preceding fall. At that time, fill several flats heaping with garden loam and leave them outside, undisturbed, for the winter. In early spring, take these flats inside and allow them to thaw, but do not disturb the soil. When it has dried thoroughly, you can pulverize it (or work it through a fine screen) and mix it with an equal amount of sand and a little lime (about a cup of lime to a bushel of soil-sand should be enough). This mixture will make a good starting medium. Many nurseries use various combinations of sand, peat, and vermiculite, using no soil at all. Start with the standard mixture, and then experiment to find the combination that works best for you.

Table 6. Garden Companions

Vegetable	Likes	Dislikes
Asparagus	Tomato, parsley, basil, calendula	
Bush bean	Potato, cucumber, corn, strawberry, celery, summer savory, petunia	Onion
Pole bean	Corn, summer savory	Onion, beet, kohlrabi, sunflower, broccoli, cabbage
Beet	Onion, kohlrabi, broccoli, cabbage	Pole bean
Cabbage family (including cauliflower, kale, kohlrabi, broccoli, Brussels sprouts)	Aromatic plants, potato, celery, dill, camomile, sage, peppermint, mint, rosemary, beet, onion, nicotiana	Strawberry, tomato, pole bean

Table 6. Garden Companions (continued)

Vegetable	Likes	Dislikes
Carrot	Pea, leaf lettuce, chives, onion, leek, rosemary, sage, tomato, radish	Dill
Celery	Leek, tomato, bush bean, cauliflower, cabbage, pea	
Chives	Carrot	Pea, bean
Corn	Potato, pea, bean, cucumber, pumpkin, squash	
Cucumber	Bean, corn, pea, radish, sunflower, borage	Potato, aromatic herbs, pea
Eggplant	Bean	
Leek	Onion, celery, carrot	
Lettuce	Carrot, radish (lettuce, carrots, and radishes make a strong team when grown together), strawberry, cucumber	
Onion & garlic	Beet, strawberry, tomato, lettuce, summer savory, camomile, cabbage family	Pea, bean
Pea	Carrot, turnip, radish, cucumber, corn, bean, most vegetables and herbs	Onion, garlic, gladiolus, potato
Pepper	Basil, okra	
Potato	Bean, corn, cabbage, horseradish, (should be planted at corners of patch), marigold, eggplant (as a lure for Colorado potato beetle)	Pumpkin, squash, cucumber, sunflower, tomato, raspberry
Pumpkin & squash	Corn, bean, pea, borage, radish	Potato
Radish	Pea, nasturtium, lettuce, cucumber, carrot	
Soybean	Grows with anything, helps everything	
Spinach	Strawberry	
Squash	Nasturtium, corn, bean, pea, radish, borage	Potato
Strawberry	Bush bean, spinach, borage, lettuce (as a border)	Cabbage family
Sunflower	Cucumber	Potato
Tomato	Chives, onion, parsley, asparagus, marigold, nasturtium, carrot, basil	Kohlrabi, potato, fennel, cabbage family
Turnip	Pea	

Table 7. Planting Guide For Wisconsin Vegetables

VEGETABLE	—PLANTING TIME—		—SEEDS OR PLANTS—	
	Indoors at Madison*	Outdoors at Madison*	For 1 foot of row	For 100 feet of row
ARTICHOKE	March 15	May 20 (plants)		50 plants
ASPARAGUS		April 15	½ plant	50 plants
BEAN, bush, lima		May 25	6 to 8	8 oz.
BEAN, bush, green, & wax		May 10	6 to 8	8 oz.
BEAN, pole		May 10	4 to 6	6 oz.
BEET		April 15	10 to 15	1 to 1¼ oz.
BROCCOLI	March 15	May 1 (plants)		40 to 50 plants
BRUSSELS SPROUTS		May 15 (seeds)	2 to 4 seeds	1/8 oz.
CABBAGE, early	March 15	May 1 (plants)		50 to 67 plants
CABBAGE, late		May 15 (seeds)		40 to 50 plants
CARROT		April 15	30 to 40	¼ oz.
CAULIFLOWER	March 15	May 1 (plants)		50 to 70 plants
CELERIAC	March 1	April 15	2 plants	200 plants
CELERY	March 15	May 20	2 plants	200 plants
CHARD		April 15	10-15	1 to 1¼ oz.
CHINESE CABBAGE		June 20 (seeds)	15 to 20	1/8 oz.
CHIVES		Arpil 15	2 clusters	1 packet
COLLARDS		May 15		1 packet
CORN SALAD		April 15		1 packet
CUCUMBER		May 20	4 to 6	⅓ oz.
EGGPLANT	March 15	June 1 (plants)		40 to 50
ENDIVE	March 1	April 15		1 packet
FINOCCHIO		May 15		1 packet
GARLIC		April 15	4 to 6 cloves	1 packet
GROUND-CHERRY	March 15	May 10		1 packet

Depth to Plant (inches)	—SPACING— Between Rows (inches)	Between Plants (inches)	Amount for One Person	Days to Harvest
3 to 4	36	24	10 plants	65 to 80
6 to 8	36 to 40	24	30 to 40 ft.	2 years
1 to 1½	24 to 30	3 to 4	30 to 40 ft.	70 to 80
1 to 1½	24 to 30	2 to 3	50 to 60 ft.	50 to 60
1 to 1½	30 to 36	4 to 6	20 to 30 ft.	60 to 65
¾ to 1	15 to 18	2 to 3	24 ft.	50 to 60
3 to 4	36 to 42	24 to 30	2 plants	60 to 70
¾ to 1	24 to 30	12 to 18	2 plants	90 to 100
3 to 4	24 to 30	12 to 18	5 plants	60 to 70
3 to 4	30 to 36	18 to 24	12 plants	90 to 100
½ to ¾	15 to 18	1 to 2	48 ft.	60 to 70
3 to 4	24 to 30	12 to 18	4 to 6 plants	50 to 60
1/8	18 to 24	4 to 6	3 plants	115
2 to 2½	36 to 42	4 to 6	5 to 6 plants	100 to 100
¾ to 1	15 to 18	2 to 4	3 ft.	40 to 50
¾ to 1	24 to 30	6 to 10	3 ft.	90 to 100
½	14 to 16	6 to 10	3 plants	60 to 90
½	18 to 24	18 to 24	12 ft.	75
½	14 to 16	12	6 ft.	35 to 45
1 to 1½	42 to 48	4 to 6	12 ft.	50 to 60
3 to 4	36 to 42	24 to 30	2 to 3 plants	70 to 80
½	18 to 24	12	6 ft.	70
½	18 to 24	4 to 6	6 ft.	90
1 to 2	14 to 16	2 to 3	1 to 2 ft.	60 to 90
½	18 to 24	12 to 18	6 ft.	65 to 80

Table 7. Planting Guide For Wisconsin Vegetables (continued)

	—PLANTING TIME—		—SEEDS OR PLANTS—	
	Indoors at Madison*	Outdoors at Madison*	For 1 foot of row	For 100 feet of row
VEGETABLE				
HORSERADISH		April 15	cuttings	50 to 75
JERUSALEM ARTICHOKE		May 1		120 tubers
KALE		April 15		1 packet
KOHLRABI		April 15	10 to 15	1/8 oz.
LEEK		April 15		1 packet
LETTUCE, head	March 15	May 1 (plants)	1 plant	100 plants
LETTUCE, leaf		April 15	25 to 30	1/4 oz.
MUSKMELON	May 1	May 20	4 to 6	1/3 oz.
MUSTARD		April 15		1 packet
OKRA	April 1	May 15		2 oz.
ONION, plants	February 20	May 1 (plants)	3 to 4	300 to 400
ONION, sets		April 15	6 to 12	3 to 4 lbs.
PARSLEY	March 15	May 1 (plants)	1 plant	100 plants
PARSNIP		April 15	20 to 25	1/2 oz.
PEA		April 15	12 to 15	1 lb.
PEPPER	March 15	June 1 (plants)		50 to 70
POTATO, early		April 15	1 piece	9 lbs.
POTATO, late		April 15	1 piece	9 lbs.
PUMPKIN, pie	May 1	May 20 (plants)	2 to 4	1/2 oz.
RADISH		April 15	20 to 25	1 oz.
RHUBARB		April 15		35 plants
RUTABAGA		June 15[6]	15 to 20	1/8 oz.
SALSIFY		April 15		1 oz.
SHALLOT		April 15		1 lb. cloves
SORREL		April 15		1 packet
SOYBEAN		May 10		8 to 16 oz.
SPINACH		April 15	20 to 25	1 oz.

Depth to Plant (inches)	—SPACING— Between Rows (inches)	Between Plants (inches)	Amount for One Person	Days to Harvest
2	24 to 30	18 to 24	8 ft.	75 to 100
4 to 6	30 to 36	10	6 ft.	100
½	18 to 24	12 to 15	8 ft.	70
¾ to 1	15 to 18	3 to 4	5 to 6 ft.	50 to 60
½ to 1	14 to 16	2 to 3	6 ft.	100
2 to 2½	18 to 24	8 to 10	3 to 4 plants	60 to 70
¼ to ½	15 to 18	2 to 3	12 ft.	40 to 50
¾ to 1	42 to 48	6 to 8	10 to 12 plants	80 to 90
½	14 to 16	12	6 ft.	30 to 45
1 to 1½	36 to 42	24	10 ft.	90
2 to 2½	15 to 18	2 to 3	12 ft.	110 to 120
2 to 3	15 to 18	1 to 2	12 ft.	40 to 50
2 to 3	18 to 24	6 to 8	1 plant	30 to 40
½ to ¾	24 to 30	2 to 3	12 ft.	100 to 120
1½ to 2	15 to 18	1 to 2	145 ft.	60 to 70
3 to 4	30 to 36	12 to 18	2 plants	60 to 70
3 to 4	30 to 36	12	100 ft.	80 to 100
4 to 6	36 to 42	12	300 ft.	130 to 140
1 to 1½	48 to 60	15 to 18	4 ft.	90 to 110
½ to ¾	15 to 18	1	36 ft.	25 to 30
6 to 8	48 to 54	36	2 plants	2 years
¾ to 1	24 to 30	6 to 8	12 ft.	100 to 110
½	18 to 26	2 to 3	6 ft.	120 to 140
1 to 2	12 to 18	2 to 3	8 ft.	90
½	18 to 24	5 to 8	6 ft.	60
1 to 1½	24 to 30	3	12 ft.	50 to 65
½ to ¾	15 to 18	1 to 2	24 ft.	40 to 50

Table 7. Planting Guide For Wisconsin Vegetables (continued)

| VEGETABLE | —PLANTING TIME— | | —SEEDS OR PLANTS— | |
	Indoors at Madison*	Outdoors at Madison*	For 1 foot of row	For 100 feet of row
SQUASH, summer		May 20	2 to 4 seeds	2 oz.
SQUASH, winter		May 20 (plants)	2 to 4 seeds	2 oz.
SWEET CORN		May 10	3 to 4 seeds	4 oz.
TOMATO	March 15	May 20 (plants)		28 to 34 plants
TURNIP		April 15	20 to 30	¼ oz.
WATERMELON	April 1	May 10		1 packet

You may sterilize garden loam quite easily, using the microwave oven. Fill a plastic bag (up to 1½ gallon size) with soil and tie with string or a rubber band. Punch several air holes in the bag and run the oven at full power for five minutes, turning the bag once or twice.

Sowing in flats. Line the bottom third of the flat with sphagnum moss, then fill it slightly heaping with the starting medium. Level off the soil with a long board and then compress it slightly with a short and wide board so that the soil is at a level about a half-inch below the top of the flat. Make furrows with a dowel or rod and place the seeds carefully in the furrows. Sprinkle pure sand on top of the seeds to a level even with the soil. (The sand will prevent excessive moisture from encouraging damping-off disease, and will allow air to reach the seeds.) Sink the flat into a wash basin or tub of water, so that the water comes about two thirds of the way up the sides of the flat. As soon as the surface of the soil has become moist, take the flats out of the water and place them in any room of the house, out of direct sunlight. To conserve moisture, you may cover the flats with clear plastic or glass, so long as you remove the covering for at least 15 minutes daily to assure adequate ventilation. (Remove the covering permanently if fungus appears.) There are many variations of this procedure, although this one is close to the standard and is fairly reliable. You can also plant in peat pots or peat cubes, or in plant bands, to make things a little easier, but again these cost money. Try them yourself to see if results justify the extra expense.

All vegetable seeds will germinate readily at soil temperatures of 70° to 75°. Today, most Wisconsin households hold room temperatures considerably below that level, especially at night. (Cooler temperatures will still suit broccoli, onions, and other cool-weather plants, but will challenge tomatoes, peppers, eggplants, and the other warm-weather natives.) The perfect answer is a heating cable, made for the purpose and available at garden centers or through mail order catalogs. The cable is looped over the bottom of the planting flat and covered with the planting medium, and will keep the soil temperature between 70° and 75°. They are inexpensive and energy-efficient and will last for years. It is a minor investment that I can recommend highly, since it makes life so much easier for seed-starters. (Lacking a heating cable, an electric blanket can be made to serve well.)

Germination. It is always a thrill to see the first of the spring seeds push through the soil surface, indoors, in your care. This, after all, is

Depth to Plant (inches)	—SPACING— Between Rows (inches)	Between Plants (inches)	Amount for One Person	Days to Harvest
1 to 1½	48 to 60	15 to 18	2 plants	50 to 60
1 to 1½	72 to 84	15 to 18	12 ft.	90 to 120
1 to 1½	30 to 36	8 to 10	84 ft.	65 to 90
3 to 4	36 to 42	24 to 36	12 plants	65 to 80
½ to ¾	18 to 24	2 to 3	10 to 15 ft.	60 to 70
1 to 2	96 to 120	8 ft. (hills)	1 hill	110 to 120

SOURCE: O. B. Combs, *Vegetable Varieties and Planting Guide for Gardens, 1974.* Additions by myself.
*Plant about one week later in central Wisconsin, two weeks later in northern Wisconsin. Consult spring frost map for your area.
†Plant about one week earlier in central Wisconsin, two weeks earlier in northern Wisconsin, in order that roots may mature during early autumn frosts.

Table 8. A Typical 20' x 50' Vegetable Garden Plan for Wisconsin.

Distance from end of Garden	Crop	Planting Date*	Suggestions for Planting
Row 1 1'6"	Parsley	April 15 (seed)	First 2 feet of row
	Chard	April 15	Next 3 feet of row
	Cavalier, radish and parsnip	April 15	Seed together 7 feet
	Pepper	June 1	3 plants
Row 2 3'6"	Spinach	May 1	
	Late carrot	July 1	Carrots follow spinach
Row 3 5'0"	Cavalier, radish	May 10	
	Late carrot	July 1	Carrots follow radishes
Row 4 6'3"	Onion	April 15 (seed) or May 1 (plants)	
Row 5 8'3"	Cauliflower	May 1	Cauliflower interplanted with lettuce and followed by Chinese cabbage
	Buttercrunch head lettuce (plants)	May 1	
	Chinese cabbage	July 10	
Row 6 10'3"	Buttercrunch head lettuce (plants)	May 1	Lettuce interplanted with cabbage
	Late cabbage (plants)	July 1	
Row 7 12'3"	Early cabbage	May 1	Cabbage interplanted with lettuce plants and followed by turnip
	Head lettuce (plants)	May 1	
	Turnip	August 1	
Row 8 14'0"	Pea	April 15	Two rows, 6 in. apart
Row 9 15'9"	cavalier radish	April 15	Radishes followed by cucumbers
	Cucumber	June 1	
Row 10 17'6"	Pea	April 15	Two rows, 6 in. apart
Row 11 19'9"	Spinach	April 15	Spinach followed by tomatoes
	Tomato (seed)	April 15	Sow seeds in hills when spinach is planted
	or		
	Tomato (plants)	May 20	Set plants in spinach row, 2 ft. apart if staked; 3 ft. unstaked

Table 8. A Typical 20' x 50' Vegetable Garden Plan for Wisconsin (continued)

Distance from end of Garden	Crop	Planting Date*	Suggestions for Planting
Row 12 22'0"	Pea	May 10	Two rows, 6 in. apart
Row 13 24'3"	Spinach	April 15	Spinach followed by tomatoes as in row 11
Row 14 26'6"	Pea	May 10	Two rows, 6 in. apart
Row 15 28'0"	White Icicle radish	April 15	Radishes followed by beans
	Kentucky Wonder pole bean	June 15	
Row 16 29'0"	Scarlet Globe radish	April 15	Radishes followed by beans
	Kentucky Wonder pole bean	June 15	
Row 17 31'0"	Spinach	May 1	Spinach followed by beans
	Green bush bean	July 1	
Row 18 32'6"	Wax bush bean	May 10	
Row 19 34'0"	Green bush bean	May 10	
Row 20 35'6"	Early beet	April 15	Beets followed by turnips
	Turnip	August 1	
Row 21 36'9"	Cavalier radish	May 1	Radishes followed by corn
	Sweet corn	June 10	
Row 22 38'0"	Early carrot	April 15	
Row 23 39'3"	White Icicle radish	May 1	Radishes followed by corn
	Sweet corn	June 10	
Row 24 40'6"	Onion (sets)	April 15	
Row 25 41'9"	Sweet corn	May 10	Corn followed by radishes
	Scarlet Globe radish	August 10	
Row 26 43'0"	Leaf lettuce	April 15	Lettuce followed by radishes
	Scarlet Globe radish	August 10	
Row 27 44'3"	Sweet corn	May 10	Corn followed by radishes
	Scarlet Globe radish	August 20	
Row 28 45'6"	Spinach	May 10	Spinach followed by lettuce
	Fall leaf lettuce	August 10	

Table 8. A Typical 20′ x 50′ Vegetable Garden Plan for Wisconsin (continued)

Distance from end of Garden	Crop	Planting Date*	Suggestions for Planting
Row 29 46′9″	Sweet corn	May 10	Corn followed by lettuce
	Fall leaf lettuce	August 10	
Row 30 48′6″	White Icicle radish	May 10	
	Late beet	July 10	
50′0″	End of garden		

SOURCE: O. B. Combs and John A. Schoenemann, *The Vegetable Garden*, University of Wisconsin-Extension Special Circular 117.

*NOTE: Planting dates given are for Madison; plant about one week later in central Wisconsin, two weeks later in northern Wisconsin.

the beginning of your garden. When this stage is reached, remove any covering and place the flat in a sunny—preferably a south—window. At this time, also, reduce the amount of water (still watering from the bottom—never by pouring water on the soil surface) so that the roots will be encouraged to go seeking their own water and thus grow strong. But never allow the flat to become completely dry. Moistness—not wetness or dryness—is the key.

Seedlings at this early stage seem to be a paradox. On one hand, they are obviously delicate, mere slips of life; on the other, their vigor is amazing, each slip seeming to fight for its place among all the others. If they are eventually to find a place in the garden, they need proper conditions of light, temperature, spacing, and moisture.

Light. This is the critical factor. Insufficient light duration and intensity, in fact, are probably the chief contributors to seedling failure. Young seedlings need 16 to 18 hours of good light each day. And since Wisconsin receives considerably less in very early spring, this means that some supplemental light should be provided.

For my seedlings, I use two inexpensive fluorescent workshop fixtures, each holding two 48-inch tubes. These lights easily handle six flats of seedlings, enough to stock my 40-by-30-foot garden with plenty of seedlings left over. I turn the lights on shortly before sundown, each day, and keep them going for four to five hours, in order to reach the total minimum daily allotment of light. If the day is very dark, I may keep them on all day long, especially if the seedlings are growing quickly.

During the day, you can increase natural light intensity by 30 percent or more by setting up a light-bouncing board just behind the plants, so that the sun is reflected off the board and onto the "dark side" of the plants. The board can be a simple piece of cardboard covered with aluminum foil, or one painted with a flat white paint (which reflects more light, more evenly, than glossy white). Quarter-turn or half-turn the flats every day, to keep plants growing straight.

Many gardeners have asked about the special plant-growing fluorescent tubes, which of course are very expensive. University tests at both North Carolina State and Cornell indicate that they offer no real advantage over ordinary fluorescent tubes. Just use a variety of different tubes (half warm-white, half cool-white) in each fixture for a good light spectrum balance.

Fluorescent tubes are cool and will not burn plants. Thus, you may keep them very close to the tops of growing seedlings—as close as one inch. With chains, you can raise the fixtures as plants grow. Or, if your fixtures are permanently installed, you may arrange plant supports (boxes, bricks-and-boards, etc.) that may be lowered to achieve the same effect.

Your seedlings, given ample light, will make controlled and stocky growth. Without sufficient light, they will grow tall, spindly, and weak, unable to support themselves. (Note: If your tomato seedlings develop legginess, you may rescue them by transplanting them very deeply—up to the first leaves—in another flat or in plastic pots. The stem portion you bury will form roots. But be sure, also, to provide more light to prevent further legginess. You may use the same technique with peppers, eggplant, and broccoli.)

Temperature. A constant temperature of 70° to 75° is perfect for germinating seeds. But after they have germinated, unplug the heating cables and give them lower temperatures, shooting for 60° to 70° during the day, 55° at night. Cool-weather crops (cabbage, cauliflower, onions, broccoli. etc.) will benefit from temperatures somewhat lower than those for the warm-weather plants. Too much heat, just like too little light, will cause seedlings to become leggy and weak.

Spacing. Your seedlings need room to grow. If they are cramped by each other, all will suffer. Impeded air circulation, as well as actual physical constraints (root competition), may result in the loss of all seedlings. Crowding also encourages damping-off disease, which easily can wipe out an entire flat overnight. The obvious solution is to thin out seedlings so that no one touches another. As they grow, they will

need several thinnings before they are finally transplanted into the open garden.

Seedlings may be thinned by pulling up some with a pair of tweezers. Unless you want to replant these seedlings, however, it is far better to simply snip off the unwanted plants at the soil line, using a pair of manicure scissors. Pulling seedlings out of the flat may disturb the soil and break the tender roots of the plants you want to save. Snipping is also a quicker and simpler method.

Moisture. Here, we include both soil moisture and atmospheric moisture, or humidity. Both are important. The soil should be kept constantly moist—never soggy, never dry. Be sure to offer proper drainage, because water can collect at the bottom of the flat and rot the plant roots, even though the surface seems to be moderately moist. You may keep flats moist by misting them every morning.

Humidity is critically important. too. The ideal situation is a south-facing room, equipped with a room humidifier, that can be closed off from the rest of the house or apartment. Lacking an ideal location, you must do everything you can to assure good humidity. Set containers of water around the seedlings, so that the water slowly evaporates into the air. Put pans of water on radiators, or above heat vents, to hasten evaporation and increase room humidity. Or set the flats on top of shallow pans filled with water (but don't let the water actually touch the flats). Try to mist the seedlings a few times every day during this critical growing stage, but do not mist at night, as temperatures are dropping in the room.

Last, keep the seedlings away from cold drafts. Much cold air will come from windowpanes during the night; if your flats are right next to the window, they may be adversely affected. To prevent damage, close the curtains at night. Flats should not be situated immediately above heat vents, either. Strive at all times for even, moderate temperatures for growing seedlings.

Enriching the soil. Seeds, as we have said, do not need a nutrient-rich soil to germinate.

In fact, a starting medium that is too rich will be detrimental to the germination process—especially of tomatoes. The seedlings are not able to use soil nutrients until their first true leaves appear. The first "leaves" you will see are actually the cotyledons that come from the seed structure. They cannot perform photosynthesis and cannot take advantage of soil fertility in any case.

When the first true leaves appear. however (the second set you will see coming from the center of the plant), it is time to give the seedlings a richer soil mixture, for they will then be able to operate as true plants. There are three ways in which you can do this: (1) Add compost tea to the original starting medium after the first true leaves have appeared, thus introducing nutrients to the mixture; (2) make the top half-inch layer of the original medium a mixture of peat and sand, overlaying a more fertile mixture. The seeds will germinate in the infertile mixture, and the roots will penetrate to the fertile layer as the first true leaves are showing. You may experiment with either of these methods, but remember that most professionals will transplant when the first true leaves have appeared; (3) transplant to flats.

Transplanting to flats. The soil mixture for the transplanting flat should be the same as for the starting flat, except that a little well-screened compost should be added and mixed in thoroughly. The mixture should still be kept lean, however, so a slight handful of compost for each flat should be plenty. The idea here is to encourage the roots to search for food and thus grow large and strong. If the mixture is too rich, the roots will not develop well, the stems will grow tall, spindly, and weak, and the chances of ultimate failure will increase drastically.

Dampen the soil before transplanting, in both the starting flat and the transplanting flat. Remove the seedlings very carefully from the starting flat, keeping the seedlings two inches apart in both directions. Plant them to the original depth, in holes that you have poked with a small stick, and firm the soil carefully around the young roots. Keep the transplants out of direct sun until they show signs of active growth. Most plants will not be bothered by the transplanting process, although some may wilt from shock, but they will recover in a day or two. Some plants seemingly cannot take transplanting at all, however, and I have tried to identify these when discussing the individual vegetables earlier in this chapter. Generally, you will want to start indoors the seeds of tender varieties which take a long time to mature, such as cabbage, head lettuce, broccoli, eggplants, tomatoes, and peppers, while there is not much sense in spending this time with leaf lettuce, radishes, beans, peas, and other vegetables that can either be planted very early in spring, or that come to maturity in 60 or 70 days or less. Those varieties that should be started indoors,

but do not take well to transplanting, should be started in peat pots, peat cubes, or plant bands, so that they can be moved without disturbing their roots.

Transplanting outdoors. For each vegetable, plan carefully the date on which you will transplant it into its final garden location. It is best not to crowd this date, for your seedlings can still make good progress indoors if all conditions are right, while a late spring frost can quickly undo all your efforts should you set them out too soon.

About two weeks before the setting-out date, begin the hardening-off process. This is simply the practice of exposing the young plants gradually to the outside environment, in order to minimize shock. Begin by setting the flats outside in the midday filtered sun, protected from

Young cabbage seedlings might look limp, wilted, and near death for the first few days after transplanting. Generally, however, they recover nicely and grow with amazing speed after the weather turns hot.

Onion plants started from seeds in a home-made flat.

the wind, for a half-hour. Gradually expand this time outdoors until, on the day before transplanting, they remain outside until dark, only then being brought inside. (If you have a cold frame, you should use it for the hardening-off process, keeping the lid closed at night and opening it for longer and wider periods each day.)

On the day of final transplanting, remember to protect the young plants against direct sun, strong wind, and excessive cold. The ideal day should be cool and cloudy. If you cannot find a day such as this, then do the best you can to protect the plants. Never let the sun shine directly on the exposed roots. Prepare the beds carefully. The top several inches of the garden bed should be raked as finely as possible, and the soil should be loose. Keep the rows straight, using pegs and strings as guides, if necessary, not only for the sake of neatness but to retain the proper planting distances. Pay strict attention to the recommended distances both in the rows and between the rows. It may look as if you have all the room in the world when you are putting in new plants, and the temptation to crowd in a few more plants is

strong. Along about August, however, you will be sorry if you had yielded to temptation in May. Crowded plants do not produce well.

Several hours before transplanting time, soak all the pots or flats with water. They are going to have a difficult time in drawing up water for the first few days, and this presoaking will assure that they will go into the ground holding all the water their tissues can absorb. The soaking will also keep root breakage to a minimum and help the roots hold on to some water.

Don't remove the seedlings from their pots or flats until you are ready to set them into the ground. If they are allowed to lie on the ground, bare-rooted, for 15 or 20 minutes. they may well go into severe shock. (Cabbage seedlings always go into shock, no matter what you do. Generally, they lie limply for a day or two, then recover with amazing speed.)

My method is to dig a very large hole, about 15 inches deep, for each tiny seedling. I put a heaping double handful of composted manure in the bottom of the hole, then fill up the hole with ordinary garden loam, into which I set the plant. Along about the middle of June, when the plant's roots discover the compost, it makes an amazing growth spurt, and its root system by then is deep and strong, resistant to drought.

If you have grown your seedlings in peat pots—the kind with fine plastic netting around them—be sure to tear off the netting before you set the plant into the ground. I know that the manufacturer's directions don't include this advice. I also know that I have, in spring, dug up last year's peat pots, finding that the netting had not even given a thought to dissolving. In every case, the plant's roots had managed to break through one small part of the netting and had made all its progress from that point.

Set your seedlings into the ground at a somewhat lower level than they were in the flat or pots. Especially if the plants are leggy and weak, this technique will help them to form better root systems. In the case of tomatoes, the technique can be exaggerated, all to the benefit of the plant. I generally tear off the bottom two sets of leaves and trench in the plant at an angle, burying about half of the stem. The plant will look a little strange when you first plant it, angling halfway to the ground and only half as tall as it once was—but it will soon straighten up and head for the sky. Best of all, the stem portion you bury will quickly develop roots, and those roots will result in a larger plant and many more tomatoes in the months ahead. (I also pinch off any blossoms on tomatoes when I plant them. At this stage of the game, you want root development—not fruit.)

Do not fertilize seedlings for at least two weeks after you plant them. Fertilizer at this stage will encourage quick and weak growth, making the plant susceptible to injury or death from cold winds, insects, and diseases.

Provide plenty of water, both as you transplant (soak the hole several times, as you are working with it) and for several weeks afterward. Young seedlings, which have grown up indoors, must adjust their chemistry to handle outdoor breezes. Winds quickly carry away moisture from plant tissues, and the plant's roots cannot draw up water easily at this stage.

Remember that cutworms can slice through all your seedlings in a single night's activity.

Buy the little cutworm collars, or use orange juice concentrate cans or some other homemade protective device.

After transplanting, water the plants thoroughly and—if possible—provide some protection against both sun and wind, at least for a few days. If you have not used all your seedlings, return them to the house. If any of your outdoor-planted seedlings do not make it, they can then be replaced. If you mulch the plants, pile it high around each plant for the first few days. A straw mulch can be set very lightly to cover the plants, offering good protection from the wind while filtering the strong sunlight. The mulch can be pulled back gradually over a period of a week. After that, the plants can be treated normally. Keep a good mulch and keep the garden reasonably free of weeds.

Presprouting Seeds

One of the problems of planting beans, cucumbers, corn, squash, and other directly seeded vegetables in May, in Wisconsin, is that the soil often has not had a chance to warm up thoroughly. even though the air temperature may be 70° or higher. Often, the seeds just lie buried and dormant, when they could be making good progress in the warm air temperatures.

The answer to the problem is in presprouting seeds. In this process, the seeds are germinated indoors, under controlled conditions, then are planted in sprouted form. The procedure gives the plants as much as a two-week headstart, and—because you do not have to allow for nongerminating seeds—the tedious job of thinning seedlings is greatly reduced.

You may presprout all seeds that are planted in May, including flowering annuals. The practice is especially recommended for slow-sprouting seeds such as parsley, beets, delphinium, and larkspur.

The procedure is simple. It requires only small plastic bags and milled (shredded) sphagnum moss, which contains a natural chemical defense agent against diseases that can kill seeds as they sprout. Ordinary peat moss should not be substituted, since it lacks this disease-inhibiting agent.

Sphagnum moss is dry when you buy it, and it is difficult to moisten. Remove a small amount from the bag and roll it up in a towel. Then, moisten the roll and wring it to force moisture into the dry moss. Let it stand wet for an hour, then wring it again. The moss should be moist, but not soggy.

Mark a small plastic bag with the kind and variety of seeds and the date of seeding. Add a cup of moist moss and a pinch of seeds. Shake to mix. Twist and fold over the top and seal with tape or twist-tie wire. Put the bag in a warm place, around 70° to 75° for tomato, eggplant, and pepper seeds, 65° for cool-weather seeds.

Be ready to plant the sprouts when about half of them have germinated. If rain delays planting, slow down the germinating process by placing the bag in a cool room.

Sprouts can be killed by exposure to wind or sunlight. Prepare the furrow before separating the sprouts from the moss. Work quickly to scatter the sprouts down the furrow, making sure that they do not touch each other. Cover them lightly with sifted compost, and soak the rows.

Sprinkle the rows lightly two or three times daily until shoots begin to show above the soil, then gradually decrease the frequency of watering. Don't worry about sprouts being upside down or sideways in the furrow: they know which direction to go.

Presprouting, incidentally, is hardly a new idea. The American Indians were doing it with bean seeds, long before the first European settlers caught on to the idea.

Last Year's Seeds

Should you throw away last year's packaged seeds? Probably not. If they have been kept in a spot free from excessive heat, there is every chance that they are still viable and capable of producing good crops. Here are the reasonable viability periods of some common garden vegetable seeds:

Two years: Corn, onion, parsnip, soybean, salsify.

Three years: Bean, leek, parsley, pea.

Four years: Carrot, mustard, pepper, tomato.

Five years: Broccoli, cabbage, cauliflower, kohlrabi, lettuce, okra, pumpkin, radish, spinach, turnip.

Six years: Beet, eggplant, melon, squash.

Eight years: Celery.

Ten years: Cucumber, endive.

Many seeds will last for considerably longer periods of time. If you have any doubts about your seeds' viability, try a germination test. Count out 20 seeds or so, and place them on a layer of sterilized cotton in a saucer. Put another layer of cotton on top, and soak both layers with water. Pour off any excess. Keep the cotton damp throughout the test. Some seeds take only a day to germinate, others take several weeks. Lift the top layer of cotton every day to check for sprouting and to let some air in. If mold appears, take off the top layer permanently, but keep the bottom layer moist and in a dim or dark place. If all, or nearly all. of the seeds sprout within a reasonable time, you can count on the viability of the rest. If only half germinate, you may still use the seed if you sow twice as thickly as recommended. If less than 25 percent germinate, do not use that seed.

Saving Garden Seeds

Why try to save your own garden seeds, when packets of them are available in stores every spring?

There are several reasons for experimenting in this activity. First, all the seeds you save will replace those you would otherwise buy. The savings will be only a few dollars for the average backyard gardener—but might really mount up for those tilling a half-acre or more.

Then, there are some plants we occasionally grow for which seeds are not commercially available, or are difficult to locate. We might wish to perpetuate a particular strain of flowering plant that we found on a vacation trip, or a plant that a foreign visitor presented to us. In these cases, a basic knowledge of seed collecting is rewarding, indeed. There are dedicated gardeners throughout the U.S. who collect, grow, and preserve heritage varieties, ones that that the big seed companies have forsaken in favor of improved hybrids. This is nothing less than an attempt to preserve the gene pool of our vegetative food supply. If you want to learn more about seed saving and heritage plants, send a self-addressed and stamped envelope to Kent Whealy, Seed Savers Exchange, R.R. 3, Box 239, Decorah, IA 52101. There is also an excellent 33-page book on the subject, *How to Save Your Own Vegetable Seeds*, by the Heritage Seed Program of Ontario, Canada. It is available for $8.95 from the Territorial Seed Co., 20 Palmer Ave., Cottage Grove, OR 97424.

Most of us, I suppose, are ever looking for ways to feel (if not actually be) self-sufficient. I suspect that gardeners, especially, feel this way. What would happen if we were left on our own, for any reason, with no access to the good old garden center or mail-order catalog? In the world of self-sufficiency, food production is obviously critical. And seed collection and storage are necessary to food production, just as during the time of our pioneer forebears.

A fourth group of seed collectors are actually trying to develop new and superior varieties of flowers and vegetables. They will find no insights in the following advice, which is directed toward us amateurs and tinkerers.

If you want to collect and save seeds from some of your annual vegetables and flowers, May or June is the time to begin thinking about it. Identify the plants that interest you, then mark those that are the healthiest, for they are likely to produce the healthiest seed.

The first no-no involves hybrid plants, whose seed you should not bother to save. An F1 hybrid seed, the kind most often sold, is the result of careful inbreeding of two parent plants of different genetic makeup. The F1 (first generation) hybrid will produce the best characteristics of both parents, but the seed saved from that plant will tend to revert toward the characteristics of one parent or the other. The result, every time, will be an inferior plant. So, check your varieties, look them up in the seed catalog if you must, and eliminate all hybrids from this project.

Next, be advised that some vegetables— including root crops, parsley, cabbage, and Brusels sprouts—are biennials, meaning that they will not produce seeds until the second year. Unless you want to try to store their roots over the winter and replant them the following season strictly for seed production, do not bother with them.

The matter of cross-pollination is frequently overstated. Contrary to the belief of some, pumpkins will not cross with cucumbers, a cantaloupe cannot cross with a squash or watermelon, and a cucumber hill may safely be established next to a zucchini hill. In order to cross-pollinate, two plants must be of the same species. Closely related members of pumpkin and squash families may cross-pollinate, but pollination between families is impossible. And, of course, different varieties of corn cross-pollinate quite easily.

If cross-pollination does occur, that season's fruit is not likely to be affected greatly, but it is unwise to save seed from a cross-pollinated plant. If you plan to save seed from any vegetable, it will be best not to plant another variety of the same vegetable nearby, to keep the strain as pure as you can.

Seeds should be collected from plants when the fruits are fully mature (often more mature than we like for eating) but before they have started to rot. Fleshy fruits—cucumbers, tomatoes, peppers, etc.—should have gone past prime eating stage before their seeds are collected. Beans should be allowed to dry on the vine. Plants with seeds that scatter—lettuce, onions, and okra—should have a paper bag tied over their seed heads so that the seed may be collected easily. (Make pinholes in the bag for air circulation.)

There are various methods for cleaning seeds, most of them practiced for hundreds of years on farms, before the modern seed-breeding industry made things easy for us. Dry seeds are easy to handle, simply by shelling, winnowing, or screening. Seeds to be separated from pulpy fruits (tomatoes, berries. etc.) require a slightly messier operation.

After a sufficient drying period (the seeds should be as dry as possible, down to about a 5 percent moisture content), the seeds are stored for next year's planting. The process is simple, for most plants, and the chief reward is a comforting feeling of security, the knowledge that, if you really had to, you could produce your own quality food from year to year, with no help from the national agribusiness superstructure. Your garden can be self-sustaining. And to many people, in a very large way, that's what gardening is all about.

Vegetable Gardening Without a Garden

Container gardening—the growing of plants in tubs, crocks, barrels, sacks, etc.—is a boon for apartment dwellers. But this form of gardening has recently attained popularity even among families in large-lot homes and on farms, since it offers special challenges and extra rewards.

Most container gardens are oriented toward ornamental annuals, which can be grown quickly and easily to brighten rooftops, patios, porches, balconies, steps, and windowsills. It is no trick to grow a few tubs or large pots of marigolds, coleus, petunias, or geraniums. But the real challenge is in growing vegetables and using containers that would otherwise be assigned to the local landfill site.

Your choice of containers is limited only by your imagination. You can use old washtubs, half-barrels, that plastic wash bucket that sprang a leak, coffee cans, milk cartons, tires, wading pools—anything that will hold a few inches of soil. The container should have drainage holes, so that water will not collect in the bottom and rot the roots of growing plants. But if the container cannot be drilled for drainage (a ceramic crock, for example) or if you cannot allow drainage for some other reason (it would not be nice to let muddy water drip on your downstairs neighbor's grilling steaks), then you can line the bottom of the container with a few inches of gravel, which will collect excess water. A thin layer of charcoal on top of the gravel will absorb impurities and keep the soil sweet.

Nearly all container vegetables and ornamentals require only six to eight inches of soil for good growth. The exceptions are cabbage (which produces a long taproot), carrots, and large varieties of tomatoes, broccoli, Brussels sprouts, and cauliflower. These will do well in 10 to 12 inches of soil.

Your container garden will need at least six hours of sun daily, so choose your location carefully. The more sun, the better results you will have. Many times, you can staple aluminum foil to a large sheet of cardboard and bounce sun around a corner for extra light.

Also use a good planting medium. I recommend one third potting soil or ordinary garden soil, one third sand, and one third composted manure, with a little bone meal thrown in—about a heaping handful to the bushel.

Water and fertilizer are critically important to container plants. They must be watered every other day, unless rainfall has taken care of the job, and they should be fertilized about once every ten days (use a fish emulsion solution).

The varieties you choose are important. Plant breeders, responding to the increasing popularity of container gardening, have developed some great dwarf and compact vegetable varieties especially for the purpose.

Give yourself the best chance for success by choosing varieties carefully. Here are some to consider:

Cabbage. Dwarf Morden, Baby Head, Little Leaguer (all dwarfs); Stonehead (a standard variety, good for larger containers).

Carrot. Tiny Sweet, Midget, Little Finger. Space them two inches apart in six to eight inches of soil.

Cucumber. Baby, Little Minnie, Mini, Tiny Dill Cuke, Patio-Pik. Provide little trellises for climbing, or let them hang from baskets.

Eggplant. Morden Midget (dwarf); Jersey King, Early Beauty (standard varieties). Stake plants.

Bibb lettuce. Tom Thumb, Buttercrunch.

Leaf lettuce. Any variety.

Cantaloupe. Minnesota Midget. The fruit measures only four inches across and is very sweet. Vines are only three feet long.

Watermelon. Petite Sweet, New Hampshire Midget, Lollipop, Golden Midget, Market Midget. Provide trellises.

Tomato. From the smallest to the largest— Tiny Tim, Small Fry, Pixie, Presto, Patio. Stake and tie.

Turnip. Tokyo Cross.

Beet. Ruby Queen. Grow them quickly and pick them young and tender. Mix wood ashes into the soil and water them heavily.

Radish. Any variety except long-rooted ones.

Spinach. Any variety.

Swiss chard. Ruby.

Bean. Any bush variety will do well in 10 to 12 inches of soil. Train pole beans up the side of a wall or fence, or let them weave through balcony rails.

Endive. Any variety.

Onion. Sets may be planted in shallow containers, spaced one inch apart. Thin plants as the season progresses, using the young onions as scallions.

Squash. There are several compact forms of zucchini. Give them 10 to 12 inches of soil. Support them with a trellis or let them hang from baskets.

Pepper. Any standard variety will do well in ten inches of soil, if fertilized heavily. The foliage is attractive and may be interplanted among flowers. Bell varieties need full sun, but Hungarian wax varieties will do well with only six hours daily.

Caring for Vegetables through the Season

Weed control. A weed is a plant out of place. All weeds serve several good purposes, and some weeds are fully as valuable as some of the plants we cultivate. A large part of the weed "problem," in fact, is our very attitude toward them.

Our general aversion to weeds is another of our values shaped over the years by Madison Avenue. The vision of the spotless green lawn, and the perfectly clean rows of vegetables, is one to which we have been taught to aspire, if we are to win the respect of our peers (who, of course, have been taught the same thing). A perfect expression of this misshapen attitude, I think, is the "dandelion gun" which has become popular among many suburban lawn owners. This gun has a real trigger that shoots a dose of herbicide into the heart of a dandelion plant. ("The roots don't come back!" says the TV announcer.)

No, the roots don't come back—and neither do the plant nutrients that the dandelion captures from deep beneath the topsoil. This is one service that weeds perform. Like any other plant, they bring up minerals from the earth, storing them in organic form that can be used by other plants. And because the taproot of the dandelion goes so deeply into the soil, it brings up nutrients that otherwise would be leached away.

(The dandelion, incidentally, is a versatile little plant. It bears cheerful yellow blossoms in profusion, as you know. But its tender young leaves may be used in early spring salads, offering good amounts of vitamins A and C, iron, and potassium. Its roots have long been used as a coffee substitute, and the plant is the source of a favorite wine in rural America. Throughout history, the dandelion has been used to combat a variety of physical ailments. Now, how can you hate a plant like that?)

Weeds are also a great soil conditioner, their roots penetrating the soil, breaking it up, keeping it loose, providing food for beneficial soil life, creating air and water spaces, and in general making the soil a better living place for plants of all kinds.

Euell Gibbons, the most famous American weed fancier (*Stalking the Wild Asparagus*, etc.) could gather up a good dinner in any weed patch. He did it quite easily in New York's Central Park. We can do the same here in Wisconsin, even by choosing among the most common of weeds. Burdock, cattail, lamb's-quarters, milkweed, peppergrass, pigweed, pokeweed, purslane, sorrel, not to mention wild forms of onions, lettuce, leeks, asparagus, watercress, and garlic—all are edible and healthful foods.

All this is not to say that we should give our lawns and gardens completely over to weeds. It is to say that we should take a new look at weeds, examine our long-held values concerning them, reflect, reappraise, and perhaps emerge with a new view that does not automatically classify all weeds as dread adversaries.

Our goal, then, is to control weeds, not to eliminate them from our gardens. And with this goal in mind, it becomes clear, also, that herbicides are completely unnecessary in the home garden. You can cultivate a 40-by-30-foot vegetable garden, without chemical weed controls, and spend no more than an hour a week in hand weed control.

The two secrets to weed control are proper cultivation and heavy mulching. After you have harvested all vegetable crops in the fall, till the ground and leave it in a rough state, so that many weed seeds are exposed to the elements or gathered up by birds. If possible, till again, several weeks later, to destroy more seeds. In spring, till the entire vegetable garden as soon as the soil is dry enough to be worked. A second tilling in spring will be even more effective.

Mulching techniques are covered in Chapter 2, starting on page 35. For weed control in the vegetable garden, the best mulch is one of hay or straw, which is abundant throughout Wisconsin. Be sure to put it on thickly, or it won't serve to smother weeds. If you cannot get enough mulch for the entire garden, it is better to apply it thickly on part of the plot, and to hand-cultivate the other part, rather than to apply a thin layer that will let weeds through, yet impede cultivation. Lay the mulch as soon as the young plants are up and the ground has warmed up enough for each of the vegetables. (Warm-weather plants such as tomatoes, peppers, and eggplants should be mulched last.) Until it is time to lay the mulch, keep weeds out of rows with a hoe or cultivator, or, on large plots, with a tiller.

During the growing season, you should go through the entire garden about once every week, hand-pulling weeds that grow right up against vegetable plants. Since slugs and snails sometimes hide under mulch, it is best to keep the mulch several inches away from the plants. If you mulch heavily, and never let weeds grow too large, the containment effort should be a minor one.

Side-dressing. Quite often, the difference between a mediocre harvest and an outstanding one is side-dressing. Most gardeners have heard of side-dressing but have never bothered to practice it. But, then, most gardeners have average gardens.

Side-dressing is simply the midseason fertilizing of plants. The fertilizer is usually dug into the soil to the sides of the plants, thus the name.

Vegetables need an extra supply of nutrients as they are making their big growth spurt, or as they are flowering. Use aged compost or manure, but do not use fresh manure, which can easily burn the roots. If you have a supply of fresh manure, use it to make manure tea, for which I will give directions shortly.

Root crops, including beets, carrots, turnips, and parsnips, should not be fertilized with manure or compost, since the high nitrogen content of these materials will encourage leafy growth at the expense of good root development. For root crops, side-dress with a combination of bone meal and wood ashes, which will provide good amounts of phosphorus and potash. Also see that these crops have plenty of soil moisture during their period of quick development.

Exactly when to side-dress is a question that has received much attention in gardening books and magazines, with advice so contradictory that many gardeners throw up their arms in confusion and simply forget about the whole thing. The answer is actually a simple one. Side-dress vegetables when they need it— when they begin to grow quickly or when they are forming blossoms and fruit. In any case, it is better to side-dress at the wrong time than to not side-dress at all.

Beans, peas, potatoes, and cucumbers should be side-dressed about a week after their first blossoms have appeared. Tomatoes, peppers, and eggplants need a good dose just after they have set fruit. Squash and watermelons will benefit from side-dressing just as their vines begin to grow vigorously.

Broccoli, cabbage, cauliflower, and Brussels sprouts should be dressed during their big initial growth spurt in June or early July. Onions need extra nutrients as their bulbs begin to expand.

The actual technique of side-dressing is no great trick. For individual plants such as tomatoes, peppers, eggplants, cabbages, etc., just dig out a circular trench, three inches deep and about four inches wide, keeping four to six inches away from the stem of the plant. (Always be careful not to disturb the roots.)

Fill the bottom of the trench with an inch of aged manure or compost, then replace the soil, forming a low circular ridge around the plant. Tamp down the ridge and water the area thoroughly.

For row crops, such as onions and beans, dig trenches along both sides of the row and proceed as before.

Manure tea. If you are using fresh manure, make it into manure tea before using it. Just fill a burlap sack with the fresh manure and sink it into a barrel or trash can full of water. It should be in a sunny location and away from the house. Within a day, bubbling and fuming will begin, as billions of bacteria work away at fever pitch. When there is no more sign of activity in the barrel, the job is done and the liquid may be used to side-dress plants. Just pour it carefully around the individual plants, or close to plants along both sides of rows. (If the ground is crusted, break it up with a hoe so that the tea will be absorbed easily.)

Side dressing often is the difference between an average garden and a great garden.

Staking and tying. My feelings on staking and tying of garden plants may be summarized in three words: least is best. I would rather let my tomatoes run free over a bed of mulch than to spend hours in staking and tying up their vines. I plant bush beans rather than pole beans. And I avoid flowering plants that must be staked.

Nevertheless, supports are needed for some plants, especially if garden space is limited and plants are to be trained upward. Tomatoes, for instance, will yield more fruit per square foot of garden space when they are staked and tied— but will have higher yields per plant if not staked. Pole beans, which require supports, have higher yields per square foot of space than bush beans, although, if bush beans are planted in double rows, the difference becomes slight. Whether or not to stake, then, becomes a matter of individual preference, often depending on the amount of garden space available.

In all cases, stakes should be driven into the ground at the time that seedlings are transplanted. Driving in the stake next to a half-grown plant invites root damage. For tomatoes, two-by-two-inch stakes provide the needed support for the heavy fruit. A six-foot stake, extending four and a half feet out of the ground and set a few inches from the plant, is sufficient. As the vines grow, they are tied to support an upward growth pattern. Use thick twine or torn bed sheets, which will not easily injure the vines. In all cases, tie the twine tightly to the stake and loosely to the vine. If you notch the stake with a rasp, the twine will not slip.

For pole beans, longer stakes are needed. In the country, the trunks of unwanted young saplings are ideal for the purpose. Urban gardeners will more likely use eight-foot two-by-two-inch stakes. Whichever are used, they are generally driven into the ground around the bean hill, three or four stakes to the hill. and tied together at the top. tepee style. Twine may be wrapped around the poles, at two-foot intervals, to give the vines extra climbing support.

Peas are usually trellised. The most simple structure is a length of four-foot chicken wire stapled to stakes, which are spaced four feet apart along the row. (If you are growing Sugar Snap peas, be advised that—contrary to package advice—their vines may easily grow to six feet or more in length.)

Some other vine crops—including cucumbers and small-fruited squash—may also be trellised, if space is at a premium. In addition, garden centers offer a variety of support structures, including tomato cages, which are rather expensive but will last indefinitely. Be certain, before investing, that the space between the wires is large enough for you to reach into, to collect the fruit.

If you do stake some plants each year, you may wish to make your own permanent supports, which will be attractive as well as useful. Your two-by-two-inch stakes may be cut, pointed, notched, and then painted with a flat dark green paint. You may even drill holes in them. to allow twine to run through. They should last for years, cared for properly, and

they will add to your garden that professional touch that brings admiration from neighbors, friends, and in-laws.

Thinning. The practice of thinning—the removal of some plants in a row to make room for others to grow—is not a favorite garden chore, but a necessary one with crops that are open seeded—beans, carrots, radishes, lettuce, beets, peas, corn, etc. If carrots, for instance, are to grow two inches apart, it would not do to plant one seed every two inches, since not all will germinate. We sow them much more closely, then thin out the row after the plants have germinated.

Exactly how closely to sow seeds—to assure enough viable seedlings yet reduce the time spent in thinning—comes only with experience. You may be more sure of seed germination, however, if you presprout seeds (see page 138), and then your thinning time will be reduced. You may also buy "seed tapes," which have seeds imbedded in a narrow strip of biodegradable material, correctly spaced for easy thinning. I have considered these to be an expensive gimmick, although I have yielded to temptation (in the name of research, I tell myself) and used carrot tapes. I believe that carrots are the most difficult of all crops to thin.

Thinning out seedlings may be done with thumb and forefinger, with a pair of tweezers, or with a pair of small scissors. Large-plot gardeners sometimes use a metal lawn rake, which pulls out many seedlings at once, at more or less regular intervals—an effective, if not very tidy, technique. If you do not plan to replant the seedlings you pull, I recommend that they be cut or pinched off at ground level, so that the roots of the remaining plants are not disturbed. If you pull the seedlings, be sure to water the row several hours before doing the job, so that soil and root disturbance is held to a minimum.

Many seedlings removed may be used in salads or stews, including onions, beets, lettuce, carrots, radishes, and all leaf crops. Winter onions, which you hope will grow to very good size, may be planted very closely together in spring, the thinnings used as scallions. Radishes, quick to germinate, are often used as row markers for other crops. The radishes are thinned out as they reach edible size, leaving room for the slower-growing crop to expand. The radishes further serve to break up the soil and keep it loose for the remaining crop.

Watering and soil moisture. Wilting, stunted plant growth, and retarded fruit development are the common effects of insufficient soil moisture. Tomatoes suffer blossom-end rot when exposed to a very dry period after a wet period. Peppers simply drop their blossoms if the soil becomes too dry.

Supplying ample soil moisture can be as simple as watering the garden thoroughly when it becomes too dry. If your garden is small enough, and reachable by hose, then be sure to do the job right. Don't sprinkle the garden every night. Rather, water no more often than once every five days, but then soak the ground thoroughly, to a depth of four inches. Here's why:

Plants have built-in mechanisms to combat drought. They undergo definite physical and chemical changes in every cell, enabling them to survive fairly long periods of dryness. The leaf pores (stomates) will close, to slow down transpiration of water out of the plant. The leaves will curl, to conserve what moisture they hold.

If you water lightly, then let the plant become exposed to drought, you will do it more harm than good, since you will shut off its natural defenses while providing water only to the surface roots. With no defenses—and no water—bottom roots will die.

Further, a season-long habit of frequent sprinklings will encourage plants to develop shallow root systems. Then, in time of drought, the plants will be unable to search deeply into the soil for the water they need.

In any garden, large or small—but especially in the larger plot where watering is impractical—your best weapons against drought are a good loam soil, heavy mulch, and deep fertiliz-

ing. Even if you can water your garden, you will save water (and money) by adopting good soil management principles.

The texture of your soil is vitally important to its water-holding capacity. The coarser the soil, the less is its ability to hold water. A sandy soil will hold only about 0.75 inches of water per foot; a fine sandy loam will hold 1.25 inches; and a silt loam, clay loam, or clay will hold from 2.5 to 3.0 inches. If your soil is sandy, you must watch moisture levels very carefully—and for the long run, you should begin to incorporate all the organic matter you can into that soil, to improve its water-retention properties. (See Chapter 1 for soil improvement tips.)

In a drought, the soil dries from the top down. A week of drought might dry out about two inches of soil. But a good mulch will reduce surface evaporation greatly—by as much as 50 percent.

Your third ally against drought is deep fertilization. When drought strikes and the soil begins to dry out at the upper levels, plant roots begin to seek moisture at deeper levels. This means that they will draw their nutrients from those deeper levels, too, since nutrients are transported through the roots by water. If the soil is deficient in nutrients at those deeper levels, the plant will suffer accordingly. When a plant suffers during drought, it is not simply because it cannot get water—it is also because the little water it receives carries few nutrients. The answer is to carry on a year-round system of deep fertilization, including plenty of compost which should be spaded or tilled as deeply into the soil as you can manage. Such a program will increase the soil's water-holding capacity, while providing a source of deep-lying nutrients. It will be a veritable bank account of nutrients that your garden plants can call upon in time of need.

Vacation care. Unless you take special precautions, you might return from a two-week vacation to find your garden in total shambles. Radishes and leaf lettuce may bolt to seed, heads of broccoli will burst into useless bloom, and weeds may quickly take over the entire plot. If you spend a few hours in your garden before leaving town, however, you can cut your losses to virtually nothing.

The first thing to do, before leaving on a summer trip, is to clear all the remaining spring crops from the garden—leaf lettuce, peas, radishes, and spinach. They will all become worthless during a July hot spell, and so they should be removed and replaced with succession crops—beans, cucumbers, carrots, Chinese radishes, or late cabbage. By the time you return from your trip, it will be time to thin out the new plantings.

Next, pick off all the blossoms from beans, zucchini, and cucumbers. The plants will become revitalized in your absence, send out more blossoms than before, and produce a crop just as large—if not larger—at the time you want to harvest.

If any of the tomatoes are turning pink, remove them from the plants, wrap them in newspaper, and store them in your refrigerator until you return. They will then ripen on the windowsill. On the plant, they will become overripe and slow the development of younger fruit. (You may also take the ripening tomatoes with you, allowing them to ripen *en route*.)

If your broccoli and cauliflower have formed heads—even small ones—cut them and freeze them for later enjoyment. Broccoli will form lateral heads after the main head is cut, and these laterals—just as delicious, albeit smaller—will be ready as you return from vacation. If you do not cut the main head before you leave, it will probably go into full blossom, making the plant totally worthless.

All the root crops—onions, potatoes, carrots, turnips, etc.—will continue to mature satisfactorily in your absence. Spring beets, however, might bolt to seed, thus ruining the texture of the root. Pick them and store them in the refrigerator before you leave town.

Next, go through the entire garden and remove any plant parts that have been affected by insects or diseases. These things spread quickly, as you know, and by removing affected leaves and stems, you will lessen the possibility of disaster.

Then, remove all weeds—totally, thoroughly, getting up as many of the roots as you can. A good weeding is an essential vacation prerequisite.

Next, be sure that the garden is well mulched. A deep mulch will not only hold down weeds but protect your garden against possible drought in your absence.

Then, if the garden is dry, soak it thoroughly just before you leave town, giving it more than the normal amount of water. If you have been mulching all along, of course, you won't have to water at all.

Last, as a precautionary measure, dust your beans, cabbage, broccoli, cauliflower, and Brussels sprouts with rotenone. In the event of a cabbageworm attack your plants will be protected at least until the first good rain. You may also use Thuricide or another *Bacillus thuringiensis* preparation for protection against cabbageworm. Both rotenone and *B. thuringiensis* are of extremely low toxicity to warm-blooded animals.

If all this sounds like a lot to do, it isn't, really. Two people can perform the entire prevacation chores in three hours, in a good-size (40-by-30) garden. And, after all the work you will have put in to bring the garden to the brink of heavy production, it would be a shame to let it run amok during your vacation.

Sixty-Seven Vegetables for Wisconsin

Here are 67 vegetables, some common and some uncommon, that will grow in Wisconsin. I have grown many of them personally, but I certainly have not grown all of them, and I imagine it would be difficult to find anyone who ever has. The information given for these 67 vegetables, then, is necessarily drawn from a variety of sources—from my own experience, yes, but mainly from government and university reports, from the works of other garden writers, from the pages of *Organic Gardening* magazine, from the personal advice of gardening friends and Extension agents, and even from newspaper articles.

All the information given here is accurate, or at least as accurate as such a compilation can be. Because of space restrictions, the cultural directions are brief. Remember, though, that these directions should be supplemented by the information given in the Planting Guide, which will give you the space between plants, space between rows, approximate planting dates, number of days to harvest, and other valuable data. If you would like still more information about any of these varieties, check your library or bookstore for a good vegetable encyclopedia, or ask your county agent, who might have a pamphlet giving full cultural directions.

Then, a word about the recommended varieties given for each vegetable: Those followed by an asterisk (*) are those recommended for growing in Wisconsin in the pamphlet *Vegetable Cultivars and Planting Guide for Wisconsin Gardens,* prepared by O. B. Combs and since revised by Helen C. Harrison and Astrid C. Newenhouse of the University of Wisconsin-Madison. These varieties, or cultivars, have been tested at the University or Wisconsin experimental plots, passed the tests with flying colors, and are probably the most reliable varieties you can plant. For dependability, then, look for the asterisk.

This pamphlet is revised annually to include new varieties and is available from your county agent at no charge. Those without an asterisk have not been so recommended, but they give every indication of being suitable for Wisconsin growing.

Those followed by a dagger (†) are especially recommended for growing in northern Wisconsin by Eugene E. Anderson, Area Community Development Agent, University of Wisconsin-Extension.

Amaranth

Amaranth is the most nutritious vegetable you can grow in your garden. It is an exceptionally rich source of calcium, iron, and vitamin C; a very rich source of potassium, vitamin A, and riboflavin; a rich source of niacin; and an above-average source of protein. There are two kinds of amaranth—grain and vegetable—and it is the vegetable amaranth we are concerned with here. It is a quickly growing annual that may be used like spinach, raw in salads or steamed as a potherb. Amaranth leaves also make a savory addition to soups and stews.

Although amaranth has been grown for human food for more than 4,000 years, it has only recently received serious attention as a crop for North American gardens. This is one leafy green that does best in hot weather, making it a good succession crop to follow spinach. It will not do well when summers are damp and cool, and it is very sensitive to frost.

Soil. Loose, rich, well-drained soil with a good supply of nitrogen is best.

pH. 6.0-8.0.

Culture. Sow seed outdoors when all danger of frost is past, or start plants indoors three weeks before the frost-free date. Plant outdoors when danger of frost has passed. Thin to six inches between plants in beds or rows. No mulching is needed between plants because of quick growth. The crop is ready to be harvested in about 70 days. Harvest the leafy rosettes at top of plant as they appear, when plant is four to six inches tall. Continue to harvest the rosettes as they develop, again and again through the growing season. They can be frozen like spinach.

Varieties. There are none from which to choose. Both Burpee and Park Seed sell amaranth under the name "tampala," Nichols under the name "edible amaranth spinach," and several Asian catalogs under the name "hin choy."

Artichoke

Thanks to the introduction of an exciting variety, Grande Beurre, gardeners can now grow globe artichokes in Wisconsin with a reasonable expectation of success. This is not the easiest of vegetables to grow in this hostile climate, but, with some attention and a pair of crossed fingers, you can enjoy your own artichokes the very first season after planting from seed.

The traditional American artichoke, Green Globe, produces no edible flower heads during the first season, and so it must be carried over as a perennial. This is possible in warmer parts of the country but difficult here. At the same time, it cannot stand intensely hot weather, and it also rots easily under a heavy winter mulch. Its requirements are so demanding, in fact, that commercial production is limited almost exclusively to the Monterey Bay region of California, where the winters are mild and the summers are consistently cool. While driving through that region, I saw acres and acres of thriving artichokes (not without a touch of envy, since artichokes are a personal passion).

Grande Beurre, however, is different. It will produce edible heads the very first season, from 50 to 80 percent of its seedlings. Researchers at the Organic Gardening and Farming Research Center, in Pennsylvania, harvested edible artichokes at about the time the first tomatoes ripened. Another gardener in the Berkshires of western Massachusetts—which has a climate not dissimilar to our own—harvests artichokes beginning about the second week in August, and continues to harvest them until frost. If your growing season is 100 days or more, you can grow Grande Beurre.

Soil. Artichokes need a very fertile soil, well composted, well limed, and with good drainage.

pH. 6.0-6.5.

Culture. Start seeds indoors early in the spring, at the same time you start tomatoes, broccoli, and cabbage. Germination will be improved if you store seeds in the refrigerator two weeks before planting. After the first true leaves have appeared, transplant to individual containers. These should be deep ones—four to five inches—because the seedlings quickly develop long roots. From that point until transplanting time, treat the seedlings as you would tomatoes.

Transplant seedlings to the open garden at the same time you set out tomatoes, after all danger of frost has passed. The leaves can take temperatures as low as 28°, but any frost that enters the ground will kill the crown and surface roots.

Traditional varieties, planted in long-season areas, can grow as high as six feet and spread out considerably. But Grande Beurre, grown in Wisconsin, will not likely grow to more than two feet tall, spreading two to three feet across. Seedlings, then, should be planted two feet apart in rows that are deeply prepared, with compost dug in to a depth of 18 inches.

Do all you can to encourage quick growth. Never allow the soil to dry out; at the same time, avoid soggy soil. Side-dress plants with fish emulsion every three weeks during the growing season, or use a mixture of blood meal (for nitrogen) with bone meal, ground limestone, or wood ashes (for calcium). Both are important to good artichoke production.

Keep the plants mulched with hay throughout the season, especially when the weather turns hot. If you are harvesting good crops as the cool days of autumn arrive, remove the hay mulch and substitute one of black plastic, which will absorb more heat during the day and retain much of it at night.

For the following year's crop, you may save the roots of your best bearing plants. Cut the tops down to within two inches of the crown, then dig up the roots carefully and brush away the soil clinging to them. Repot them in the basement, using large pots or wooden boxes, and keep them over winter in a cool, bright spot. Water the roots just enough to keep them from shriveling, until it is time to set them out the following spring. You may also harvest healthy side shoots, if you get a good piece of root along with each shoot.

Special tips. The artichokes we buy in supermarkets are often old and tough. Californians know that the best artichokes are young and tender, no more than three inches in diameter. Perhaps, thanks to Grande Beurre, Wisconsin gardeners will come to know this, too.

Varieties. What else? Grande Beurre (available from Thompson and Morgan).

Asparagus

It takes several years to establish a producing asparagus bed, even when roots instead of seeds are planted. But, properly cared for, an asparagus bed will last a lifetime. Asparagus is the first vegetable to be brought to the table in spring, usually in late April or early May, and the harvest may continue up until July 1.

Soil. Asparagus prefers a sandy loam but will do well even in heavier soils, if they are well drained.

pH. 6.0-7.0.

Culture. Select a sunny corner of the garden, one with rich, deep, well-drained soil. In early spring, as soon as the ground can be worked, dig a trench ten inches deep and ten inches wide. (A rotary tiller can be used for easier trench digging.) Line the bottom of the trench with three inches of well-rotted compost, including plenty of old manure. Dig this into the bottom of the trench to a depth of at least six inches. Set one-year-old crowns two feet apart in the row and cover with two inches of well-rotted and screened compost. Water well. Fill the trench very gradually throughout the summer with a mixture of screened compost and good topsoil, until it is full by September 15. A bed prepared in this careful manner will give roots a good start and will support the plants for many years to come.

Do not cut any spears the first year, but let them grow into the ferny brush that will establish the planting for future years. In the second year, you may cut spears for the first several weeks but not after that. During the third year, you may cut spears up until the middle of June, after which you should leave them alone. After the third year, you may make a full harvest, cutting up until July 1 but not after.

Asparagus does not need much fertilizing. since its roots are so deep and vigorous, drawing nutrients from six feet in any direction. But you might adopt the practice of hilling the rows in spring and side-dressing with a mixture of compost and either limestone or wood ashes.

Do not remove the ferny brush in fall, but let it die down naturally, cutting it only in the following spring. A winter mulch of hay will prevent frost from damaging the roots, and it will prevent heaving, which tends to bring the roots slowly to the surface.

Special tips. If you maintain a fairly large bed, sow a cover crop of cowpeas or soybeans after the cutting season has ended. Sow between the asparagus rows, and till under the cover crop in fall for soil enrichment.

Varieties. Mary Washington*†, Waltham Washington*, Viking* (all open-pollinated). Jersey Gem*, Jersey Giant*, Jersey Knight* (all hybrids).

Bean (bush, green)

Bush beans (also called snap beans) are a most rewarding crop, easy to grow, productive, simple to harvest, and suitable for both canning and freezing. They are a good source of vitamin A.

Soil. Bush beans thrive in almost any soil, from light sand to heavy clay.

pH. 6.0-7.5.

Culture. Treat seeds with a nitrogen inoculant before planting to give them a faster start. After the young plants have grown to about three inches high, thin until they are four to six inches apart. Cultivate lightly with a hoe during the season, being careful not to disturb the shallow roots. A light mulch may be applied after the plants are established and thriving. Beans should be picked before they have matured, when the pods are fairly small and the tips are soft. Regular picking is important, since the plant will stop producing if the seeds are allowed to mature.

Special tips. Instead of making one large planting of bush beans, make several plantings, separated by two-week intervals. This practice will assure a continuous supply of beans throughout the summer and early fall.

Trouble-shooting. Snap beans won't flower when daytime temperatures exceed 90°. Be sure to stagger plantings, as suggested above, so that the plants don't all come into blossom at the same time. If poor germination of seed is the problem, chances are that you planted seed before the soil had warmed up sufficiently. Plant a little later in the season, or warm up the bean rows with a layer of black plastic, then remove the plastic before seeding.

Varieties. Bush Blue Lake 94*, Bush Romano*, Contender*, Derby*, Hystle*, Top Crop*, Tendergreen*†, Earligreen*, Tendercrop*†, Gardengreen*† (mosaic tolerant), Executive* (mosaic tolerant), Astro* (mosaic tolerant), Provider* (mosaic tolerant), Tenderette* (mosaic tolerant), Bush Blue Lake 274*, Speculator*.

Container varieties. Any will do well in 10 to 12 inches of soil. Provide support for pole varieties.

Bean (bush, wax)

Wax beans are yellow podded instead of green, but otherwise there is little difference in their use or taste. Culture is the same as for green bush beans.

Varieties. Earliwax* (mosaic resistant). Pencil Pod*, Goldrush*, Kinghorn*†, Cherokee*†(mosaic tolerant), Gold Crop* (mosaic tolerant), Midas* (mosaic tolerant), Eastern Butterwax, Honey Gold (mosaic tolerant).

Bean (pole, green)

Pole beans have the same general taste as bush beans. They require a longer time to mature, but the gardener who is pinched for space will certainly want to include them, since their yield is higher.

Soil. Pole beans have the same general soil and climatic requirements as bush beans, except that they seem able to thrive in heavier soils.

Culture. The traditional method of planting pole beans is to drive seven-foot stakes into the ground, hilling up some soil around the base and planting six seeds (inoculated) in the hill around each pole. The hills should be 18 to 24 inches apart, although some gardeners plant

much more closely. Rows are three feet apart. After the seeds have produced young plants, thin to three per hill, and be sure that the vines get a good start up the pole. Some gardeners erect the poles in tepee fashion, building veritable cones of pole beans. Others stretch washline horizontally between vertical poles, to provide even more climbing room for the vigorous vines. Begin with traditional poles, and then experiment with your own devices.

Special tips. All beans fix nitrogen in the soil and thus are valuable soil builders. When clearing garden wastes after the last harvest, cut the bean stalks at ground level, but do not tear up their roots. It is the roots that hold the nitrogen. In the following season, plant a nitrogen-loving vegetable where the beans stood—early beets or cabbage, cauliflower, spinach, or white potatoes. All will benefit from the bean's legacy of nitrogen.

Varieties. Kentucky Wonder*†, Blue Lake*†, Romano*†, Kentucky Wonder Wax, Kentucky Blue*.

Bean (bush. lima)

Lima beans are native to warmer regions and are not always easy to grow here in Wisconsin. They require a slightly more acid soil than snap beans, and long, warm days. They generally take from 10 to 20 days more to mature than bush or pole beans.

Soil. Limas do well in a light, but rich, garden loam.

pH. 5.5-6.5.

Culture. Select the sunniest spot in the garden for limas. Plant seeds (inoculated) only when the soil has warmed up thoroughly, or else the seeds might well rot in the ground. The soil surface cannot be hard and crusty or the young seedlings might be unable to push the large seed halves through the surface. After the plants have bloomed and the tiny pods have been set, be careful not to disturb the plants for about a week, for the young pods drop off easily. A large dog running through the lima bean row at the wrong time can decimate your crop in seconds. The plants also need extra moisture after they have bloomed, but it should be applied by irrigating the rows or hand watering along the roots with care—never by training the hose on the plants or dragging the hose between the rows where it might brush up against the plants.

Special tips. Even when you do everything right with limas, they might respond with luxuriant leafy growth and a scant crop of beans, especially if the soil is rich. This is a difficult crop for most gardeners, and many in Wisconsin will not want to assume the high risk of failure.

Varieties. Fordhook 242* †, Thorogreen* †, Henderson*, Thaxter (baby limas), Baby Potato, Burpee's Improved Bush, King of the Garden (a pole variety).

Bean (other)

Although bush pole and lima beans probably comprise 90 percent of the garden beans grown in the United States, many others are both interesting and valuable for their nutritive content. Following are some varieties that Wisconsin gardeners might want to try. The cultural requirements of all are similar to those for green bush beans, except where noted.

Adzuki bean. The Adzuki has been gaining in popularity in recent years, principally because of its extremely high protein content —up to 40 percent. It is a small plant that matures in 90 days, producing thin pods and small dark red beans. Adzuki can be used as a green snap bean or its seeds may be dried and stored for winter use. It is also good for sprouting, because of the small size of the beans.

Fava bean. The broad, flat fava is a favorite baking bean although it may also be used as a green shell bean, like limas. It matures in 85 to 90 days and does well in cool weather. The large seeds take some time to germinate and should be soaked overnight before planting.

Great northern white bean. Another good baker, the great northern can also be used as a green shell bean at 65 days, although the crop matures at 85 days.

Jacob's cattle bean. This is the white bean with red speckles, having the same uses and requirements as great northern.

Maine yellow eye. A good baker, grown exclusively for drying. It matures in 92 days and will do well in cool areas.

Mung bean. A popular bean for drying and later sprouting, easily grown in Wisconsin.

Soldier bean, Navy pea bean. Both are standard white baking beans grown exclusively for drying. Soldier bean is the larger of the two and needs about one third more room than green bush beans. Both soldier and navy pea beans mature in 85 days.

Pinto bean. This Mexican native does best in warm weather and requires 90 days to mature, probably limiting success to the warmer areas of the state.

Red kidney bean. It requires a 100-day season but is the easiest of all dry beans to grow. A favorite for chili and other Mexican dishes.

Romano bean. Also called Italian pole bean, it is grown like other pole beans. Romano produces broad, flat pods that are useful in many Italian recipes. Pods may be picked while young and tender, for use as snap beans, or left to mature for use as green shell beans. They require only 66 days to mature. A bush variety. Roma, requires only 50 days.

Scarlet runner bean. Here is a remarkable bean that every gardener should try. It has long been the most popular edible green bean in England. Its strong vines can be trained on walls or trellises, where they will grow 10 feet or higher. They produce spectacular red flowers that attract hummingbirds. The beans are produced in rough-looking pods, which are actually quite tender when picked while young for use as snap beans. The beans can also be used as green shell beans, later in the season, or can be left to mature (88 days) for use as dry beans.

Some others you might wish to investigate are French horticultural bean (65-70 days). red Mexican bean (85 days), and white Dutch runner bean (88 days).

Beet

Beets are a rewarding garden crop, relatively easy to grow, fast developing, and requiring little space. They do especially well in the cooler regions of the state. We grow them for the red roots, which are a good source of vitamins B, and C, but the beet tops are good, too, as a source of vitamins A and C and iron.

Soil. Beets do well on nearly any well-composted soil, so long as it is rich in nutrients. Beets are notorious consumers of potash, and for this reason you should incorporate either hardwood ashes or potash rock in that part of the garden you have reserved for beets, before planting in the early spring.

pH. 5.8-7.0.

Culture. Seeds can go into the open ground very early, at the same time as peas. You can thin the young plants by picking the baby beets to use in salads. Sowings made every few weeks during the season will give you a continuous crop throughout the summer and into fall's heavy frosts—but very hot weather might force them into bolting and woodiness.

Special tips. Late-planted beets can be harvested just before the first severe frost of the autumn. Packed in sand and kept barely moist at a temperature of 35 to 40 degrees, they will last for several months, probably into January.

Varieties. Big Red*, Burpee Golden*, Chioggia* (striped), Kleine Bol*, Red Ace*, Early Wonder*†, Perfected Detroit*, Detroit Red†, Ruby Queen*†, Vermilion, Cylindra†, Spring Red (slow to bolt), Early Red Ball, Crosby Egyptian, Red Pak (good for canning), Detroit Dark Red, Garnet, Crosby Green Top, Long Season (80 days), Pacemaker II* (hybrid), Gladiator (hybrid).

Container variety. Ruby Queen.

Broccoli

Broccoli is a highly nutritious vegetable. It is not difficult to grow in Wisconsin, and the mature plant will be quite resistant to the first fall frosts, thus extending the growing season beyond that of many other vegetables. Broccoli is one of the few vegetables that we grow for their flowers, for it is the bunches of flowering buds and their tender stems that we pick to eat.

Soil. Broccoli needs a fertile and well-drained soil, rich in organic matter and lime.

pH. 6.0-7.0.

Culture. The broccoli plant will grow quickly during hot weather, but once the heads begin to form, the plant prefers cool nights. This preference makes broccoli a good succession crop, perhaps following a planting of early spinach. You can buy plants from most nurseries and local garden centers, or you may start seeds indoors about six weeks before transplanting time. When the heads begin to form, you might side-dress the plants with a strong compost tea. Keep a mulch around the plants once they have become well established (spoiled hay is good for these large plants). and give them extra water if the weather becomes particularly hot and dry.

Special tips. The leaves of the broccoli plant are particularly susceptible to attack by the cabbageworm. The worm doesn't attack the edible portions of the plant, however, and therefore doesn't cause much concern. The cabbageworms can be picked off by hand, or, if the infestation is great, you can control them with rotenone. If cabbageworms, plant lice, or aphids get into the heads, it is best to cut the heads into small pieces and drop them into a fairly strong solution of salt water for a few minutes. The insects will float to the top, and the broccoli, after having been washed, will be perfectly good to eat.

Varieties. Emperor*, Green Belt*, Spartan Early*†, Crusader* (hybrid), Premium Crop* (hybrid), Green Comet*† (hybrid), Green Valiant*, Packman*, Raab* (cutting), Waltham 29*, Royal Purple Cauliflower'*, Cleopatra, Italian Sprouting, Green Mountain (recommended for short-season areas where nights are cold), Bravo, Green Hornet, Green Comet, Early Purple Head.

Brussels Sprouts

Brussels sprouts have been a prized vegetable in America for more than a hundred years and in Europe for several hundred. They do well in Wisconsin, like other members of the cabbage family, because of our cool nights. Excessive heat, however, might force growth to the point where the heads will become loose and leafy instead of tight and firm, as they should be.

Soil. Brussels sprouts like a fairly heavy soil, well drained and well supplied with compost and lime. On sandy soils great care must be given to heavy fertilization and extra water.

pH. 6.0-7.0.

Culture. Sow seeds in the open garden after the danger of heavy frost has passed. Or, sow seeds later in the season for a fall crop. When the young plants are about three inches high, they should be thinned and transplanted to the recommended distances. A mulch will help to moderate the soil temperature, keeping growth at just the right pace. When the little heads begin to form on the axils of the leaves, give the plants an application of compost tea. When the heads begin to mature, cut off the lower leaves (below the heads) to facilitate harvesting. The tangy flavor of Brussels sprouts is greatly enhanced after the plant has been touched by a few light-to-medium frosts.

Varieties. Captain Marvel*, Jade Cross (hybrid)*†, Jade Cross E (slightly taller than Jade Cross), Prince Marvel*, Early Morn, Long Island Improved, Green Pearl (120 days).

Cabbage

The rightful head of the cabbage family is cabbage itself, an old Wisconsin favorite. At the turn of the century, when traveling photographers made their rounds of Wisconsin rural areas, a favorite late summer picture was the one of the entire family gathered around a display of their garden's harvest. And the picture was never complete without at least one mammoth cabbage head, often set directly in front of the proud and dour head of the family. Cabbage is, indeed, a garden product you can be justly proud of. In the home garden, you can produce heads that weigh 20 pounds or more by giving the plants plenty of compost and plenty of water. And few vegetables are more versatile than cabbage. Cooked with pork roast or corned beef, cut up

into crisp slaw, made into sauerkraut, or just eaten raw in chunks, cabbage returns all the effort put into raising it, many times over.

Soil. Like other members of its family. cabbage prefers a rather heavy loam, rich in nutrient matter. Few plants feed more heavily, so generous applications of compost, including plenty of manure, are essential. If the soil is sandy, care must be taken to keep it well watered during the growing season, for cabbages are heavy drinkers as well as eaters.

pH. 6.0-7.0.

Culture. Start seeds indoors about six weeks before transplanting time, or buy plants at your garden center. Set them out when danger of heavy frost has passed. The early varieties are smaller than the late ones, and they must be picked as soon as they are firm, or else the heat of midsummer will force a seed head to form, destroying the quality of the head. The late varieties, which are larger and require considerably more time to mature, do not demand early picking, since they will mature as the weather turns cool. The late varieties can stand a couple of light frosts. Like Brussels sprouts, in fact, the flavor of cabbage is enhanced by an early frost or two.

When planting cabbage, work aged compost at least eight inches into the ground for best results. The roots will go down three feet or more. if they can, to draw moisture to quench their heavy thirst. When you do apply water during dry spells, soak the ground thoroughly—never sprinkle. During the growing season, give plants a couple of applications of compost tea, fortified with dried blood. The dried blood, which is rich in nitrogen, will give the plants an extra boost when they need it most. It is also a good idea to plant cabbages where last year's peas or beans stood, since the nitrogen that these legumes leave in the soil will be eagerly received by the cabbage plants.

Special tips. Those pretty yellow and white butterflies that you see darting around your young cabbage plants are up to no good. They are laying eggs that will hatch the dread cabbageworm. This is a good time to get the children interested in collecting butterflies— providing that the kids are old enough to avoid stepping on the young plants. After the worms have appeared and have begun to eat huge, gaping holes in the leaves, they can be controlled with rotenone if there are too many to pick by hand. But do not be too concerned when holes appear on the outer leaves. The cabbage head grows from the inside out, and the head will be good even when the outer leaves look ragged. The other major attacker of early cabbage is the root maggot, which can be controlled by placing tarpaper discs around the stems of the young plants at the soil surface. The discs are inexpensive and can be purchased at most garden centers.

If maturing heads begin to split, slice through half of the taproot at the base of the plant, to reduce water uptake. Some gardeners simply twist the cabbage head until the taproot snaps.

Cabbages can be stored for a short time in a cool cellar, by pulling out the head, getting as much of the root as possible, tying a paper sack around the head, and hanging it up by the root. Or, you may store them underground, covering them with layers of soil and straw to protect them against freezing. Further storage hints are given in the table on page 181.

Varieties. Jersey Wakefield* (earliest), Wisconsin Golden Acre* (second earliest), Gourmet* (hybrid), Sanibel* (hybrid), Jersey Queen*, Market Dawn* (hybrid), Wisconsin Golden Acre*†, Badger Market*†, Market Topper* (hybrid), King Cole* (hybrid), Market Prize* (hybrid), Guardian* (hybrid, resistant to black rot), Defender* (hybrid, resistant to black rot), Greenback*†, TBR Globe*†, Little Rock* (hybrid), Sanibel* (hybrid), Excel* (hybrid), Roundup* (hybrid) (the foregoing listed in order of earliness; all resistant to yellows), Vangard (Savoy)*, Savoy Ace* (hybrid), Savoy King* (hybrid), Ruby Ball*, Stonehead*†.

(Note: So many varieties of cabbage are commercially available—more than 50 are offered in the Stokes catalog alone—that I have listed only those recommended specifically for Wisconsin.)

Container varieties. Dwarf Morden, Baby Head, Little Leaguer (all dwarfs), Stonehead (a standard variety good for larger containers).

Carrot

Carrots have a long and distinguished heritage, going back to the time of the ancient Greeks. They are a rich source of vitamin A and have long been a popular garden vegetable. It is not difficult to grow carrots, but it is considerably more difficult to grow good-looking carrots. They require far more personal attention than most garden vegetables, although many gardeners think that the final product is worth the extra effort.

Soil. Carrots will grow in most soils, but they prefer a sandy loam that is free from stones and lumps. These obstructions will inhibit the growth of the carrot (which is a taproot) and will cause it to be misshapen. If your soil is heavy, you had better choose among the half-long varieties. The long varieties require about a foot of well-prepared soil of fine texture. In any case, the soil should be well supplied with compost and should be given an application of lime, well worked in, before planting.

pH. 5.5-6.5.

Culture. Carrots can be planted as soon as the soil can be worked in spring. They are slow to germinate and must be thinned so that the individual plants are one or two inches apart, depending on the variety. This is a slow and tedious job which, once done, will prompt you to sow carrots more thinly next time. In order to avoid having all the carrots mature at once, successive plantings can be made up until about July 15 in Wisconsin. After the initial thinning, made when the young seedlings are about two inches tall, the plants may be further thinned throughout the season. (Use the young carrots in salads.) In fall, the last of the mature carrots should be dug and stored just before the first hard frost. They are particularly suitable for storage in an underground root barrel.

Special tips. Try interplanting radishes with your carrots. Sow the radishes very thinly (perhaps two seeds to the inch), right in with the carrot seeds. The radishes will germinate first and will be picked before they begin to crowd the carrots. The early-germinating radishes serve another purpose in that they will mark the row until the carrots show their foliage later on.

Trouble-shooting. If you have had trouble growing perfect, long-rooted carrots in heavy clay soil, try the mound method. Work plenty of aged compost and ample amounts of sand into the carrot row, then work in some wood ashes for added potassium. Next, use a garden rake to form a seven-inch mound along the length of the row. Flatten out the peak of the mound gently with a spade, then dig your seed furrow. Sprinkle a thin layer of wood ashes in and along the furrow (to deter nematodes and maggots), then sow the seed, cover the furrow, and tamp to assure good seed contact with the soil. Put a hay mulch over the entire mound (to prevent the soil from washing away), but do not mulch directly over the seeds. The seven-inch mound will offer a perfect, light growing medium for the carrots. Never walk on the mound, and do watch soil moisture carefully throughout the season, because mounds do tend to dry out quickly. (The mound method may, of course, be used with other long-rooted crops.)

If your carrots split open in the soil, the cause probably is that a period of heavy rain followed a dry period. The carrot, with its drought-fighting chemistry in full operation during the dry spell, could not cope with the flood of water suddenly received. The answer is to keep soil moisture even by providing a deep mulch and regular watering during droughts.

Half-long varieties. Lucky B*, Nantes* (less likely to become bitter, some resistance to aster yellows), Red Cored Chantenay*†, Scarlet Nantes†, Spartan Bonus* (hybrid), Danvers 126*, Coreless Amsterdam†, Baby-Finger Nantes, Touchon Deluxe, Pioneer*, Oxhart†.

Long varieties. A Plus* (hybrid), Golden State* (hybrid), Imperator*†, Ingot* (hybrid), Gold Spike, Gold Pak†, Spartan Sweet, Canuck, Spartan Fancy, Gold Pak, Ultra Pak, Waltham Hicolor, Orlando Gold* (hybrid; highest of all carrots in Vitamin A).

Container varieties. Tiny Sweet, Midget, Little Finger (space two inches apart in six to eight inches of soil).

Cauliflower

Cauliflower is an interesting plant to grow, both challenging and rewarding. It should not be attempted unless you are prepared to give it the special attention it requires, and its needs are quite specific. Like broccoli, it is the flower of the plant that we covet. Many gardeners are willing to spend the time to grow perfect flowers for both the eye and the palate.

Soil. Cauliflower is perhaps the heaviest feeder of the garden, even hungrier than cabbage. Be sure that the soil is well supplied with all nutrients, particularly nitrogen. Cauliflower will do well where beans or peas grew in the previous year, since these legumes leave nitrogen stores behind. Lime should be incorporated deeply before planting.

pH. 6.0-7.0.

Culture. The plant does best during cool and moist weather and is a voracious drinker of water. Apply a mulch as soon as the young plants are set out, and never let the soil become dry. Do not disturb the roots in cultivating, or else the heads will grow unevenly and become fuzzy. Either a late spring frost or a lack of nitrogen can cause premature heading, in which case the plants should be pulled out and discarded.

Special tips. When the heads are about two and one-half inches in diameter, tie the outside leaves loosely over the heads to shade them from the sun. This will result in the pure white heads that are prized by growers. This bleaching process may be started later, depending on which expert you listen to, even as late as a week before harvesting.

Succession plantings may be made, although late plantings must be given even more water than early ones. The keys to good cauliflower are heavy composting and heavy mulching.

Varieties. Alverda* (green), Polar Express* (hybrid), Snow Crown* (hybrid), Snow King*† (hybrid), Snowball Imperial*, Self Blanche* (no tying needed), Early Snowball†, Snowdrift†, Super Snowball†, Extra Early Snowball, Super Junior, Snowmound (developed for fall crops), Idol Original, Perfected Snowball, Clou, Snowball-Y* (shows resistance to downy mildew), Silver Cup 45* (hybrid), Igloo, Early Purple-Head†, Royal Purple, Violet Queen* (hybrid).

To bleach the heads of cauliflower, tie the outer leaves loosely over the heads, to shield them from the sun.

Celeriac is an unusual but rewarding root crop, long popular in Europe but just making itself known in Wisconsin.

Celeriac

This vegetable, sometimes called knob celery, is more popular in Europe than in America, but it has caught the fancy of some Wisconsin gardeners to the point where it can now be found in some garden centers. It is related to celery and it has a similar taste. The difference is that we grow celeriac for its enlarged root crown, which the Europeans prize for soups and stews. The sliced root can also be used in salads.

Soil. Celeriac likes a fertile, well-limed, and rather heavy loam. (The heavier soils provide ample supplies of water, which are needed for the plant's success.)

pH. 6.0-7.0.

Culture. Celeriac requires less care than celery, and it is easier to grow. If your local seed dealer or nursery cannot supply seed, it may be ordered from one of the larger mail order seed houses such as Stokes, or Harris. Seed is sown about eight weeks before transplanting time, which is about May 15 in Madison, June 1 in Superior. It is a slow grower, requiring 110 to 120 days, but it can take a few light frosts without apparent damage. Set three- to four-inch seedlings six to eight inches apart in rows two feet apart, and apply a light mulch to conserve moisture. Roots can be harvested when they have reached two inches in diameter. After the first light frosts in fall, and before a really hard frost, the remaining roots can be dug and stored either in an underground root barrel or in a cool basement, where they should be packed in moist sand.

Varieties. Brilliant*, Mentor*, Prague*, Alabaster Prague* (120 days), Large Smooth Prague (110 days), New Giant Prague (115 days).

Celery

The ancestors of modern garden celery come from the marshes of Western Europe and Northern Africa, and celery still grows best in a marshy soil which supplies plenty of water and plenty of lime. It may be grown successfully in any soil, however, if moisture and fertilization requirements are met. There are two common types—golden (or yellow), which was much preferred until recent years, and the green variety, which we see most often in supermarkets under the label of Pascal celery.

Soil. Celery likes a fertile soil, rich in all elements, and plenty of water. A generous application of well-rotted manure before planting will virtually assure a good crop.

pH. 6.0-7.0.

Culture. Seeds are slow to germinate and to grow, so that indoor sowings should be made a full nine weeks before setting out the plants in May or June. If you have a cold frame, seeds may be started even earlier, indoors, and set into the frame to harden off along about April, giving you larger plants with which to start the outdoor growing season. Be careful not to break the taproot when transplanting, for this can injure the plant, perhaps fatally. It is best to sow seeds in peat pots, which can be put into the ground, pot and all, thus eliminating any possibility of root injury. The surface of the seeding soil should be kept damp at all times. (Since a damp surface is one of the major causes of damping-off disease, you may now wonder how to prevent the problem with celery. The answer is to apply a light sprinkling of washed sand on the bedding surface. The seeds can germinate through the sand, and the damping-off disease cannot function in this medium.) Water the peat pots by placing them in a shallow tray of water until the surface becomes damp. In the garden, keep a light mulch around the plants and do not let the soil become dry. During hot spells, water the soil around the plants, but do not direct water on the plants themselves. The foliage should not be wet unnecessarily.

Special tips. Celery is a heavy potash feeder but will react badly to excessive nitrogen supplies. The potash can be supplied by sprinkling hardwood ashes alongside the plants several times during the growing season. The rains will wash the ashes down to the shallow roots. You can bleach the stems if you wish, by sliding a four-inch drain tile down over the plant,

or by staking up boards on each side, or simply by wrapping the stems loosely with several layers of newspaper. Care must be taken not to suffocate the foliage with the bleaching material that you use. Begin the bleaching process when the plants are fully mature. About a week of cover should do the job.

Golden varieties. Golden Self-Blanching*†, Golden Plume, Cornell 619.

Green varieties. Summer Pascal*†, Utah 52-70*, Utah Early Green, Florida 683, Slow Bolt, Tendercrisp, Beacon, Florimart.

Chard

Chard, often called Swiss chard, was described by Aristotle as early as 350 B.C. It is an ancestor of the beet, to which it is closely related, although it is grown for its large and tender leaves which are cooked and eaten much like spinach. (The tender stems may also be cooked and served like asparagus.)

Soil. Chard will grow well in any good garden soil so long as it is planted in a sunny and open place, and it will repay your efforts by aerating your subsoil. The vigorous roots go as far down as six feet, breaking up the subsoil and improving drainage wherever they grow.

pH. 5.8-7.0.

Culture. Few plants are easier to grow. Sow seed in the open garden as soon as the soil has warmed. Rows should be 18 to 24 inches apart, and later the plants should be thinned to ten inches apart in the row. Chard may be picked as soon as the leaves are large enough to make the picking worth your while, and it will continue to grow even after being cut.

Varieties. Large White Ribbed*†, Fordhook Giant*†, Rhubarb*†, Dark Green White Ribbed, Lucullus†, White King, Burgundy Swiss Chard, Charlotte* (red), Fineleaf* (red).

Container variety. Ruby.

Chicory

Chicory might as well be three plants instead of one, because different varieties are grown for entirely different purposes. Early varieties are grown and eaten like lettuce, such as radicchio (q.v.). Other varieties are picked in fall, stored, and sprouted in the basement for winter greens.

Still other varieties are grown for their roots, which are prized as a coffee additive or substitute. Depending on its use, chicory is sometimes called French endive or coffee weed. It is an interesting and easy plant to grow—so easy, in fact, that it can easily become a bothersome weed if it is not checked.

Soil. Any deeply prepared, reasonably fertile, and loose garden soil is fine for chicory.

pH. 6.0-7.0.

Culture. The handling of chicory varies widely, depending on the variety grown. The asparagus type is sown in early spring and

grown, picked, and eaten much like leaf lettuce. The Witloof variety, which we know as French endive, is the one that provides winter salads, and for cultural directions I turn to the Harris seed catalog:

"Witloof Chicory (usually called 'French Endive' but more properly 'Belgian Endive') makes an appetizing and delicious salad and is easy to grow. Sow seed outdoors in May or June and dig the roots in the fall. Trim tops and place in sand in a warm dark place in winter. The roots produce large tender white sprouts . . . and they have an unusual and delightful flavor."

When growing varieties for use as a coffee additive or substitute, dig the large roots before the first really hard frost. The plant is very

A side-dressing of wood ashes will supply the potash these young celery plants need for vigorous growth.

tolerant to frost, however, and you need not rush to rescue roots at the first warning from the weather forecaster. The roots are dried thoroughly, ground, and stored in jars for later use.

Spacing requirements are not given here, because they vary so widely, depending on the variety grown. Instructions are on every seed packet, however.

Varieties. Witloff*, Witloff Improved (both for French endive, 110 days), Magdeburgh Improved (for coffee, 100 days), Cicoria Catalogna (asparagus type, 65 days), Cioria San Pasquale (salad type, 70 days).

Chinese Cabbage

Chinese cabbage does indeed come from China, where it has been grown for several thousand years. Its thin and tender leaves fold together and grow upward in a cylindrical shape, and they are good either in salads or cooked as greens. The taste is fresh and delicate.

Soil. A rich, light loam, well supplied with compost, is best for Chinese cabbage.

pH. 6.0-7.0.

Culture. This is definitely a cool-weather crop. In Wisconsin, which is apt to have several prolonged hot spells during any summer, it is best to sow seeds during the latter part of June or early July, so that the plant will mature during the cooler days of August and September. When the young plants are thinned, the rejects may be used in salads. Give the plants a good mulch and make certain that the soil does not become dry during rainless periods.

Since it is important to force quick and tender growth, an application of well-rotted and screened manure or compost tea will be beneficial during the growing season. The manure should be worked in very lightly at the sides of the plants, taking great care not to injure the roots.

When the plants reach maturity, they may be cut and used as needed. After the first light frost, all plants may be dug up by their roots and stored In a cool cellar or in the cold frame.

Remove the outer leaves, pack the plants in layers separated by straw, and cover with soil.

Varieties. Blues*, Early Hybrid G* (may be seeded early), Nerva (hybrid; slow to bolt), China Express (hybrid; slow to bolt), Michichli*† (seed after June 20), Springtime, Summertime, Wintertime (the last three, hybrids).

Chive

Chives are ridiculously easy to grow and are welcome additions to soups, sauces, salads, omelets, and hundreds of other dishes.

Soil. Chives like a rich, coarse soil, with plenty of small pebbles and plenty of compost. They may not do well in heavier soils, but you can easily cater to their needs, since they take up so little space.

pH. 6.0-7.0.

Culture. The easiest way to grow chives is to buy a couple of pots of the growing plants, which are offered in many large supermarkets. In winter, keep the pot in a sunny window, keep it watered (but not soggy), and cut the tops of the slender onionlike leaves as you need them. In spring, divide the small bulbs and plant them outside in a sunny location. The plant is a perennial, producing very attractive blue flowers, and is not at all out of place in the perennial flower bed. Throw a mulch over the plants after they have died down in winter, and they will reappear the following spring and every spring thereafter. Or, you may wish to dig up a potful of the plants after the first light frost for kitchen use.

Varieties. There are no varieties to speak of. Seed is offered in some catalogs.

Collards

Collards are generally ignored in the North, for reasons unknown to me. They are regarded as a Southerner's substitute for cabbage, which cannot grow well in the heat of the South, but actually the flavors of the two are quite different. Collards are heavy producers, and they are easy to grow. They are usually boiled like other greens, often with ham hocks. They are rich in vitamins B and C and in minerals.

Soil. Give collards a deeply tilled, rich soil with plenty of moisture and nitrogen for fast, tender growth .

pH. 6.0-7.0.

Culture. Collards are large plants, growing to 30 inches or more in height. Rows should be three feet apart, with plants two feet apart in the row. Plant them in the space where early peas were harvested, or (at the same time as cabbage) in another part of the garden where they will get full sun all day long. They are heat loving, of course, but they are tolerant to light frosts in the autumn, too. Quick and tender growth is important here, and so a midseason application of nitrogen-rich compost tea, or a side-dressing of compost, will spur them along. Harvest the whole young plants, or, with older plants, cut the outer and lower leaves first, before they become tough.

Varieties. Champion*, Flash*, Georgia*, Southern† (75 days), Vates*† (80 days).

Corn Salad

This is a quick-growing salad green (45 days) that's favored by a special few. It has a mild flavor and goes well in salads with stronger-tasting greens such as watercress. It resembles spinach in appearance.

Soil. A good garden loam, well supplied with compost and lime, will suit corn salad just fine.

pH. 6.5-7.0.

Culture. Corn salad is a fast grower and is fairly hardy, but it cannot stand summer heat. Therefore, it is best to plant it either with the earliest crops (April 15 in Madison) or in late August for an early October crop. A light covering of straw will protect fall plantings from frosts, so long as the frosts are not too severe. Rows should be 16 to 18 inches apart, and plants should be four to six inches apart in the row. The leaves should be harvested before the seed stalk forms, or else the leaves will become tough.

Varieties. There is no choice of varieties.

Cress

Cress (also called peppergrass or winter cress) is a name given rather loosely to several members of the mustard family. All are valued as greens, because of their tangy flavor, and many are worth growing for this reason. Cress is especially rewarding because it is about the only garden plant that grows faster than the weeds—as few as ten days to maturity. This will be the first salad green you will harvest in the early spring.

Soil. Any fertile, well-drained garden soil will be fine for cress.

pH. 6.0-7.0.

Culture. Sow thickly, in rows one foot apart, as soon as the soil can be worked in early spring. Cress runs to seed quickly, and so it must be harvested when ready, but you can keep a constant supply by sowing a few more feet of row every three or four days for at least a month. Fall sowings of the quick-growing variety may be made as close as three weeks from the date of the first average killing frost in your locality. If you like cress particularly, you may make sowings in the cold frame as late as October, harvesting into November.

Varieties. Fine Curled (peppergrass, 10 days), Extra Fine Curled (45 days), Curled (45 days).

(See also Watercress.)

Cucumber

Cucumbers are fun to grow because there have been so many new varieties introduced in the past several years. One of the most interesting is the burpless, a slicing cucumber that does (or, rather, doesn't do) just what it says. Cucumber varieties are grouped into those recommended for slicing and eating fresh and those intended for pickling. Wisconsin's warm summer days and breezy nights are perfect for cucumbers, which have most trouble flourishing in hot, humid, and still weather.

Soil. Cucumbers succeed in a well-drained sandy loam that is well supplied with compost, lime, and moisture.

pH. 6.0-8.0.

Culture. These are tropical plants, very sensitive to frost in either spring or fall. They are one of the last plants to go in, after all danger of frost is past. Cucumbers are generally planted in hills or mounds spaced according to directions for the particular variety. A mulch should be placed between the hills and can be drawn in closer to the hills after the young plants have established themselves. This will give the vigorous vines a soft bed on which to rest their fruit and will keep down weeds and conserve moisture. It is difficult to cultivate cucumbers without injuring the shallow roots or cutting into the vines, hence the special value of the mulch.

Special tips. Bees are necessary to cucumber production, since they must carry the pollen from the male to the female flowers in order for fertilization to occur. In order for perfect fruit to form, the female flower must be pollinated on the first day that it is ready, otherwise the cucumbers will be misshapen and wasplike in shape or will not form at all. A spell of cold and rainy weather can hinder bees, resulting in poor pollination and a poor crop.

It is vitally important that cucumbers be picked every day. They form their fruits very rapidly, and if the fruits are allowed to ripen on the vine, the plant will wither and die, for it will have completed its life cycle. But if you keep picking before the fruits reach maturity, the plant will continue to produce right up until frost.

Trouble-shooting. When nighttime temperatures dip below 55°, blossoms may drop from plants, resulting in a poor crop. Stagger plantings, so that blossoms don't all appear at one time. Bitterness in cucumbers is often caused by irregular watering or rainfall, which stresses the plant. Use a heavy mulch to keep soil moisture even. The burpless varieties resist bitterness better than others.

Pickling varieties. SMR 18*, Calypso*, Carolina*, Pioneer* (all resistant to mosaic and scab), County Fair* (hybrid; resistant to scab, mosaic, cucumber beetles; nonbitter; also good for salads and slicing), Napoleon*, Regal*, Vert de Massy*, Liberty*, Improved Chicago Pickling, Spartan Dawn, Triple Purpose (scab, mosaic, and powdery mildew tolerant), Salty (highly tolerant to scab, mosaic, powdery and downy mildew), Wisconsin SMR 12, Wisconsin SMR 18, Double Yield Pickling.

Slicing varieties. Armenian*, Dasher II* (hybrid), Lemon Apple* (round), Meridian*, Gemini*†, Spartan Valor*† (hybrid), Marketmore 76*† (all resistant to mosaic and mildew), Sweet Slice* (resistant to mosaic and scab; nonbitter), Spartan Salad* (resistant to scab, mosaic, and cucumber beetles; nonbitter), Burpless* (hybrid), Burpee*, Raider*, Salad Bush* (hybrid), Challenger F-1 (hybrid), Marketer, Longfellow, Triumph F-1 (hybrid), Straight 8, Long Marketer, Windermoor Wonder, Tablegreen, Spacemaster (bush type).

Container varieties. Patio-Pik*, Baby, Little Minnie, Mini, Tiny Dill Cuke.

Eggplant

The eggplant traces its ancestry back to Asia, where it is grown as a perennial in tropical regions. Our climate dictates that we grow this handsome vegetable as an annual, to be set out among the latest of our garden plants. The purple varieties are the ones we are used to, because they are the ones we see in supermarkets, but the Europeans have long preferred the white varieties for their better taste.

Soil. Eggplant is related to both tomatoes and peppers, and its requirements are similar. It likes a medium or sandy loam, well drained and rich in nutrients. It is a heavy feeder.

pH. 6.0-7.0.

Culture. Young plants of the purple varieties may be purchased at nurseries and garden centers at planting time, or seeds may be started in flats or peat pots about 10 weeks before planting time. Because of their extreme sensitivity to cold weather (even several degrees above the frost level) it is a good idea to provide some kind of covering for the young plants for the first week or two outdoors. After the young plants have become well established, put down a thick mulch in order to preserve valuable moisture and keep a constant soil temperature. Along about the end of July or the beginning of August, the plants will benefit from a side-dressing of compost or compost tea. They need not be fully ripe in order to be picked. In fact, they are best used before fully ripening (during which time they begin to turn from purple to brown). In September, keep your eye on the weather forecasts and pick all remaining fruits before the first frost. They will keep for some time if stored in a cool and dark place.

Standard varieties. Early Beauty* (hybrid), Black Beauty†, Mission Bell*, Long Tom*, Black Magic*, Black Oval*, Royal Knight*, Dusky* (the last six, hybrids), Faribo Hybrid, Applegreen, Royal Knight, Blacknite, Burpee (hybrid).

Asian varieties. Agora*, Ichiban* (both hybrids).

White varieties. Ghostbuster* (hybrid), White Beauty.

Container varieties. Morden Midget*, Jersey King (hybrid), Early Beauty. (The first is the only dwarf variety.)

Endive

This plant is similar to lettuce in both appearance and culture, but its flavor is far stronger. It is sometimes called *escarole*, although the two are actually different plants. Escarole's flavor is somewhat milder. In any case, it should not be confused with *French endive*, which is actually chicory.

Soil. Any good garden soil will support endive, so long as its nutrient content is fairly high.

pH. 6.0-7.0.

Culture. Endive is grown much like lettuce, with seeds sown in the open ground as soon as the soil can be worked. Unlike leaf lettuce, however, endive requires 85 to 95 days to mature. Some gardeners follow early lettuce with endive, although care must be taken to shade the young plants from excessive sun and heat. Successful culture depends on forcing quick and succulent growth, and thus plenty of moisture and feeding are necessary. If the soil is well composted to begin with, extra feeding will not be necessary. Otherwise, apply a side-dressing of compost six weeks after planting. The heads may be picked as soon as they are large enough to make picking worthwhile.

Special tips. Many gardeners prefer to blanch the heads about two or three weeks before picking them for use. The blanching makes the leaves more tender and less pungent, but it also reduces the vitamin C content. To blanch the heads, pull up the outer leaves and tie loosely over the top, just enough to exclude light, but not enough to exclude air. The same effect may be promoted by placing large flower pots over the heads.

Varieties. Broadleaf Batavian*, Salad King*, Green Curled†, Full Heart Batavian*, Florida Deep Heart*.

Container varieties. All are good.

Finocchio

Finocchio, fairly popular in Europe but little known here, has a pleasant aniselike flavor and is used either as a cooked vegetable or fresh in salads. It is related to fennel, and in fact it is sometimes called sweet fennel or Florence fennel, although it grows and is used quite differently from true fennel, which is an herb. It grows from a large bulblike structure, looking much like celery, and it is this base structure that is most highly prized, although the stalks can be eaten also. Finocchio is difficult to find locally. Harris, however, offers the seeds in its catalog.

Soil. Plants do best on a well-drained, average loam, well composted and well supplied with lime.

pH. 6.0-7.0

Culture. Sow in rows 18 to 24 inches apart and, later, thin the young plants to six or eight inches apart in the row. About three weeks before harvesting, the soil should be drawn up around the plants to blanch the bulbs.

Variety. Mammoth.

Flowers, edible

Brightly-colored blossoms dress up nearly any dinner or salad plate, and it certainly helps if those blossoms are edible. In Wisconsin, the list of edible flowers includes nasturtium, johnny jump up, anise hyssop, clary, calendula, kablouna, signet, Butterblossom zucchini, Lemon Gem marigold, and Tangerine Gem marigold.

Garlic

Every garlic-loving family should plant at least a few sets each year. Garlic does not take up much room, and it is easy to grow. Fresh garlic from the garden—plump, juicy, and flavorful—is entirely different from the dried bulbs purchased in supermarkets. And, of course, your own bulbs can be dried, braided, and hung in the kitchen for year-round use.

Soil. Any soil that is good for onions will support garlic. This means a good, loose loam, well drained and well supplied with moisture. Even sandy soils can support garlic if enough organic matter is incorporated into the soil.

pH. 6.0-7.0.

Culture. Garlic can be grown from seed, but the home gardener will find it easier to plant sets, which are the cloves that together comprise the bulb. Every clove will grow an entire bulb. The sets are planted at the same time and in the same way as onions. With garlic, however, it is important that you give the cloves a cold treatment. Several weeks at 50° should do the job. You can use the refrigerator, but be sure the cloves don't freeze. The plants should mature in about 90 days. After the tops have turned yellow and begun to die down, the bulbs may be pulled, dried in a shady place, and stored like onions or braided and hung indoors.

Varieties. There is seldom a choice of varieties. However, Nichols Garden Nursery does offer an interesting *Elephant Garlic*, which is said to produce bulbs weighing one pound or more, milder in taste than ordinary garlic.

Gourd

Few varieties of gourds are edible, but we often include them in the vegetable garden for their unusual, decorative, and sometimes useful fruits. Every children's garden should include gourds, since they are easy to grow and fun to dry and use afterward. There are dozens of varieties, too many to list and describe here, but some large seed companies list a wide array in their catalogs. Stokes, for instance, lists 14 individual varieties, and most seed companies offer mixed packets of both large and small gourds. One variety I will mention is *Luffa cylindrica* or *Lagenaria leucanthe,* otherwise known as the dishcloth gourd. The cellulose of this gourd is similar to that of cotton, and the inner mass, carefully removed, can be used just as any ordinary household sponge. Bath shops sell luffa sponges for four or five dollars each, but you can grow your own for practically nothing. Luffa is offered by Henry Field, Gurney, and R. H. Shumway, among others.

Soil. Gourds do best on a well-drained loam, but will grow in most soils except heavy clays.

pH. 6.0-7.0.

Culture. Gourds need full sunlight and about 100 growing days. Given these requirements, they are vigorous growers when planted nearly anywhere. Most varieties are good climbers and are often used to screen in the southern sides of porches, offering cooling shade during August's hot days. Some people plant gourds in bare, ugly spots, since they are fairly attractive ground covers.

Seeds can be started indoors, about April 15 in Madison, and transplanted outdoors whenever it is safe to put out tomato plants. Or the seed may be planted directly into the open ground around June 10. If the vines are to grow along the ground, be sure to apply a hay mulch so that the fruits will not be flat and discolored from lying on the ground. Better still, tie up soft washline for them to climb, or plant beneath a trellis that receives plenty of sun. Northern

Wisconsin residents may have trouble growing gourds in any case, because of the short season, but they are certainly worth a try.

Special tips. From the Stokes catalog, we get drying instructions: "Pick fruit carefully from the vines when completely ripe. [The rind should be hard when your fingernail presses into it—J. M.] It is most important not to injure or bruise the fruit when handling. Wash each gourd with a strong disinfectant, to remove dirt and fungi that might cause rotting. Spread the fruit out evenly, so that they do not touch each other, in a dry, well-ventilated place. Turn the fruit regularly during the drying period, which usually takes three to four weeks. When completely dry, wax with ordinary floor wax and polish with a soft cloth."

Small varieties. Aladdin's Turban, Bicolour Pear, Miniature Bottle, Miniature Ball, Crown of Thorns, Flat Striped, Spoon, Striped Pear, White Pear, Orange Warted.

Large varieties. Cave Man's Club, Dipper or Birdhouse, Large Turk's Turban, Wild Cucumber, Luffa.

Edible variety. Italian Edible.

Ground-Cherry

The ground-cherry, also called husk tomato or strawberry tomato, is closely related to the Chinese lantern plant. Both are members of the Physalis family. The edible variety offers small cherrylike fruit encased in a husk and is used extensively in pies. Ground-cherries are hardly the most popular of garden crops, but they have long been treasured by some, and they are an interesting plant to grow. A related crop is the Tomatillo (q.v.).

Soil. Like tomatoes, ground-cherries like an open, well-drained soil. They do best on a sandy loam that is well supplied with nutrients.

pH. 6.0-7.0.

Culture. Start the seeds indoors toward the end of March and transplant to the open garden after all danger of frost is past. Space according to directions on the seed packet. The fruits may be picked when they have turned yellow.

Variety. True Yellow*.

Horseradish

When I was a boy, the horseradish man used to come through the alleys with horse and cart every Saturday morning. He would grind the roots from the back of the wagon—15 cents for a half-pint jar. And, if you were daring enough to take a good sniff from the jar while carrying it home, your sinuses took an instant and jolting cleaning that no modern-day cold remedy can hope to match. Fresh horseradish is difficult to come by these days—the commercial products seem so tame—but you can bring back the old days in your own garden if you reserve a little corner of it for horseradish.

Soil. Horseradish needs a deeply prepared and rich sandy loam with plenty of room to grow long, straight roots.

pH. 6.0-8.0.

Culture. Although horseradish is a perennial plant, and many gardeners do carry plantings over from year to year, the prize roots are usually grown as an annual. This does not mean that you must buy cuttings each year, since you may easily save your own in the fall and store them over winter in a root cellar for planting the following spring, as you would potatoes.

Prepare the planting area as early in spring as the ground may be worked. Root cuttings that you bring home from the garden center, or receive by mail order, will be straight-cut at one end (the thicker end) and slant-cut at the other end. Space the cuttings 10 to 12 inches apart in the row, placing them at a 45° angle, the straight-cut end about three inches below the surface, the slant-cut end trailing down into the soil. If you reverse the position of the root (in effect, planting it upside down) results will be poor. Pack the soil firmly against all roots, leaving no air spaces. Although rows should be two to three feet apart, you may plant double rows, the plants only 12 inches apart, then leave about 30 inches between the double-row plantings.

Mulch the rows after active growth has started and apply liquid fertilizer or compost tea late in August and into September, when the plant makes its most important growth. Do not harvest roots until after a few hard frosts in late fall, for they will not attain their desired pungent flavor until then. If you mulch the roots heavily in fall, you may continue to harvest throughout the winter, so long as the ground has not frozen hard. If it does, you may begin to harvest again as soon as the spring thaw allows a garden fork to penetrate the ground.

Special tips. If you want to save root cuttings for next year's crop, do it while you harvest roots in late fall. Cut the best-looking lateral roots, those nearer the top of the main root. Make a straight cut, close to the main root, and then slant-cut the far end. Tie the cuttings in bunches and pack them in moist sand, as you would carrots. Store the bunches in a root cellar where the temperature is close to 32° and keep the sand just moist enough to prevent the roots from drying out. If you have no root cellar, you may pack them in sand, in a wooden box, and bury the box two feet under ground, outdoors. The roots will be in good shape for planting when spring rolls around.

To prepare horseradish, clean the roots well, remove the brown outer skins with a vegetable peeler, and grind the white roots thoroughly with a meat grinder or food processor. For every cup of grated horseradish, add one-half cup of white vinegar and one-fourth teaspoon of salt. Mix well and store in jars in the refrigerator. Your next corned beef and cabbage dinner should be one to remember!

Variety. Bohemian (offered by J. W. Jung).

Jerusalem Artichoke

The Jerusalem artichoke does not come from Jerusalem, and it is not an artichoke. The word Jerusalem, used here, is actually a corruption of the Italian word *girasole*, meaning "turning toward the sun," and the word "artichoke was tacked on because someone apparently thought that this vegetable tasted like globe artichokes. (It doesn't.) Were I to rename the plant, I would call it the "sunflower potato" because it is a member of the sunflower family (producing attractive yellow blossoms in summer), and because the food part of the plant is the brown tuber, which resembles a potato. The plants are amazingly prolific, once established, and they will come up year after year. They are cooked and eaten just like potatoes, and their flavor is mild and slightly nut-sweet.

Soil. Jerusalem artichoke will do well on nearly any kind of soil except very heavy clays. They do better, in fact, on poor soils lacking nutrients, since too much nitrogen forces great top growth and small tubers.

pH. 6.0-8.0.

Culture. Select a sunny, out-of-the-way spot for Jerusalem artichokes, for they spread rapidly and will gladly take over the garden if you let them. They grow six to eight feet high and can be used as a rather attractive screen. Or plant them in soil that won't grow much of anything else. The tubers are planted much like potatoes, one eye to a cutting, and are set a foot apart in rows two to three feet apart. Planting should be done at the same time as potatoes—April 15 in Madison—and you should never have to plant them again. They are best dug after the first frost in fall. Harvest up to two-thirds of the crop without worrying about depleting next year's supply. They can be stored like potatoes or left right in the ground and dug when needed, right up until the ground is too hard for digging.

Special tips. Jerusalem artichokes are a good potato substitute for those on diets, or for those who must restrict their intake of carbohydrates. There are virtually no carbohydrates in the tubers, since this plant stores its carbohydrates in the form of insulin, and there is little sugar. There are virtually no calories, either—as few as 22 in a full pound of freshly dug tubers. As the tubers are stored, however, the insulin is gradually converted into sugar, and the tubers then may contain as many as 235 calories in a pound—which still makes it a low-calorie vegetable. The Jerusalem artichoke is a good source of both potassium and thiamine in the diet.

Varieties. There is no choice of varieties. (If you have trouble locating seed tubers, contact Nichols Garden Nursery.)

Kale

Kale is the richest in vitamins of all the common potherbs. A member of the cabbage family, it is easy to grow if given proper conditions, and it is a heavy yielder. We grow it for the large leaves, which can be used in salads when they are very young and tender, or, more commonly, boiled with ham.

Soil. Since quick and succulent growth is essential for high-quality leaves, the soil should be rich and loamy. A liberal application of compost before planting will pay rich dividends.

pH. 6.0-7.0.

Kohlrabi

Culture. The growing directions given for collards can be used in growing kale, since the two are so closely related. Kale is highly resistant to both heat and cold, so that it can be planted any time from early spring right up to eight weeks before frost. It matures in about 55 to 70 days and is especially good as a succession crop, perhaps following peas, since a couple of early autumn frosts improve the quality and taste of the leaves. The roots are shallow and widespread, making it chancy to work the soil with a hoe. Instead, apply a heavy mulch to protect those shallow-lying roots from drying out. A couple of midsummer applications of compost tea will spur along the rapid and tender growth you seek.

Varieties. Lacinto*, Dwarf Green Curled*†, Tall Green Curled Scotch (tender after exposure to frost), Dwarf Curled Scotch†, Dwarf Blue Curled Vates*, Green Curled Scotch, Ornamental*, Red Russian*, Squire*, Vates*.

Kohlrabi

Kohlrabi has been described as a "turnip growing on a cabbage root," and that seems to be an apt description of this unusual member of the cabbage family. It grows well in Wisconsin, for it likes cool weather, and it is one of the few vegetables that gardeners like to grow and then, for some reason, don't like to eat. The problem, perhaps, is that we don't pick and eat it early enough. The bulbs and roots should be harvested while they are still young and succulent—not after the plant has attained full maturity, and has become tough and woody. Harvest when the bulbs are no more than two inches in diameter, or even when they are as small as golf balls. Slice both bulbs and roots for raw salads, or steam them as a cooked vegetable.

Soil. Like other members of the cabbage family, kohlrabi likes a richly prepared loam, well supplied with moisture, for quick and tender growth.

pH. 6.0-7.0.

Culture. Seed is sown into the open ground in early spring, at the same time as onions and carrots. Because successful growth must be quick growth, ample nutrients and water are essential. Apply a good mulch as soon as the young plants are established, to conserve moisture and also to protect the young and shallow-lying roots. Cultivation can easily injure these roots, which spread laterally just under the soil surface, but a good mulch will make cultivation unnecessary. If the plants seem to be slow in growing, stimulate them with a few midseason applications of a strong manure tea. The two big kohlrabi cautions: Don't let them grow slowly, and don't harvest them too late.

Special tips. If the kohlrabies are growing faster than you can use them, pick them anyway and store them either in a cool basement or underground, surrounded by straw. They will keep cool underground during summer, and they will not freeze there during winter. Late-harvested kohlrabies can also be stored in a cold frame up until December.

Varieties. Gigante*, Grand Duke* (hybrid), White Vienna*†, Purple Vienna*†.

Leek

If you like to use cooked onions in recipes but the onions don't like you, leeks might be just the thing you are looking for. They are very onionlike, but milder in flavor and effect. Many French recipes call for leeks, too, for their subtle enhancement of stews and other dishes.

Soil. Any good garden soil, well composted, will grow leeks successfully.

pH. 6.0-7.0.

Culture. Leeks are planted from seed instead of sets, but otherwise culture is the same as for onions. Sow seed sparingly in early spring, in a fully sunny place. Make rows 20 inches apart and thin the young plants to three or four to a foot of row. During the growing season, continue to hill the soil up around the growing stems, to blanch them. We grow leeks not for a bulb but for the thick and tender stems. A few side-dressings of rich compost during the season will help along the growth of this rather slow-growing plant. Harvest

when they are large enough to make the harvesting worth your while. They can take a few good frosts in autumn and can be stored in a root cellar.

Special Tips. If your growing season is too short for leeks, you can cut down the growing time by starting the seeds inside and transplanting them. Sow seeds six weeks before transplanting time (April 15 in Madison). When setting the young plants into the open ground, trim off one half of their roots and one third of the tops. Then set them in a shallow trench well lined with aged compost.

Varieties. American Flag*, Giant Musselburg* (90 days), Otina*, Pancho*, Titan (early, 70 days), Elephant (85 days), Swiss Special, Conqueror.

Lettuce

Lettuce is certainly our most popular salad green. There are four major groups: loose-leaf or nonheading; butterhead; crisp-head or cabbagehead; and cos or Romaine. All are easy to grow in Wisconsin except crisp-head, which is difficult to grow almost anywhere in the U.S. except in the mountains of the west.

Soil. Lettuce needs a well-drained soil, well supplied with compost. It will grow well in either sandy or clay loams, but either must be kept moist for the quick and succulent growth needed for successful production.

pH. 6.0-7.0.

Culture. Lettuce needs warm days and cool nights for optimum growth. Crisp-head lettuce is especially particular in this respect, often failing to form heads if the weather turns hot at heading time. All lettuce can be grown best in an area where the sunlight is filtered for at least part of the day, or on a northern or western slope where the sun's rays are indirect. If part of your garden lies in the afternoon shadow of a large tree, use this spot for lettuce.

Loose-leaf culture. This is the easiest and quickest to grow. Sow seed in the open ground in early spring, spaced according to directions. Thin the rows by cutting leaves for salads as you need them. Make successive plantings for as long as a month, but do not expect to get good results when the weather turns hot.

Butterhead culture. This lettuce forms a soft and loose head. Plant seeds thinly in the row and later thin out the plants to the distances recommended for the particular variety. To avoid the danger of midsummer heat, you can start plants indoors, in the cold frame, or in peat pots, transplanting them into the open garden as soon as the weather permits.

Crisp-head culture. The secret of growing head lettuce lies in getting a very early start and then praying for cool weather when the plant gets ready to head-up. Sow seeds in flats indoors, in a cool but sunny window, about the middle of March. Thin the plants carefully, so that no plant touches another. Keep the soil damp, but not soggy, and do not let the young plants suffer from dry household air. When the first true leaves have formed, transplant the seedlings to flats or peat pots, being careful not to disturb the roots any more than necessary.

Transplant the young plants into the open garden as early as possible—no later than April 15 in southern Wisconsin, May 1 in the north. Lettuce may appear to be extremely tender, when in reality it is fairly hardy and will not be bothered by a few light frosts. Cover with hot caps if a heavy frost threatens. (Note: If you have a cold frame, you may begin plants indoors as much as a month earlier, transplanting to the frame about a month before setting them into the open garden. Harden off the plants by admitting air to the frame on mild afternoons.) Once in the garden, planted in well-composted rows, lettuce needs plenty of moisture. And, even after all your early work and special care, you still must worry about damaging hot spells. As a precaution, you might construct a light wooden frame along the row, over which you can stretch cheesecloth or open lath to act as a sun filter. Build the frame early in the season, and add the shading material only when you need it.

Cos culture. Cos or Romaine lettuce is a tall-growing type, with long spoon-shaped leaves that fold gracefully in toward the center of the plant, naturally bleaching the inner leaves. It is highly prized in French and Italian restaurants as a crisp salad lettuce, and is not too difficult to grow. Its culture is the same as for the butterhead varieties. The seed is sown thinly in early spring, and plants are thinned out to stand about eight inches apart in the row. The plant takes 66 to 75 days to mature, but may be harvested before maturity, if you so choose.

Loose-leaf varieties. Baby Oak*, Fanfare*, Grand Rapids*, Lollo Rossa*, Red Fire*, Oak-leaf*, Ruby*, Salad Bowl*, Waldmann's*.

Butterhead varieties. Buttercrunch*†, Summer Bibb†, Pirat*, Red Riding Hood*, Butter King*†, White Boston, Dark Green Boston, Bibb, Tom Thumb Midget.

Crisp-head varieties. Crispino*, Great Lakes 659†, Fulton*, Pennlake†, Minilake, Ithaca*, Montello*, Victoria*, Imperial (recommended for muckland), Fairton, Evergreen (frost-resistant late variety).

Cos varieties. Paris White, Paris Island*, Rosalita*, Rubens*, Valmaine, Sweet Midget.

Container varieties. Tom Thumb, Buttercrunch (both bibb varieties). Any variety of leaf lettuce, Sweet Midget Cos.

Mushroom

Mushroom culture, which is conducted indoors under very exacting conditions, will not be treated in this outdoor gardening book. (Park Seed, for one, offers an indoor growing kit.) However, Stokes offers a variety called Lambert's that is grown outdoors, under the lawn. The technique involves rolling back a piece of sod four inches deep, in a shady area, sprinkling the mushroom spawn on the soil surface, and then replacing the sod. The mushrooms grow through the sod and can be harvested in about seven weeks.

Muskmelon

Many varieties of muskmelons will grow well in Wisconsin. Some are similar to the cantaloupe and may even be sold under that name in stores, but the true cantaloupe is native to warmer regions and is not widely grown in the United States. Most supermarket "cantaloupes" are actually nutmeg melons.

Soil. Muskmelons grow best in a light, well-drained soil, rich in nutrients. They will not do well in clays.

pH. 6.0-7.0.

Culture. All melons need full sunshine and a large number of warm days to reach sweet maturity. They might not do well in Wisconsin's northern areas, particularly where long stretches of cool and sunless days will retard their growth. Most varieties require 85 days or more, and this period can be extended if the weather does not cooperate.

Melons are very sensitive to frost, and plants should not be put into the open garden until all danger of frost is past. The long maturity period, then, dictates that seeds be started indoors, in plant bands or peat pots. In southern Wisconsin, start seeds indoors around May 1 (they germinate only at temperatures above 65°) and transplant into the open garden around May 20. Apply compost liberally to the outdoor planting area before setting in plants. The best method is to put a layer of compost or rotted manure about six inches under the soil, covering this with a three-inch layer of good garden loam. Firm the plants in well, and the roots will soon find the nourishing compost with no chance of "burning."

Melons do best when grown quickly, and to grow quickly they need full sun and plenty of water and fertilizer. Anything less will not produce perfect melons. Work plenty of compost into the planting hill or row, and give the plants adequate water while the vines are making their big growth spurt and while the fruits are developing. But when the fruits are nearly ripe, hold back on water. Doing so is said to produce sweeter fruit.

Planting is traditionally done in hills. We usually plant seven or eight seeds or seedlings in a circle around the hill, then thin down to the best three or four vines. But you may plant them in rows just as well. Set a pair of plants every 18 to 24 inches along the row and allow six feet between rows. The vines will quickly fill the space.

To prune or not to prune melon vines (and vines of tomatoes, cucumbers, and squash, for that matter) is a subject of long debate among gardeners. On one hand, more of the plant's energy will go into fruit production if vines are pinched back. On the other, the fruit really gets its sugar content from the leaves. So where does that leave us? The one kind of pruning that is recommended is tip-pinching of the main trailing vine. This will encourage the production of lateral shoots, and it is only the laterals that produce fruit.

Sometimes the difference between a perfect melon and a flat-tasting one is a deficiency of boron and magnesium in the soil. You may correct the situation by watering the plants several times during the season, adding two tablespoons of epsom salts and one tablespoon of household borax to each gallon of water. Apply this solution when the vines are growing most quickly and again when the fruits are between one and two inches in diameter.

Special tips. How can you tell when a melon is ripe? Thumping is the traditional method, but it is unreliable. A better way is to apply gentle pressure with the thumb between the fruit and the base of the stem. If the fruit separates easily from the stem, the fruit is ripe. Chill the melons and eat them the same day they are picked. The difference between your own vine-ripened melons and the supermarket kinds—which are picked green and shipped from distant states—is tremendous.

Varieties. Earlisweet* (hybrid), Earliqueen* (hybrid), Gold Star* (hybrid), Supermarket* (hybrid), Delicious 51*†, Harvest Queen*†, Iroquois*†, Saticoy*† (hybrid), Spartan Rock†, Harper* (hybrid), Star Trek* (hybrid), Zenith* (hybrid), Pride of Wisconsin, Honey Rock, Mainrock, Sugar Rock, Early Delicious, Sungold Casaba, Hales Best Jumbo, Milwaukee Market, New Yorker, Burpee, Samson, Canada Gem, Tangiers* (hybrid; cantaloupe/honeydew). (All marked with an asterisk are fusarium resistant.)

Container variety. Minnesota Midget. (The fruit measures only four inches across and is very sweet. Vines are only three feet long.)

Mustard

Mustard is grown in the home garden for its leaves, which are used as potherbs, much as are collards and kale. They are quick-growing plants and very heavy yielders. There are quite a few devotees of mustard greens in Wisconsin, although the crop is not as popular as kale. The home gardener can also harvest the seeds. which are widely used as a pickling spice.

Soil. Because of the quick-growing nature of the plant, it likes a heavy loam, well drained and well supplied with nutrients. Tender growth depends on a large supply of available nutrients.

pH. 6.0-7.0.

Culture. Seed is sown in the open ground in the early spring—April 15 in Madison. Thin the plants by harvesting some of the leaves for table use. The plants will mature in 45 to 60 days. They can stand dry weather, but particularly hot weather may send them bolting to seed, destroying the quality of the leaves. Harvest the greens while they are young and tender. Cut off any flower buds that might appear.

Varieties. Giant Long Standing Southern Curled*†, Mustard Spinach or Tender Green, Green Wave*†, Giant Curled.

Okra

If you have never eaten okra, you might find it difficult to become accustomed to its consistency, which is somewhat mucilaginous, but there are many okra devotees who are willing to reserve parts of their gardens for this unusual vegetable.

Soil. Okra will thrive in a variety of soils, but only if they are well drained. Drainage is, by far, the most important soil consideration.

pH. 6.0-7.0.

Culture. Okra is a rapid-growing plant, maturing in less than two months. It is a heavy feeder, however, and should be planted in a fully

sunny place that has been well composted and manured. Plenty of available nutrients will give you a faster-growing and more successful crop. Sow seeds lightly in rows or plant in hills after all danger of frost is past—at the same time as beans. A rainy week immediately after planting may well rot the seeds, for they do rot easily, and will necessitate your replanting. After the plants are several inches tall, thin them to stand 18 to 20 inches apart, choosing the healthiest and most robust for your permanent finalists.

Pick the pods when they are young—one to four inches—and use them as quickly after picking as possible. Even if you do not plan to use the pods, pick them every day. If the pods are allowed to remain on the plant, they will mature and the plant will stop producing for the season. Okra can be canned, frozen, or dried for later use, and it is excellent when pickled.

Varieties. Emerald*†, Clemson Spineless*†, Perkins Mammoth Long Pod.

Onion

Onions have been cultivated, treasured, and savored since ancient times. They are Robert Louis Stevenson's "rose among roots," and even if they don't remind you much of roses, you will have to admit that culinary life would be mighty dull without them.

Wisconsin gardeners can grow onions from sets, plants, or seeds. It is most difficult to grow them from seed in most parts of the state, but if you master the technique you will have increased your options to include dozens of varieties that are simply not offered in set or plant form. Summer onions are usually grown from sets. Those for late fall use and winter storage are usually grown from plants or seeds.

Multiplier onions, like shallots and garlic, divide underground to form a bulb cluster. There are both yellow and white multipliers, both good for use in salads or as "pearl" onions in soups and stews. The *Egyptian onion*, which is also a multiplier, forms a cluster of sets at the top of the flower stalk, and also divides underground. They are very hardy, and can be used as a perennial onion patch, providing green onions both in the late fall and early spring.

Soils. Onions need a deeply prepared, fertile, rather loose, and well-drained soil for best results. They will not do well in heavy clays that turn to hardpan in the absence of rain.

pH. 6.0-7.0.

Set culture. Sets are little pickling onions that are used to produce either scallions (when picked while they are young) or cooking onions (later in the season). The sets traditionally offered in supermarkets and garden centers are those of the Ebenezer type (white or yellow) that are perhaps the easiest of all onions to grow. The first thing to remember is to avoid particularly large sets when buying them. The large ones may look good, but they tend to produce seedstalks, big necks, and undersized onions.

Avoid also the very small, shriveled-up sets that obviously lack vigor. Instead, look for plump, medium-sized sets that have not yet sent out shoots. They will produce the best onions.

Plant the sets carefully, in their natural position (root end down). There are differences of opinion on planting depth, some advising to plant two to three inches deep, others preferring to let just the top of the set protrude above the soil. I have always covered them with about a half-inch of loose soil, with good success, but you might experiment by planting different rows to different depths and comparing harvests. Give them ample moisture and keep the onion patch entirely free of weeds. In five weeks or so, the onions can be pulled and used as scallions. Or, you may leave them in to use as white or yellow cooking onions later on in the season.

These sweet Spanish onions will grow much more quickly if they are mulched and kept free of weeds during the season.

Plant culture. Plant onions are bought in bunches, usually 50 to 100 slender plants in a bunch. Red slicer onions of the Bermuda type are grown from plants, and so are the large yellow and white sweet Spanish varieties. Like sets, they are planted early in the spring to their natural depth. They can be thinned out by picking every other one after 50 to 60 days, giving the remaining plants room to expand. You do, however, run the risk of disturbing the roots of the remaining plants by adopting this procedure. Thin very carefully and gently. Planted April 15, the onions should be fully mature by the middle of August or the beginning of September. A few light frosts will not hurt them.

Seed culture. Few home gardeners have much luck in planting onions from seed, but you might be the happy exception. In Wisconsin's muck regions, on the other hand, onions grown from seed are the rule rather than the exception. The seed is sown thickly in rows in early spring, and the young plants are thinned to stand two to three inches apart. From that point, they are treated just as sets or plants, keeping the rows free from weeds and assuring ample moisture. The rows should be cultivated frequently, to keep the soil loose and to allow air to reach the roots, and those large-growing bulbs that threaten to "pop out" of the soil should be hilled-in so that just the tops of the bulbs show.

Special tips. Pinch off the flower buds from all onions as soon as you see them. If you can recognize the seed stalk coming from the neck of the onion, in fact, it is better to cut the stalk right then, to prevent the neck from becoming large and stunting the bulb. (This advice does not apply to multiplier and Egyptian onions.) When the tops begin to wither and fall over, the onions are mature. When most of them have reached this stage, you can knock down the others. Pull the onions a few days later and leave them on top of the ground for a few days, so that they can be cured naturally by the sun and the wind. Then, gather them up, cut off the tops to within an inch from the bulbs, and spread them out on a large table, under cover,

in an outdoor and airy place. They can stay there to complete their curing until a heavy frost is forecast. On that day, take them indoors and store them for the winter in a cool and dry basement, or perhaps in a well-ventilated attic. You can store them in open containers—orange crates are perfect—or you can hang them from the rafters in netting.

Trouble-shooting. If your storage onions tend to rot in the ground, or shortly after harvest, the problem might be that you have planted the sets too deeply. The neck of the maturing onion should be above the soil line, so that when you do harvest, the neck will be well on the way to the level of dryness needed for successful storage. Be sure also to cure the onions well before storing them

Set varieties. Ebenezer*† (white or yellow), Stuttgarter.

Plant varieties. Sweet Spanish*†, Early Harvest*, White Bermuda† (all hybrids, for late summer and early fall use only; do not store well), Red Slicer or Hamburger.

Seed varieties. Abundance†, Early Harvest*, Hickory* (fusarium resistant), Nugget* (fusarium resistant), Hustler*, Spartan Banner 80*. (All are hybrids.) Early Yellow Globe, Southport White Globe, Southport Red Globe, Downing Yellow Globe, Autumn Spice, Crystal White Wax (Bermuda variety), White Spanish Green Bunching (forms clusters of small onions), Yellow Globe Danvers, Sweet Spanish, Yellow Spanish (hybrid), many others in various seed catalogs. (Note: Certain varieties may be unavailable in some years, because of the uncertainty of seed supply.)

Container varieties. Sets or transplants may be planted in shallow containers, spaced one inch apart. Thin plants as the season progresses, using the young onions in salads.

Parsley

There are two types of parsley generally grown here, the more common of which is curled, the kind found beside your mashed potatoes in the restaurant. The other is the flat-leaf Italian type that has grown in popularity in recent years. A third type—Hamburg, or turnip-rooted parsley—is grown for its roots as well as its tops, and is not often found in home gardens.

If you occasionally buy parsley in the supermarket, then plant some, by all means. Parsley can be grown with ease in the vegetable garden, or it can form an attractive border in the herb garden or even in the flower bed. It does not take up much room, and it dries and freezes well, but it is slow growing and requires patience. One packet of seed will supply all you will need for the year.

Soil. Any average garden soil will support parsley, although a good nitrogen supply will increase the yield.

pH. 5.0-7.0.

Culture. Parsley is one of the slowest of plants to germinate. Even when presoaked in lukewarm water, the young plants usually do not emerge from the ground for four weeks or more. Marian Coonse, an organic gardener and commercial parsley-grower, tells of an ancient legend saying that parsley seed must "go to the devil and back again seven times before seedlings can emerge above the ground." Gardeners waiting for parsley to germinate in the spring might well be tempted to believe in this legend.

Ms. Coonse foils both the devil and the parsley seed, however, by freezing the preplanted seed in aluminum flats. One of those disposable baking pans will do fine. The seed is planted in the flat, in the usual way, and is watered. Then aluminum foil is wrapped over the top of the flat, which is then placed into the deep freeze for a week or so. Shortly before outdoor planting time (that is early in spring, as soon as the ground can be worked), the flat is removed from the freezer and placed in any spot at room temperature. Do not lift off the foil top until after the second day, then lift it and peek in to see if germination has taken place. When the first of the seeds have germinated, the top may be removed. As soon as the plants have four leaves, they may be transplanted either into the garden or into peat pots for later transplanting outdoors. Ms. Coonse says that the cold treatment reduces germination time to less than a week.

Gardeners who do not mind waiting for the seven trips to the devil may plant parsley in the usual way, sowing seed early in spring. After it does germinate. parsley makes good progress and will produce from June until frost. It is a biennial plant and may be carried over to the second year, if mulched heavily over the winter.

Special tips. When heavy frost threatens, carefully dig up the parsley, getting all the roots, and pot it. Bring it indoors and cut all the foliage down to the crowns. Freeze the foilage for future use. Then place the pots in a sunny window and provide periodic watering. New growth should begin and should provide fresh parsley for the family all winter long.

Varieties.Forest Green*, Moss Curled*†, Perfection*, Darkie*, Hamburg (edible roots, similar to a small parsnip), Banquet, Plain Italian Dark Green, Deep Green, Bravour, Extra Triple Curled, Champion Moss Curled.

Parsnip

The lowly parsnip may not be the world's favorite vegetable, but it has one thing going for it: The parsnip is the only vegetable that actually likes Wisconsin's autumn freezes! The flavor of this root vegetable is greatly improved by a couple of hard freezes, and in fact you can leave parsnips in the ground until just before the ground freezes too hard to allow them to be dug. If the Badger State ever adopts an official vegetable, it just might have to be the parsnip.

Soil. Like all deeply growing root crops, parsnips prefer a deeply prepared, loose and somewhat sandy loam. Heavy clays will inhibit root growth. As a slow grower, the parsnip is not a particularly heavy feeder, but its progress will be aided by a good application of aged manure, made before planting time.

pH. 6.0-8.0.

Culture. The seed is slow to germinate and will be aided by soaking it overnight in cool water. Sow thickly in rows as soon as the ground can be worked in early spring, and scatter a few radish seeds in the row to act as a marker. (You will harvest the radishes just as the parsnips are making some good progress.) Apply a light mulch in order to conserve soil moisture, since the seed must remain damp in order to germinate at all. Thin the young plants to two to three inches apart in the rows, and then increase the thickness of the mulch to avoid weeding for the rest of the season. Parsnip is a long-season crop—100 to 120 days—but you will never have to worry about fall frosts. Begin to harvest after the first hard freeze, and continue for as long as possible.

Varieties. Model*†, All-America*†, Hollow Crown.

Pea

Few garden crops are as highly prized as peas, which are one of the earliest vegetables to appear on the table, usually in June. Peas take up a lot of garden space, and they do not yield heavily for the space they take. Therefore—unless you have all the garden space in the world—it is best to use them as a succession crop (first in line) or a companion crop. As a succession crop, peas can be followed by any heat-loving, quick-growing crop, such as beans. In fact, runner beans can use the same trellises you have erected for peas. Or, peas can go in between the rows of tomatoes, corn, or squash, as a companion crop, and they will be harvested before the other plants need much growing room. (The old pea vines, in fact, can be cut and used as a mulch for the long-season plants.) Peas must go in early, however, to take advantage of these techniques. If you wait until the middle of May to plant, the peas will not have matured in time for you to plant most succession crops, and they will have interfered with the growth of companions.

The 1979 introduction of the All-American Sugar Snap was one of the most successful vegetable introductions of all time. Full-size pods, they can be eaten right off the vine, pod and all, used raw in salads, or lightly steamed. Sugar Snaps are delightfully sweet, decidedly a pea for all purposes.

Soil. Peas like a loose, sandy loam, well supplied with compost and manure for fast growth.

The parsnip—should it become Wisconsin's official state vegetable?

pH. 6.0-8.0.

Culture. Plant peas in the early spring, as soon as the ground can be worked. A few light frosts will not hurt them. Treat the seeds with a bacterial inoculant (available at all garden centers) before planting. If you want really fast germination, spread the seeds out in a shallow pan in a dark place and line the bottom of the pan with water, so that the peas are just half covered. Just as sprouts begin to show, plant them in the open garden. (Inoculate just before planting.)

The garden pea is a trailing plant and will appreciate a trellis to climb on. The trellis will afford the plants optimum sun and air and will also make harvesting easier (not necessary with dwarf varieties). Mulch the plants

Sugar Snap

after they have become established, to keep the soil cool.

It might take some experience in order to tell just when to pick peas for optimum quality. They should be picked as soon as the pods are filled, but before they become really hard. Edible-podded peas (snow peas) should be picked just as the peas become visible, forming little bumps on the pods.

Trouble-shooting. Peas will not flower when daytime temperatures exceed 90°. Plant them early in the season for best production. If your area often experiences early hot spells, consider Wando, which is a heat-resistant variety.

Dwarf varieties. Alaska*†, Frezonian* (fusarium wilt resistant), Early Frosty*, WR Surprise* (fusarium wilt resistant), Wando*†, Thomas Laxton*†, Green Arrow*, Little Marvel†, Frosty†, Lincoln. (Many gardeners report success with Lincoln after failure with other varieties.)

Tall-growing varieties. Alderman*†, Perfection (wilt-resistant).

Edible-podded varieties. Dwarf Gray Sugar*†, Oregon Sugar Pod II* (both dwarfs), Mammoth Melting Sugar*† (tall-growing), Little Sweetie (dwarf), Super Sweetpod (tall-growing).

Sugar Snap types. Sugar Ann* (dwarf), Sugar Daddy*, Sugar Snap*.

Peanut

Peanut country is in Virginia, not Wisconsin. Nevertheless, gardeners in the southern half of our state may dabble in peanuts with some expectations of success, if they follow the rules.

Soil. Peanuts have traditionally been a poor-soil crop, grown in areas unsuited for nitrogen-loving plants. An excess of nitrogen, in fact, will lead to too much top growth and a poor crop of peanuts. They do, however, respond to an application of compost made before planting time. In Wisconsin, plant peanuts only on a loose and sandy loam, with a southern exposure, in full sun.

pH. 6.0-7.0.

Culture. Peanuts require a 120-day grow-ing season. If yours is much shorter, your chances for success are reduced proportionally. Prepare the soil deeply, keeping it loose, after the sun has warmed it thoroughly in May (around May 10 in Madison). Plant the peanuts in mounds, as you would squash, four kernels to a mound, about 1½ inches deep. Keep the mounds 18 to 24 inches apart, in rows two to three feet apart. (You may add several weeks to your growing season if you start seeds in peat pots and transplant in early May—but be very careful not to disturb the roots.)

Germination of seed planted outdoors may be slow—up to two weeks, if the weather is cool and rainy. When the plants are about six inches tall, begin to cultivate the soil, to knock out weeds and keep it loose. After the plants are about a foot high, begin to hill up the plants as you would potatoes, bringing the soil up high around each plant to the base of the bottom branches. Lay a loose mulch around the plants after they have been hilled. Small flowers will soon appear in the axils of the leaves. These inconspicuous flowers will soon bend toward the soil, fade, and bury themselves in it. New seeds will be formed underground which, of course, are the new peanut crop.

From the point of mulching, you should not disturb the plants until harvest, which will be after the first hard frost has killed the tops of the plants in October. Then, lift out each plant from the soil with a garden fork, shake the soil loose, and pick off the peanuts. Look in the hole for any that may have dropped. The peanuts should be placed in shallow trays and stored in a cool and dry place—perhaps in the attic—to cure. After about two months, they will be ready for roasting. Place them, one-deep, in a shallow pan or on a cookie sheet and roast in a 300° oven for 20 minutes. Then place them on wooden trays to cool. For peanut butter, simply add a little salt and run them through the meat grinder or food processor a couple of times.

Varieties. Early Spanish (earliest variety to mature), Mammoth Virginia (the type usually seen in stores), Early Virginia.

Pepper

The garden pepper is a long-season crop that needs warm and sunny days. The secret of suc-cess in Wisconsin is in setting out large plants in the spring and giving the plants the sun and nourishment they need to come to maturity. There are two general types—the sweet pepper, usually represented by the bells, and the hot or pungent pepper, of which there are many vari-eties. Because peppers react so sensitively to differences and variations in soil, climatic, and weather conditions, it is especially important that only tried varieties be planted in Wiscon-sin, if you hold high hopes for success. The foliage of the plants is bright and attractive, so they may be included in flower borders or among landscape plantings.

Soil. Peppers will grow in most good garden soils, but they prefer a loose and sandy loam that provides good drainage and good aeration. A generous application of compost before plant-ing will benefit the crop. Magnesium and phos-phorus are particularly important.

pH. 6.0-7.0.

Culture. Seeds may be started inside about ten weeks before transplanting time, or estab-lished plants may be purchased at any garden center in May or early June. Set plants outside as soon as all danger of frost has passed in a location where they will receive full sun. Mulch the plants immediately, to keep the soil moist and the weeds down. The first peppers should be ready for harvest in August.

Trouble-shooting. If nighttime tempera-tures drop below 55°, blossoms may drop from plants—and, of course, no blossoms, no pep-pers. Buy yourself some insurance by stagger-ing plantings, so that not all blossoms appear at the same time.

Early sweet varieties. Ace* (hybrid), Canape* (hybrid), Cheese*, Gypsy* (yellow), Lipstick*, Pimiento*, Yellow Belle* (yellow).

Midseason sweet varieties. Ariane* (orange), Bell Boy*, Corona (green/orange), Golden Bell* (yellow), Hybelle*, Islander* (purple—turns green when cooked), Lady Bell*,

Ma Belle*, North Star*, Purple Beauty* (purple—turns green when cooked; all the previous are hybrids), Sweet Cherry* (pickling), Yolo Wonder B.

Hot varieties. Hungarian Wax*†, Habanero*, Mexi Bell* (hybrid, bell-shaped), Ole*, Spanish Spice* (hybrid), Super Cayenne* (hybrid), Super Chili* (hybrid), Long Red Cayenne*†, Goldspike*, Hot Portugal*, Serrano, Jalapeno.

Hottest varieties. Thai Hot, Habanero.

Container varieties. Any variety will do well in ten inches of soil, if fertilized heavily and given good sun.

Popcorn

Popcorn is a fun crop to grow, even though it cannot possibly be justified on a dollars-and-cents basis since the commercial variety is so inexpensive. But the kids will love to see their very own popcorn growing in the garden. If nothing else, it will demonstrate to them that their favorite snack foods are not really born in a plastic bag in the supermarket, but, like all life, come from the sun and the soil.

What makes popcorn pop? It does so because the corneous endosperm (the shell) is hard and rigid, unlike sweet corn and most field corn. When heated, this endosperm (which becomes hard only after the corn has dried) confines the steam which is formed from the moisture inside the kernel, until the pressure becomes great enough to explode the kernel. If popcorn does not pop well, it may be either because the kernels are immature and not hard enough, or because they have been stored in warm temperatures where they have lost moisture. Do not store popcorn in a cabinet above a stove or oven.

Soil. Wisconsin is good popcorn country, along with the entire Mississippi Valley. Any good loam or sandy loam will grow popcorn, and its nutrient demands are not particularly high.

pH. 6.0-7.0.

Culture. Popcorn is grown just as sweet corn, the seed sown in the open garden after danger of frost has passed. Some authorities advise earlier planting, since the seed is so slow to germinate. However, University of Wisconsin horticulturists specify May 10 in the southern part of the state, May 24 in the north. Keep the corn patch free of weeds—mulch it, if the area is not too large, or run the rotary tiller between rows—and hope for bright and not-too-wet weather, which produces the best popcorn.

Do not harvest the ears until they have dried out well in the fall. Then, pick the ears, shuck them, and store them in a dry place where air can circulate around them—a table in a well-ventilated attic is good—or tie them up with strings and hang them in any room in the house. After a month or so, give one ear a trial popping. If results are unsatisfactory, wait for a few weeks and try again. After the corn has proved suitable for popping, it may be shelled and stored in air-tight jars.

Varieties. Minihybrid 250 White Hulless, Faribo, Fireside, Hybrid Gold, Snow Cloud (hybrid), Tom Thumb, Purdue 202 Yellow Hybrid (long-season; not suitable for north), Strawberry Popcorn, White Cloud.

Potato

Every vegetable gardener should find room for at least a few rows of potatoes. If you want to keep potatoes over the winter and lack the garden space, perhaps you can borrow a spare piece of land from a farmer friend, in which you can grow all the potatoes your family can use from autumn through the following spring. Suppose that you want to plant 300 linear feet of potatoes. Preparing the soil, planting, and mulching will take nearly a full day of labor for two people on some cool Saturday in April. After that effort, however, little work is necessary. You should visit the patch every week or so, to check for insects or disease and perhaps to rearrange the mulch. But your work is essentially finished until harvest time. Your 300 feet of row should provide from 10 to 20 bushels of potatoes, which can easily be stored in a cool and dark cellar at no expense. Potato growing is a smart investment, and potatoes fresh from the garden are vastly superior to those found in supermarkets.

Soil. Potatoes will grow on nearly any average garden soil, even soils that are too poor in nutrients to grow other crops. In Wisconsin, they thrive on sands, loams, and muck soils. An ideal soil, however, will be one that is rich in nutrients, well drained and well supplied with air pockets. As with other root and tuber crops, a hard clay will make tough going for potatoes. Last, professional growers much prefer an acid soil for potatoes, not necessarily because alkalinity decreases yields, but because it encourages scab. The scab does not hurt the quality of the potato, but it does blight the skin, making it unattractive to the eye and rendering the potato unsuitable for baking. The easiest way to lower your soil's pH is to grow a green manure crop of soybeans, plowing them under in the fall. Plant potatoes there in the following spring. (Other ways to lower the soil's pH are given on page 19.)

pH. 4.8-6.5.

Culture. Potatoes should never be planted in the same place two years in a row, or following tomatoes (which are members of the same family and carry some of the same diseases). Be sure to buy certified disease-free seed potatoes for planting—not those that have begun to sprout under your kitchen sink.

The day before you plant, cut the seed potatoes so that there is at least one eye to each cutting and plenty of flesh around the eye (which the sprout will use as food). Let these dry overnight. The next day, till the soil well and make rows at the recommended distances. Well-aged compost can be incorporated at this time, but never fresh manure, which can easily burn the seed potatoes. (Ideally, the manure should have been tilled under the previous fall.) Dig very shallow trenches, with the tiller or with a hoe, and lay the potatoes in, eyes up. Cover the potatoes with soil, and then hill up the soil along the rows lightly, so that the seed potatoes are about four inches beneath the soil. (Later, weeds may be killed easily by leveling the rows with a hoe, being careful not to break the potato sprouts.) Mulch this area deeply, with 10 to 12 inches of hay, but keep the mulch very loose directly above the rows where the sprouts will emerge. The mulch will eliminate weeding and will keep the soil moist and cool, which is very important to successful potato production.

A good harvest of potatoes in the cellar is like money in the bank. Beg, borrow, or rent space for potatoes this year. (Shown above are Katahdins, a good late variety for Wisconsin.)

When the majority of the tops have withered and turned brown in the late season, the potatoes are mature and ready for harvest. Dig them with a garden fork or spade, and dry them in a cool and airy place, out of the sun. A day or two of drying should do the job. Then, clean them and store them in a cool and dark place. They will keep well for several months, since this is their natural rest period, but after that the storage conditions are critical. A temperature of 34 to 41 degrees is necessary to prevent sprouting during the winter.

Special tips. A novel way of growing potatoes—well worth trying—is outlined by Mrs. Lois Hebble of Decatur, Indiana, in *The Complete Book of Composting*:

"In the fall I choose a very wide strip of garden where I want my potato patch to be the next year. Leaves are piled all over this spot almost three feet deep.

"By spring they have packed down and already the earthworms are hungrily working up through them. When the time is right, I plant the potatoes by laying them in long rows right on top of the leaves. The potatoes are then covered with twelve or fourteen inches of straw. Sometimes I have to put a little more on later on if I see any potato tubers sticking through.

"When it is time to dig the potatoes, I just pull the mulch aside and harvest. The potatoes are the best-tasting, smoothest and largest I have ever grown. I might add that so far I have never seen a single potato bug on the potatoes I grow this way."

Early varieties. Dark Red Norland*, Early Gem*† (scab-resistant), Norland*† (tolerant to scab), Irish Cobbler, New Norgold Russet, Anoka.

Midseason varieties. Goldrush* (russet), Russet Norkotah*, Superior*†, Haig* (both scab resistant), Chippewa.

Late varieties. Katahdin* (white), Oneida* (tolerant to scab), Yukon Gold* (yellow flesh), Red Pontiac*†, Kennebec*† (white), Sebago*† (white or russet; russet is scab resistant). Late varieties may be questionable in northern Wisconsin.

Pumpkin

Horticulturally and botanically speaking, pumpkins include a lot of vegetables that most of us would call squash. It just so happens that the pumpkin family includes acorn squash, crooknecks, zucchini, white scallops, and other squashlike varieties. We won't bother with horticultural distinctions here, but we will call pumpkins those big yellow-orange globe-shaped things that we use either for pies or jack-o-lanterns. We will include all the other horticulturists' "pumpkins" where they, through common usage, properly belong—under the heading of "squash."

That done, I will make a plea for pumpkin growing, which is both fun and rewarding. No crisp Wisconsin autumn would be complete without its share of pumpkin pies, and of course no Halloween could pass without its glowing jack-o'-lantern. Both will be more satisfying when the pumpkins come from your own garden. They do take up a lot of room, but you might be able to grow some, using no extra room at all. (See "special tips" below.)

Soil. Pumpkins will do well in a variety of soils, but they like best a sandy loam that is well supplied with rotted manure.

pH. 6.0-8.0.

Culture. Plant pumpkins after all danger of frost has passed. They are traditionally planted in hills, spaced according to directions for the particular variety. Add a few shovelsful of rotted manure to each hill and mix it in well, to give the plants a vigorous start. In a few weeks, the plants should be thinned out, again according to directions on the seed packet. After that, they need very little additional care, since they grow vigorously and are not bothered by weeds to any great extent.

If you are shooting for a champion-sized jack-o'-lantern, you will do well to allow only one pumpkin to grow from a plant. Otherwise, nature will take its course and produce more but smaller pumpkins. A midseason application of compost tea will also spur growth. And, if you want to avoid having a flat and mottled side to the jack-o'-lantern, provide it with a soft bed of hay mulch and place it upright when it is very young (being careful not to strain its connection to the vine). Choose among varieties known for large size, such as Big Moon, Atlantic Giant, Prizewinner, and Big Max.

Special tips. Many gardeners with space limitations use sweet corn and pumpkins as companion plants. Plant pumpkins in every third row of corn, spaced eight to ten feet apart in the rows. As soon as the corn is picked in July or August, knock down the stalks so that the pumpkins can have full exposure to the sun. This method will not produce results equal to those of a separate pumpkin patch, but good success can still be attained, and at a great saving in space.

Pie varieties. Small sugar*†, Cinderella*, Spookie*, Spirit*.

Jack-o'-lantern varieties. Autumn Gold*, Baby Bear*, Baby Boo* (white, miniature), Cinderella*, Ghost Rider* (hybrid), Howden*, Jack Be Little* (miniature), Limina* (white), Oz* (hybrid), Prizewinner* (average size 75-80 lbs.), Halloween*† (hybrid), Spirit*, Trick or Treat*, Connecticut Field, Big Max (another giant variety).

Radicchio (red chicory)

Radicchio is an Italian heading chicory, a slightly bitter-tasting and colorful salad ingredient that has recently become popular in trendy restaurants. The tight heads grow as large as a softball and are colored dark red with prominent white veins

Soil. A loose, well-drained garden loam, well supplied with moisture, is best for radicchio.

pH. 6.0-8.0.

Culture. In Italy, radicchio is traditionally planted in fall, but here in winter wonderland it is planted either in late May or early June, or in mid-July so that it will mature as cool weather arrives. Hot weather causes it to bolt. If you cut off the heads at ground level around the first of September, new sprouts will emerge for a second fall crop.

Varieties. Red Verona (the standard), Early Treviso* (most dependable in Wisconsin), Rossana*, Red Treviso, Castelfranco, Giulio. (The Cook's Garden catalog has several of these varieties. Address: P.O. Box 535, Londonberry, VT 05148.)

Radish

Radishes are said to be the easiest of all garden vegetables to grow, and yet many gardeners have trouble with them. If you do, the trouble may lie in one of three areas: (1) *Timing*. Radishes must be planted as early as possible in the spring. Hot weather will make the roots pithy, misshapen, and generally worthless. Their ideal growing temperature is around 45°. (2) *Nutrient supply*. Radish soil should be well composted and moist, so that the plants can grow quickly and tenderly. Slow growing radishes become hot and woody. (3) *Spacing*. Too many gardeners sow the seed too thickly, and then fail to thin the plants properly. Crowded seedlings will not develop at all. Avoid these three pitfalls, and radish production should be as simple as everyone says it is.

Trouble-shooting. If your radishes taste a lot hotter than they should be, they are probably coming to maturity too late in the season, when hot weather has arrived. Try earlier planting, or earlier harvesting when roots are young and tender.

Soil. Radishes do best on a loose and fertile soil of any kind—one that will not bake hard in the absence of rain. Do not add extra nitrogen; it will only increase top growth.

pH. 6.0-8.0.

Culture. As early in spring as the soil can be worked, sow seeds thinly in the row. The experts recommend 20 to 25 seeds to a foot of row, but I think that this is too many. The seeds will germinate within a couple of days, and if some areas don't show any plants after a week, it is a simple matter to bring out the seed packet and reseed those areas. After the plants have developed their first true leaves, thin the plants so that they are one to two inches apart in the row. Then no more care is needed, except that you will want to cultivate with a hoe between rows to keep out weeds. Sow new seed every week for a month, for a continuous supply. After that, the weather will turn hot, making it unsuitable for radish growing.

A second group of radishes, called *winter radishes*, is planted in July and August for a fall crop. These are quite a bit larger than the early varieties, but just as crisp and flavorful.

Red varieties. Cavalier*†, Cherry Belle*†, Early Scarlet Globe*†, Easter Egg* (hybrid), Red Prince* (fusarium wilt resistant). Crimson Giant, French Breakfast, Red Boy, Stop Lite, Comet, Scarlet King*.

White varieties. White Icicle*†, Burpee White, White Globe Hailstone.

Winter varieties. Round Black Spanish*, April Cross*, New White Chinese, China Rose Winter, Chinese Rose, and Chinese White. They mature in about 55 days.)

Container varieties. Any variety except long-rooted ones.

Rhubarb

Every garden should have a little corner reserved for rhubarb. This hardy perennial, once planted and established, needs virtually no care at all. It will continue to come up year after year, producing tender stalks that you can turn into tart and juicy pies in the middle of spring. Later in the season, you can enjoy strawberry pies—but we depend on rhubarb to initiate the fresh pie-baking season. (One caution: Do not let the kids nibble on the leaves, which contain large concentrations of poisonous calcium oxalate.)

Soil. Rhubarb will grow on almost any soil, but really prefers a sandy loam.

pH. 6.0-7.0.

Culture. You can probably get some root divisions from a friend who has plenty of rhubarb. Explain that your taking some of the root will benefit his or her plants, since all rhubarb should be dug up and the roots divided and replanted every five years, anyway. The plant should be dug up in early spring, before

growth starts. Break apart the roots so that each division will have one bud on the crown and a root—or, if you can't identify a bud, simply divide into several good-sized clumps. Replant the divisions, so that the bud is just covered with soil. When you replant your share, prepare a generous hole, 12 inches deep, and incorporate plenty of aged compost into the soil. This will give the plant a good start and will feed it for several years. You may begin to harvest two years after planting and every year thereafter.

Commercial growers have traditionally spread a few forksful of rotted manure over the plants each fall, letting it seep into the ground over the winter and into the following spring. The home gardener should adopt this practice and may work any remaining manure into the soil in the early spring.

Varieties. McDonald*†, Canada Red*†, Valentine*, Chipman's Red.

Rutabaga

The rutabaga is similar to the turnip in taste and in culture. The rutabaga usually grows larger, and its flesh is more dense. Rutabagas are also planted later in the season in order to enable them to be harvested as a fall crop. They mature best in nippy weather, explaining the late planting date (June 15 in southern Wisconsin, one to two weeks earlier in the north). Rutabagas are a good crop for winter storage. They may be stored just as potatoes are, or they may be packed in moist sand and kept in a cool basement. They are also suitable for pit storage outdoors. The rutabaga is not the most popular of vegetables, but it is favored by some, and its nutrient content is quite high.

Soil. Rutabagas prefer a loam or a rather heavy sandy loam, well composted and well drained.

pH. 6.0-8.0.

Culture. Rutabagas should be planted from June 1 to June 15 in Wisconsin, in order for them to mature when the first autumn frosts arrive. Sow the seeds in the open ground and keep the area free of weeds, at least until the plants have established themselves. The quality of the roots will be better if they are harvested after a few frosts—but do not allow the roots to freeze in the ground, or else their keeping qualities will be impaired.

Varieties. Laurentian*† (90 days), American Purple Top Yellow (85 days), Altasweet* (92 days), American Purple Top*, Macomber.

Salsify

Salsify (also called oyster plant, for its oyster-like flavor) is a root crop, similar to parsnip but not quite as large. It is not a popular vegetable in Wisconsin, although our climate is well suited to its production. Salsify is used in the kitchen much as turnips and parsnip. If you favor these two vegetables, you might give salsify a whirl.

Soil. Salsify likes a well-drained and loose soil, such as a sandy loam, well composted and well aerated. Since the roots grow six to eight inches long, the soil should be prepared deeply.

pH. 6.0-8.0.

Culture. Sow seed in the open garden in the early spring, as soon as the soil can be worked. Make the rows 20 inches apart and thin the plants to stand four or five inches apart. Mulch the rows after the plants have established themselves, in order to keep the soil moist and cool and to discourage weeds. The roots can be dug for use anytime that they have grown large enough to make the digging worthwhile. Like many root crops, however, their flavor will be improved by a few brisk autumn frosts. They may be stored in moist sand in the cellar or in an outdoor root pit.

Varieties. Mammoth Sandwich Island*†.

Shallot

Shallots are large, sweet, and mild-flavored onions that are often called for in French recipes. Some seed houses and nurseries offer them under the name of multiplier onions. They grow much as garlic does, each plant producing several cloves which eventually form a bulb. The plants may be pulled at any time, and the cloves may be separated and used as bunching onions (scallions).

Their soil requirements and culture are the same as for other onions. Stokes offers sets for planting under the name of multiplier onions.

Soybean

Soybeans are probably the most underrated vegetable crop of all, deserving far more garden space than they have been given up until now—not only in Wisconsin but in all parts of the country. Here is a crop that grows easily in almost any kind of soil and requires almost no care during the season. The beans can be cooked and eaten fresh, much like lima beans. They can be sprouted and eaten in salads. They can be frozen. Or they can be dried and stored for use anytime during the year. They are very high in nutritional value, offering high levels of complete and usable protein (one cup of cooked soybeans equaling the protein content of one-quarter pound of meat), the B vitamins, calcium, phosphorus, and iron. When sprouted, soybeans even offer significant levels of vitamin C, making this bean a complete nutritional package. And after the plant has offered all this to us, it continues to serve. Plowed under in the fall, the plants add their precious nitrogen stores to the soil, improving the garden for the season to come. Soybeans are, in fact, often grown for a green manure crop alone—but considering the quality of the harvest, it seems a shame not to use all those power-packed little beans. The Chinese have depended on soybeans for centuries as a meat substitute. I have no doubt that soybeans will continue to grow in popularity here and all across America.

Soil. Soybeans prefer a well-drained and sandy soil. but will grow well on nearly all soils except heavy clays that do not offer good drainage. The plant's nutrient demands are not high. It will return more nutrient matter to the soil than it removes.

pH. 6.0-7.0.

Culture. Sow seed in a composted area after all danger of spring frost has passed—about the same time as bush beans. Allow three feet between rows and thin plants to stand one foot apart in the rows. They are vigorous growers and need plenty of room. The plants will mature in about 100 days. If you are going to dry the beans, let them mature on the vines until the pods have turned yellow. For freezing or eating fresh, pick them while the pods are still tender and green but well rounded. Freeze them like peas. To dry the mature beans, spread them on pans and put them in the oven for 30 to 60 minutes at 135°. Cool them and place in bags or jars for storage. They can be used for your favorite baked bean recipes.

Varieties. Bansei, Kanrich, Giant Green Soy†. (If you have trouble ordering seed, try Burpee or Burgess.)

Soybeans are a vegetable of the future, but many Wisconsin gardeners are learning of their versatility right now.

Spinach

Spinach is one of Wisconsin's favorite cool-weather crops. The idea is to give spinach plenty of water and nitrogen, grow it fast, and harvest it before hot weather comes along. The heat will send it bolting to seed, destroying the tender quality of the leaves. It can be followed by a fast-growing and heat-loving succession crop, such as bush beans.

Soil. Spinach will grow well in a wide variety of soils. The most important factor is the pH level. Spinach cannot tolerate an acid soil, and so enough limestone should be incorporated into the area to bring the soil up to the recommended level. (A soil test will tell you the current pH level.) The soil should be prepared deeply and should be well composted. Nitrogen is especially important to fast and tender growth.

pH. 6.5-7.0.

Culture. Sow seed in the open ground as soon as the soil can be worked. Thin plants in the row according to recommendations, and then begin to pick for table use by cutting every other plant in the row, giving the others a chance to spread out. A mulch is especially important for keeping the soil cool and weeds down. Spinach planted on April 15 should be completely harvested by June 1, when hot weather begins to set in.

Trouble-shooting. If your spinach habitually bolts to seed before producing a good harvest, hot weather is probably the cause. The answer is to plant the crop earlier in the season, or plant in August for a fall crop. Also consider a heat-resistant variety such as New Zealand.

Varieties. Long Standing Bloomsdale*†, King of Denmark*†, Melody* (hybrid), Wisconsin Bloomsdale*† (resistant to downy mildew), Tyee* (hybrid), New Zealand*† (summer "spinach"), America, Giant Nobel.

Container varieties. All varieties are good.

Squash

Most of our popular squashes are actually pumpkins, botanically speaking. These include most summer varieties, including zucchini and the scalloped varieties, and fall squashes such as the acorn. True squashes include the hubbards and butternuts. Here we will treat all these as squashes, since they are thought of as such, despite botanical differences.

Squashes have been popular in Wisconsin since the time of the pioneers. The great conservationist John Muir speaks enthusiastically of squashes in his uncompleted autobiography, *The Story of My Boyhood and Youth.* As a boy living on a Columbia County farm in the 1840s, he recalls the amazement he felt upon planting a few seeds in a sandy corner of the farm and later harvesting wagonloads of huge and sumptuous squashes. The common nineteenth-century photo of the family's garden harvest nearly always included a mammoth hubbard, which was both a source of pride and a good winter keeper.

There are many varieties to choose from, and these are usually divided into summer and winter groups (those picked and eaten during the summer, and those stored for winter use). If you have the space (squash is a greedy consumer of ground), it is a good idea to plant at least one summer and one winter squash.

Soil. Squash prefers a sandy loam, well aerated and well drained, but it also needs rich amounts of nutrients for vigorous growth. The soil should be well composted before planting.

pH. 6.0-8.0.

Culture. Squash, which is thought to be a native of tropical America, can be planted only when the ground has warmed up and all danger of frost has passed. The seeds are planted in hills three to four feet apart in both directions. Eight to ten seeds are planted in each hill, and later the plants are thinned out to three or four per hill. The strong runner vines will soon spread and crowd out most weeds, and the plants will need no more of your care after they have established themselves.

Summer varieties. Peter Pan*, Tromboncino*, Early Prolific Straightneck*, Scallopini* (hybrid), Seneca Butterbar* (hybrid), Early

Summer Crookneck (resistant to squash bug), Delicious Green, Mammoth White Bush Scallop, Vegetable Marrow Bush, Cocozelle (and many others).

Summer zucchini varieties. Aristocrat* (hybrid), Clarimore* (hybrid), Ghada, Greyzini*† (hybrid), Chiefini*† (hybrid), Diplomat, Zucchini Select, Black Jack, Caserta, Black Breauty, Gold Rush* (hybrid; yellow)

Winter varieties. Burgess Buttercup*, Honey Delight* (hybrid), Sweet Mama* (hybrid), Table Queen*† (acorn, resistant to squash bug), Table King* (nonvining), Table Ace* (nonvining), Bush Ebony* (bush-type plant), Special Butternut, Waltham Butternut*†, Buttercup*† (bush type), Mooregold*†, Gold Nugget*, Kindred*, Hungarian Mammoth (giant variety, 120 days), Baby Hubbard, Warted Hubbard (110 days), Golden Hubbard, New England Blue Hubbard (110 days), Perfection, Delicata ("sweet potato" squash), Blue Hubbard (110 days), True Hubbard, Butternut (resistant to squash bug), Butternut Ultra* (hybrid), Early Butternut* (hybrid), Waltham Butternut*, Emerald Bush Buttercup* (hybrid; nonvining), Hercules (butternut type).

Acorn-type varieties. Jersey Golden Acorn (super-rich in vitamin A), Cream of the Crop* (white), Table Ace* (non-vining), Table King* (nonvining), Table Queen*.

Container varieties. Give zucchini or summer crookneck 10 to 12 inches of soil. Support them with a trellis or let hang from baskets. Prune back non-fruiting vines.

(See also pumpkin.)

Sunflower

Sunflowers (*Helianthus*) are attractive, in a rugged sort of way, and productive, too. Their seeds are rich in protein, calcium, phosphorus, and the B vitamins. They were grown for their seed by the American Indians and also by many European peoples. Sunflowers make an effective screen in the late summer, and they will provide birdseed for the winter. Several varieties of edible sunflowers are suited to Wisconsin, some growing to a height of 12 feet or more.

Soil. Sunflowers will grow in most soils, but they prefer a loose and sandy loam, well fertilized and well supplied with water.

pH. 6.0-8.0.

Culture. Plant seed one foot apart, in rows three feet apart, around the middle of May. (They can tolerate a few light spring frosts.) When the plants have become established, thin them so that the plants are three feet apart in the row. If the soil has been composted before planting, the plants will grow quickly and vigorously and should come to maturity in about 120 days. When the birds begin to eat the seeds, you know they are ready for harvesting. Cut off the heads

Dan Miller of Madison grew these enormous sunflower plants for fun and as a source of winter bird feed.

with enough stalk attached to enable them to be tied into bunches. Hang the bunches in any airy place to dry. In a month or so the seeds should come loose quite easily, and they may then be placed in jars or plastic bags for storage.

Varieties. Mammoth Russian, Mingren, Giganteus (10-ft. plants). There are also some ornamental varieties, some dwarfs, listed in various catalogs.

Sweet Corn

Sweet corn brought home from the roadside stand is good, but it cannot compare to the ears that are picked from your own garden, husked, and whisked away to the cooking pot without delay—and here is why: The sugars in sweet corn are very delicately balanced. As soon as the ear is separated from the stalk, chemical changes begin which quickly reduce the quality of the kernels. Corn that is as little as three hours old has already lost a significant amount of its quality, and if it is a day old, you might as well buy canned or frozen corn in the supermarket. The trick is to get the corn from the stalk to the cooking pot as quickly as possible. And if you can't use yours immediately, be sure to store it in the refrigerator, unhusked, until cooking time. Follow the same "rush" rule when freezing corn.

Varieties are placed into one of three groups—early, second early, and main crop. Some gardeners plant all three, so that the supply lasts from midsummer right up until frost. Many modern hybrids have an especially high sugar content. These "extra-sweet" or "super-sweet" cultivars should be planted well away from other sweet corn varieties for best results.

Soil. Corn will grow well in most soils. although it prefers a loose, well-drained loam. If your soil is heavy, stay with the late varieties. In any case, work plenty of compost into the soil before planting, for corn is a heavy nitrogen consumer.

pH. 6.0-.0.

Culture. Sweet corn can be planted about the time of the last killing frost. It is better to plan your corn patch to occupy a block of the garden, rather than one or two long rows. The plants should be in close proximity with each other, to aid pollination, and a long, single row makes pollination particularly difficult. (Without pollination, of course, no corn is produced.)

Plant in rows according to spacing directions for the specific variety. Right after planting, lay a mulch between the rows, but not right on top of them. As soon as the plants are six to eight inches high, gently mulch between the plants. This is a lot of work, especially for a good-sized patch, but it will eliminate hours of weeding and cultivating during the super-hot days of July and August. A good mulch will also eliminate the danger of injuring the shallow roots in cultivating. If the roots are disturbed at any time during the growing season, the development of the ears can be affected. Corn, which appears to be so rugged, is in many ways a very delicate plant.

If you do not want your corn to come in all at once, plant one fourth of it every week for four weeks. You will then assure yourself of a continuous crop. Even when doing this, however, divide the corn patch into four quarters instead of four long strips, to aid pollination.

Special tips. Many gardeners have been disappointed to harvest ears that are stunted, only half filled, or not filled at all. Here are some of the causes of such failure: (1) Too-close planting. Corn needs room to develop properly. Do not plant closer than the distances recommended for the variety. If you are pinched for space, grow one of the midget varieties. (2) Insects. The corn earworm is hatched on the corn silk and feeds on it while it works its way into the ear. One strand of silk is attached to each embryo kernel, and each kernel must be pollinated in order to develop. If the worm eats the silk strand before it has received pollen, its kernel will not develop. For control, go through the corn patch every fourth day and cut off all the silks that have been out for more than a day, and apply a few drops of mineral oil into the top of the ear. These silks will already have done their pollinating job, and the worms will be dumped along with the silk you cut off. (3) Excess rain. A rainy day may make the pollen sticky, preventing it from being released from the tassels. This is often the cause of incompletely filled ears, but there is not much you can do about it. (4) Acid soil. Check yours; add lime if necessary. (5) Lack of nutrients or moisture. Compost thoroughly before planting; apply a good mulch.

Early varieties. Early Sunglow*†, Seneca 60*, Improved Spancross*†, Golden Rocket*, Early Extra Rocket*, Sprite*, Butter and Sugar* (these last two, white and yellow kernels mixed), Golden Miniature, Earlivee, Spancross, Garden Treat, Sunny Vee (many others).

Second early varieties. Golden Beauty*†, Early King*†, Gold Rush*†, Honey Cream* (white and yellow kernels mixed), Seneca Warrior*, Bellringer*, Extra Early Super Sweet (many others).

Main crop varieties. Early Gold* (hybrid), Reward, Reknown* (hybrid), Tango* , Genesis*, Jubilee*, Terminator*, Cornucopia*, Excellency* (all the foregoing, hybrids),Wisconsin 900*†, Wisconsin 909*, Jubilee*†, Foremost*, Mellogold*, Sugar Daddy*, Sugar King*, Target*, Pacer*, Midway*, Golden Cross Bantam†, Sweet Sue* (white and yellow kernels mixed), Super Sweet Illinichief* (extra high sugar), Summer Treat, Barbecue, Gold Rush, Morning Sun, Marcross, Improved Carmelcross (and many others).

Extra-sweet varieties. Sugar Buns*, Lyric*, Amaize*, Sugar Ace*, Bodacious*, Miracle*, Incredible*, Delectable*, Ambrosia*, Kandy King* (all hybrids).

Super-sweet varieties. Nordic*, Radiance* (bicolor), Fortune*, Debonair*, Sweetear*, Sweettooth*, Phenomenal* (bicolor), Camelot* (white), SuperSweet Jubilee*, Zenith* (all hybrids).

Corn for cornmeal. Large-space gardeners who want to make their own cornmeal may do it easily, by letting their sweet corn mature and dry, then grinding it into meal. Or, special varieties may be planted especially for cornmeal.

Recommended are the open-pollinated varieties Blue Corn, Hickory King (white), Longfellow Flint (orange), Reid's Yellow Dent, Mandan Bride (recommended for flour), and Rhode Island White Cap (white flint).

Sweet Potato

Sweet potatoes are rich in both vitamins A and C—a nutritious addition to any vegetable garden. Although sweet potatoes are a southern crop, they have enjoyed commercial success in central Wisconsin, and they have become popular additions to many home gardens in recent years. The secret of success lies in choosing the right varieties for Wisconsin and in treating the soil properly.

Soil. The sweet potato, a native of hot and often dry climates, has learned to send its roots deep into the soil to bring up both moisture and food. Large yields, then, depend on a subsoil in good condition. Compost applied to the topsoil will help to increase yields, also, but sweet potatoes have traditionally been grown on poor soil. Excess nitrogen will promote luxuriant top growth, but will reduce yields. Often. the best crops have sparse and stunted-looking vines.

pH. 5.5-7.0.

Culture. Sweet potatoes are grown from plants that are set 15 inches apart in rows 30 to 36 inches apart. Plants are not set out until the weather has actually become warm—the first week of June, in southern Wisconsin. Make a shallow furrow for each row, and line it with compost or aged manure. Then, pull up the soil with a hoe or rake so that there is a 10-or 12-inch ridge of loose soil running all along the row. Set the plants in the ridge, with the roots four or five inches under the soil. (If you are wondering why this special treatment, it is to enable the tubers to be harvested with ease later in the season.) Keep the sweet potato patch free of weeds until the vines are vigorous enough to take care of themselves, and then do not disturb the plants until harvest time. They will never need water.

Do not harvest the sweet potatoes until the first frost is forecast. Then, before frost hits, dig them with a spade or garden fork, leave them to cure on the ground for an afternoon, and then take them in and store them in a warm room for ten days to three weeks. After that, move them to a cooler spot (50° to 60°) where the humidity is relatively high (up to 75 percent) for the winter. They should receive good ventilation all during the curing and storage periods.

Varieties. Centennial*, Jet*, Vardaman*, All Gold*, Gold Rush*.

Swiss Chard See chard.

Tomatillo

This Mexican native (*Physalis ixocarpa*) is closely related to the ground cherry (q.v.), and in fact is often called the Mexican ground cherry. It is an annual, growing three to four feet both in height and width, profusely yielding ¾-inch yellow flowers and edible yellow fruits borne within golfball-size brown paper lanterns that split when fruits are ripe. Many people consider tomatillos to be an essential ingredient in Mexican salsa, and they are also used in chili rellenos, guacamole, and other Mexican recipes.

Soil. An average, well-drained garden loam is fine for tomatillos.

pH. 6-7.

Culture. Grow the same way as for ground cherries (page 117).

Varieties. Purple*, Toma Verde*.

Tomato

Surely no vegetable crop is more popular in the Wisconsin home garden than tomatoes. And why not? Garden-fresh tomatoes are delicious, easy to grow, heavy yielding, and can be preserved in dozens of different ways. You can grow any of scores of different varieties in Wisconsin—pear-shaped, heart-shaped, apple-shaped, plum-shaped—red, pink, yellow, or white—cantaloupe-sized or cherry-sized. You can put them in salads, stews, and sandwiches, on hamburgers, in a thousand casseroles. You can "put them by" by the dozens of quarts, to help you make all the chili and spaghetti you will want from now until next tomato season. You can make tomato juice, tomato paste, tomato sauce, tomato preserves, chili sauce, catsup, pickled tomatoes, spicy salsa, and chutney. You can fry them green in butter. You can make them into tomato aspic, tomato surprise, tomato soup, stewed tomatoes, stuffed tomatoes. You can use them in countless recipes, and you can take the extras to friends when you visit.

Perhaps best of all, you can simply sit down in the garden by your favorite plant and just eat a tomato right off the vine. No other experience will better bring home the real reason why we dig, hoe, rake, and sweat in the sun from April until October of each year. That first ripe tomato is the answer, pure and simple and sweet. (My favorite? Rutgers is my sentimental choice. I grew up with it and still think it's the best tomato of all time.)

Incidentally, you might wish to know exactly why your home-grown tomatoes taste wonderful, while supermarket tomatoes have virtually no taste at all. For one thing, commercial varieties are bred for uniformity and toughness in shipping, not for flavor and texture. The tomato that can bounce off a cement floor is a tomato destined for your supermarket bins. They are also picked green, which prevents the fruit from completing the six ripening stages that provide maximum flavor and texture. Then, they are refrigerated in trucks in their long trip to the market. At 40°, a tomato's flavor is destroyed in only two days. The lesson? Grow your own tomatoes, and never store them in the refrigerator.

Soil. Tomatoes will grow on a variety of garden soils, although they do best on a sandy loam. Two things they will require are good drainage and good aeration. The soil should be loose.

pH. 6.2-6.8.

Culture. Tomatoes can be planted indoors from seed, then transplanted about eight weeks later. In this way you will have your choice of scores of varieties. And, if your seedlings do not develop as you had hoped, you can always buy plants at the garden center or nursery at planting time, choosing among the tried and true varieties that are offered there. Early varieties should be planted three feet apart in either direction; later varieties need more room and should be planted from four to five feet apart. If you are cramped for space, you will want to train your tomatoes on poles or trellises, in which case you may plant more closely—18 to 24 inches apart in rows two to four feet apart. Midget varieties can be planted more closely.

Tomatoes should be planted in an open place, for they need full sun for maximum growth and production. The soil should be well

Wire cylinders for tomatoes will conserve garden space, keep the fruit off the ground, and hold mulch snugly around the plants.

composted in advance of planting, and an extra handful of well-aged compost may be thrown into the planting hole before you set in the plant. Never plant tomatoes in a spot where puddles form, for this indicates poor drainage and a great possibility of bacterial wilt, stunting, and fruit rot. Good air circulation is equally important, since this will help to prevent leaf-blighting fungus diseases and fruit decay. To avoid disease, don't plant tomatoes in the same spot twice, or where potatoes grew the season before.

Set healthy plants in the open garden after all danger of frost has passed. If you plan to stake the plants, drive in the stake at planting time and tie the young plant to the stake (tightly around the stake, but loosely around the plant). After that, allow just two main shoots to grow, pinching off any side shoots, until the plants have reached about two feet in height. Then you may allow more side shoots to develop. Keep the shoots tied to the stake as they grow. In this way, you will get larger tomatoes with less chance of the fruit cracking.

Mulching is a good idea in any case, but it is especially important if you do not stake your tomatoes. (Your total yield, if you do not stake, will be more for each plant but less from a given area of ground.) A bed of clean straw mulch will keep the fruits out of direct contact with the ground and will prevent much fruit damage. It is especially important here in Wisconsin, where garden soils do not warm up thoroughly until late June, that you apply the mulch at the proper time. Do not apply it until your soil is thoroughly warm—and that might not be until a full month after you have set out plants. Mulch acts as a soil insulator. For tomatoes (as well as other warm-weather crops), the idea is to lock in the warmth, not the cold.

Your tomato harvest should last from late July or early August right up until the hard frost hits. You can protect the fruit from light frosts by covering the plants with burlap during the night. But before that first hard, killing frost hits, go out and harvest all the green tomatoes, large and small, and bring them in. The small ones can be used for pickling and for relish. The larger green tomatoes can be wrapped in newspaper, stored in shallow, open boxes, and will ripen in the dark for several weeks. The larger green ones can also be covered with salt and flour and fried in butter. They are delicious that way.

Trouble-shooting. In Wisconsin, where rainfall patterns are unpredictable at best, tomatoes are especially susceptible to blossom-end rot. If you reach down to pick a bright red tomato from the vine, only to find it blackened and rotten at the bottom, your plants have probably been affected by blossom-end rot.

It is caused not by any organism, but by the physiological conditions of the soil and the plant. Specifically, the cause is a lack of oxygen in the soil. This lack causes damage to the fine root hairs of the plant, and then the roots are unable to bring up enough water to fill the needs of the plant. Since the blossom-end of the tomato is farthest from the source of water, it is the first to rot. After it has, fungus organisms often invade the fruit, causing white or gray-colored rot.

The sad irony of the situation is that the lack of water in the tomato may be caused by too much rainfall, which will injure the root

A heavy straw mulch pays rich dividends with tomatoes.

hairs by oxygen starvation. The same disease may be caused by a prolonged drought. Thus, either too much or too little rain may cause blossom-end rot, especially if conditions had been very favorable earlier in the season.

Blossom-end rot is less likely to occur if the soil is well supplied with calcium. If your soil tests below 6.0 on the pH scale, it is likely to be deficient in calcium. You may also discourage blossom-end rot by improving the drainage and moisture-holding capacity of your soil. This is done by adding all the organic matter you can to the soil, improving it year by year. After blossom-end rot has struck, there is little you can do to save the fruit. Remove all affected tomatoes (it can happen with peppers, too), cut away the rotted portions, and use the unaffected portions, which will still be good to eat. If white or gray rot has entered the fruit, however, discard the entire tomato.

If nighttime temperatures drop below 55°, or above 75°, tomato blossoms may drop from the plant, resulting in poor fruit set. To guard against the chance of loss, be sure to plant several varieties, and stagger the plantings of each individual variety. Remember, too, that most open-pollinated tomatoes mature at different times throughout the season, whereas most hybrids are designed to blossom and set fruit all at one time. They are designed for commercial production, first, for home gardeners, second.

Cracking of fruit results when a warm and rainy period follows a dry spell. Mulch heavily to keep soil moisture even. Sunscald can spoil fruits exposed to long periods of direct sun.

Early varieties. Springset*, Spring Giant*, Early Girl*, Jet Fire*, Star Shot* (all hybrids), Wayahead†, Earliana, Fireball, Burgess F1 Hybrid Number 1, Burgess F1 Hybrid Number 2.

Main crop. Glamour*†, Heinz 1350 (resistant to fusarium and verticillium wilts), Campbell 1327 (resistant to fusarium and verticillium wilts), Cardinal (hybrid), Jet Star* (hybrid, resistant to fusarium and verticillium wilts), Better Boy* (hybrid, resistant to fusarium and verticillium wilts and nematodes), Supersonic* (hybrid; resistant to fusarium and verticillium wilts), Burpee's Big Boy*† (hybrid), Beefeater* (hybrid; resistant to fusarium and verticillium wilts and nematodes), Terrific* (hybrid), Fantasic* (hybrid), Beefmaster* (hybrid), Floramerica*, Wisconsin Chief, Wisconsin 55, Glamour, Bonny Best, Oxheart, Burgess Trip-L-Crop Climbing (grows 10 to 20 feet high when staked), Crackproof, Marglobe (wilt and rust resistant), Rutgers (wilt and rust resistant), and many others.

Paste varieties. Roma* (resistant to fusarium and verticillium wilts), San Marzano, Vita Italia*, Nova, Red top.

Yellow varieties. Golden Delight* (early), Jubilee*†, Sunray*†.

Small-fruited varieties. Chello*, (hybrid; yellow), Gardener's Delight* (hybrid), Gold Nugget*, Patio*, Pixie* (hybrid), Ruby Pearl* (hybrid), Small Fry*† (hybrid; resistant to fusarium and verticillium wilts), Presto* (hybrid), Sweet 100* (hybrid), Bitsy* (hybrid), Tiny Tim†, Whippersnapper*, Burgess Early Salad* (hybrid), Yellow Plum, Red Cherry.

Greenhouse forcing varieties. Ohio MR12 Pink Forcing (TMV), Ohio WR7 Pink Forcing, Ohio WR25 Pink Forcing (wilt tolerant).

White variety. White Beauty (low acid content).

Container varieties. Tiny Tim, Small Fry, Pixie, Presto, Patio (from the smallest to the largest).

(Gardeners who want to survey the most comprehensive list of tomato varieties should write for the catalog of the Tomato Growers Supply Company, which describes 250 varieties and gives some good growing tips, as well. The address: P.O. Box 2237, Fort Myers, FL 33902.)

Turnip

Turnips are best grown fast and eaten young. The larger they get, and the warmer the weather gets, the more unpalatable they become. Tender, young turnips, however, have a zesty flavor all their own, and they make a welcome addition to the dining table in June and July.

The turnip tops are also prized as a potherb. In fact, a farmer once told me, only half in jest, that his family eats the turnip tops but he feeds the roots to the livestock. I say, eat 'em both.

Soil. Turnips are not particular when it comes to soil types, but they do like a loose soil, well drained and well composted. A large supply of available nutrients will spur the quick growth that is essential to producing tender roots. The soil should be deeply prepared, as with any root crop.

pH. 6.0-7.5.

Culture. The culture of turnips is similar to that of rutabagas. Plant in early spring, as soon as the ground can be worked. Thin plants when they have grown their first true leaves, and then apply a good mulch in order to keep the ground moist and cool. Harvest the roots before hot weather sets in, and follow with a planting of bush beans.

Trouble-shooting. If turnips develop a "too-hot-to-enjoy" flavor, chances are that they are coming to maturity during hot weather. The answer is to plant them earlier, harvest them while they are young and tender, or switch to July plantings, so that the roots can come to maturity as early autumn's cooler weather arrives.

Varieties. Purple Top White Globe*†, Purple Top Strap Leaf (earliest variety), Cow Horn, Tokyo Cross*.

Vegetable Spaghetti

Vegetable spaghetti is actually a pumpkin with a novel twist. The squashlike fruit is cooked whole, then split in half. The pulp, which is in long strings like spaghetti (but tastes like squash), is then removed and eaten. Served either hot or cold, it is said to be delicious. It has been used in the Orient for many years.

Soil. Vegetable spaghetti, like squash, likes a sandy loam, well drained, well aerated, and well composted.

pH. 6.0-8.0.

Culture. The culture for vegetable spaghetti is the same as that for winter squash (see squash).

Varieties. There is no choice of varieties. Nichols offers seeds.

Watercress

Many people have the idea that watercress will grow only along the banks of streams, shaded by overhanging trees. Not true! Anyone can grow watercress in a largely shaded spot, if the plants are watered thoroughly every day. You might try watercress in your own garden, or somewhere else around the house, especially if you love it as much as I do.

Soil. Watercress has no particular soil requirements.

Culture. Experiment with conditions around your home. Remember that watercress will grow where there is plenty of clean and cool water, and where there is plenty of shade. Some people sink pots of watercress in tubs of water, changing the water daily by running the hose in the tub for several minutes. If you have a stream running through your place, of course, the task should be easier.

Start seeds in a mixture of garden loam, a little ground limestone, and some sifted wood humus. (Wild watercress uses wood humus from nearby trees.) Keep the soil moist at all times, keep it cool, and give it only partial sun. When the young plants have grown large enough to handle, they may be placed outdoors. If you are planting them in a stream, choose a protected place close to the bank where they will not wash out. May is a good time for planting outdoors in Wisconsin. You might have trouble in getting the bed established in a stream, but keep on trying, for once watercress is established, it will provide cuttings each spring and fall thereafter.

(Note: If you can find wild watercress, remember that the plants can also be propagated by rooting the cuttings in water.)

Varieties. There is no choice of varieties. Harris and Stokes offer seed.

Watermelon

In our grandfathers' time, watermelons were difficult or impossible to grow well in Wisconsin.

Now, thanks to the new short-season varieties, we can grow all the melons we want—smaller than the Georgia varieties, perhaps, but just as cool and sweet on a hot summer day.

Soil. Watermelons are a warm-weather plant, no matter what the variety, and they prefer a sandy soil that warms up quickly and stays warm. Nutrient content of the soil is not too important—and, in fact, an excess of nitrogen will grow luxuriant vines and small fruits. More important is the number of hot and sunny days in the growing season.

pH. 6.0-7.0.

Culture. The culture of watermelons is the same as that of muskmelons. Plant them on a southern slope, if possible, and certainly in full sun.

Varieties. Blue Belle*, Mirage*, Paradise*, Royal Jubilee*, Royal Peacock*, Sweet Favorite*, Top Yield*, Summer Festival* (all the foregoing, hybrids), Sugar Baby*†, Black Diamond*, Charleston Gray†, Crimson Sweet*†, Petite Sweet* (the last three, resistant to anthracnose and fusarium wilt), Yellow Baby* (hybrid), Yellow Cutie* (hybrid), Jubilee*, Wilt-Resistant Klondike, Congo, Wilt-Resistant Dixie Queen†, Dixie Queen F1 Hybrid, Family Fun F-l Hybrid, Winter or Xmas, Northern Sweet, New Hampshire Midget†. (All mature in less than 100 days.)

Container varieties. Petite Sweet, New Hampshire Midget, Lollipop, Golden Midget, Market Midget. (Provide trellises.)

Herbs

Every garden should include some herbs. Most are not difficult to grow, and together they offer a variety of rewards, both practical and pleasing. Herbs can be used to add zesty or delicate flavorings to nearly all recipes. They can be used in sachets for imparting delicate aromas to drawers and closets, and many people use herbs for medicinal purposes. Here, we will focus on culinary herbs, not the medicinals or "simples," as they were once known. A good book on the latter, however, is Margaret B. Kreig's *Green Medicine*.

History. For most of recorded history, herbs served a place of great importance—as medicines and cosmetics, first, and as condiments only secondarily. Until the present century, in fact, herbs served as perfumes, salves, deodorants, magic potents, holy objects, and both curative and preventive medicines. Every civilization depended on herbs for most or all of these purposes. Even today, many of our modern medicines are derived from herbs, and these plants still function in some of their older roles. In Italy, for instance, an herb still serves as a lover's signal. If an Italian maiden places a pot of basil in her window, it is a sign to her lover that he is expected.

Where to plant herbs. Most herbs are attractive and low growing, and thus suited for inclusion in many garden areas. They can be planted in the vegetable garden, in a special herb garden (formal, as in the grand gardens of seventeenth- and eighteenth-century Europe, or informal), in hanging pots on the patio, in tubs on the rooftop, in among the flower borders, in rock gardens, or simply in small and odd spaces anywhere on the home grounds. They do require full or nearly full sun (except for a few, which are noted in the listings that follow), and their mature heights should be checked before they are interplanted among flowers or vegetables. Some herbs, such as fennel, commonly grow to five feet or more in height.

Herb culture. The nature of herbs varies as widely as that of vegetables. Some are annual, some biennial, and many are perennials. Some are planted from seed, others from nursery plants or divisions of roots. Some are grown for their seeds or flowers, but most are grown for their leaves, which are rich in essential oils. Generally, herbs favor a well-drained soil, not too acid and not too rich. The oils of these plants develop slowly, and a soil that is too rich in nutrients may well spur rank growth and diminished quality. Herbs should be nursed along slowly, as they are in their natural settings. For the same reason, they do not require frequent watering. This, too, will spur too-rapid growth and a lowering of leaf quality. Last, the perennial herbs should be planted together, so that they will not be disturbed during the spring planting of the annuals.

Twenty-Five Herbs for Wisconsin

The following 25 herbs are nearly all of the culinary variety. They include some of the most popular herbs for growing in this part of the country, but they certainly do not represent a comprehensive list. *Taylor's Encyclopedia of Gardening*, for instance, lists 58 culinary herbs, and their list is far from comprehensive. Most of the data used to compile this list comes either from Charlotte Dunn's pamphlet (Special Circular 132, *Herbs*) distributed by the University of Wisconsin-Extension Programs (available from your county agent), and from other listings. If you would like more information on herbs of any kind, I recommend that you write to the Herb Society of America, 9019 Kirtland Chardon Road, Mentor, OH 44060. Ask for a list of publications.

Anise

Characteristics. Slow-growing annual; grows to 18 inches; white flowers.

Culture. Plant from seed in moderately rich, well-drained sandy soil. Thin plants to stand six to eight inches apart. Plant in sunny place.

Harvest. Gather on dry summer day after seeds develop. Place seed heads on frames of stretched cheesecloth or netting for air circulation. Place in cool shed or room. When dry, remove seeds from stems and seal in bottles.

Uses. Green leaves and seeds can be used in salads, beverages, soups, chowders, meats, games and poultry, breads, and cakes. In Holland, seeds are steeped in hot milk as a sleep inducer.

Basil (Sweet)

Characteristics. Annual; dark green leaves with clove-pepper aroma and flavor. Grows to 24 inches; white flowers. Good border plant.

Culture. Plant in well-drained, medium-rich soil. Likes sunny, sheltered location. Space mature plants 12 inches apart. Give plants some protection from the wind. Several shearings from top three to four inches of plant can be made during the season.

Harvest. Cut plant when starting to flower. Hang for drying in warm, dry, dark room. Crush flowering tops and pack in closed containers.

Uses. Superb for tomatoes and tomato dishes, in soups, and with meat, fish, and vegetables. Use in salads and in egg, cheese, rice, and spaghetti dishes.

Borage

Characteristics. Attractive annual; grows to 15 inches or more; white or blue flowers.

Culture. Plant seeds and thin young plants to stand 15 inches apart. Likes medium-rich soil, full sun. This plant matures in six weeks, and so several sowings should be made for season-long supply.

Harvest. The leaves are usually used while still green, when their oils are in high concentration.

Uses. Adds piquant, cucumberlike flavor to salads and drinks. Blossoms are used as garnish for drinks.

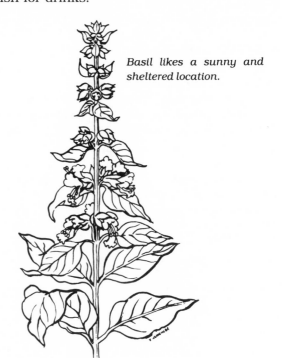

Basil likes a sunny and sheltered location.

Burnet, Salad

Characteristics. Hardy, sprawling perennial; grows 12 to 18 inches high; white or rose flowers.

Culture. Sow seed as an annual, in full sun, and later thin plants to stand 12 inches apart. Likes a poor and dry soil.

Harvest. Use younger leaves fresh, for flavoring in salads. Harvest plants when flower buds have formed.

Uses. Adds a cucumberlike flavor to salads. Good also for herb teas.

Caraway

Characteristics. Biennial; feathery foliage and creamy white flowers; grows 24 to 36 inches high.

Culture. Plant seeds in light soil in full sun. Later, thin plants to stand six inches apart. Seeds will not be produced the first year; however, if seeds are sown in fall, the plant will produce seeds the following year.

Harvest. Same as for anise.

Uses. Seeds are used in breads, cakes, cookies, potato salad, and baked fruit; add to ragouts and homemade cheese.

Chervil

Characteristics. Annual; resembles fine-leaved parsley. Tastes like parsley and fennel combined. Grows to 18 inches; white flowers.

Culture. Plant seeds in early spring in moderately rich soil. Needs some shade. Space mature plants nine inches apart.

Harvest. Pick leaves for fresh use or dry them late in season. Flavor of leaves is captured best, however, when they are frozen.

Uses. Add leaves fresh or dry to salads, salad dressings, meats, soups, omelets, and stews. Combine with butter sauce when basting chicken for broiling.

Chive

(See page 112.)

Coriander

Characteristics. A biennial that must be grown as an annual in Wisconsin. Plants grow to two feet in height; pinkish-white flowers; disagreeable odor.

Culture. Plant seed in light, medium-rich soil, in full sun. Space mature plants to stand ten inches apart.

Harvest. Seeds should be harvested as soon as they are ripe. Flavor develops when seeds are dry. See anise for drying directions.

Uses. Seeds taste and smell like orange. Use in baking, poultry dressings, and French salad dressing.

Costmary

Characteristics. A tall-growing perennial that will spread rapidly if not checked. Grows to five feet; yellow flowers.

Culture. Plant seeds in spring, and thin plants to stand 12 inches apart. After the first year, root divisions may be made to propagate the plant. Likes sun but will tolerate some shade.

Harvest. Gather and dry leaves when flower buds have formed in late season.

Uses. Has strong aniselike flavor. Use sparingly in green salads, poultry dishes, some jellies. Some people use it for herb teas.

Dill

Characteristics. Annual; grows two to three feet tall, with feathery foliage and yellow flowers.

Culture. Plant seed in sandy, well-drained soil, in full sun. Needs wind protection. Space mature plants eight to ten inches apart.

Harvest. Seed should be harvested as soon as it is ripe. Cut entire plant and hang to dry, or dry on screens.

Uses. Fresh plant, flower heads, and/or seeds are used for vinegar and pickling. Leaves can flavor soups, sauces, fish, and lamb. Cook with beans, sauerkraut, cabbage, cauliflower. Mix into potato salad, macaroni, coleslaw.

Fennel

Characteristics. A tall-growing perennial (treated like an annual in Wisconsin). Grows to five feet: yellow flowers.

Culture. Sow seed in early spring and thin mature plants to stand 18 inches apart. Needs full sun and good soil. The heavy flower heads will need support.

Harvest. Cut leaves at any time for fresh use. Harvest plants in late season.

Uses. The thick stems can be used like celery. Seeds and leaves give a licorice tang to fish sauces, chowders, soups, and pickles. Use seeds for breads and tea.

Geraniums, scented

Characteristics. Scented geraniums are easy-to-grow tender perennials. They are rapidly gaining in popularity as attractive potted or garden plants that may be used in hundreds of recipes. The scents available include apple, apple cider, chocolate-mint, cinnamon, coconut, ginger, lime, lemon, nutmeg, orange, rose, rose-mint, rose-lemon, strawberry, eucalyptus, pineapple, and more, according to the Madison Herb Society. They may be used to make jelly, cookies, flavored syrups, sugars, and honey, infused butters, teas, and as flavorings in numerous recipes. They may also be used as aromatic ingredients in potpourris, sachets, and home-made cosmetics. The world of scented geraniums is a fascinating one, well worth exploring.

Culture. Start plants from seedlings or cuttings. Grow them in pots or in the open garden, in a spot that receives maximum sun. For best concentration of aromatic oils, keep plants somewhat on the dry side, but never allow them to dry out completely. They need little fertilizer. Prune back the plants when you bring them in for the winter.

Harvest. Trim and use leaves as needed.

Lavender

Characteristics. A tall-growing perennial raised almost exclusively for its fragrance.

Culture. Can be grown from seed but more successfully from plants or cuttings. Plant in gravel or sandy, well-limed soil, in full sun. Must be grown in poor soil to produce optimum fragrance. Needs winter protection.

Harvest. Same as for anise.

Uses. Place in small cloth bags for scenting linen and clothes closets.

Lemon Balm

Characteristics. A perennial growing to 24 inches, with white flowers. Has a sweet, aromatic, lemonlike odor and flavor.

Culture. Plant seed in early spring in partial shade. Likes a moist and moderately rich soil. Thin plants to stand 18 inches apart.

Harvest. Use fresh leaves at any time; harvest plant in late season.

Uses. Use fresh leaves as you would mint, in salads, beverages, and teas. Good for iced tea. Use also with fish, lamb, and beef. Leaves can be dried and used in tea.

Lemon balm adds lemony zest to iced tea, and is excellent when used with fish.

Marjoram (Sweet)

Characteristics. An annual, growing into a small (12-inch) bush, producing white flowers.

Culture. Sow seed in early spring, in medium-rich and dry soil. Seedlings require shade until well started, then full sun. Space mature plants six to ten inches apart.

Harvest. Same as for basil.

Uses. Leaves can be used with poultry, meats, egg dishes, poultry stuffings, soups, potato salad, creamed potatoes, and string beans. Rub leaves on meats before roasting.

Mint (Spearmint)

Characteristics. A perennial with a refreshing odor and purple flowers. Grows to 12 inches. An invasive and aggressive plant. Keep it contained.

Culture. A friend may part with some young plants for transplanting, or you might find them growing wild in heavy soils. Plant these in rich and moist soil, 12 inches apart. Thin beds and renew every three or four years. Do not allow stalks to go to seed before using the aromatic leaves.

Harvest. Use fresh leaves at any time. Gather in the morning after dew is gone, but before hot sun dries flavoring oils. Dry as recommended for basil.

Uses. A perennial favorite for iced tea. Adds flavor to jellies. Use as a garnish to fruit cups and salads. Excellent with lamb, peas, and cream of pea soup. Use to make mint sauce. Dried, it can be sprinkled on fresh fruits, peas, or squash. Combine with lemon balm for delightful "lemint" vinegar. Crush fresh leaves before using.

Oregano

Characteristics. A perennial growing to 20 inches, with pink flowers.

Culture. Plant seed (or, preferably, root divisions) in early spring, in fairly dry soil, in full sun. Space mature plants to stand 12 inches apart.

Harvest. Use leaves fresh at any time; harvest plants as flowers begin to open.

Uses. A favorite in Spanish, Mexican, and Italian dishes. Rub fresh leaves on veal and lamb before roasting. Add to goulash, stews, sauces, and soups. The dried leaves of oregano can be used in a variety of recipes calling for it.

Parsley

(See page 125.)

Rosemary

Characteristics. A tender, slow-growing perennial with pale blue flowers grown as an annual in Wisconsin. Leaves have spicy odor.

Culture. Plant seeds in early spring, in well-drained and highly limed soil. Seeds are slow to germinate, but may be started indoors in March. Needs full sun and wind shelter. Space mature plants 18 to 36 inches apart, or so they do not crowd each other. If the plant is potted in the garden, it can easily be taken indoors for the winter.

Harvest. Same as for basil.

Uses. Fresh or dried leaves should be used sparingly in cream soups, poultry, stews, and sauces. Blend with parsley and butter and spread on chicken breasts and thighs when roasting. Add to water when cooking peas, potatoes, turnips. Sprinkle dried and crushed leaves on meats before roasting or broiling.

Saffron (Fall-Blooming Crocus)

Characteristics. Annual; low growing: lilac-colored flowers.

Culture. Best to buy bulbs. Plant in well-drained soil in sheltered spot. Space mature plants six inches apart.

Harvest. Same as for basil.

Uses. Add very small amounts of dried flower stamens to sauces, cookies, rice, chicken, cakes, gravies, and biscuits.

Sage, Garden

Characteristics. Perennial shrub growing to 24 inches; gray leaves and blue flowers.

Culture. Soak seeds for a few hours to aid germination. Plant in full sun, in sandy or well-drained soil. Space mature plants to stand two to three inches apart.

Harvest. Cut when just starting to flower, then handle according to directions given for basil.

Uses. Mix with onions for stuffing pork, ducks, and geese; use with fish. Rub powdered leaves on ham and pork loins. Good in soups and salads. Use with egg and cheese dishes. Some people use sage tea for relieving sore throats.

Savory (Summer)

Characteristics. Annual; grows 12 to 18 inches; pink flowers; weak stems might need support.

Culture. Plant seeds in moderately rich, rather dry soil, in full sun. Make several sowings three weeks apart. Space mature plants to stand six inches apart. Does not transplant well.

Harvest. Same as for basil.

Uses. Fresh or dried leaves are used in meat loaf, hamburger, beef stew, biscuit and dumpling batters, egg dishes, pea and bean soups. Use on fish and pork, and in cooking beans, peas, cabbage, and sauerkraut. Good for stuffings salads, and sauces for veal and poultry.

Sesame

Characteristics. Annual growing 18 to 72 inches, depending on the variety. (Probably the best is Renner Number 1, a nonshattering commercial variety.) Lavender flowers.

Culture. Sow seed in medium soil, in full sun. Space mature plants to stand six inches apart.

Harvest. Seeds cannot be sown until all danger of frost has passed, and crop takes from 90 to 100 days to mature, making it a risky venture for any but southern Wisconsin gardeners. Harvest pods when seeds are ripe. Dry in airy place, shake seeds loose, and store in jars.

Uses. Add seeds to breads and cakes. Grind and mix with nuts, figs, poppy seed, or honey to make a healthful candy.

Shallots

(See page 135.)

Tarragon, French

Characteristics. A hardy perennial, treated as an annual in Wisconsin. Grows to 24 inches; yellow flowers. The French variety is far superior to Russian tarragon, which is larger, easier to grow, and virtually tasteless. Russian tarragon may be grown from seed, but French tarragon cannot.

Culture. Start root cuttings indoors or transplant root divisions 12 inches apart in full sun. Likes medium soil and some protection from wind.

Harvest. Use fresh leaves at any time. Harvest plant when the small flower heads begin to open. Dry for storage.

Uses. Many French recipes call for tarragon. Use fresh or dried leaves with egg and cheese dishes, poultry, steak, and fish. Add to green salad and salad dressings, and to tartar and lemon-butter sauces. Rub roasting bird inside and outside with fresh leaves.

Thyme

Characteristics. Perennial; grows to 12 inches; lavender flowers.

Culture. Plant seed, cuttings, or divisions in sandy or well-drained and well-limed soil, in full sun. Space mature plants to stand eight inches apart. Clip back each spring for bushy growth.

Harvest. Cut leafy tops and flower clusters when plants are in bloom. Then dry according to directions given for basil.

Uses. Probably the most versatile of herbs. Often blended with other herbs. Leaves can be used in meats, poultry stuffing, gravies, soup, egg dishes, cheese, and clam chowder. Good with tomatoes and cheese canapes, and many other recipes.

You can also get herbs—especially the perennials—simply by finding other growers in your area and then swapping. Perennials spread naturally, and the beds usually must be trimmed back each year anyway. Be there with containers in hand!

Fruits, Berries, and Nuts—Perennial Providers

My faith is all a doubtful thing,
Wove on a doubtful loom,
Until there comes, each showery spring,
A cherry-tree in bloom.
                              —David Morton 1886-1957

5 Who has to be convinced of the value of a cherry tree? In spring, it thrills our senses with a flood of delicate, white blossoms. All summer long it provides cooling shade and green beauty. And then, as if that were not enough, in late July or early August it offers us all the bright and succulent fruits of its boughs, which we can preserve to enjoy throughout the year.

Granted, here in Wisconsin that cherry tree is likely to be a sour cherry, for our winters are too severe to play a proper host to the sweet varieties. Similarly, most of us can virtually rule out peaches, apricots, many pear and apple varieties, and scores of other fruits that can be grown only by our southern neighbors. Only in Wisconsin's extreme southeast corner is the choice of fruit trees really a wide one.

What does that leave for the rest of us? It leaves a tempting variety of fruits to satisfy nearly any home gardener. We have apples aplenty—tangy Courtlands and McIntoshes the most popular, but also more than a dozen other varieties that will do well even in the coldest reaches of our state. We have pears—not suited to commercial production, but some varieties—including the popular Bartlett—that are fine for the home garden. Plums are not difficult to grow here, and some of us can even try a few apricot varieties with a good expectation of success.

Then there are berries and grapes, many of which respond to the zest of Wisconsin's climate with a pure and tangy flavor produced in few other sections of the country. Strawberries are by far the most popular of these. In June, it is difficult to take a country drive without being invited by a sign to "pick your own" at a nearby farm or orchard. As good as these are, your own will taste even better. Not far behind are grapes, which also respond well to the Wisconsin climate. The varieties that do well here are generally those that have been developed in the cooler sections of the northeast, in New York and Massachusetts. Raspberries are so easy to grow that gardeners have difficulty keeping them in check. And then there are currants, trouble-free and great for jellies—and gooseberries, which make a pie that is beyond comparison, reserved for the special few who are wise enough to include this fruit in their garden plans.

Last among the perennial providers are the nut trees. You can harvest nuts in the wild every autumn, looking for butternuts, hazelnuts, hickories, black walnuts, and—if you are lucky—a few remaining American chestnuts. These wild-growing trees are native to Wisconsin, and they may be cultivated on your own land with relative ease. In addition, the Chinese chestnut, which found sudden popularity in America after the blight wiped out nearly all of our native chestnuts, can be grown in most areas of the state. The advantage of growing nut trees is that they generally grow much larger than fruit trees, and thus serve much the same

USDA Plant Hardiness Zone Map

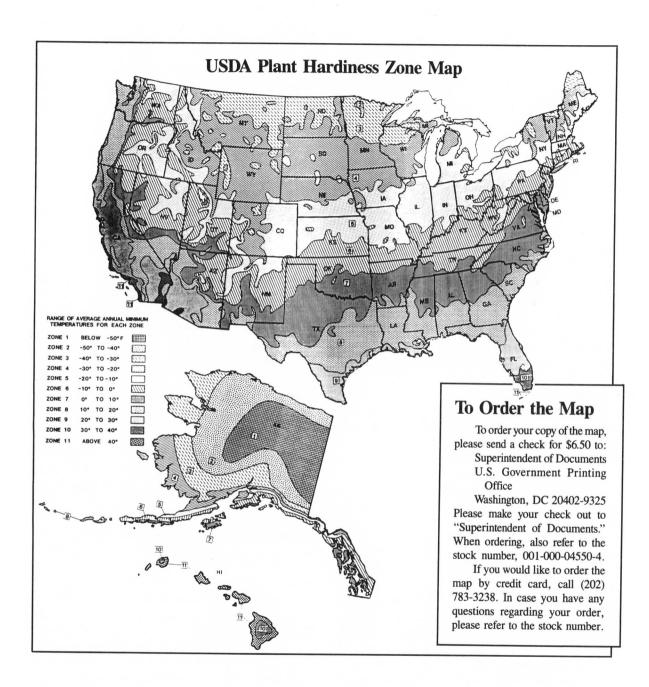

RANGE OF AVERAGE ANNUAL MINIMUM
TEMPERATURES FOR EACH ZONE

ZONE 1   BELOW −50° F
ZONE 2   −50° TO −40°
ZONE 3   −40° TO −30°
ZONE 4   −30° TO −20°
ZONE 5   −20° TO −10°
ZONE 6   −10° TO   0°
ZONE 7   0°   TO   10°
ZONE 8   10°   TO   20°
ZONE 9   20°   TO   30°
ZONE 10   30°   TO   40°
ZONE 11   ABOVE 40°

To Order the Map

To order your copy of the map, please send a check for $6.50 to: Superintendent of Documents U.S. Government Printing Office

Washington, DC 20402-9325 Please make your check out to "Superintendent of Documents." When ordering, also refer to the stock number, 001-000-04550-4.

If you would like to order the map by credit card, call (202) 783-3238. In case you have any questions regarding your order, please refer to the stock number.

purpose as shade trees, but are bothered far less by insects and diseases than are fruit trees.

Planning for Maturity

Size is important. Most fruits and nuts are not very particular about soil requirements, and so the paramount consideration in planning is site and size. A full-size apple tree will require up to 40 feet of room in both directions—1,600 square feet in all. You can grow a generous family garden in this space and, if you are pinched for space, you had best think in terms of the smaller berries or dwarf varieties of fruit trees. When planning, think ahead 20 years.

Nut trees grow to enormous sizes. A full-sized, mature apple tree will grow to 30 feet or more in height, but a good hickory will grow to 100 feet. Chestnuts, on the other hand, are lower and bushier, and will require less room. The general rule is to plant all standard-size fruit trees 50 feet apart from each other, except for chestnuts. which can be planted 30 feet apart.

Berries and grapes, of course, require less room. Strawberries can fit nicely into the vegetable garden, in a patch of their own, or even in a colorful strawberry barrel or "pyramid patch," a space-saving arrangement of progressively elevated and diminishing circles of soil, raised by the use of circular aluminum strips. The strawberries are planted on the "steps" of the pyramid. Raspberries, currants, and gooseberries are cane and bush fruits, and should be planted on the edges of the garden where they will be out of the way. The foliage of raspberries is not particularly attractive, but currants can serve ornamental purposes in many places on the home rounds. Grapes are attractive plants, also. Their vines can be used to cover arbors. climb up over porches on trellises, or form pleasant screens for backyard privacy. Both bush fruits and grapes, however should not be planted right up to your neighbor's lot line, unless you have some sort of an arrangement whereby he or she will not resent the spreading plants.

Effect of trees on plants. Remember that trees will cast significant shadows after a few years, and that they should not be planted where they will reduce the amount of sunlight to the vegetable garden or to flower plantings. Another major consideration is the great expanse of the root structure of all trees. The roots will spread far beyond the outermost branches (the drip line) and can easily compete for nutrients with your less-robust garden plants, both vegetables and flowers.

Insects and disease. Last, remember that the highly developed commercial varieties of most fruit trees are generally very susceptible to attack by both insects and disease, even though breeders in recent years have worked to develop resistant cultivars. There are methods to assure good harvests of healthy fruit without resorting to chemical pesticides, but these natural control methods are often time-consuming to apply and sometimes not fully effective. Your choices, then, often come down to either spraying heavily and often, or remaining organic and spending the time to research and apply natural control methods. If you have both the will and the time, the latter choice is a practicable one.

Soil and site. Since the roots of trees drive deeply into the earth to bring up both nutrients and moisture, the condition of the topsoil is not particularly crucial, except perhaps during the first few years when the tree is becoming established. If you are working for maximum fruit production, however, there are some rules you should observe:

1. Plant trees in a well-drained soil, to enable you to feed them more effectively. Compost will wash down to the roots, if the soil is well drained.

2. Avoid low-lying frost pockets, which can lead to both fruit damage in early autumn and the winterkill of buds. Avoid equally the planting of fruit trees on the top of a hill, unprotected from the wind. They can dry out quickly here, and strong spring winds can strip the tree

Table 9. Planting Distances, Heights, and Bearing Times for Fruit Trees

	Planting Distance, Each Way (ft.)	Mature Height (ft.)	Years to First Crop	Years of Bearing
Apple, standard	35-40	20-25	3-10	50-100
Apple, semi-dwarf	12-15	12-15	2	30-60
Apple, dwarf	10-15	8-10	1-3	25-50
Apricot, standard	20-25	15	3-4	10-25
Apricot, dwarf	10-12	8-10	2	8-10
Cherry, sour, standard	20-25	20	3-4	15-25
Cherry, sour, dwarf	10-12	8	2	8-12
Cherry, sweet, standard	25-30	30	3-4	15-25
Peach, standard	20-25	20	3-4	20-25
Peach, dwarf	10-12	8-10	2	10-15
Pear, standard	20-25	30	3-4	25-75
Pear, dwarf	12-15	12-15	2-3	15-40
Plum, standard	20-25	20	3-4	30-40
Plum, dwarf	10-12	8-10	2-3	15-20

of blossoms (and the possibility of fruit) in a short time.

3. Plant on hillsides, if you can—preferably on a northern or eastern slope—to avoid winter damage and late spring frost injury.

4. Give the tree maximum sunlight. Sunlight is very important to production, and a site that offers full sun is also likely to offer good air circulation. which is also important.

5. The soil should be slightly on the acid side for best production.

How to Buy a Good Tree

Any tree you buy should be vigorous, showing good signs of growth. It should be young and stocky—not spindly and overly tall—and it should be entirely free of disease and injury. Choose a variety that you know is resistant to disease, insofar as possible, and be absolutely sure that yours is a self-fertilizing tree, unless you plan to plant two or more compatible varieties in close proximity. If you plant a single, self-sterile tree, you will get no fruit.

The safest way to buy a good fruit tree is to know a good nursery and to trust their judgment. Mail order trees may appear attractive in

the catalogs—and there is a good chance of success with these—but any young tree will suffer some shock in being transported, most of the damage coming from dryness. You might pay a little more in buying locally, but you will be able to examine your tree, see it growing, and be assured that it was raised in the area where you will plant it. When you consider that you are planting a tree to last for several generations, the difference of a few dollars does not seem very significant.

Choosing the proper variety of any tree, bush, or other permanent planting depends greatly on where you live. On the USDA Hardiness Zone map (page 153), three zones—3, 4, and 5—fall within Wisconsin. Many varieties that can thrive in Zone 5 will winterkill, or at least issue poor crops, in areas farther north. Wisconsin's prime fruit tree zone stretches along our souther tier of counties, then up the shore of Lake Michigan and up around Door County, as well as along the southeastern shore of Lake Superior, where lake effect mitigates the worst of winter temperatures.

This chapter will offer guides to selection among different varieties. Before making a final selection and purchase of any tree, however, you should check with your nursery and, if you feel that you should, ask your county Extension agent to confirm the recommendation. If, for instance, you live in a low-lying lake area, you might discover that you can plant more varieties than are indicated in the following general recommendations. The warmer air on the leeward side of a large body of water often creates a narrow "fruit belt," which simulates the climate of an area many miles to the south.

Dwarf Trees and Espaliers

Dwarf fruit trees are a boon for the home gardener. They take up far less room than their full-sized counterparts, and yet they yield fruit of fully equal size and quality. They are easier to care for, simply because they are smaller, and they begin to bear at a much earlier age (although their life-span is shorter).

Dwarf trees are nothing new. The Europeans have bred and cultivated them for hundreds of years, for the same reasons of space conservation that we grow them today. Modern plant breeders have, furthermore, now developed semidwarf varieties to fill in the gap between dwarfs and the full-sized trees. While dwarfs may grow to a mature height of five to 10 feet, and full-sized fruit trees to 30 feet or more, the semidwarfs grow in the 12- to 15-foot range. They are large enough to produce significant amounts of fruit, but not so tall as to frighten you when you are harvesting fruit from the upper limbs.

A dwarf tree is developed by grafting the bud of a standard variety onto the rootstock of a dwarf variety that bears imperfect fruit. Because the rootstock determines the size of the tree and the bud determines the character of the fruit, plant breeders have combined these two to get the best of both worlds.

Espaliers. Espaliers, which also have been popular in European gardens for hundreds of years, are fruit trees whose branches are especially trained to predetermined shapes. They are grown against walls, or against trellises or some other structure, so that they virtually have only

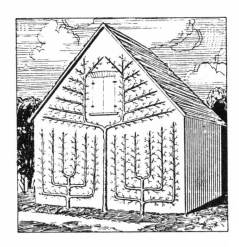

two dimensions—height and width—instead of a rounded three. They are grown from dwarf rootstock especially chosen for the purpose, and the grafting of the bud is done to assure the proper shape and number of the branches. After they are planted, they must be carefully trained, pruned, and supported. The shape of the espalier can be modified, but not much beyond the basic shape for which its initial grafting has prepared it.

Henry Leuthardt, the founder of a nursery in Long Island, New York, and a leading American pioneer of both dwarf and espalier trees, gave this good advice on the care of espaliers:

"Espaliers will grow wherever other fruit trees will grow. They need about six hours of intense sun per day in order to grow well and bear a good crop of fruit. If trees get sun from 10 a.m. on, it is sufficient—but, do not plant a tree in a location that receives sun until 10 a.m. only, for it is not enough. However, if you desire the espalier for decorative purposes only, or if you do not care about the quantities of fruit the tree will bear. you may plant the trees where they receive less sun.

"A tree that has been espaliered attains its permanent pattern and the owner should refrain from bending the main structure into his own design. Vertical-type espaliers will not expand in spread, but will continue to grow in height. Horizontal types will continue their spread, but making additional height depends upon the nature of the tree. Fan-shaped espaliers will grow in spread and height but desirable size may be obtained by pruning."

Planting dwarf varieties. The soil and site for dwarf varieties should be about the same as for their big half-brothers, although a little more attention might be paid to the site selection. They should be planted in an open and sunny place, and yet in one that offers at least some protection from strong north winds. Avoid both frost pockets and the tops of hills. City-lot gardeners should not have to worry much about these factors, since surrounding buildings and trees will offer good protection, but country gardeners might have to give the matter considerable thought.

The actual planting should be done according to the recommendations given for planting other trees. although the dimensions of the hole should be proportionally smaller.

For the first few years, you might wish to wrap the trunk in order to offer winter protection, using special elastic wrap available at nurseries and garden centers. And, you might wish to wrap a fine wire mesh around the base of the trunk to protect it from rodents, especially if you live in the country. Dwarf varieties require very little pruning, although crossing limbs and competing limbs should be eliminated at an early stage. All dwarf trees will appreciate a good straw mulch. and otherwise will require the standard care recommended for other fruit trees.

When planting dwarfs and espaliers. a vitally important thing to remember is to plant with the graft-union above the ground.

The graft-union is the point at the bottom of the trunk where the bud of the standard variety has been grafted to the dwarf rootstock. You will recognize it easily by the differences between the two woods. Also, there is a noticeable knob at that point. If you plant the graft-union below the ground, the standard bud will form its own roots, and you will end up with a full-sized tree.

When to Plant

All fruit trees, including dwarfs and espaliers, are best planted in the spring in Wisconsin. Further south, fall-planted trees can withstand the ensuing winter, but our winters are not so kind. Plant early in the spring, soon after the last average frost date In your area.

Pollination

Will you have to plant more than one tree of a kind in order to assure pollination and fruit development?

It depends. Peaches, nectarines, sour cherries, and European plums are self-fruitful, meaning that you need plan no more than one tree to assure fruit production. At the same time, you will get larger crops if more than one tree is planted.

On the other hand, apples, apricots, Japanese plums, sweet cherries, and pears require cross-pollination, and you must plant more than one of each tree class. If you simply don't have room for two apple trees in your backyard, however, look to the neighbor's yard for possible help. If there is a nearby apple tree, pollination will be effected. Pollinating bees, after all, don't observe property lines.

If you are in doubt, ask the nursery person who sells you the tree. Mail-order catalogs will tell you whether you need two of any particular tree for cross-pollination.

How to Plant a Tree

"It is better to plant a one-dollar tree in a five-dollar hole, than to plant a five-dollar tree in a one-dollar hole."

I don't remember who said that, but it must have been said a long time ago, considering the price of trees today. Nevertheless, those words should be remembered. The scrawniest and barest sapling can be made to grow, if provided with a good root environment, while the hardiest of nursery trees can wither and die because of improper planting. Take the time to do the job right.

The hole should be dug about three feet deep, and wide enough to accommodate the tree's roots easily when they are spread out naturally on the ground. Most roots are cut back at the nursery, and so the diameter of the hole will probably be from three to five feet.

It should be emphasized that this will require a lot of digging, not easily accomplished. In planting a tree, you can expect to move forty bushels or more of soil, and then you will have to move it back. Doing the job properly will take at least three hours, and you should have a helper after you are ready to set the tree into the hole.

After the hole has been dug, take a crowbar and break up the subsoil at the bottom of the hole and around the sides. This is especially important if the soil is packed and hard. Your service here will make it much easier for the young roots to push into the soil and get themselves established. Work aged compost into the loosened subsoil, adding a few good handfuls of bone meal. Then, line the bottom of the hole with four inches of good garden loam. If the loam is not particularly rich, you may add some aged compost to it. Never use fresh manure.

(A mistake made by many people is to add gravel to the hole in an attempt to improve drainage. This actually causes problems for the tree, because it traps water under the roots and makes the tree stand in saturated soil.)

You are now ready to set in the tree. If the tree's roots are encased in a burlap ball, simply make a mound of soil in the bottom of the hole

and set in the tree, well centered. If the tree has come in a tub or container, remove the tree from the container as gently as possible, trying not to disturb the roots, and set it into the hole. If the tree's roots are bare, trim back any broken ones past the point of the break, spread out all the roots in their natural positions, and set the tree in as gently as possible on a mound of soil, so that the roots may dip downward naturally. Bare-root trees should be planted only when they are leafless and dormant. Be sure that the root system does not dry out before planting.

At this point, you should call for your helper. Someone has to hold the tree upright while the other works with the roots in the hole. If you are going to stake the tree, now is the time to drive in two supporting stakes at opposite ends of the hole. Drive them about one foot into the bottom of the hole and allow five feet of stake above the soil line. (Adding the three-foot depth of the hole, this means a nine-foot stake.) By driving in the stakes at this stage, you will avoid injuring any of the roots.

Check the tree now, to see whether it will be at its proper planting depth when the hole is filled in. If it is too low in the ground, mound soil under the roots until it is at the proper height. Remember, though, that it will settle just a little as you fill in around the roots. Now, begin to pack the soil around the roots. One person holds the tree steady, while the other fills in good garden loam, very gently and very carefully, around the roots. Allow no air pockets, for they will injure the roots. During the filling operation, flood the hole with water several times while the other person gently rocks the tree just slightly, so that the movement of soil around the roots will fill in any air pockets.

When the hole is finally filled, soak it very thoroughly. Then come back in an hour and work the soil around the tree into a slight basin or saucer, so that rainwater will be directed toward the trunk. Now is the time also to wrap the trunk with tree wrap, which will help to prevent summer sunscald and winter drying, and to place wire mesh around the base of the trunk to foil rodents that otherwise might nibble the tender bark during the winter. After you have finished these wrappings, you may attach the trunk of the tree to the supporting stakes. using hose-covered wire.

You are finished.

In a few days, mulch the tree with hay or aged compost, clear out to the drip line. (If you are planting the tree in a lawn, of course, you will not want to do this.) Keep the mulch two feet away from the trunk, however, to remove rodent nesting places.

Fertilizing

Unless your soil is particularly poor, you should not have to fertilize your fruit trees to obtain normal production. You will, however, increase production if you do provide additional nutrients. Manure is the traditional fertilizer for fruit trees, but you may substitute good compost if you cannot obtain manure. In the orchard or field, the manure is simply spread beneath the tree, out to the drip line, and allowed to seep into the soil with the rains. This method has obvious disadvantages on a city lot. Here, dig small holes (about 18 inches deep) around the tree, spacing them fairly evenly out to the drip line. Save the sod for replacement later. Nearly fill the holes with manure or compost, cover this with a two-inch layer of topsoil, and replace the sod. This is a two-hour job, per tree, but it does not have to be done more than once a year. The only disadvantage is that the grass on top of the holes might well turn emerald green and grow twice as quickly as the surrounding grass—which should tell you something about manure. Dig next year's holes in different spots.

Many gardeners with small orchards also grow cover crops to help provide nutrients for the trees. Plant a winter cover of vetch or clover, and turn it under with a rotary tiller in the spring. (More information about cover crops is given on page 12.) Never fertilize in late summer or fall, since this practice will stimulate new and tender growth going into winter, when the new wood can be destroyed by subzero winds.

Summer Care

Many gardeners, having planted a tree, think that it needs no further care to flourish. In truth, the first summer is a critical time for the young tree, as it attempts to adapt to its new environment.

If your garden needs water, you may be assured that your tree saplings need water, too, during that first summer. Provide it during times of drought. You might also provide a thick mulch around the tree, to conserve moisture and keep down weeds. The mulch should extend out to the tree line, but should be kept eight inches away from the trunk to avoid problems with mice. Check carefully for signs of insect and disease damage that first year, too, and take proper action early on, to avoid big problems later.

Sunscald. This is a problem in winter. The sun is lower in the sky in winter, so its rays hit the trunk at nearly a right angle. If there is snow on the ground, the reflection intensifies the glaring of the sunlight, heating the tree bark to dangerously high temperatures. And this can cause premature flow of the tree sap.

"When this occurs in the late afternoon on the southwest side of the tree," cautions Stark Brothers experts, "it's only a short while before the sun goes down. Then the temperature quickly drops below freezing and this rapid temperature change causes the injury."

To prevent sunscald, wrap the trunk with the white stretchable wrap sold by nurseries and garden centers for the purpose. The wrap will protect the trunk in both summer and winter. Its white color reflects, rather than absorbs, heat from the sun. Commercial fruit growers often whitewash the trunks of their older trees with a white latex paint.

Pruning Fruit Trees

Many gardeners approach pruning with trepidation, fearing that they will injure or kill the tree, or at least deform it irreversibly. Actually, if a tree needs pruning, even a rather bad job of it is likely to be more beneficial than not pruning at all. Far from injuring a tree, pruning rejuvenates it. The removal of the more undesirable limbs will stimulate the growth of the others, since they will receive a proportionately larger share of moisture from the roots. Too-heavy branches will be cut back, thus lessening the danger of breakage and real injury. More light will filter down to the tree's leaves and fruit, improving production and aiding the health of the entire tree. You should be no more afraid to prune your fruit tree than you are to prune your lawn, which in fact you do every time you mow it.

The one danger you must guard against is infection. You can help to prevent it by sterilizing your tools before pruning, by making your cuts sharp, clean, and close to the trunk of the tree, by painting the exposed wood of large cuts (over two inches) with one of the products designed for this purpose, and by pruning in very early spring, before the leaves have come out and before there are disease spores in the air. (The other advantage of early spring pruning is that you can see the branches in far greater detail than you can after leafing has occurred.)

Fruit trees should be pruned every year, to remove dead wood, to eliminate weak and broken branches, to train the tree into a pleasing and productive form, to eliminate crossing or competing branches, to control the height and width of the tree, and, by all of these, to increase fruit production.

For the first few years of your tree's life, pruning should be directed mainly toward establishing a good framework that will make the tree strong in maturity. Lateral branches should be allowed to grow from the main leader (nursery term for the young trunk) only insofar as they are spaced evenly, both above and below each other, and around the tree's main leader. The lateral branches should, in general, be well balanced, and you can control this balance by careful and early pruning.

Eliminate, also, those branches that form a small angle with the trunk. The crotches of these branches will be weak and subject to injury. Favor those branches that form a wide angle (60° to 90°) with the trunk, since these will be the strongest.

Never allow any branch to compete with the main leader, or the tree might develop a forked leader, or trunk, that will be subject to splitting in later years. Encourage the development of one clearly defined trunk. If such a competing branch has already developed, prune it just above the first good lateral branch, so that the branch will be trained outward instead of upward.

If several branches develop very close together on a limb, prune out all but the strongest one.

Once you have decided upon the main lateral limbs you wish to encourage, do not prune the growth that comes from these limbs, for the fruit will form on this new and tender growth. Prune only if any of these small branches threaten to disrupt the general form of the tree,

Work compost into the soil out to the tree's drip line; only in this way will you be sure to get nutrients down to the active, outer roots.

or if they grow so numerous as to exclude sunlight and impede air passage.

Pruning is an art, one that will come with practice and with a great deal more detailed information than can be offered in these pages. There are several good books on the subject, and your county Extension agent has illustrated pamphlets. Your interest in pruning will, of course, depend on the number of trees you grow. But no matter how inexperienced you may be, do not neglect this important job because of fear of hurting the tree. Make your plans and do the job as well as you can.

When Trees Won't Bear

If your fruit tree is of bearing age and shows no signs of bearing, the trouble might lie in one or more of several areas:

1. **Lack of pollination**. If the tree is not self-fruiting, it will need another tree of the same variety, or a compatible variety, planted near it. Consult your nursery.

2. **Lack of nutrients**. Apply compost in one of the two methods described earlier in this section.

3. **Nitrogen excess**. An overabundance of nitrogen forces luxuriant leaf growth and discourages fruit development. It is unlikely if organic fertilizing methods are used.

4. **Severe pruning.** If lateral branches are stripped of all spur growth in spring pruning, neither blossoms nor fruit will develop.

5. **Frost damage**. A very heavy frost after trees have blossomed in spring can destroy many or all blossoms, depending upon the severity of the frost and the hardiness of the tree.

6. **Lack of hardiness**. Blossom buds of fruit trees form during the season preceding their blooming. If the tree variety is not hardy in your area, severe winter temperatures can kill the embryo and the pistil in the flower bud. Even though the bud might open the following spring, it will not set fruit. Do not count on trees that are not hardy in your area.

Controlling Insects and Disease

Commercial fruit growers employ a continuing program of chemical control for the insects, fungi, bacteria, and viruses that commonly attack trees and plants. Apple trees are sprayed as many as 16 times in a season. For commercial production of fruit, chemical control is probably necessary, at least at the present time and under the present market structure, since we lack the full technical capability, including disease-resistant varieties, to meet the threats of insects and disease by natural means. Not that commercial growers could not raise good market fruit without chemicals—they could—but natural control methods require far more time to apply, and the commercial grower could not turn to them and still compete in the present market structure.

My organic friends (those more organic than I, that is) might dispute the foregoing statement—and they would have ample fodder for their counterattack, for there are commercial fruit growers today who are operating organically and making a living at it. Most of these pioneer orchard people, however, sell to small specialty markets—stores that advertise and sell organically grown products—and the significantly higher prices that organic fruits bring are testimony enough to the high costs of raising and marketing them.

Home gardeners, however, are in a completely different boat. They will have only a few fruit trees, perhaps a dozen, perhaps only one. They can afford to forgo chemical poisons in favor of natural controls and can produce beautiful fruit in so doing. The difference is that home gardeners do not count their time as an expense of producing food, as commercial growers must. They raise fruit trees because they like to raise fruit trees, and the time spent in working with their trees is rewarded—both immediately, in the outdoor activity and reflective solitude, and later on, when they enjoy the fruits of their harvest. And, because they are organic gardeners, they have the further consolation in that they have produced food without contributing to the poisoning of the earth, sky, and waters.

Principles of Prevention

Before turning to specific insects and diseases, there are some principles of prevention that should be noted carefully and followed rigorously. Their application might well reduce insect and disease problems by half.

1. **Disease-resistant varieties**. Diseases of fruit are most difficult to control, even with chemicals. That is why it is vitally important to buy disease-resistant varieties whenever possible. Resistance characteristics are detailed in the listings of individual fruits.

2. **Clean cultivation and proper pruning**. It is extremely important to keep a clean garden in order to remove the nesting and breeding places of many harmful insects and other pests. All diseased plants should be sunk immediately into the hot center of the compost pile to destroy the disease organisms. If there are too many, they should be burned or discarded in a place where they will not affect other trees. Cankers (lesions of the bark) and diseased limbs should be cut away promptly. before the disease spreads, and open wounds in trees should be painted immediately. Fungus on trees must be removed early. Pruning must be carried out regularly to open the tree to air and lessen the chances of moisture-loving fungus propagation. Loose bark must be scraped off to remove hiding places for insects.

Weeds should be controlled, since they harbor many destructive insects, such as the tree hopper. In fall, gather up leaves and put them into the compost pile. Apple scab fungi live through the winter in the leaves you fail to collect. Keep the garden free of all debris, containers that will collect water, old boards lying on the ground, fallen fruit, and brush piles.

3. **Birds and toads**. Do everything you can to attract birds to your garden. The amount of fruit they eat is small in comparison with the quantities of harmful insects they devour. Feed the birds during the winter, build houses or nesting shelves for them, provide water, and go so far as to leave out bits of string and hair in the spring to encourage the birds to build nests in your yard.

Equally effective, if you can get them, are toads. A toad will eat up to 10,000 insects over a summer. Most of these are garden pests, such as slugs and cutworms, but toads eat caterpillars, too, some of which can find their way to your fruit trees. You would do well to put some of the neighborhood kids to work in rounding up toads for your garden. A toad house can be built by overturning a flower pot, knocking out a door in it, and screwing it slightly into the ground. Keep a sunken pan of water nearby (the toad must sit in it to drink, since he drinks through his skin) and be sure to put both the toad house and the water under a protective bush. If you treat your toads right, they might decide to like your place and stay around for a while. If so, you will have gained valuable new allies.

4. **Beneficial insects.** There are also beneficial insects that, although they do no harm to your trees and plants. will wreak havoc on those insects that do. Chief among these is the ladybug or lady beetle, which feasts voraciously on aphids, scales, and other soft-bodied attackers of plants. Ladybugs can be purchased by mail order, as can praying mantids. These large and formidable-looking insects exist solely on a diet of insects—aphids, caterpillars, and a large assortment of other destructive insects, both large and small. Among other helpful insects are wasps, aphid lions, grasshopper maggots, assassin bugs, dragonflies and damselflies, ground beetles, minute pirate bugs, spiders, and syrphid flies. Learn to identify these insects, and recognize them as friends. (More on this topic, in Chapter 9.)

General Control Measure

In addition to specific control measures for specific insects (which are covered in Chapter 9), there are some general measures that you can carry out on a regular basis to keep down the populations of many insects that attack fruits. These general controls will help to stop trouble before it begins.

1. **Sticky bands.** Some worms and insects are unable to fly, and therefore they crawl up the trunk of the tree to do their damage. Chief among these are the female inchworm moth and the tent caterpillar. Ants also carry aphids up the trunk into trees. You can control these vertical migrations by the use of bands of sticky material, going under the names Tanglefoot, Stickem, and others. The insects that attempt to cross the bands become stuck in them and are destroyed.

Other insects will be induced to hide in a band of corrugated cardboard, the kind that ordinary cartons are made from. Staple a band of cardboard around the trunk of your tree, inspect it regularly, and then remove and destroy it when necessary.

2. **Traps.** Night-flying moths can be killed in large numbers by the use of light traps and insect electrocutors, both commercially available. These traps tend to be expensive and are not particularly pleasant to have around (the electrocutor, for instance, makes a chilling zap sound every time it disposes of a victim), but they do trap thousands of moths that otherwise would lay eggs and breed hundreds of thousands of hungry caterpillars.

3. **Dormant oil spray.** An annual application of dormant oil spray on fruit trees is perhaps the most dramatically effective of the perfectly safe insect control measures. The oil does not poison the insects on contact, but alters their immediate environment so that it is impossible for them to survive. It is harmless to humans and other warm-blooded animals while it is being used, and it will not affect the leaves or fruit of the tree.

Organic gardeners in various parts of the country have reported success in using a 3 percent miscible oil dormant spray to control a broad spectrum of chewing, sucking, and scale insects, including aphids, red spiders, thrips, mealybugs, pear psyllas, mites, and the eggs of codling moth. Oriental fruit moth, various leaf

rollers, and cankerworms. Most of these insects are troublesome in Wisconsin.

The time to apply dormant oil spray is in the early spring, before leafing has occurred, perhaps at the same time that you prune your trees. The oil forms a light film over insect eggs and the coverings of scales, and literally suffocates the hatching insects. Since the oil is harmless, you will not have to worry about putting on too much—but when you buy dormant oil spray, be sure it is not mixed with Bordeaux mixture, arsenate of lead, or other deadly chemicals that can be potentially hazardous to the person who sprays the trees.

4. **Safe insecticides.** Dormant oil spray can be termed an insecticide, because it does kill insects. Two other safe insecticides for occasional use in the fruit orchard are derivatives of plants—Ryania, a powder made from the roots of the South American plant *Ryania speciosa*, and rotenone, made from a combination of several tropical plants. Both are "natural" insecticides. Ryania is effective against cranberry fruitworm, codling moth, Oriental fruit moth, and some other insects that injure fruit trees. Rotenone is used mainly against pests in the vegetable garden and is of little use in the orchard.

Still another safe insecticide is based on a natural, microbial agent, *Bacillus thurngiensis*, which is effective against oakmoth larvae, cankerworms, and tent caterpillars on all trees. (Brand names include Biotrol, BioGuard, and Thuricide.) All of these safe insecticides may be used without fear of poisoning people or pets, or even birds, but none should be used except when real insect troubles appear and cannot be controlled by the general methods previously mentioned.

Major Insect Pests of Fruit

Listed below are the insects that are most likely to attack your fruit trees, vines, canes, shrubs, and plants. Actually, there are literally hundreds of potentially harmful insects, any of which can do damage from time to—but these are the major attackers whose presence might call for special measures. Suggestions for the control of many of them will be found in the chapter devoted to insect control, beginning on page 236.

Apples: Rose chafer, picnic beetle, apple maggot, curculio, tent caterpillar, scales, codling moth, red-banded leaf roller, apple aphid, eye-spotted bud moth, fruit tree roller, oystershell scale, European red mite.

Blueberries: Rose chafer, picnic beetle, apple maggot, curculio, tent caterpillar, some scales.

Cherries: Aphids, buffalo treehopper, plum curcullo, tent caterpillar.

Currants: Currant aphid (leaf louse), currant borer, currant worm.

Grapes: Grape-berry moth, grape cane girdler, grape leafhopper, rose chafer.

Pears: Codling moth, New York weevil, pear leaf blister mite, pear psylla, San Jose scale.

Plums: San Jose scale, plum curculio.

Raspberries: Raspberry cane borer, raspberry root borer.

Strawberries: Slugs, strawberry crown borer, strawberry leafroller, strawberry weevil.

Major Fruit Diseases

Many of the fungi, bacteria, and viruses that produce disease in fruit can be controlled by the same methods recommended for the control of insects. This means the selection of disease-resistant varieties whenever possible. clean cultivation throughout the garden, regular and proper pruning, annual dormant oil spraying, the prompt removal of fallen fruit, and—only as a last resort when all other methods have been exhausted—pesticide application.

Full directions for the chemical control of fruit diseases are readily available at the office of your county Extension agent. Here we will list some of the major diseases of fruits, keys to their recognition, and some nonchemical means of specific control. Using these control methods, in addition to the general controls previously listed, the home gardener will seldom have to resort to chemical controls.

Apples

Apple powdery mildew. This is a fungus that overwinters in the bud of the apple blossom. It becomes active in the spring, when leaves appear, spreading a gray, powdery mildew over the leaves and twigs. Fruit may be stunted and cracked, showing fine russet-colored lines.

Prune out the twigs that appear to be heavily infested and dispose of them immediately. McIntosh is a favorite Wisconsin variety that's somewhat resistant to apple powdery mildew.

Apple scab. This disease is caused by the fungus *Venturia inaequalis*, which overwinters in leaves that lie on the ground. Spores are released into the air in spring, affecting the new growth. Brown spots appear on the fruit, and the fruit may be stunted and cracked. Leaves will show the same brown spots.

The major methods of control are the removal of fallen leaves in autumn and the cutting out of heavily infested twigs during regular spring pruning. Nova Easygro, Redfree, Prima, Priscilla, and Jonafree are all resistant varieties.

Fire blight. See under pears. There are now many resistant apple cultivars.

Cedar apple rust. Symptoms are bright orange spots on apple foliage and to a lesser extent on fruit. A related fungus, quince rust, attacks Courtland apples, causing a hard green lesion on the fruit. The disease goes back and forth between apple trees and red cedar trees. You can prevent attack by keeping apple trees at least one mile from any red cedars, or by selecting resistant varieties (mentioned a little later on).

Blueberries

Few diseases of blueberries have proved troublesome in the home garden. Any that might begin to appear should be eliminated by the prompt pruning of the affected branches and twigs.

Cherries, Sour

Diseases are rarely a major problem with sour cherries grown in the home garden. One that might prove bothersome is brown rot, a fungus that attacks and rots the fruit thoroughly. Keep a close watch on the developing fruit and remove any that show signs of rot. The fungus can work clear through the fruit and into the twig and so the twig should be removed also. Be sure to pick up all fruit and leaves that have fallen prematurely, for these are likely to be diseased.

Currants and Gooseberries

Anthracnose. Although currants and gooseberries are virtually trouble-free, they may be subject to occasional attack by any one of several diseases, among them anthracnose, which is characterized by dark brown and sunken spots on the fruit. Control rests in pruning out and removing affected branches promptly.

Crown gall. This disease attacks the plants at the soil level. It will not actually kill the plant or interfere greatly with its production. If it does, the plant should be uprooted and replaced.

Mildew. This fungus might prove bothersome if the weather is particularly cool and wet and if the bushes are planted under large trees. Control mildew by removing the cobweblike substance from the top surfaces of the leaves and by opening up the plant to greater sun and air by judicious pruning.

Cane blight. This is a fungus disease that attacks when the bushes are heavy with fruit, causing the entire cane to wilt. Again, the affected canes should be removed promptly so that the disease does not spread. Clean cultivation and conscientious pruning are especially important to the prevention of this fungus disease.

Grapes

Black rot. This fungus disease affects both the leaves and the fruit, as well as the blossoms. Light spots appear on the grapes when they are half-grown, and the fruit gradually turns black and shrivels up.

Remove any affected fruit during the season, and be sure to remove all plant wastes after the season is over. The fungus overwinters in the parts of the plant it has affected. By removing all these wastes, you will drastically reduce next year's spore population.

Downy mildew. This fungus is particularly bothersome in wet seasons, since it requires plenty of moisture in order to flourish. The first sign of infestation is the appearance of pale, yellow blotches on the upper surfaces of the leaves. The blotches will grow in size and will eventually turn brown. The fruit will be affected, too, being covered with a white mildew. Older fruit will turn brown if the disease is not checked.

Remove affected plant parts promptly, and prune vines properly each year in order to promote plenty of sun and good air circulation. The varieties Fredonia, Niagara, and Delaware are very susceptible to downy mildew.

Pears

Fire blight. This bacterial disease, also called pear blight, can affect apples as well as pears. As its name implies, the affected portions of the tree look as if they have been burned black, including the leaves, flowers, twigs, and fruit. The infection enters the blossoms at pollinating time, often being carried by bees.

It is crucial to keep an eye out for fire blight, and to cut away the diseased parts of the tree well below the infection. Burn the waste promptly. Pears are rarely grown commercially in Wisconsin because of fire blight, which can wipe out an orchard in short order. One or two trees in the home garden, however, are far less likely to be affected. Nevertheless, constant checks and, if needed, immediate surgery are the best answer to fire blight.

Pear scab. Similar to apple scab in appearance, effect, and control is pear scab. There are resistant pear varieties, some of which are suitable for growing in Wisconsin. Check with your nursery to see which are recommended for your area.

Plums

Brown rot and black knot. These diseases, which rot and destroy the fruit, can most easily be controlled by clean cultivation, prompt removal of fallen fruit and leaves, and, especially, careful and proper pruning. Prune away all branches very close to the trunk or larger branch from which they grew, and paint even small cuts on plum trees to prevent infestation. Remove all diseased material promptly and burn it.

Raspberries

The United States Department of Agriculture gives these six steps for the general control and prevention of all raspberry diseases. All six make very good sense:

1. Choose disease-resistant varieties.
2. Plant only healthy stock.
3. Plant black or purple varieties in fields that have not recently been used for tomatoes, potatoes, or eggplant. (Note: These vegetables are subject to many of the same diseases, and may spread them to raspberries.)
4. Remove old canes after harvest.
5. Keep the field clean of weeds and fallen leaves.
6. Destroy seriously diseased plants. Use pesticides when needed.

These measures alone will probably make others unnecessary. Nevertheless, there are some specific diseases of raspberries that you should watch out for:

Anthracnose. See under currants and gooseberries.

Cane blight. See under currants and gooseberries.

Mosaic. This is a virus disease, and a serious attacker of raspberries. You can recognize it in the young leaves by the mottled yellow and green patches. Later in the spring, green blisters will appear on the leaves, surrounded with yellowish tissue. The entire plant is stunted, and the fruit will be ruined by a severe attack.

Check the plants often and dig out any that are diseased. Burn the waste immediately, to prevent spread of the disease. Latham is the standard variety of red raspberry in Wisconsin, and fortunately it is fairly resistant to mosaic. Newburg, a variety suited to southern

Wisconsin, is also fairly resistant. All black raspberries are very susceptible to disease, including mosaic, and are planted only at the gardener's peril.

Raspberry leaf curl. This virus disease is usually confined to wild raspberries and black raspberries, but it can spread to the red varieties. Canes become stunted, leaves curl, turn yellowish, and eventually become stiff and brittle. For control, remove and burn all affected plants. More important, never plant red raspberries near black or wild varieties.

Spur blight. A fungus disease that attacks red raspberries, spur blight can be spotted by infestation appearing first on the buds nearer the ground. Brown or purple spots will appear at the buds. Soon, the buds shrivel and become inactive. For control, remove infected canes promptly and destroy them.

Strawberries

Black root rot. This is a disease that seems to affect roots that are not healthy in the first place. Roots turn black, rot, and die, killing the plant. The best answer to black root rot is to buy healthy plants and then to plant them in good soil, well drained and well composted. Premier and Catskill, two varieties that do well in Wisconsin, show resistance to this disease.

Fruit rot. This is a fungus that attacks the ripening fruit during rainy periods. For control, keep the plants mulched with straw, to keep the fruit off the wet ground, and pick all ripe fruit after a rain, to prevent the spores of the disease from spreading to the green fruit.

Leaf scorch. Small reddish-brown or purple spots are the clue to this disease. Heavy clay soils that remain wet after rain will produce susceptible plants, and so the best prevention is to assure good drainage before planting strawberries.

Leaf spot. This is a fungus disease characterized by spots on the plant's leaves. The spots begin as purple ones, gradually changing to tan, and then to white. Wet weather and frequent rains will help to spread the spores of this disease.

The best prevention is to choose resistant plants. In Wisconsin one of the most popular of the resistant varieties is Premier, although there are others.

Fruit Tree Varieties for Wisconsin

When choosing a fruit tree, you should be guided by two major considerations: First, a variety that is hardy in your area; and second—among those hardy varieties—one that bears fruit that your family really likes. It is surprising how many people actually plant fruit trees when they have little or no idea of the actual characteristics of the fruit.

When it comes to hardiness, no rigid lines exist. Some varieties are definitely hardy in your area, some don't stand a chance, and many are in that gray area in between. Peaches, for instance, are not recommended for growing in Wisconsin because they are supposedly not hardy here. Nevertheless, many Wisconsin gardeners have grown peach trees for years, and they harvest beautiful fruit annually. The fact is that the official recommendations, which come from university research centers and are published in the pamphlets distributed by your county Extension agent, are usually geared not to the home gardener but to the commercial fruit grower. Of course, it would be foolish for a farmer in Stevens Point to plant an acre of peach trees and hope thereby to establish a successful commercial enterprise. At the same time, the home gardener in Wisconsin's milder areas can plant peach trees with a good expectation of success. You must choose the very hardiest of peach varieties, of course, and you must not gamble more than you can afford to lose. Chances are, however, that the extent of your loss will be irregular fruiting, smaller size of fruit than could be obtained further south, and occasional winter or spring killing of blossoms and resultant loss of fruit for that season. The trees, though. will have an excellent chance to survive, grow to maturity, and produce enough peaches to make any gardener proud and happy.

The fruit variety recommendations that follow are on the conservative side, nearly all based on research conducted by horticulturists of the University of Wisconsin. Their recommendations are solid ones, based on years of experience, research, and trials made in many parts of the state. To these, I have added other varieties that, according to reports from other growers both here and in other states, appear to stand an excellent chance of thriving in Wisconsin.

Apples

Although Wisconsin is known throughout the nation for its sour cherry production, there are more apple trees than cherry trees here, and a large part of the reason is that apple trees are so popular in home gardens. The choice of varieties is a wide one.

Following are some apple varieties recommended in the bulletin *Apple Cultivars for Wisconsin,* by T. R. Roper and E. J. Stang (Bulletin No. A2105) and *Home Fruit Cultivars for Northern Wisconsin,* by B. R. Smith and T. R. Roper (No. A2488), both bulletins available from your Wisconsin county Extension office or from Cooperative Extension Publications, Rm. 245, 30 N. Murray St., Madison, WI 53715; phone 608 262-3346. From these bulletins, I have selected only varieties that are hardy enough to grow in all parts of the state.

Lodi. Ripens early August. A large green-to-yellow apple with soft flesh and tart taste, used for cooking. Not a good storage apple, or keeper. Susceptible to apple scab; very susceptible to cedar apple rust and fire blight.

McIntosh. Originated in Canada, from a chance seedling on the McIntosh homestead. Now the most popular apple in Wisconsin. Matures the second week in September. A handsome large red apple with tender, juicy, aromatic flesh. A heavy annual producer that comes into bearing quite young. Very subject to scab, but very resistant to rust. A good all-purpose apple, a favorite at farmers' markets. A good keeper.

Jerseymac. A McIntosh-type apple that matures in mid-to-late August. Yellow skin with red overcolor, medium to small fruits with firm, mildly tart, white flesh. Excellent flavor for eating fresh, but not a good keeper. Very susceptible to scab, very resistant to rust, susceptible to blight.

Cortland. Resembles McIntosh with lighter red skin color and firmer flesh. Another very popular Wisconsin apple. Generally ripens just after McIntosh. A good keeper. Very susceptible to scab, and somewhat to rust and blight.

Northwest Greening. Originated in Waupaca County from a chance seedling. Matures in late September. A very large and smooth-skinned fruit, waxy yellow or greenish. Fresh yellowish, firm, juicy, with slight aroma. A good keeper. One of the best baking and cooking apples. Somewhat susceptible to scab, rust, and blight.

Spartan. A British Columbia native apple, ready for harvest in early October. Fruit is deep red with white flesh. A good, sweet, eating apple and a good keeper. Resistant to rust, but somewhat susceptible to scab and blight.

Macoun. Matures with Spartan. Fruit is deep red with white flesh. A firm, crisp, juicy, and sweet all-purpose apple, and a moderately good keeper. Very susceptible to scab, resistant to rust, susceptible to blight.

Empire. Matures with Spartan. A deep-red apple with creamy flesh, firm, crisp, and sweet. For eating fresh. A good keeper. Very susceptible to scab, but resistant to rust and blight.

Haralson. Originated in Minnesota. Matures in early October. Fruit is medium to large with red striped skin and creamy white, crisp, juicy, and tart flesh. An all-purpose apple and a moderately good keeper. Susceptible to scab, but somewhat resistant to rust and blight.

Honeygold. Matures just after Spartan, in the second week of October. A yellow-skinned apple with creamy, crisp, juicy, and blandly sweet flesh. A Golden Delicious-type apple for harsher climates. A moderate keeper, susceptible to scab, rust, and blight.

Fireside/Connell Red. A Minnesota native. Matures with Honeygold. A large apple with red over yellow skin, creamy, crisp, juicy, and sweet flesh, good for eating and cooking. A good keeper. Susceptible to scab and blight, but resistant to rust.

Nova Easygro. Matures in mid-to-late September. A large apple with red blushed skin and creamy, firm, slightly juicy, sweet flesh. A moderately good keeper, best for fresh eating. It is the most resistant of the hardy apples, very resistant to scab and resistant to rust and blight.

The following apples are also disease-resistant, but are somewhat less hardy than the varieties listed above, which are hardy throughout the state. The following are hardy in all but USDA Zone 3, the very coldest section of Wisconsin.

Redfree. Matures in mid-to-late August. A bright red apple with white to creamy flesh. Crisp, juicy, and mildly tart to sweet, good for both fresh use and cooking. A moderately good keeper, and its quality improves in storage. Very resistant to scab and rust, and resistant to fire blight.

Prima. Matures in early September. Red on green skin with white to cream flesh. Soft texture with mild flavor, for eating fresh and cooking. A moderately good keeper. Very resistant to scab, resistant to blight, but very susceptible to rust.

Priscilla. Matures the second week of September. Medium to large fruit with red over yellow skin and white-to-green flesh. A crisp, coarse, and sweet eating apple, and a good keeper. Hardy only in Zone 5. Very resistant to scab and rust, resistant to blight.

Jonafree. Matures mid-to-late September. Medium to small fruit with red skin and pale yellow flesh. Crisp, juicy, mildly tart taste. For fresh use. Moderately good keeper. Resembles Jonathan but is hardier. Very resistant to scab, and resistant to rust and blight.

Liberty. Matures in early October. Medium-to-large fruits have purple-red skin and light yellow flesh. Crisp, juicy, sprightly flavor, moderately tart, like McIntosh. A good all-purpose apple. Very resistant to scab and rust, resistant to blight. One of the best disease-resistant apples.

Apricots

Several varieties of apricots can be grown with good chances of success in Wisconsin's warmer regions.

Wilson Delicious. Perhaps the hardiest of the apricots. Large, excellent-tasting fruit. Good for eating fresh, canning, cooking, freezing, and drying.

Stark Earli-Orange. An early freestone variety with firm and juicy fruits. The tree is handsome and makes a nice ornamental. Offered by Stark Brothers.

Sungold and **Moongold**. Both developed at the University of Minnesota and both available from Farmer Seed and Nursery. Sungold ripens in early August, bears golden, freestone fruit, is attractive both in spring bloom and autumn color. Moongold has a sweeter flavor, is good for jam and sauce, and bears slightly earlier. Each needs cross-pollination, which can be supplied by the other.

Cherries

Sour cherries are the pride of Wisconsin's Door Peninsula, but they can be grown in most parts of Wisconsin, the chances for success increasing with the mildness of the winters. Although sour cherries are generally considered fit only for pies and baking, many people love to eat them fresh, with a bit of sugar sprinkled over them. They freeze and can beautifully.

Montmorency. Originated in France. Medium-red, large fruit; tart and rather firm flesh. Trees generally uniformly productive annually. The most popular sour cherry in Wisconsin. Zone 5 and the southern part of Zone 4.

North Star.* Originated in Minnesota. Tree small, very hardy in wood and fruit bud. Can be grown in areas too cold for Montmorency. Zones 5 and 4.

Meteor.* Originated in Minnesota. A large cherry with a light red skin. Tree is both hardy and attractive. Zones 5 and 4.

Early Richmond. Medium-size fruit, bright red color. A good producer, bears at an early age. Fruit ripens early. Zones 5 and 4.

Cherries, Sweet

A few sweet cherry varieties might be tried, with no guarantee of success, in Wisconsin's Zone 5. For the adventurous:

Schmidt's Biggareau. Similar to the popular Bing, which is less hardy. Large, very dark red fruit. Excellent for eating fresh.

Venus. A relatively new variety. Deep, glossy red fruit, highly resistant to cracking. Good-quality flesh. Tree is medium size, spreads freely and openly, needs little pruning.

Van. Similar to Bing in color, flavor, form, and firmness. One of the hardiest of the sweet cherries.

Emperor Francis. Large, high-quality, medium-red fruit. Resists cracking during wet seasons. Tree is medium size. Good producer.

Peaches

All the peaches are not down in Georgia. Most Wisconsin gardeners can grow peaches of excellent quality. This was not true in years past, but modern breeders have discovered and developed varieties that stand an excellent chance of producing in all but the top third of the state.

Wisconsin. This variety was developed from a chance seedling found growing in central Wisconsin, where it had survived many severe winters without injury. It is a large, firm, freestone variety with yellow flesh.

Marquette. This tree originated in Michigan's northern peninsula, where winters are pretty severe, too. The fruit is a freestone of medium size, white flesh. and excellent quality.

Reliance. Perhaps the hardiest peach variety of all, Reliance was developed at the University of New Hampshire, where winters equal our own in severity. This variety has survived winters of 25 degrees below zero and has produced full crops in the following season.

Polly or **Eskimo**. Developed at Iowa State University, this variety has survived temperatures of 15 below. It might be the hardiest of the white-fleshed varieties.

(Other varieties that show some evidence of hardiness include Goldray, Golden Jubilee, Cresthaven, Kalhaven, New Sun Haven, Champion, Sunapee, and Frost King.)

Pears

As mentioned previously in this chapter, pears are not often grown commercially in Wisconsin because of the high incidence of fire blight. They are, however, popular in many home gardens, where the investment is smaller and the trees can receive close and regular attention. Most pears are not self-fruiting, and so you must either plant two trees or be certain that a single tree has been specially grafted to be self-pollinating.

According to Malcolm N. Dana, Elden J. Stang, and Daniel L. Mahr, in their bulletin *Pear Production in Wisconsin* (Bulletin No. A2072), pears may be grown successfully in the southern third of the state. The hardiest pear cultivars, they say, will tolerate winter temperatures down to 25° below zero. Cultivars such as Bosc, Anjou, and Bartlett will tolerate temperatures to -20° or slightly lower. These grow well in areas near Lake Michigan in the southern third of the state and along the Mississippi River Valley as far north as La Crosse, but may be injured in harsh winters.

From that bulletin, here are the recommended pear cultivars for Wisconsin home gardens:

Parker. Originated in Minnesota. Tree upright, fairly hardy. Susceptible to fire blight. Fruit large, roundish, yellow-blushed red; flesh whitish and juicy. Quality fair. Season mid-to-late September. Needs cross-pollination.

Flemish Beauty. Originated in Belgium. Tree vigorous, often spreading, quite hardy. Fruit medium in size, roundish; flesh yellowish white, firm, juicy, and sweet, quality very good. Season late September. Needs cross-pollination for best results and is an excellent pollinator for other varieties.

Clapp's Favorite. Originated in Massachusetts. Tree large, upright, generally productive and hardy. Susceptible to fire blight. Fruit much like Bartlett, but ripens at least a week earlier than Bartlett. Chief fault of the fruit is that it softens at the center when ripening on the tree. Must be picked about 10 days before it ripens. Needs cross-pollination.

Bartlett. Originated in England. Tree medium size, upright, fairly hardy and productive. Is susceptible to fire blight. Probably the most popular variety. Fruit matures in September, is large, clear yellow, and smooth. Flesh is white, juicy, and of good quality.

Bosc. A high-quality pear. Has buttery sweet flesh, very good general quality. The skin is brownish and heavily russeted.

Lincoln. Medium to small fruit. Flesh is coarse and granular but sweet. Lincoln matures in mid-September and is among the hardier cultivars.

Seckel. Fruit is small, skin is smooth, yellowish-brown, sometimes russetred. Flesh is juicy with an aromatic spicy flavor and good general quality. Matures in early October. Seckel and Bartlet are not pollen compatible, and so another cultivar should be used as a pollen source for these cultivars. *Seckel is resistant to fire blight.*

Anjou. A large, blocky, winter pear with excellent fresh-eating quality. This is the standard commercial winter pear. Anjou is not highly productive, but the fruit quality is excellent. It is susceptible to fire blight and is only moderately winter-hardy.

Luscious. Medium to small fruit, shape similar to Bartlett. Flesh is creamy white, juicy, very sweet, and of good quality. Has proven hardy in limited tests in Wisconsin. Matures in early October. Is resistant bur not immune to fire blight.

Plums

Plums are perhaps the easiest of tree fruits to grow in Wisconsin. Many are hardy throughout the state. They are not particular about soil type, and they require relatively little pruning. Further, varieties such as Mount Royal, Stanley, and Wisconsin Prune are excellent for canning. There are two groups—red and blue. The following recommendations and descriptions are from the Smith and Roper bulletin, *Home Fruit Cultivars for Northern Wisconsin:*

Blue (European or Prune) Plums

The following blue plum cultivars do not require cross-pollination.

Mount Royal. Very good, hardy blue plum for southern Wisconsin. Small, round, attractive fruit. Clingstone type. Good for fresh use, canning, and freezing. Ripens early September.

Stanley. Late blooming, heavy annual producer. Good growth habit, hardiness, and productivity. Freestone type with sweet, rich flavor. Yields are heavier if planted with Mount Royal. Excellent for fresh use and processing. Moderately hardy.

Red Plums

The following red plum cultivars require cross-pollination. The cultivars Kaga or Toka will serve as a pollinizer for the following red cultivars.

Underwood. Round fruit is medium-sized with red skin and yellow flesh. Clingstone type. Good quality. Very hardy tree. Ripens early to mid-August, extending over a long season.

LaCrescent. Small, red-blushed, yellow fruit. Excellent for fresh use and very good for jam. Freestone type. Tree is vigorous, very hardy and productive. Ripens mid-August.

Pipestone. Very large, red-fruited cultivar with yellow, sweet, clingstgone flesh. Tree is very hardy and productive. Ripens about mid-August.

Alderman. Large, burgundy-red fruit. Clingstone type with soft flesh and sweet, slightly astringent flavor. Excellent quality for fresh use and preserves. Ripens the third week in August. A new introduction from Minnesota.

Superior. Excellent quality, large red fruit. Clingstone type. For fresh use and preserves. Unless hand-thinned, tree tends to overload, resulting in small fruit. Moderately hardy. Ripens late August.

Kaga. Bright red fruit is small to medium-sized. Clingstone flesh is firm, meaty, and characterized by a strong but pleasing flavor. Good for fresh use and cooking. Tree is small, hardy, and productive. Ripens early August.

Toka. Small-to-medium-sized red fruit with sweet, somewhat spicy flavor. Clingstone type. Extremely hardy. Ripens mid-August.

Cherry Plums

Cherry plums are small-statured trees resulting from hybrids between sandcherry and Japanese (red) plums. They are extrelely hardy and early to ripen, and will begin to bear in one to two years. They require a pollinizer. Cherry plums tolerate most soil types. To maintain productivity and longevity, prune to encourage one-year-old wood.

Opata. One of the hardiest and most productive of the cherry plums. Purple-green fruit with greenish yellow, juicy, clingstone flesh. Good for fresh use and cooking. Ripens mid-August.

Oka. Largest of the cherry plums and also the least hardy. Medium-sized, clingstone fruit with deep reddish purple skin and flesh. Good for fresh use and sauce. Ripens mid-to-late August.

Sapalta. Fruit is dull reddish purple, somewhat clingstone and of excellent quality for all uses. Tree is small, very productive, and hardy. Ripens late August.

Red Diamond. Freeston type fruit is maroon with firm, ruby red flesh that is very sweet. For fresh use or preserves. Compact growth habit and very hardy.

Compass. Fruit is small and dark purple-red with yellow clingstone flesh. Juicy and sweet but somewhat astringent. Good for fresh use or processing. Vigorous, productive, vase-shaped tree. Ripens late August to early September. Used as a pollinizer for all other cherry plums.

Growing Small Fruits

Small fruits can fit into many spots around the home grounds. Grapes, blueberries, currants, and gooseberries are often planted near lot lines in city gardens, where they provide some privacy as well as food. Strawberries are usually worked into the vegetable garden, although they can occupy their own spot in nearly any sunny place. Rhubarb, watermelons, and muskmelons are considered fruit by those who eat them, although growers usually treat them as vegetables. In this book, you will find cultural directions for all three in the chapter devoted to vegetables.

Blueberries

Blueberries have long been native to Wisconsin, especially in the northern and central regions of the state, and there is no reason why nursery-bred stock will not do well in our home gardens. If you pay attention to a few precautions, you can harvest quarts of the luscious berries each year.

The three general types of blueberries are lowbush, highbush, and half-high hybrids. Of the three, the last is perhaps best suited to home production in our climate. Blueberries will tolerate winter temperatures to about 20 below zero without much problem. Much below that, the fruit buds (which are formed during the previous season) begin to die off and the crop will be diminished. A high snowbank, however, will protect plants from severe temperatures. You can create this bank easily, with a snowblower, but be careful not to break the branches by piling on wet, heavy snow.

Blueberries ripen in from 60 to 90 days after blossoming, depending on the variety. If the growing season is under 100 days, the earlier lowbush or half-high hybrids should be planted.

Soil. Blueberries will grow in most good garden soils, so long as they are loose and well

drained. The one important soil requirement is acidity. Blueberries need a pH of 4.2 to 5.5 to produce normally. If your soil is on the alkaline side, it can be corrected for blueberries by incorporating plenty of leaf mold to a depth of 15 inches. Choose the more acid leaves for this purpose, such as sugar maple, white oak, or red maple. White ash leaves should not be used, since their pH is about 6.8. (See page 19 for more complete directions on correcting soil pH.)

Culture. Plant the bushes in late April or early May in a fully sunny place. The soil should be well composted and the compost should include peat and sawdust, but no lime. Set the plants about four feet apart in both directions, and then mulch them with an acid material such as sawdust or peat. They should need no fertilizer after that, although they will respond to an annual application of compost tea. In the first year, give them an application about four weeks after planting, and another when the blossoms have faded. Most important is the mulch. Experiments at the Ohio Agricultural Experiment Station showed that mulched blueberries outproduced the unmulched plantings by 80 to 152 percent! In other words, you might be able to double your production simply by adding a mulch.

Pruning. Prune away only dead or broken branches for the first two or three years. Then, to maintain productive plants, thin out the plants annually by cutting out some older branches that may not be productive any longer and the very slender ones that also will not produce well. Harder pruning will produce fewer but larger berries.

Varieties. There are eight varieties recommended for Wisconsin gardens by G. C. Klingbell, professor of horticulture at the University of Wisconsin. The first two in the following list are half high hybrids, and the remaining six are highbush varieties. They are listed in order of their hardiness, from the most hardy to the least hardy: Northland, Bluehaven, Bluecrop, Rubel, Earliblue, Rancocas, Berkeley, and Pemberton.

Here are the same eight varieties, this time listed in order of their ripening (from earliest to latest): Earliblue, Northland, Bluehaven, Rancocas, Bluecrop, Berkeley, Pemberton, and Rubel.

Finally, here are the same eight again, this time listed in order of the size of their fruit, from largest to smallest: Berkeley, Bluecrop, Earliblue, Bluehaven, Pemberton, Northland, Rancocas, and Rubel.

A little scanning will indicate that perhaps Bluecrop—a highbush variety—might be the best bet for Wisconsin. It has the second-largest fruits of the eight, is third in the hardiness category, and ripens in a time only slightly longer than average.

In their bulletin, *Home Fruit Cultivars for Northern Wisconsin,* Smith and Roper suggest the following five "half-high" cultivars for trial: Northcountry, St. Cloud, Northblue, Northsky, and Friendship. (The last is a new introduction from the University of Wisconsin.)

Currants, Gooseberries, and Elderberries

Currants, gooseberries, and elderberries are listed and discussed together because the culture of these three plants is identical, as are their insect and disease problems (which are few). The uses of the fruit are similar, as well. They are all used extensively for jellies and jams. Some people love the tart taste of fully ripe currants, eaten fresh with a little sugar sprinkled on them, while almost everyone likes gooseberry pie and elderberry jam.

These are easy fruits to grow. They will do well even in partial shade, and they respond well to Wisconsin's cool climate. They are little bothered by insects and disease, and they make attractive foliage plants and hedges.

(Note: There are control zones in Wisconsin in which currants and gooseberries have been eradicated. Check with your county agent before planting either.)

Soil. Currants and gooseberries will grow in any average garden soil. They will respond nicely to an annual application of compost tea or manure tea, although they are not particular in this respect.

Culture. Plants can be propagated by making cuttings from one-year-old canes in the fall, or by setting out nursery plants in the spring. The plants should be set four feet apart in rows six feet apart in late April or early May. The roots of these plants are shallow and easily injured by cultivation. It is best to keep them mulched with hay or straw to keep down weeds without cultivation.

Currants turn red early in the season, but are best when they turn dead ripe (mid- to late August in southern Wisconsin). They are at their sweetest then and perfectly suitable for eating fresh.

Pruning. Annual pruning in the early spring or mid-fall is a good practice for both currants and gooseberries. The best fruit is produced by canes two, three, or four years old. Prune away the older ones in order to direct the plant's energy to the producing canes. Also prune out very slender, broken, and diseased canes.

Current varieties. Red Lake, Cherry, Wilder, White Imperial (sweet-flavored), Minnesota 71.

Gooseberry varieties. Welcome, Pixwell, Downing, Poorman.

Elderberry varieties. Adams, Johns, Nova, York.

(*Jostaberry* is a new fruit that crosses black currant with gooseberry. The fruit is sweet like a ripe gooseberry, but with a touch of sharper currant flavor. It is a heavy producer, and very hardy, ripening in early July.)

Grapes

If you are planting grapes in a new location, it will be worth your while to do the job well, for you are planting for future generations. A good grape arbor, well cared for, will last for 50 or 60 years, possibly more. And, if you have inherited an older planting, it will again be worth your while to take good care of it. Even an ancient, unproductive vine can usually be rejuvenated, using proper pruning and fertilizing methods.

The blue varieties have long been the most popular in Wisconsin, possibly because they are the easiest to grow here. But some green and red grapes will do well here, too, in all but the coldest regions of the state. Grape growers in extreme northern Wisconsin will find the going hard, except in those isolated areas of mildness along Lakes Michigan and Superior. Even in the coldest reaches of Zone 3, however, three blue varieties—Moore's Early, Fredonia, and Van Buren—may be grown successfully. Production might not be so high as in more southerly areas, but these varieties are certainly worth trying on a small scale.

Soil. Grapes will thrive in any average garden loam. They will not do well in very light sands or heavy clays. Sandy loams and gravelly or clay loams are especially recommended.

Culture. Vigorous two-year-old vines are best for planting, although one-year-olds are entirely satisfactory. You may also start your own plants by either layering or rooting hardwood cuttings. Both methods are explained in *Growing Grapes in Wisconsin*, an informative publication available free from your county Extension agent.

Spring planting is recommended in Wisconsin. Choose a sunny location, preferably on a gentle, southern slope. Plants may be set in as soon as the ground can be worked. Holes 12 to 14 inches deep and 16 inches in diameter should be dug 8 feet apart (10 feet for Worden, Concord, and Niagara varieties). Mix in some aged compost (including bone meal or ground granite rock, if you have it) into the soil at the bottom of each hole. Trim back the top of the plant until only one strong cane remains. Then trim that cane back so that only two buds remain. Apply a mulch of hay or straw.

You will need no permanent support for the vines during the first year. In the second year, some sort of trellis will be necessary. Unless you are using an ornamental trellis (such as might be constructed at the side of a porch), you should drive eight-foot support stakes two feet into the ground and string two horizontal wires

through them. Considering that the grape planting is a 50-year proposition, the posts might well be metal ones. There are several commercial vinyards in Wisconsin, and you might tour one of them just to see the planting arrangement. A good one is the Wollersheim Winery, on Hwy. 188, just south of Hwy. 60, near Prairie du Sac.

Fertilize the vines each spring by digging compost into the soil, but don't add too much nitrogen, which will stimulate foliage growth and cause poor cluster formation. Be sure, too, to mulch the vines. At the Ohio Agricultural Experiment Station, straw-mulched grapes yielded 25 percent more than their unmulched counterparts.

Pruning. The real key to growing grapes is pruning. Unpruned grapes will produce so much fruit that it will not ripen well. The fruit will be of poor quality, and the growth of the canes will be impeded. Proper pruning, however, will maintain the balance between cane growth and fruit production that is necessary for good production.

There are several traditional methods of pruning grapes. Here we will consider only one—the Kniffin system—which is the most popular system used east of the Rocky Mountains and certainly the most popular in Wisconsin. We are indebted to Professors G. C. Kingbell, E. K. Wade, and C. F. Koval, of the University of Wisconsin, for the following explanation of the Kniffin system:

First year. After planting, cut back the strongest cane to two buds and remove all other canes. Shoots will arise from the buds. Select the most vigorous shoot and tie it loosely to a temporary, five-foot stake set next to the plant. Remove other shoots. The selected shoot will become the permanent trunk of the vine.

Before the second spring, erect a permanent trellis. Set durable wood or steel posts 16 to 20 feet apart in the row and run two strands of No. 10 galvanized wire between the posts. Run one wire 30 to 36 inches above the ground and a second about two feet above the first wire.

Fasten the wires so they can be tightened each spring.

Second year. How much pruning you do the second year depends on how the vine grew the first year. If the cane is long enough, tie it to the top wire of the trellis and cut it off just above the wire. If the cane will not reach the top wire, cut it back just above the lower wire and tie it.

If the growth doesn't reach the lower wire, or appears weak, cut the cane back to two buds as you did at planting time. Vigorous growth will generally follow.

After tying the vines to the permanent trellis, remove the temporary stakes.

Third year. Third year pruning depends on the training the vines got during the second year. Canes which were tied to the top wire should have developed side branches during the growing season. Select four of these canes, two for each wire, and cut them back to four or five buds. Remove all other canes. Tie two canes to each wire, one to the right and one to the left of the trunk.

Canes cut back at the lower wire should have produced several canes. Extend one cane, tie it to the top wire and cut it off at that height. Select two canes for the lower wire. Cut them back to four or five buds and tie them loosely to the wire—one to the right and one to the left of the trunk. Remove all other canes.

Canes that were cut back to two buds should have produced enough to reach the top wire. Prune them the same as vigorous second season plant.

Fourth year prune for fruiting. By the fourth year the vine should be well established and producing a considerable fruit crop. Prune now with fruit production in mind.

Grapes are borne on shoots from buds produced the previous year. High production of good-quality fruit depends on balancing the fruit load with the productive potential of the vine and providing for new fruiting canes for the following year. The fruiting shoots arise from selected canes left on each wire. The potential canes for the following year's fruiting shoots should arise from spurs on the arm of the vine.

For the fruiting, select canes arising on an arm or as near the trunk as possible. Choose four canes, one on or near each arm if possible. The ideal fruiting cane is about the size of a pencil. Leave five to ten buds on each cane (depending on the vigor of the vine) and remove the remaining growth. Tie each cane loosely to the trellis.

Also leave one or two "renewal spurs" (canes cut back to two buds) near each fruiting cane. The shoot growth from the renewal spurs becomes the fruiting canes for the following year. After you select fruiting canes and renewal spurs, cut out all other growth and deadwood.

Prune the mature vines in this way every year before growth starts. This insures you of new fruiting wood as near the trunk as possible.

Pruning neglected vines. Generally, neglected vines have too much deadwood, and the fruiting wood is too far from the main stem. Old vines don't produce many grapes. But they can rapidly be rejuvenated by pruning. Quite often there are young canes arising from the roots. Select a single cane, tie it to the top wire, and treat it as a vigorous, second-year cane. Remove all the remaining parts of the vine.

If complete renewal isn't desirable, remove as much as possible of the old, nonfruiting wood to encourage new growth near the main stems or trunk. You can select several fruiting canes even though they are some distance from the main trunk. Old vines generally have large root systems and are able to support about twice as many buds as young vines.

Blue Varieties:

Concord. Fruit large and of good quality when mature. Generally ripens too late in Wisconsin to obtain best fruit quality. Vines are vigorous and productive. Hardy in southeastern counties only.

Worden. Good quality, large berries. Ripens about seven to ten days earlier than Concord.

Crop improved if pollinated by another variety. Vines of medium vigor. Hardy in southeast third of state, including Door County.

Fredonia. Ripens about three weeks before Concord. Vigorous and hardy, but susceptible to mildew. Hardy in all but the extreme northwest counties.

Van Buren. Berries smaller than Concord, and of good quality. About as early as Fredonia. Vines fairly vigorous. Hardy only in the southeast region, including Door County.

Moore's Early. Berries often drop early. Fair quality. May be just slightly earlier than Fredonia. Vines of medium vigor. Hardy in all but the extreme northwest counties.

Beta. Fruit small with only fair quality. Hardy, vigorous, and productive. Used mainly for jelly. Hardy throughout the state.

Valiant. Blue, medium-sized, tart fruit in small clusters. Quality better than Beta. Used primarily for jams and jellies. A vigorous grower and producer. Ripens about the second week in August. Hardy throughout the state.

Foch. Small, bluish-black fruits used to make very good quality Burgundy-type wines. Leading red wine grape among commercial growers in Wisconsin. Vines are very vigorous and hardy throughout the state.

Blue Jay. Fruit about size of Concord, of fair quality. A vigorous grower and producer. Hardy in all but the extreme northwest counties.

Amber (Green) Varieties:

Portland. Fruit of fair quality. Ripens with Moore's Early. Hardy in extreme southeast counties only.

Niagara. Fruit of fair quality. Ripens just before Concord. Vine vigorous but only moderately hardy; susceptible to diseases. Suitable for extreme southeast counties only.

Moonbeam. Fruit quite large, fair quality, bland. Vine vigorous and hardy. Suitable for all but the extreme northwest counties.

Edelweiss. Medium-size berries with good flavor, primarily used fresh. Usually matures by early September. Hardy in all but the extreme northwest counties.

St. Pepin. Excellent multi-purpose grape. Needs some winter protection and requires a pollinizer, but cannot pollinize other cultivars. Ripens in early to mid-September. Hardy in all but the extreme northwest counties.

La Crosse. White grape very similar to St. Pepin, but does not require a pollinizer. Good for winemaking. Harvest early to mid-September. Hardy throughout state.

Red Varieties:

Swenson Red. Medium-sized fruit with very high quality, fruity flavor, and thin skin. For fresh use. Susceptible to mildew. May require some winter protection. Matures mid-to-late September. Hardy in all but the extreme northwest counties.

Delaware. Fruit small, of excellent quality. Ripens with Worden. Vine tender and lacks vigor. Requires heavy pruning. Hardy in extreme southeast counties only.

Brighton. Fruit tender and attractive. Ripens with Worden. Vine fairly hardy and vigorous. Requires cross-pollination to set fruit. Hardy in extreme southeast counties only.

Red Amber. Fruit smaller than Concord, sweet, of good quality. Vine moderately vigorous. Hardy in all but the extreme northwest counties.

Raspberries

Raspberries are very popular in Wisconsin, both because their fruit is so luscious and because they are easy to grow in all corners of the state. All you need for raspberries are average growing conditions and a fair amount of room for the spreading canes.

Black raspberries can be grown in Wisconsin, but they are not generally recommended because they are so very susceptible to disease and, in any case, they are not hardy in the colder regions. Red varieties are the only kind cultivated extensively throughout the state. There are some yellow cultivars, which really are variations of the red berries, and which have all their characteristics.

Soil. Raspberries will grow well in any average garden soil, from sandy loam to clay. In fact, the subsoil is more important, since the plants send their roots deep into the subsoil to bring up moisture. If raspberries are planted over hardpan, the roots will be prevented from getting the necessary moisture to combat drought.

Culture. There is no need to buy nursery plants if you have a friend who owns a raspberry patch. The plants are simple to propagate by suckering. Red raspberries send up suckers—new shoots—from the underground stems or roots. These suckers may be dug up at any time during the season. Try to hold on to as much of the root as you can, take the suckers home, and transplant them into your garden. They may either be transplanted into a nursery, where they will build up strength before being transplanted into permanent locations the following year, or they may be set into their permanent locations at once. Red raspberries are easier to propagate than nearly any other fruit, and the removal of the suckers will not harm the parent plants in any way.

The advantage to buying and planting nursery specimens are several. You will be assured disease-free plants, and you will have your choice of many different cultivars, so that you can choose the berry that's just right for you. Since the raspberry patch should thrive for many years to come, these are important considerations.

Suckers may be planted at any time. Nursery plants are usually planted in the spring, as soon as the ground can be worked. Choose a sloping area and avoid frost pockets when choosing a site, particularly if winters are especially severe in your area. The ground should be tilled to a depth of six inches, and plenty of aged compost should be worked into the soil at the bottom of the holes. Holes should be dug two to three feet apart, and as wide as necessary to accommodate the spread-out roots with ease. Apply a mulch of hay or straw after planting.

Thinning. Raspberries are thinned, rather than pruned. The roots and crowns of this plant are perennial—but the canes are biennial, i.e., they grow one year but do not produce; they produce fruit the second year; and they die soon after fruiting. The first group of canes to be pruned away, then, are those that have just produced fruit. Their job is done, and their continued presence will just impede the development of the plant. You can prune away year-old canes anytime after they have fruited, from mid-summer right up into fall, or even during the following spring. It will be easiest right after fruiting, however, since they will be easier to identify at that time.

The second group of canes to be pruned away are those that must be pruned in order to thin the plant. Ideally, after fall pruning, each plant should have only four to eight canes, and they should be spaced four to six inches apart at the soil line.

To attain this ideal, prune away first the broken or diseased canes. Then prune away the most slender canes, which will not bear well in any case. Then, prune away any that are growing too close to your most robust new canes.

All cuts should be made as close to the crown as possible (without cutting into the crown, of course) and as cleanly as possible. Clean cuts are important to the prevention of disease. A small pruning shears will do the job, but a sharp pocketknife will probably do a better job.

Red Varieties:

June. Fruit bright red, medium-sized, round, attractive, of fair quality. Fruit requires careful handling. Begins to ripen about ten days before Latham. Plants fairly hardy and often slow to produce suckers. Hardy in the southeast, including Door County.

Latham. The standard variety for all of Wisconsin. Originated in Minnesota. Fruit attractive light red but turns dark when over-ripe: large, roundish, and quite firm, but inclined to crumble; mildly flavored. Good quality, ripens late. Plants vigorous, upright, productive, and hardy. Will grow in a wide range of soils and climate. Hardy throughout the state.

Boyne. Vigorous and productive, with medium- to large-size fruit of very good quality. Ripens late June. Hardy throughout the state.

Haida. Fruit is larger, firmer, and sweeter than Boyne, but somewhat less hardy. Ripens one week after Boyne. Hardy in all but the very coldest sections of the state.

Reveille. Large, soft fruit has very good flavor. Ripens early, and is hardy throughout the state.

Nordic. Fruit is superior to Boyne in flavor and firmness. Is more resistant to anthracnose than Boyne. Hardy throughout the state.

Festival. Very attractive fruit with firm flesh. Excellent for fresh use, but only fair for freezing. Immune to mosaic virus and tolerant to spur blight. Ripens midseason. Hardy throughout the state.

Redwing. Fresh fruit is firm and of high quality. Freezing quality is only far. A productive fall-bearer, not recommended for short-season areas.

Amity. Moderately firm fruit, moderately vigorous and productive. A fall-bearer, not hardy in the extreme northwest. Matures too late for short-season areas.

Fallgold. Good winterhardiness and vigor. Yellow fruit is somewhat soft but of excellent quality. For fresh use. Ripens in July for summer crop and late August for fall crop. Not recommended for the northern tier of Wisconsin counties.

Rose Hips

Rose hips are not commonly grown in Wisconsin, or anywhere else in the United States for that matter. They are well worth mentioning, however, for one very important reason: They are among nature's richest sources of vitamin C—40 to 60 times richer, for instance, than oranges. They are grown commonly in the Scandinavian countries, where long winters increase the human body's need for vitamin C, and where short summers rule out many other natural sources of this vitamin. Rose hips can be made into jams and jellies, into tart and delicious teas and juices, or they can be dried for winter use. They can be combined with other fruits to make healthful pies, and their extract

can be added to many drinks as a vitamin C booster.

All roses produce hips, which are actually the seed pods or fruits produced after the blossom dies, but the best variety for producing edible hips is *Rosa rugosa*. This variety's foliage is not attractive, and so it will not serve well as an ornamental. However, it can make a fast-growing and effective hedge. Set plants of *Rosa rugosa* two feet apart, for making a hedge, but remember that individual plants will spread to five feet in diameter and more than ten feet in height. Plants are set out in spring. *Rosa rugosa* is hardy and is seldom bothered by insects or disease. Plants are offered by Farmer Seed and Nursery and by Wayside Gardens.

Strawberries

Strawberries are unquestionably the most popular small fruit grown in Wisconsin. And, in terms of the number of people who grow strawberries, they are the most popular fruit of any kind.

The reasons for the strawberry's popularity are obvious. They are easy to grow in every part of Wisconsin (all the following recommended cultivars are hardy throughout the state). Our cool climate is well suited to this fruit, which responds with firm, and flavorful berries. There are scores of varieties to choose from, for every taste and climate. They are the first fruit of the season to be brought to the table (if you discount rhubarb), and for that kindness they are doubly treasured.

Soil. Strawberries will do well in most garden soils, so long as they are well drained. They do not require much fertilizer—and, in fact, an excess in nitrogen will produce luxuriant foliage and scant fruit. Spring-planted berries will benefit by soil that had been well manured the previous fall, but further fertilization during the season is unnecessary. The exception will be those strawberries that are grown on very sandy soil. Since light sand cannot hold nutrients well, several applications of compost tea or manure tea during the season will be appreciated by the plants.

Culture. Strawberries should be planted in early spring, as soon as the soil can be worked. Depth of planting is vitally important. The plants should be set deep enough to bring the soil up to the crown, but not over the crown or the young leaves that should then be growing from it. Dig the hole to the proper depth, and wide enough to accommodate the roots easily when they are spread out naturally. Put a small mound of soil in the center of the hole and set the plant on this mound, so that the roots drop down naturally. Then, fill in soil around the roots, packing it gently but firmly so that all the roots come into contact with soil. Water the plants thoroughly after they have been set in.

The spacing of plants depends on the variety and the cultivation method chosen. Strawberry plants send out runners that root and produce "daughter" plants. These daughters grow into full-sized plants that will bear in the future. Since each plant remains viable for only a few years, it is important to cultivate these daughter plants, in order to keep the bed fresh and productive year after year. The space that you allow between plants and between rows, then, depends upon the mature size of the mother plants and the number of runners that you will permit to develop. The average variety can be planted 12 to 18 inches apart in rows 18 inches apart. Runners are then permitted to the extent that they do not crowd each other or the mother plants. An overcrowded bed will cut production severely.

Although strawberries do not require heavy fertilization, they do require soil moisture throughout the growing season, and especially during their entire fruiting period. As for all garden plants, any water applied should be given in occasional, long, soaking doses—never in frequent sprinkles. More important, plants should be mulched as soon as they have been put into the ground. Hay or sawdust are the recommended mulching materials for strawberries.

Harvest the berries as soon as they are ripe, even the undersized or overripe ones that you will not use. Only in this way will the plants continue to produce to the limit of their capacity.

Varieties. There are two groups of strawberries—June bearers and everbearers. As their name implies, the June varieties—which are more popular—produce a large crop starting in mid-June and continuing for about three weeks. (The season is from two to three weeks later in central and northern Wisconsin.) The everbearers, however, set and produce fruit at a slower and steadier pace, from June up until the first snows fly. Strawberry-loving gardeners often plant both kinds, using the June crop mostly for freezing and preserves.

Because there are so many varieties suitable for Wisconsin's climate, I will list here only those recommended by our University of Wisconsin horticulturists. But I do suggest that you look into the wide world of strawberries by requesting the catalogs of one or more of the mail-order nurseries that specialize in berries. These include Conner, Brittingham's, W. F. Allen, and Rayner Brothers. In addition, you should see what your local nursery or garden center has to offer. But remember that those varieties recommended in catalogs "for home gardens only" are likely to be far better than those suitable for commercial production. What commercial growers gain in shipping qualities, they lose in succulence and eating quality. The berries you grow at home should be head and shoulders above the supermarket varieties.

(In Wisconsin, a fungus disease called Red Stele is the bane of strawberry growers. Infection is worst in heavy and poorly-drained soils, and most active in cool weather. Look for varieties that are resistant.)

Early June Bearers:

Sunrise. The fruit is medium-sized, orange red, firm, subacid in flavor, but not good for freezing. Plants are vigorous and produce many runners. Sunrise is resistant to verticillium wilt, leaf scorch, and some races of red stele, but is susceptible to leaf spot.

Premier. A good plant maker with fair vigor. Generally a good producer of bright, moderately firm fruit. It is widely grown in Wisconsin as a standard early variety.

Early-Midseason June Bearers:

Earliglow. Moderately productive cultivar. Fruit is firm and has very good flavor. Resistant to root diseases and moderately resistant to leaf diseases.

Crimson King. Vigorous and productive. Fruits are large but somewhat soft and marginal in quality. Good tolerance to leaf scorch and leafspot. Resistant to several races of red stele.

Cyclone. Fruit is medium but variable in size, of good quality, but somewhat soft in wet seasons and subject to mold. It is fairly good for freezing. Cyclone is somewhat resistant to leaf spot and scorch under Wisconsin conditions.

Redglow. Maintains fair fruit size during the season. Fruit is moderately firm, deep red and very glossy, and above average for freezing. Plants are vigorous and produce many runners. They do best in 18-inch-wide rows. Susceptible to leaf spot and red mites, but resistant to red stele.

Robinson. A vigorous grower and plant maker. Yields are high. Fruit is large in size and of fair quality. Ripens about one week later than Premier. It is adapted to a wide range of conditions and is widely grown in Wisconsin. Not recommended for shipping or freezing.

Wisconsin 537. A vigorous grower and good plant producer, generally a good berry producer. Fruit is medium to large in size and of good quality. Ripens about a week later than Premier. This variety is rated high for quick freezing. It has a history of being susceptible to the "yellows," but this can be controlled in the home garden by routing those plants showing the disease.

Midseason June Bearers:

Catskill. Fruit is large, irregular, moderately firm, bright red, and glossy. It is mildly subacid, of good quality, and fairly good for freezing.

Catskill is very vigorous and productive, but susceptible to leaf spot and virus diseases.

Cavendish. High yield potential. Fruit is medium red, firm, and very large. For fresh use. Resistant to red stele.

Midway. Fruit is medium-sized, firm, deep red, and glossy. It is subacid, of good quality, and satisfactory for freezing. Plants are moderately vigorous, fairly productive, and prolific runner producers. Midway is resistant to common races of red stele and moderately resistant to scorch and leaf spot.

Late June Bearers:

Badgerbelle. Fruit is large, moderately firm, and medium glossy red with prominent yellow seeds. It is of fair to good quality and is satisfactory for freezing. Plants are vigorous, hardy, produce many runners, and yield good crops. Badgerbelle has some resistance to leaf spot.

Honeoye. Highly productive. Large, attractive fruit good for fresh use and freezing. Tolerant of leaf powdery mildew but susceptible to red stele and angular leafspot.

Sparkle. Fruit is medium-sized, becoming smaller in late season, and dark red. It has excellent flavor and is excellent for freezing. Plants are vigorous, productive, hardy, and have many runners. Sparkle is fairly resistant to leaf spot and red stele, but susceptible to virus diseases and cyclamen mite.

Blomidon. Berries are glossy, medium to dark red, very large and well formed. Excellent flavor for fresh use, freezing, and preserves. A productive plant, resistant to leaf scorch and leaf spot but susceptible to red stele.

Glooscap. Widely planted, mid- to late-season cultivar. Fruit is large and dark glossy red; flavor is good for fresh use, freezing, and preserves. A productive and vigorous plant. Resistant to leaf scorch and leaf spot but susceptible to soil-borne diseases.

Everbearing Varieties:

Ogallala. Vigorous and productive early-ripening berry. Dark red fruit are somewhat soft, medium-size, and highly flavored. Good for freezing. Resistant to leaf spot and tolerant of drought.

Superfection, Gem, or Brilliant. These varieties are virtually identical. Fruit is large and of good quality. Plant is vigorous and quite hardy. Does best in sandy loam soils.

Ozark Beauty. Fruit is large, sweet, firm, and has good flavor. Plants are good yielders, with fair runner production. A good freezer.

Fort Laramie. Medium-size, bright red fruit with a sweet flavor. A vigorous plant, tolerant to leaf spot and leaf scorch, but leaves are very susceptible to mildew.

Quinault. Medium-large, deep red, soft fruit. Very good for fresh use and preserves; fair for freezing. Very productive. Resistant to leaf spot and leaf scorch, but susceptible to mildew. Moderately hardy.

Day-Neutral Strawberries

The following two cultivars are called day-neutral, because they produce regardless of the day length (which is the factor that causes June berries to fruit in June). These plants produce two crops each year, one in mid-summer and another in the fall.

Tribute. Bright red, medium-size, firm fruit. Good for fresh use and processing. High-vigor, medium-sized plant. Resistant to many leaf and root diseases.

Tristar. Sweet, firm, glossy fruit with a deep red color. Moderate-vigor, medium-size plant. Bears an earlier crop the year of planting. Adapted to hanging baskets.

Storing Fruits and Vegetables

Go to the ant, thou sluggard; consider her ways, and be wise: Which having no guide, overseer, or ruler, Provideth her meat in the summer, and gathereth her food in the harvest.
—Proverbs, 6:6-8

6 Of the traditional food storage methods—canning, freezing, pickling, drying, and root cellaring—we will treat only the last two in this chapter. Ample advice on canning, freezing, and pickling is found in cookbooks, government publications, and booklets of equipment manufacturers, and there is no need to repeat that advice here.

Drying and root cellaring, however, are two old ideas whose time has come again, as we seek to conserve the earth's dwindling resources. Drying requires some energy from an oven or food dryer (at least here in Wisconsin), while root cellaring requires none at all. Both have advantages and disadvantages, when compared with each other and with canning, freezing, and pickling.

Harvesting for Flavor and Quality

All expert opinion agrees that only the best of fruits and vegetables should be reserved for preservation and storage—and this is good advice. Your fruits and vegetables will never improve in quality when stored, and so you should begin only with perfect specimens. Blemishes, soft spots, cuts, and scrapes may have allowed disease organisms to enter the fruits and vegetables. If they are stored, the disease may easily ruin an entire batch. (One rotten apple *can* spoil the whole bunch.)

Pick vegetables while they are at their peak of flavor, while slightly immature, and before their sugars have begun to turn to starch. Fruits should be picked while fully ripe, but before they begin to lose good texture. Vegetables for root cellar storage should be picked as late in the season as possible, so that a warm Indian summer will not shorten their lives. Herbs should be harvested when their essential oils are at a peak of concentration in the leaves. Usually, this point is reached just before the flower of the plant has opened.

Drying

Food drying has enjoyed a new wave of popularity in recent years, to the point where a food dryer is now a standard piece of equipment in many kitchens. Drying is not only a low-energy storage method, but also a boon to the growing number of families dedicated to camping and backpacking, to whom every ounce of equipment—and food—is important.

The single goal of drying is to remove most of the water content—from 80 to 90 percent—from the food, and in so doing make it impossible for bacteria and other organisms to grow there. As water is withdrawn, so of course are weight and bulk.

The disadvantages of drying are several. Most vegetables suffer a loss of taste, and, upon being reconstituted with water, never regain good texture. The exception is the bean; many kinds have long been dried for storage.

Fruits, including apricots, apples, cherries, plums, grapes, and pears, retain good taste when dried, but of course their texture is changed. In some cases, and for some purposes, it is actually improved. Dried apricots, for instance, are far more suitable than fresh apricots for backpacking trips. Prunes and raisins, which, after all, are only dried plums and grapes, have secured a food category all their own.

Both fruits and vegetables suffer significant losses of vitamins A and C, and lesser losses of other vitamins. On a pound-for-pound basis, however, vitamin content is higher, since water is lost and the flesh of the fruit or vegetable is then in concentrated form.

Herbs take especially well to drying, since their flavor is in their essential oils, which remain with the leaves after water is removed.

Outdoor Drying

In some sections of the country, foods are easily dried outdoors in the sun. Not so in Wisconsin, where our high humidity makes this method difficult or impossible. The Wisconsin gardener must depend on a food dryer (commercial or homemade) or an oven where the temperature can be maintained at 140° or lower.

Equipment. Any homemade dryer must include removable, shallow, wooden trays (not metal) contained in any structure in which temperatures may be controlled. Home-built dryers use a variety of heat sources, including heat lamps, gas plates, electric hot plates, even light bulbs. Each square foot of tray space will hold from one and one-half to two and one-half pounds of food for drying.

The average oven will hold about six pounds of food for drying, unless extra racks are added.

Preparation. An anti-oxidant will prevent your fruit slices (especially apples) from turning brown. Supermarkets offer commercial preparations, but you can make your own by adding a teaspoon of crystalline ascorbic acid (which is nothing more than pure vitamin C, available at pharmacies) to a cup of cold water. Apples, which oxidize quickly, may need a stronger solution.

Blanching vegetables is essential before drying them. They should be blanched in steam, in a large pot containing a wire basket, or in a pressure cooker, until each piece is heated through. The blanching stops the ripening process and preserves color, texture, and taste. Mushrooms need not be blanched, and onions should not be blanched if they are to be used only for seasoning.

The drying operation. Nearly all fruits and vegetables can be dried in from three to twelve hours at temperatures ranging from 120° to 160°. The more thinly that fruit and vegetable pieces are sliced, or the smaller they are chopped, the more quickly they will dry. For most vegetables, the drying temperature is set fairly low for the first hour, then increased to a minimum of 140°, where it remains until the food is nearly dry. It is then lowered again as the drying process comes to completion. Food should be checked periodically during the process, turned several times on the trays, and the trays themselves should be rotated if the food on some is drying more quickly than that on others. When drying food in an oven, keep the door slightly open if you have trouble containing the temperature to the desired level, and keep the trays as far as possible from the heat source.

When food is dry. Fruit, when sufficiently dried, should feel leathery on the outside but should be moderately moist on the inside—much like the dried fruit that you buy at a store. Vegetables should be more thoroughly dry, to the point of brittleness. When the food is ready, store it in any airtight containers and keep it in a cool, dry spot. A root cellar is ideal.

To reconstitute dried fruits and vegetables, simply add one and one-half cups of boiling water to each cup of food. After several hours of soaking, they should be ready for use.

Table 10. A Guide to Drying Fruits and Vegetables

Vegetable	Preparation	Blanching Time (min.)	After Blanching	Drying Temp. (F.)*
Asparagus	Use top 3 in. of spears	10		130-160°
Beans, green shell	Shell beans	15-20		130-160°
Beans, snap	String, slice into narrow strips	15-20		120-150°
Beets	Remove tops, blanch whole	30-45	Dice or slice ½-in. thick	120-150°
Broccoli	Slice or cut into small pieces	10		120-150°
Brussels sprouts	Slice ½-in. thick	12		120-150°
Cabbage	Slice ½-in. thick	5-10		120-140°
Carrots	Slice ½-in. thick	10-15		120-150°
Celery	Slice stalks crosswise, ½-in. thick	10		130-150°
Corn	Husk, remove silk	10	Remove kernels	140-165°
Mushrooms	Slice ½-in. thick	none		130-150°
Onions	Peel; slice ½-in. thick	5-10		130-140°
Peas	Shell	15		130-160°
Peppers	Slice ½-in. thick; remove seeds	10		120-150°
Rhubarb	Slice crosswise into 1-in. strips	3		130-150°
Spinach	Cut strips 2-in. wide	5		140-150°
Squash, winter	Slice pulp into 1-in. strips	10		120-150°
Squash, summer	Slice ½-in. thick	7		120-150°
Tomatoes	Quarter	5	Remove skins and seeds; strain out most juice	120-150°

Fruit

Apples	Pare; core; slice ¼-in. thick; coat with anti-oxidant		130-150°
Apricots	Half; remove pit; slice ½-in. thick; coat with anti-oxidant		130-150°
Cherries	Remove stems; pit, drain juice		120-140°
Grapes	Remove stems; blanch 2 min.; drain juice		120-140°
Peaches	Half; remove pit; blanch 2 min.; remove skin; slice ½-in. thick; coat with anti-oxidant		130-150°
Pears	Skin; core; cut into slices ½-in. thick		130-140°
Plums	Remove stems; pit, blanch 10 min.; drain juice		130-150°

*Begin drying at low temperature; after one hour, raise gradually to high temperature; change to low temperature when food is almost dry. If temperature cannot be regulated, keep at 140°.

Drying herbs. Herbs are easy to dry without special equipment. After you have cut the plants, bring them indoors to dry. Rinse them quickly in cold water, then blot them dry with a paper towel and place them on trays of wire mesh or netting and allow them to dry thoroughly in an airy place for three or four days. When the leaves have become brittle (they will crumble when rubbed between thumb and forefinger), store them in clean, dry jars of other airtight containers.

Another drying method involves the use of small, brown paper bags, the kind sold in stores for school lunches. After the plants have been dried for a day on wire mesh or netting, tie them together at the bottom stems and hang them upside down in the bags. Tie the top of the bags shut around the stems, so that the leaves do not touch the sides, and hang the bags in an attic or another little-used room. In this way, the essential oils are not allowed to dissipate in the air, the plants are kept free of dust, and yet they receive enough air to dry thoroughly. After a month or two in the bag, they should be thoroughly dry. Roll the bag in your hands in order to free the leaves from the stems, and then open the bag and empty the crushed leaves into jars for storage.

An excellent book on food drying is *Dehydration Made Simple*, by Mary Bell, a Wisconsin writer and expert on food drying.

Root Cellaring

Root cellaring is a broad term, and its principles can be used by nearly anyone. You do not have to have a special room in a dirt-floor cellar to practice root cellaring (although it would be nice to have one). City people can do it as well as their country cousins. You can benefit from root cellaring even if you don't have a large garden, since you can buy produce at harvest time, at bargain rates, and store it through the winter at absolutely no cost in energy.

Not all garden produce can, or should, be stored in a root cellar. In the futuristic scheme of things, there will still be room for canning tomatoes and freezing berries. But since root cellaring is energy-free, there is an obvious advantage to using its principles whenever you can.

Despite blistering summer heat and icy winter blasts, the earth, just a few feet under its surface, remains cool and dark all year 'round. It is said to remain a constant 52°, although I can't vouch for Wisconsin's ground temperature. In any case, it is the ground's constantly cool temperature that is the basis of root cellaring. As Mike and Nancy Bubel point out in their book *Root Cellaring*, a good root cellar should provide the three conditions most necessary to prolong the storage life of the roots and leafy vegetables it will contain: *low temperature, high humidity,* and *darkness*. That's all. It's that simple. Building a root cellar is not complicated, but the proper place in which to build it is critical.

You can build a root cellar outdoors, in a hill, or simply on any flat ground surface. You can build it in a cement basement or tuck it away under the basement steps. You can dig it into the floor of your backyard tool shed, or in the crawl space under your front porch. For some vegetables, you can utilize unheated attics or spare rooms, with no building effort required at all. All you must do is find the best conditions for the storage of each vegetable you have.

As with any new endeavor, it's best to start small. Even with the best of research, you are bound to make some mistakes along the way, and it's better to lose a small amount of food than a large one while you are experimenting.

The ideal temperature for storage is 32° to 40°. A temperature as high as 50° is permissible, but foods will not last as long. The ideal humidity is 90 to 95 percent. It is easier to approach this level outdoors than indoors, but there are tricks you can use to increase humidity, even indoors. Darkness, although essential, should present no problem.

The root cellar can be built indoors, in your own cellar or basement, or outdoors nearly anywhere. If you live in an old house, you might already have a dirt-floor room that was once a root cellar. If modern heating has made it too warm for root cellaring, correct that with wall and/or pipe insulation, and a tight-fitting door.

Or, perhaps you can use an old coal bin that can be sealed off from the rest of the basement. Ventilation is important, too. If the room does not have a window to the outside, then you will have to ventilate it yourself.

If you have a cement basement, the project becomes more complicated. You will have to partition off a small room on the north side of the house, insulate it well to keep out heat, and provide wood flooring, shelves, and the proper ventilation, which will include both an inlet for fresh air and an outlet for stale air. If your basement requires major alterations for root cellaring, consult the book *Root Cellaring*, by Mike and Nancy Bubel (Rodale Press) for good advice. It contains detailed directions and drawings for building two different basement root cellars.

Some vegetables require less rigid conditions of storage, and you can probably find an ideal place to keep these without going to any extra work. Pumpkins, winter squash, and sweet potatoes do well at 50° to 60° with 60 to 70 percent humidity. Perhaps a corner of the basement, far removed from the furnace, would be ideal. Onions and garlic, on the other hand, will do well at 35° to 45° at 60 to 70 percent humidity. You might find that an unheated but insulated attic offers the perfect conditions, or a north-facing sunporch. The crops that do demand 32° to 40° and high humidity include white potatoes, cabbage, apples, pears, endive and escarole, carrots, beets, parsnips, celery, Chinese cabbage, salsify, winter radishes, kohlrabi, leeks, and horseradish.

Outdoors, your options are opened up. The problem there is to keep out the cold, rather than the heat, and that's always easier. Also, maintaining high humidity is no problem at all.

A home storage pit made by covering a barrel with straw and earth.

Table 11. Energy-Saving Storage of Fruits and Vegetables

Commodity	Place to Store[1]	Storage Period	Temperature[2]	Humidity
Vegetables:				
Dry Beans and Peas	Any cool, dry place	As long as desired	Cool	Dry
Late Cabbage	Pit, trench, or outdoor cellar	Through late fall and winter	Cool	Moderately moist
Cauliflower and Broccoli	Any cold place	2 to 3 weeks	32°	Moderately moist
Late Celery	Pit or trench; roots in soil in storage cellar	Through late fall and winter	Cool	Moist
Endive	Roots in soil in storage cellar	2 to 3 months	Cool	Moist
Onions	Any cool, dry place	Through fall and winter	Cool	Dry
Parsnips	Where they grew, or in storage cellar	Through fall and winter	Cold; freezing in soil does not injure.	Moist
Various Root Crops	Pit or in storage cellar	Through fall and winter	Cool	Moist
Potatoes	Pit or in storage cellar	Through fall and winter	See text	Moist
Pumpkins and Squashes	Moderately dry cellar or basement	Through fall and winter	50° to 60° F	Moderately dry
Sweet Potatoes	Moderately dry cellar or basement	Through fall and winter	55° to 60° F	Moderately dry
Tomatoes (mature green)	Moderately dry cellar or basement	4 to 6 weeks	55° to 60° F	Moderately dry
Fruits:				
Apples	Storage cellar, pit, or basement	Through fall and winter	Cool	Moderately moist
Pears	Storage cellar	Depending on variety	Cool	Moderately moist
Grapes	Basement or storage cellar	1 to 2 months	Cool	Moderately moist
Peaches	Basement or storage cellar	2 to 4 weeks	31° to 32° F	Moderately moist
Plums	Basement or storage cellar	4 to 6 weeks	Cool	Moderately moist

SOURCE: USDA data.

NOTE: 1. Always avoid contact with free water that may condense and drip from ceilings.
2. Cool indicates a temperature of 32° to 40°; avoid freezing.

Here are directions for building a simple root box, compliments of the Bubels:

"Dig a hole not too far from the kitchen door, big enough to accommodate a box about two by four feet. Construct the box out of scrap lumber to fit in the hole. Line the box with hardware cloth to keep out gnawing rodents. Arrange the vegetables on a bed of hay with straw, hay, leaves, or moss packed between the layers. Cover with a three-to-four inch layer of hay. Top with a hardware-cloth-lined lid—not hinged, just laid on top. Put hay bales on top of the lid and enjoy visiting your underground store when the roots are frozen and more snow's on the way."

That's the easiest construction. There are many variations on the theme, and the one you choose will depend on the scrap materials you happen to have on hand. You can sink a dead refrigerator into the ground, after removing the motor and the door latch—for safety. It already has good insulating powers, but you should heap bales of hay on top of the door (which should be just at the ground surface), to keep out the winter chill.

You can also simply dig a trench, two feet deep, line it with hardware cloth, and pack your vegetables away in that (always layering them with hay or leaves). Arrange boards over the top of the trench and, again, insulate the top with bales of hay. (If you don't have any bales, bagged leaves will do the job nearly as well.)

An old barrel can be sunk diagonally into the ground, so that the bottom lip comes just to the surface of the ground. Mound soil all around the barrel and pack hay around the opening. A few boards and large rocks will keep the hay in place and offer easy access during the winter.

If you have a large drain tile, you can sink that into the ground, lining the bottom of the hole with rocks and gravel for drainage. Some hay packed into the top of the tile, and an old board or two, will secure it from the top. In every case, it's a matter of taking advantage of the earth's naturally moderate temperature and insulating adequately at the access point.

Root cellaring, like food drying, is a food storage method known to our greatgrand-parents but one that we are learning all over again. As such, we are certain to make mistakes and learn by trial and error. At the same time, our technological capabilities are far greater than those our great-grandparents enjoyed, making the experimentation somewhat easier. As our energy supplies dwindle in the years ahead (and there is no reason to think that they will not) these almost-forgotten skills will become more and more important to home gardeners if they are to maintain the quality of their food supplies.

Flowers for Wisconsin—Nine Months of Glory

Such a starved bank of moss
Till, that May-morn,
Blue ran the flash across:
Violets were born!
                    —Robert Browning
                    The Two Poets of Croisic
                    (1878)

7 As vegetables provide food for the body, so do flowers offer food for the spirit. And, even though many gardeners will concentrate on vegetables and other food plants, it is inconceivable that any garden should be without its ornamental flowering plants.

Here in Wisconsin, we are fortunate to have the beauty of outdoor bloom for as many as nine months of the year. In the southern parts of the state, at least, we can look forward to the cheerful yellow blossoms of winter aconites popping bravely through the snow in early March, and the first spring crocus blooming by the middle of the month. These welcome harbingers are followed in quick succession by the other spring-flowering bulbs—snowdrops, Glory-of-the-snow, grape hyacinths, tulips, daffodils, hyacinths, and more—and by a host of wild flowers which, with just a little persuasion, will become willing volunteers in our gardens. These spring-blooming plants are quickly followed by the early-blooming perennials, including peonies, poppies, alyssum, geraniums, phlox, and scores of others. By midsummer, the annuals that you planted earlier will have created a profusion of bloom. and these—along with many long-blooming perennials and summer-flowering bulbs—can be counted on to serve right up until the first killing frost. After that, there are still the hardy and half-hardy autumn-flowering plants—notably the asters and chrysanthemums—that will fill your life with color right into October and even early November, if the season is favorable.

Even though "nine months of bloom" might be a slight exaggeration, then, it is true that only during December, January. and February are we denied completely the companionship of outdoor bloom.

What is a Flower?

The flower that we cultivate to delight our senses has a completely different purpose for the plant that produces it. For the plant, the flower contains the reproductive organs that enable it to perpetuate its species. Thus, every plant must produce flowers in order for the species to survive. Often these flowers are so small that they escape our attention. Other times we look at them without being more than dimly aware that they are flowers at all—such as in the case of cauliflower and broccoli, two flowers that we grow with scant recognition of their biological status.

Since every plant produces flowers, our choice of ornamental flowering plants for the home garden is enormous. Out of the hundreds of thousands of varieties available to us, however, we have narrowed down our choices to several thousand plants that produce blossoms large enough, showy enough, and colorful enough to capture our attention and affection. The most attractive of these have been captured by plant breeders, who have improved them by generations of breeding and crossbreeding, until the most desirable characteristics of each variety are accentuated to the fullest extent possible.

Perhaps the most outstanding examples of this breeding process are the hybrid tea roses, while at the other end of the scale are the many native wild flowers of Wisconsin. But there are disadvantages as well as advantages in growing the highly bred varieties. Hybrid tea roses, for instance, have been so finely bred that they have lost most of their natural resistance to insects and diseases. It is virtually impossible to grow them successfully without spraying,

dusting, meticulous pruning, and special winter care. A common wild flower such as the blue wood violet (*Viola papilionacea*, our official state flower), however, will grow freely and without care, once we have provided it with a suitable environment in which it can carry out its natural cycle.

In between hybrid tea roses and wood violets, there are thousands of flowering plants of all shapes and sizes, and with blooms of every imaginable color and form, from which we can choose to complete our garden schemes. If you do not want to devote the bulk of your garden-

The first crocus blooms signify the approach of spring in Wisconsin.

ing time to growing flowers, then you will pick those varieties that require relatively little care and are fairly resistant to insects and diseases. Probably, you already have some experience in flower gardening, and you have some old favorites which you call upon each year. You might wish to expand upon this group by adding one or two new varieties annually. But, if you have never grown flowers before, it will be best for you to begin with some of the easier-grown plants—spring-flowering bulbs, of course, marigolds, petunias, and zinnias among the annuals, peonies, phlox, and lilies among the perennials, and perhaps chrysanthemums and asters for fall bloom. This small sampling will provide color from early spring until the first hard frosts of fall, and these plants can be grown with little trouble from insects and diseases. Many more, of course, will fit into the easily grown category, and you have only to study a few of the nursery and seed catalogs to get some idea of the huge array of offerings. Most are well suited to Wisconsin's soil and climate, especially if they are offered by a northern nursery.

Latin Classifications

In dealing with vegetable varieties, we rarely have to call upon their Latin names. When it comes to flowering ornamentals, however, the Latin nomenclature is often useful, especially since many flowering plants have more than one common name and since so many varieties are often found within a single species which goes by a single name. The home flower gardener will sometimes use Latin names to get exactly the plant that is desired, and it will do us no harm to understand the very fundamentals of the game. A good and concise explanation of the Latin classification system appears in Norman C. Fassett's *Spring Flora of Wisconsin* (University of Wisconsin Press, 3rd ed., 1967).

Plants are grouped into species. A species is composed of all the individuals in existence which resemble each other closely enough to be considered of one kind. Species are grouped into genera, and the name of a plant is composed of the generic name followed by the specific name. Thus we have grouped under the genus *Cypripedium* the various species. or kinds, of Lady's Slipper: *Cypripedium arietinum*, the Ram's Head Lady's Slipper; *Cypripedium candidum*, the White Lady's Slipper; *Cypripedium acaule*, the Stemless Lady's Slipper. Genera are grouped into families; *Cypripedium, Habenaria, Orchis*, and various others are included in the *Orchidaceae*, or Orchid Family. Family names end in -*aceae*.

In addition, we must deal with the term *variety*. None is used more loosely in discussing horticultural matters. It can be used to refer to nearly any classification of plants, but botanically speaking, it denotes a group of plants within a species which are different from other members of the species, but not different enough to have earned individual species names. *Parthenocissus tricuspidata veitchii*, for instance, is a climbing plant of the genus *Parthenocissus* (the grape family), the species *tricuspidata* (meaning, literally, "with three sharp, stiff points"), and the variety *veitchii*, which finally identifies the plant as Boston ivy.

In addition, plant breeders and horticulturists now call cultivated varieties by the shortened term "cultivar." (A cultivar is a variety bred commercially.) In this book, I use the two terms interchangeably.

| FAMILY | → | GENUS | → | SPECIES | → | VARIETY |

That done, we will do our best to avoid Latin classifications for the rest of this chapter, preferring to stay with the common names. Boston ivy will remain Boston ivy, and *Parthenocissus tricuspidata veitchii* will be given back to the botanists.

What is a Hybrid?

Just what is a hybrid, anyway? Most gardeners have some vague idea that it is some sort of a cross between two different plants. They know that hybrid plants are more uniform than non-hybrids (called "standards") and that seed from hybrids cannot be saved and used successfully from season to season. All this is true. But for a clear explanation of a hybrid, we turn to the National Garden Bureau:

"A hybrid is the result of pollinating one specific variety of a class of plants with the pollen of another genetically different variety of that class. While a hybrid can occur by chance, within the seed industry hybrids are the result of cross breeding of carefully chosen parent plants that produce offspring (seeds) that will have special characteristics."

To accomplish this pollination procedure, the parent plants that are selected to be the females and produce seed have their pollen-bearing anthers removed and they receive only pollen from those plants that have been selected as their partners. This is done because most plants have both male and female parts and can pollinate themselves. By controlling the pollinating process, this results in the offspring having genetic characteristics from both parents. The offspring (seed) of this cross is called an F1 hybrid (F1 stands for "first filial"). The seeds from this cross will produce plants that are very uniform in plant habit, and carry a combination of traits from the parent plants.

By careful plant crossing, seed breeders have produced earlier flowers or fruits, higher-yielding crops, more vigorous bloomers, better disease resistance, and other characteristics that both commercial growers and home gardeners value. The "super sweet" sweet corn is a result of hybridization. Freely-blooming hybrid impatiens have rocketed to the top of the popularity chart among flowering annuals. Double-flowering tuberous begonias, burpless cucumbers, odorless marigolds, miniature forms of both vegetables and flowers, all are made possible by hybridization.

That's the up side. The down side is that F1 hybrids are the property of the plant breeder, who keeps the parent plants a closely guarded secret. With hybrids plants, you must depend on the seed company for your seeds. If the seed company decides to discontinue your favorite geranium, there is not much you can do about it. You cannot save your own seeds from year to year. In addition, some hybrid flowers have lost their original scents in the breeders' quest for larger and showier blooms, and some are more susceptible to disease than their open-pollinated counterparts.

With open-pollinated, or standard, varieties, you may save your own seed from year to year. The standard varieties used in gardens have become well stabilized over many generations, sometimes over hundreds of years. Many gardeners today enjoy growing and preserving heirloom plants, varieties that never appear in garden catalogs. They feel that the saving of seed is one of the most basic aspects of gardening—the striving toward individual self-sufficiency.

Not all classes of plants are hybridized. Among vegetables, bush, pole, and lima beans, snap peas, popcorn, ornamental corn, lettuce, leeks, and radish are not hybridized. Herbs are not hybridized. The list of flowers not hybridized includes alyssum, balsam, browallia, calendula, celosia, cleome, coleus, cosmos, dahlia, dusty miller, gazania, gomphrena, lobelia, marigold, nasturtium, phlox, salvia, verbena, and vinca.

Flowers primarily offered as hybrids include ageratum, begonia, geranium, impatiens, American and African marigolds, nicotiana, and petunia. In addition, many vegetables and flowers are offered in both standard and hybrid forms.

Planning the Flower Garden

There can be no recommended flower garden plan for your home, because any plan will necessarily depend on variables that only you can identify: the size and location of your house, the contour of your ground, the nature of your permanent landscape plantings, the patterns of sunlight and shade on your grounds, your soil and climate, and—most important—your individual preferences.

There are, nevertheless, a few general rules —suggestions, really—which might be considered in making any garden plan. Some are so obvious that I hesitate to even list them—and yet

I have seen one-foot marigolds struggling behind five-foot dahlias, and I have seen large tulip beds in front of houses, breathtakingly beautiful in May but creating a large brown and lifeless patch for the rest of the summer. The following rules, then, are presented both with apologies and with the hope that at least one or two of them might improve your own individual plan:

1. Plan for season-long bloom. Don't concentrate solely on spring-flowering plants, but do plant annuals among the spring bulbs as soon as they have finished blooming. The fast-growing annuals will soon hide the brown foliage of the tulips and daffodils. Don't plant masses of chrysanthemums and dahlias without some shorter-growing and earlier-blooming flowers in front of them. Marigolds, for instance, will keep dahlias colorful company until the end of August or the beginning of September, when the dahlias come into bloom, and the short-growing marigolds will not interfere with the development of the dahlias.

2. Don't scatter plants too thinly. Mass groupings of flowering plants are far more effective than single plants scattered here and there, and your garden space is conserved in this way, too. This does not mean that a grouping must comprise only one variety or species, but simply that flower beds are more pleasing than scattered flowering plants.

3. Don't be afraid to mix annuals and perennials in the same bed. You may plan a perennial bed, but do not be afraid to add annuals if they will serve the desired aesthetic purposes. In general, annuals bloom throughout the season, while perennials have an intense but short blooming season. Annuals thus can fill in color gaps.

4. Plan your flower garden to suit the character of your home and grounds. Follow natural contours of the ground. Soften harsh lines of the house with tall-growing and graceful plants, but do not make your flowers compete with the more ornate features of the house. Try to

With annuals, you can redecorate your garden every year!

visualize each plant growing and blooming in its place. Go so far as to take a color print of the house and sketch in, with oils, the flowering plants you are considering.

5. Avoid rectangular or other stiffly formal flower beds, unless you are certain that they will fit best into your scheme. Generally, gracefully curved beds are more pleasing to the eye. You can form these curves by laying down the garden hose and moving it around until you have come upon the shape that seems right. Then cut away the sod to make the bed.

6. Do not plant short plants behind tall plants. Know the varieties of the plants you buy, and know their expected heights at maturity.

7. Don't plant a monocolor garden. A "blue bed" or a "pink bed" might seem to be a delightful idea in conception, but in reality it will probably bore you stiff. There are few colors that nature cannot mix with grace. Generally, you will achieve gratifying results by using old favorites as the core of your collection, mixing colors freely.

8. Consider the family's use of the yard when planning flower beds. It won't make much sense, for instance, to plant your prize hybrid teas where your kids have traditionally played baseball, or to make the yard off-limits for family enjoyment of outdoor activities. Fit flower beds into the total scheme of home use and enjoyment.

Annuals for Wisconsin

Annuals are probably the most popular flowering plants, and for several very good reasons. They are easy to grow. They are inexpensive to buy. They require relatively little care. They produce results quickly, often blooming within a few weeks after germinating. They offer a huge variety of colors, shapes, and sizes. And many of them bloom continually from midspring until the first hard frosts of autumn. Annuals are hard to beat—but, as their name states, they complete their life cycle in one short season. Next year, they must be planted all over again.

Soil. Annuals will grow well in most good garden soils, although most prefer a loose and well-drained sandy loam that has been well supplied with compost. Annuals are plants in a hurry, since they must complete their life cycle—from their own germination to the final production of seed—in one short Wisconsin season. And, because of their urgency, they need relatively large amounts of nutrients. It will be best to dig copious amounts of compost into the annual beds during the autumn preceding spring planting. If you have not done this, however, you may dig in well-aged compost in the early spring, as soon as the ground can be worked—but in this case, it should be screened compost that will not impede the germination of seeds. Feeding during the season should be made in the form of compost tea, if it is made at all. The roots of most annuals are shallow and easily disturbed by cultivation, and so side-dressings of compost are not recommended.

Location. Most annuals do best in a sunny and open location. None will do well in total shade, but some will bloom quite well in partial shade, including the following: impatiens, coleus, sweet alyssum, snapdragon, sweet sultan, cornflower, China aster, clarkia, cynoglossum, California poppy, godetia, balsam, lupine, mimulus, forget-me-not, nemophila, flowering tobacco, pansy, petunia, schizanthus, ageratum, calendula, zinnia, cleome, cornflower, lobelia, nasturtium, and wishbone flower (*Torenia fournieri*).

If you have an area with very little sun. there are a few other considerations you should heed. First, try to remove some of the sources of the shade, if at all possible. A tree might be pruned judiciously, in order to let more light come through, or an old board fence might come down and be replaced by a wire fence. Soil drainage should be checked carefully, too, since the soil in dim places tends to stagnate and become heavy and waterlogged. Last, some authorities remind us that the white varieties of any species will do better in shade than those of different colors.

If you are faced with total shade, however, you will be better off in planting ground covers and certain perennials recommended for deep shade.

Culture. Nearly all common garden vegetables are annual plants, and are grown in much the same way as are flowering annuals. And, since we have covered the culture of garden vegetables extensively in Chapter 4, it would serve no point here in going over the same material for a second time. I refer you, then, to Chapter 4 for directions and suggestions for starting seeds, preparing seed beds, transplanting young plants and thinning them, and on weed control, watering, and general care during the growing season. In addition, the principles that were set down in the chapters on soil, on composting and mulching, and on climate and weather apply to flower growing as well as vegetable growing and should be studied carefully.

Plants or seeds? The easiest way to grow annuals is to buy young plants from a local nursery or garden center in the spring. These are usually popular varieties that are placed on sale at the proper planting time, and they are plants that will do well in your locality.

If, however, you have grown tired of the same old petunias, zinnias, and marigolds that are offered every year and wish to strike out boldly in new directions, then you might prefer to grow your own annuals from seed. The question then becomes whether to sow the seeds directly into the outdoor beds or start them indoors and transplant them later.

There is actually no need to start annuals indoors, since all will have ample time to come to flower if they are seeded outdoors after the danger of frost has passed. If you want to get an early start. however, and have blooming beds as early in the season as possible, then many annuals may be started indoors and transplanted as warm weather arrives in May or June.

The seeds to start indoors, six weeks before the date of the last expected frost (based on 50 percent chance), include flossflower (*Ageratum houstonianum*), hollyhock, love-lies-bleeding (*Amaranthus caudatus*), Joseph's coat (*Amaranthus tricolor*), Cape forget-me-not, snapdragon, wax begonia, browallia, China aster, Madagascar periwinkle, cockscomb, sweet sultan, feverfew (*Chrysanthemum parthenium*), coleus, Chinese forget-me-not, bedding dahlia, hybrid pinks, sweet William, China pink, common foxglove, blanketflower (*Gaillardia pulchella*), globe amaranth, strawflower, heliotrope, garden balsam, impatiens, burning bush, edging lobelia, sweet alyssum, ten-week stock, four-o'clock, Bells-of-Ireland (*Molucella laevis*), flowering tobacco (*Nicotiana alata*), cupflower, bedding geranium, beardtongue, petunia, annual phlox, gloriosa daisy, painted tongue, blue salvia, scarlet sage, pincushion, dusty miller (*Seneco cineraria*), French marigold, torch tithonia, verbena, viola, pansy, and zinnia.

Quite a list there—and quite a saving, since a dollar's worth of seeds will quickly grow into $20 worth of bedding plants. Then, too, you will never find many of these annuals at your garden center in May and June, since the centers sell only the most popular flowers.

A few other annuals may also be started indoors, but can just as easily be sown directly into the garden as warm weather arrives. They include pot marigold (*Calendula officinalis*), spiderflower, cosmos, Mexican tulip poppy, and African marigold.

Then, there are those annuals that should not be started indoors in any case, preferring to be sown right where they are to grow. They are bachelor's button, annual larkspur, calliopsis, California poppy, Mexican fire plant (*Euphorbia heterophylla*), snow-on-the-mountain (*E. marginata*), annual baby's breath, sunflower, morning glory, sweet pea, flowering flax, Iceland poppy, moss rose (*Portulaca grandflora*), and nasturtium. Most of these don't take well to transplanting. You may try starting them indoors, four weeks before transplanting, if you use peat pots. Then transplant them carefully, so that you do not disturb the roots. Still. they are better sown directly into the garden.

14 Popular Garden Annuals

Here are 14 recommended annuals for Wisconsin gardens. Any such list is highly selective, I realize, but I have selected these because they are all reliable, productive, vigorous, easy to grow, and virtually guaranteed to reward your efforts. All are offered in a wide variety of colors and forms. If you have never grown your own annuals, this would be a nearly perfect starter list.

Impatiens. A generation or two ago, impatiens were little more than a novelty. Today they are by far the most popular garden flower in America—a true American success story. They are colorful, in infinite shades of pink, red, orange, violet, and white. They are easy to start from seeds or cuttings, and they bloom equally well in shade or partial shade. They make a thick and colorful bed when planted in mass, but are equally adaptable to containers, window boxes, and hanging baskets. They are not particular about soil. but the most endearing characteristic is their eagerness to bloom and bloom and bloom, right up until autumn frost. Every garden should have impatiens. Indeed, it seems that every garden *has* impatiens.

Phlox. These prolific bloomers have been popular for generations as tall-growing perennials, and now gardeners can enjoy them as annuals, too. *Phlox drummondii* grows to 18 inches tall and begins to bloom in late spring, continuing all summer, in shades of red, pink, lavender, blue, and white.

Zinnia. What is it that makes zinnias an enormously popular annual flower? Could it be the vast choice of plant and blossom sizes, colors, and petal conformation? Partly. Ease of growth, heat resistance, and dependability also are important considerations. Zinnias are native American flowers, however, so perhaps they come by their number one ranking naturally. Despite blistering heat, rain, and hoards of pests, zinnias come through smiling. They come in virtually any color of the rainbow, and in both tall-growing and dwarf sizes. The only trouble they are likely to have is mildew, when the weather is cool and damp for a long period. Zinnias are native to Mexico.

Marigold. Another native American, marigolds would be at or near the top of anyone's "easy-to-grow" list. The seeds are large, easy to handle. and sprout quickly in warm, moist soil. The seedlings are easily recognizable, so you won't confuse them with weeds. Marigolds come in a wide variety of sizes. The dwarf French varieties are popular because they come in dozens of warm colors and bloom quickly. Many gardeners rely on these small plants to cover up bare soil and hide the lanky legs of taller flowers.

Petunia. Petunias can deceive beginning gardeners. They see baby plants in bloom when no larger than a teacup and refuse to believe that they can become 10 to 20 times larger in short order. So, they cram the seedlings too close together. Six weeks later, the dense mass of foliage and blossoms splits apart and caves in from its own weight, thrusting up green hummocks. Gone is the level, symmetrical flower bed they had envisioned.

Give petunias room, as much as two feet between transplants. Each plant will shoot out ground-hugging laterals. Then, over a period of many weeks, vertical branches will form, each bearing the large blossoms that go with juvenile growth. That's the way petunias perform best.

Geranium. Hybrid geraniums are actually members of the genus *Pelargonium*. They are tender perennials, but plant breeders have developed a whole series of new varieties that most of us now grow from seed as annuals. They are easy to grow, trouble-free, and they flower profusely through the summer and right up to the first hard frosts. Available in a host of shades ranging from red, through the pinks, and into white (there is now even a blue cultivar), they are favorite plants for pots, tubs, and window boxes. Further, they may be wintered over quite easily, so that you may begin with bigger plants in the following season. Take cuttings before the first frost, or cut back the plants and hold them in a cool basement over winter. Old-time gardeners used to hang them upside-down from the rafters of the root cellar.

Nasturtium. Nasturtiums are a genuine heirloom flower, among the very first seeds ordered after the colonists established trade with England. Now they hold a high place among flowers grown from seed. Nasturtiums are not only bright and beautiful, but they smell good enough to eat. Indeed, they *are* good enough to eat. Use fresh unopened buds in salads, or, if you have large crops, pickle them as capers. The full, opened blossoms are often used as plate garnishes in the fanciest of restaurants. Modern nasturtium varieties are

bred to hold their blossoms above the foliage. Colors include garnet, cherry pink, and cerise, in addition to the traditional yellow, gold, and cream shades with dark markings.

Salvia. This bright-blooming annual has grown enormously in popularity in recent years. Best known for its brilliant red blossoms, which are borne on long spikes, salvia is now available in blue and other colors, also. The modern cultivars begin to bloom only six to eight weeks after sowing, and continue all summer long. They are very resistant to heat and drought conditions, holding their color even in extreme heat.

Alyssum. No other flower can match the fragrance of alyssum. Downwind from a large bed of alyssum on a humid, fairly calm day, you can smell the perfume at 50 feet. But alyssum offers more than just a breath of spring. It is so useful and adaptable that it continues to climb on the popularity scale. Mixed colors and separate shades are available in pink, rose, lavender, purple, and white. They are perfect for rock gardens and for edging, the plants reaching four to six inches in height and spreading to a foot or more across.

Moss rose. Portulaca or moss rose is a self-reliant flower. Drought doesn't faze it, and little or no cultivation is needed. Colors include some of the most intense yellow, pink, and crimson hues found in the plant kingdom. Moss rose loves full and hot sun, but will close up its blossoms if the weather is cloudy and cool. A little-known fact about moss rose seeds is that they frequently germinate and sprout better if stored in a refrigerator at approximately 40° for two or four weeks. Pre-chilling breaks the dormancy that may cause slow sprouting. If you're lucky, moss rose will self-seed in your garden.

Snapdragon. The "jaws" of the snapdragon, which for generations have delighted children, are actually a cleverly designed trap door that opens with the weight of a pollen-laden bee. It is almost as if the snapdragon and the bee were made for each other. Snapdragons like cool weather. For spring blossoms, start seeds indoors six weeks before transplanting time. We

Table 12. Germination Time for Garden Flower Seeds

Plant	Days	Plant	Days
Ageratum	5-8	Godetia	12-15
Alyssum	4-5	Heliotrope	15-18
Anchusa	18-20	Hollyhock	15-18
Arctotis	12-15	Larkspur (annual)	15-18
Baby's breath	18-20	Lobelia	8-10
Balsam	5-8	Marigold	5-8
Butterfly weed	10-12	Mignonette	8-10
Calendula	8-10	Morning glory	8-10
Candytuft	5-8	Nasturtium	8-10
Canterbury bells	12-15	Nicotiana	18-20
Clarkia	7-10	Nigella	8-10
Cockscomb	5-8	Pansy	10-12
Columbine	15-18	Pea, sweet	15-18
Coreopsis	15-20	Penstemon	18-20
Cornflower	5-8	Periwinkle	15-18
Cosmos	5-8	Petunia	10-18
Dahlia	8-10	Phlox (annual)	15-18
Delphinium	10-15	Poppy (Iceland)	18-20
Dianthus	8-10	Portulaca	15-18
English daisy	5-8	Sage, blue	12-15
Forget-me-not	12-15	Shasta daisy	18-21
Four-o'clock	5-8	Strawflower	5-8
Gaillardia	15-20	Zinnia	5-8

used to have trouble with snapdragons bending and breaking their stems in the wind, but modern breeders have now developed varieties with shorter and stouter stems.

Morning glory. No other flowering vine can excel morning glories for quickly screening and covering unsightly objects. A vine can easily top a 20-foot pole, but can also be kept in bounds by pinching back tip growth. The huge three- to four-inch blossoms come in white, pink, rose, purple, and blue. Nick seeds with a nail file before planting them, to speed up sprouting.

Coleus. Here is one of the most colorful of all garden annuals, a plant we grow for its brilliant and multicolored foliage rather than its blossoms, which are insignificant. It seems that there are more and more leaf colors and patterns to choose from each year, making coleus one of the most popular and versatile of annu-

als. A huge bonus is that coleus performs very well in shaded areas, helping to brighten dim corners. In fact, their colors are muted when exposed to long hours of bright sun. Pinch off any flower spikes for best performance. Coleus can also be potted up and used as a house plant on a sunny windowsill.

Pansy. Perky pansies have traditionally been a biennial plant, germinating the first year, then flowering and dying the second. But now there are annual varieties, thus removing the challenge of keeping the plants over winter in northern climates. Further, the modern hybrid pansies come in a broad pallet of new colors, ranging from the traditional purple and yellow through oranges and reds, and all shades in between. These pansies are easy to raise and perfect for edging and hanging baskets, growing only six inches high.

Planting times. Started plants or seeds of most annuals should not be set outside until all danger of frost has passed. The ideal soil temperature for the germination and early growth of these half-hardy and tender annuals is 60° to 70°. If the soil is much cooler than that, the seeds will simply not germinate and seedlings will not grow larger.

Exceptions to the rule are these hardy annuals that can be set out in the early spring, as soon as the soil can be worked: baby's breath, cornflower, gaillardia, globe amaranth, phlox, poppy, salpiglossis, cleome, stock, strawflower, summer cypress, sweet alyssum, and sweet pea. Recommendations for planting times are given on the backs of most seed packets.

Removing wilted flowers. One important rule to observe in growing annuals is to remove wilted and dried flowers almost daily. If the flowers are allowed to produce seeds, the plant will have completed the final stage of its life cycle and will stop producing new blossoms. In order to keep each plant producing blossoms, then, you must remove the old flowers before they have begun to produce seed pods.

Sixty-four annuals for Wisconsin.

Table 12 lists 64 annual flowering plants that will grow well in Wisconsin's climate. This list is by no means exhaustive, but it will give you an idea of the range of annuals that is open to you. You can learn much more about the characteristics of different annuals by sending for several seed catalogs during the late winter and early spring.

Biennials

Biennials are plants that require two seasons to complete their life cycle. Generally, flowering biennials are planted during the summer of the first year, and they bloom during the second year.

The use of biennials in home gardens is not so popular as it once was, probably because the extra care they require is not thought to be worth the results they bring—and also because it is so simple and inexpensive to buy second-year biennials from the nursery, ready to bloom. Also, there seems to be a general lack of desire to prepare a bed and sow flower seeds in June and July, when we are already surrounded by blooming annuals and perennials. Last, plant breeders have developed annual varieties of some of the popular biennials, so that the extra effort in starting and overwintering plants is seldom necessary.

The most popular biennials are Canterbury bells, foxglove, hollyhocks, rose campion (these, the more hardy), pansies, forget-me-not, English daisies, and English wallflowers (these, less hardy). Others include Siberian wallflower, cup-and-saucer, steeple-bellflower, honesty, and horn poppy.

The cultivation of biennials in Wisconsin is a chancy thing, at any rate, because of our severe winter climate. In southern areas of the United States, the young plants can over-winter without much difficulty. Here, however, special winter protection is an absolute necessity. Seeds are sown in June or July, depending on the variety, and the young plants are transplanted into a cold frame in September, where they are covered with straw and left to overwinter in a dormant state. In spring they are transplanted into their permanent garden locations.

The only advantage of growing biennials in this way is that they will provide some nice color early in the season, when the annuals are just getting started. Even this advantage, however, is largely obviated by the efficient services of the local garden center or nursery, which can supply the same plants in ready-to-bloom state, at the same time of the year.

Perennials for Busy Gardeners

Perennials should form the backbone of the flower garden. They produce a maximum of bloom with a minimum of care, and they reappear year after year, soon becoming old and trusted friends.

Strictly speaking, perennials are plants that live for more than two years. Under this definition, trees and shrubs qualify as perennials—and, indeed, they are. But when gardeners

Table 13. Annuals for Wisconsin Gardens

Plant	Height (inches)	Best Uses	Remarks
Ageratum	6 to 20	Edging	Tall varieties grown for cut flowers. Good rock-garden plant. Pot and bring in house for winter bloom.
Amaranthus	36 to 72	Beds, borders	Brilliant red to deep-red leaves. Shrublike.
Anchusa	up to 18	Beds, borders	Deep blue flowers in June and July. Needs full sun.
Arctotis (African Daisy)	up to 36	Beds	Large daisylike blooms all summer and fall. Prefers sandy soil and full sun.
Baby's breath	12 to 18	Borders	Source of cut flowers and plants for drying. Grows well on alkaline soils.
Balsam	20 to 28	Bedding	Good window-garden plant. Will not tolerate wet or cold weather.
Brachycome	9 to 12	Edging, rock gardens	Profusion of small flowers all summer and fall. Prefers full sun.
Browallia	10 to 24	Borders	Blooms blue to lavender. Likes moist soil and partial shade.
Calendula	14 to 18	Bedding	Source of cut flowers. Good window-garden plant. Needs full sun, cool, moist soil.
California poppy	10 to 12	Beds, borders	Free-flowering and easy to grow. Likes sandy soil and full sun.
Calliopsis	18 to 24	Bedding, edging	Blooms quickly, lasts all summer. Needs full sun.
Candytuft	9 to 12	Edging, bedding	Good rock garden plant and filler. Select dwarf varieties for bedding.
Carnation	15 to 18	Beds, borders	Popular cut flower. Is biennial, but will bloom first year if planted early.
China aster	12 to 24	Bedding	Good source of cut flowers.
Clarkia	up to 24	Beds, borders	Easy to grow, does best in cooler areas. Prefers dry semishade.
Cockscomb	16 to 40	Bedding	Source of cut flowers and plants for drying. Will tolerate partial shade.
Coleus	20 to 24	Bedding	Perennial, really; grown for its decorative foliage.
Cornflower	16 to 36	Bedding	Source of cut flowers. New double blossoms are impressive.
Cosmos	30 to 48	Screens, bedding	Source of cut flowers. Good background plants. Needs full sun.
Dahlia (seed-grown)	18 to 40	Bedding, edging	Source of cut flowers. Blooms early. Needs good soil, full sun.

Table 13. Annuals for Wisconsin Gardens (continued)

Plant	Height (inches)	Best Uses	Remarks
English daisy	up to 6	Borders, rock gardens	Likes moist, well-drained soil, partial shade. Not really an annual, but nursery plants will bloom the first year.
Everlasting flower	12 to 36	Beds, borders	Will grow almost anywhere, but prefers dry soil and full sun.
Forget-me-not	12 to 36	Beds, borders	Source of cut flowers. Does not withstand intense heat.
Four-o'clock	20 to 24	Beds, borders	Neat, regular, closely branching; multicolored blossoms. Plant in sun or partial shade.
Gaillardia	12 to 18	Borders	Source of cut flowers and plants for drying. Needs full sun.
Geranium	up to 24	Beds, borders	Easy to grow from seed. Likes full sun.
Globe amaranth	18 to 24	Borders	Good for cut flowers and for drying. Likes hot, dry location.
Godetia	10 to 36	Beds, borders	Likes moist, cool soil and partial shade.
Heliotrope	12 to 24	Bedding	Will succeed in any good soil in full sun.
Hollyhock	24 to 96	Screens, beds	Dwarf varieties now available. Likes warm weather and full sun. Plant annual varieties early.
Impatiens	10 to 12	Bedding	Perennial grown as annual. Good plant for window gardens. Will take deep shade.
Kochia	30 to 60	Beds	Also called burning bush. Green foliage turns brilliant red in autumn.
Larkspur	18 to 48	Screens	Source of cut flowers and plants for drying. Make successive sowings for cut flowers.
Lobelia	4 to 18	Borders, edging, rock gardens	Blooms well in partial shade.
Lupine	18 to 24	Borders	Source of cut flowers. Prefers dry, sandy soil.
Marigold	6 to 30	Bedding	Most popular of all annuals. Good for cut flowers, window gardens. Likes full sun. Excessive nitrogen delays blooming.
Mignonette	6 to 18	Beds, borders	Good fragrance. Likes moist soil and partial shade.
Morning glory	(climber)	Screens	Vine grows 8 to 12 feet tall. Vigorous once started.
Nasturtium	12 to 72	Beds, borders, screens	Blooms one month after sowing. Likes full sun. Poor soil will produce more blossoms, less foliage.
Nicotiana	15 to 48	Beds, borders	Ornamental tobacco. Easy to grow, blooms profusely summer and fall. Likes moist soil and partial shade.

Table 13. Annuals for Wisconsin Gardens (continued)

Plant	Height (inches)	Best Uses	Remarks
Nigella	18 to 24	Beds, borders	Short blooming season, but a fine range of colors.
Pansy	6 to 10	Beds, borders	Source of cut flowers. Pot plants after bloom, protect for over winter. Replace with petunia for summer bloom.
Petunia	8 to 24	Bedding	Good plant for window gardens. Long blooming period.
Phlox	6 to 15	Bedding	Withstands heat. More compact than petunias.
Pink	6 to 16	Edging, borders	Source of cut flowers. Long-blooming, bright colors.
Poppy	12 to 16	Borders	Source of cut flowers. Make successive sowings for longer bloom.
Portulaca	6 to 9	Bedding, edging, rock gardens	Bright colors. Withstands heat.
Rudbeckia	20 to 24	Borders, bedding	Source of cut flowers. Loves heat.
Salpiglossis	24 to 30	Bedding	Source of cut flowers. Does not withstand heat. Blooms midsummer to frost.
Salvia	7 to 24	Beds, borders, edging	Blooms profusely and brilliantly from midsummer until frost. Best to buy started plants to set out when weather and soil have warmed up.
Scabiosa	18 to 36	Borders	Source of cut flowers. Remove dead flowers for greater bloom.
Scarlet sage	14 to 36	Borders, bedding	Short varieties bloom early and are best for Wisconsin.
Snapdragon	10 to 36	Bedding	Source of cut flowers. Dwarf varieties good for window gardens. Sun or partial shade.
Spiderplant	30 to 36	Borders, hedges	Long blooming period.
Stock	24 to 30	Bedding	Source of cut flowers. Good plant for window gardens.
Strawflower	30 to 40	Bedding	One of best plants for drying. Grows well in a variety of locations, but prefers hot sun.
Sunflower	48 to 84	Screens, borders	See cultural directions in chapter on vegetables.
Sweet alyssum	6 to 10	Edging, borders	Grow in well-drained soil. Damps off easily. Neat and free flowering. Long blooming period.
Sweet pea	(climber)	Screens	Vine, grows 4 to 8 feet long. Source of cut flowers.
Tithonia	36 to 72	Screens, hedges	A large and vigorous plant with three-inch orange-colored blossoms. Good for cut flowers.

Table 13. Annuals for Wisconsin Gardens (continued)

Plant	Height (inches)	Best Uses	Remarks
Torenia	8 to 12	Borders, rock gardens	Compact and bushy plants will do well in full sun or partial shade. Blooms during summer and fall.
Verbena	9 to 12	Bedding	Source of cut flowers. Cover spots left by spring-flowering bulbs.
Vinca	15 to 18	Bedding	Perennial grown as annual. Good plant for window gardens.
Zinnia	18 to 36	Bedding	Popular source of cut flowers. Endures heat. Foliage frequently mildews. Wide choice of colors.

(Note: In the listings above, you will see some plants—such as dahlia and geranium—that we do not usually think of as annuals. They are included because certain varieties of these species can be grown from seed and will produce as annuals. They will also be treated in later parts of this chapter, however, under the classifications in which we usually expect to find them.)

speak of perennials, they are speaking of herbaceous flowering plants whose tops die down each fall, but whose roots remain alive to produce new top growth and bloom during the following year. Some of the most popular perennials in Wisconsin are chrysanthemums, asters, delphiniums, peonies, phlox, and day lilies. But there are scores of perennials that will find a happy home in Wisconsin's rugged climate—especially if they are given a little winter protection. Your selection of varieties should be dictated only by the growing conditions in your garden and your aesthetic sense.

Planning for perennials. Since you hope to keep your hardy perennials in one location for a number of years, you should exercise considerable care in planning the beds. Perennials can be divided and transplanted, of course, but there is no sense in doing this unless and until the plant really needs it. Take into consideration, then, each variety's expected mature height, sun and shade requirements, time of blooming, and hardiness. In this section we will recommend only the more hardy perennials that can take Wisconsin's winters, although gardeners in the colder areas of the state should be conscientious in providing extra

winter protection—while those in the southern portion of Wisconsin can find many additional options in garden catalogs.

Soil. Nearly all perennials like a light, rich, and well-drained soil, one that is capable of holding adequate moisture without being heavy. It will reward your efforts to prepare the perennial beds carefully in advance. Till the soil 18 to 24 inches deep and incorporate plenty of compost, manure, peat moss (or leaf mold), and bone meal (four to seven pounds per 100 square feet).

Hardiness. Most common garden perennials are hardy in Wisconsin, although some are naturally hardier than others. The best way to discover which are definitely hardy in your area is to check with your local nursery or observe those plants in other local gardens. Don't be afraid to ask friends and neighbors about their own favorite perennials. The conversation might even lead to the neighbor's sharing some root divisions with you.

Planning for continuing bloom. Many perennials have comparatively short blooming periods, even though the blooms during these times may be spectacular. A typical example familiar to nearly all of us is the peony, which is found growing everywhere in Wisconsin because of its remarkable hardiness and vigor. Its blooming period is short—only a week or two—while that of marigolds, the popular annual, lasts from spring right up until the first hard frosts of autumn. But we grow peonies because of the breathtaking glory of that short bloom, just as we welcome marigolds for their long and cheerful service.

The perennial garden, then, should be planned so that there is some bloom during as much of the growing season as possible. The following guide will help. Remember, though, that this is a guide and not a guarantee. These perennials might bloom a week or two earlier or later, depending on which section of the state is their host. Generally, however, you can assure a continuing parade of bloom (although not continuous bloom) by choosing at least one perennial from each of the following groups:

April-blooming perennnials: Anchusa, arabis, bleeding heart, dwarf anchusa (*Brunnera macrophylia*), forget-me-not, primrose, and Virginia bluebell (*Mertensia virginica*).

May-blooming perennials: Anchusa, anthemis, arabis, armeria, artemisia, aubrietia, bleeding heart, bugleweed, day lily, dwarf anchusa (*Brunnera macrophylia*), forget-me-not, gas plant, iberis, painted daisy, primrose, trollius, and Virginia bluebell (*Mertensia virginica*).

June-blooming perennials: Achillea, agrostemma, alyssum, anthemis, armeria, artemisia, astilbe, baby's breath, balloonflower, blue flax, bugleweed, columbine, coralbells, coreopsis, cupid's dart (*Catananche caerulea*), day lily, cornflower, delphinium, forget-me-not, gaillardia, gas plant, geum, heliotrope, iberis, lychnis, myrtle, nepeta, oenothera, oriental poppy, painted daisy, penstemon, peony, pink, shasta daisy, sidalcea, snow-in-summer (*Cerastium tomentosum*), sweet William, trollius, verbena, and viola.

July-blooming perennials: Achillea. agrostemma, alyssum, anthemis, artemisia, astilbe, baby's breath, balloonflower, bee balm, blue flax, cimicifuga, columbine, coralbells,

coreopsis, cornflower, cupid's dart (*Catananche caerulea*), day lily, delphinium, gaillardia, geum, harebell, heliotrope, hosta, lupine, lychnis, lythrum, myrtle, nepeta, oenothera, oriental poppy, painted daisy, penstemon, peony, perennial pea (*Lathyrus latifolius*), phlox, physostegia, pink, scutellaria, shasta daisy, sidalcea, sweet William, trollius, verbena, veronica, and viola.

August-blooming perennials: Alyssum, anthemis, artemisia, baby's breath, balloonflower, bee balm, boltonia, cimicifuga, coreopsis, cupid's dart (*Catananche caerulea*), day lily, cornflower, gaillardia, geum, golden glow, harebell, helenium, hosta, lythrum, monkshood, myrtle, nepeta, oenothera, penstemon, perennial pea (*Lathyrus latifolius*), phlox, physostegia, pink, scutellario, sedum, verbena, veronica, and viola.

September-blooming perennials: Anthemis, artemisia, aster, baby's breath, boltonia, chrysanthemum, coreopsis, cornflower, gaillardia, golden glow, harebell, helenium, hosta, lythrum, monkshood, myrtle, nepeta, penstemon, perennial pea (*Lathyrus latifolius*), physostegia, pink, verbena, and veronica.

October-blooming perennials: Aster, chrysanthemum, coreopsis, gaillardia, nepeta, penstemon, and pink.

November-blooming perennials: Gardeners in the southern part of the state can hope for some November bloom, particularly if they take precautions against the first hard frosts. When frost is forecast, cover your favorite perennials with large plastic trash bags. Anchor the bags at the bottom so that the heat rising from the soil cannot escape readily. After the sun is well up in the sky the next day, the bags can be removed easily and the plants can again receive the warm rays of the sun. You can prolong bloom for several weeks in this way—but the day will come when you will at last have to put the perennials to bed for the winter.

Starting perennials. There are various ways in which you can build up a collection of perennial flowering plants. The least expensive is to prevail upon your friends and neighbors to share clump divisions or to give you cuttings. Perennials usually should be divided about every three years, anyway, in order to keep the plants vigorous and thriving. The best time for dividing is in the early spring, although it can be done in the fall. too, if you can do it at least four weeks before the first hard frosts. (Fall-blooming perennials, however, should not be divided in the fall.)

When a perennial has been in one spot too long, the center of its root clump becomes crowded and weak. You will want to discard the center of the clump, while dividing the vigorous outside shoots into new plants. To divide roots, dig up the entire clump, getting as much of the root as you can, wash most of the soil away, and examine the clump to see where the most vigorous growth is taking place. Make the divisions by inserting two garden forks into the clump, back to back, and gradually prying the clump apart. Try to get good-sized divisions, so that they will grow quickly. Then replant these divisions in newly prepared soil.

You can also start perennials by taking and rooting cuttings, although this is sometimes a little tricky. Select vigorous new shoots in spring and cut them as far down as possible— below the soil line, if they extend beneath the soil. Insert these in moist sand, indoors or in a hotbed, until they have established good roots. Expose the young plants gradually to outside temperatures to harden them off, until they are ready to be transplanted into the perennial beds by midsummer. (The care of young plants is covered in detail in the chapter on vegetables. The principles are the same.)

You can also grow many perennials by sowing seed in the open garden, and these often grow quickly into strong and vigorous plants, since you will not have to nurse them along. Seed is sown in either early spring, after all danger of frost has passed, or in late summer or fall, in finely prepared beds, and the young plants should be thinned and spaced according to directions for the individual variety.

You can get an earlier start by sowing seed indoors or in a hotbed or cold frame, although the added burden does not seem to be justified for plants that you hope to establish as permanent plantings.

Perhaps the safest and easiest way to start perennials (although the most expensive) is to buy started plants at a local nursery or garden center. These will have a good chance of growing, even for the beginner, and you will know that the plants you buy are suited for growing in your locality. Also, the plants will probably be in bloom when you buy them, and so you will see the exact colors of the blossoms. Buy plants that are bushy, compact, dark green, and vigorous looking.

Perennials to seed up to two months before frost: August 1-15

Achilles—The Pearl
Aquilegia—Columbine
Arabis—Rock Cress
Armeria—Sea pink
Carnation
Delphinium
Digitalis—Foxglove
Gaillardia
Garden pinks
Geum
Gypsophila—Baby's breath
Hibiscus
Hollyhock
Liatris
Linum—Flax
Lychnis (Agrostemma)—Rose campion
Physalis—Lantern Plant
Platycodon—Balloon Flower
Pyrethrum—Painted daisy
Saponaria—Soapwort
Shasta Daisy
Sweet William
Tritoma—Red Hot Poker

Perennials to seed in late fall: End of October

Gas Plant
Iceland poppy
Oriental Poppy
Pansy
Penstemon
Phlox
Primula—Primrose
Scabiosa
Viola

Assuring moisture. After your perennials have been established, they should be mulched, in order to conserve moisture and keep down weeds. The best mulch material will be one that is light, porous, and attractive. Buckwheat hulls and cocoa bean shells are two good ones that fill all three requirements. During a particularly long dry spell, you might find that the soil has become dry, despite the mulch. Water the perennials at this time, and be sure to water thoroughly and deeply. A soaker hose is perfect for a perennial bed.

Fertilizing. If you have composted the soil well during the preceding fall, you will not have to feed the plants during the season. However, they will respond to a few applications of compost or manure tea, particularly when they begin to bloom. Older plantings should be fertilized more often—once, when they have begun to make active growth in the spring, again in three weeks, and still again just as they begin to bloom. These feedings, too, can be made in the form of compost or manure tea. In addition, older plants will respond to a light side-dressing of compost in the early spring.

Staking. Modern perennials have been bred to bloom heavily, and so the taller of them will need staking for support. Any stakes will do, although the most inconspicuous will be the green cane types sold by garden centers. Tie the stems to the stake with some soft material or with green plastic strips made especially for the purpose. Loop the strip loosely around the plant stem. Make a knot between the stem and the stake, and another around the stake to secure it tightly. Do not endanger the stem by tying a knot tightly around it, or by using wire. Breeders have also begun to produce hybrids that have heavier stalks, therefore needing less staking or none at all. If you don't like the job of staking plants, look for these hybrids in catalogs.

Removing wilted flowers. As with other flowering plants, you should remove wilted flowers regularly, in order to encourage the plant to produce more blossoms.

Winter protection. All but the hardiest of perennials will appreciate a heavy winter mulch to protect their roots from hard freezing and—more important—to prevent root damage during the alternate freezing and thawing of the ground during late winter and early spring. A good mulch keeps the soil temperature at a more constant level, preventing the heaving of the ground that can tear roots apart.

Wait until the ground freezes hard before applying the winter mulch. (The summer mulch need not be removed at all.) When the ground is hard, apply a 10- to 15-inch layer of straw or hay, or even pine boughs, over the plants. When the weather has moderated in April, remove the straw, but do not remove the light summer mulch. Loosen up the summer mulch and, after the plant has made some good growth, replenish the summer mulch to make up for any that might have composted itself into the top layer of soil. The winter straw mulch which you removed can be used to mulch vegetables a little later in the season.

Three Dozen Perennials for Wisconsin

The following 36 selected perennials (with cultural recommendations based mainly on USDA materials) will constitute a well-rounded group for Wisconsin gardens. All are hardy and most are easy to grow—which is perhaps why this group includes many of the more popular perennials in this section of the country.

This list is, to be sure far from comprehensive. You can get many more ideas by scanning the seed and nursery catalogs and by checking with your local nursery. But do make sure that any other perennials you choose are hardy in your area.

In describing these plants, I give the growing height for the popular forms. Note that there are now dwarf hybrids of many of these perennials, and you can find these by studying the catalogs.

Achillea. *Achillea millefolium* (yarrow, milfoil) grows about two feet high. It looks best in borders that bloom from June to September. Achillea is grown also for cut flowers. Plant seed in early spring or late fall. Choose a sunny spot in your garden. Space plants 36 inches apart. Seed germinates in seven to 14 days. Because seed is very small, water with a mist. Achillea is easy to grow.

Alyssum. *Alyssum saxatile* (gold dust) grows nine to 12 inches high. It is used in rock gardens and for edging and cut flowers. It blooms in early spring. Alyssum is excellent in dry or sandy soil. Plant seed in early spring in a sunny spot. Space plants 24 inches apart. Seed germinates in 21 to 28 days.

Anchusa. *Anchusa italica* and *A. myosotidiflora* (alkanet) grow four to five feet high. They are used for borders and backgrounds, as well as a source of cut flowers. Refrigerate seed for 72 hours before sowing. Plant seed anytime from spring to September in a semishaded part of the garden. Shade summer plantings. Space plants 24 inches apart. Seed germinates in 21 to 28 days.

Anthemis. *Anthemis tinctoria* (golden daisy, golden marguerite, Saint John's daisy) grows about two feet high. It looks best in borders that bloom from midsummer to frost. Anthemis is grown also for cut flowers, which are slightly aromatic. You can either start plants indoors eight weeks before planting outdoors or plant seeds outdoors after the soil has warmed in the spring. Anthemis grows well in dry or sandy soil. Plant in a sunny spot. Space plants 24 inches apart. Seeds germinate in 21 to 28 days.

Arabis. *Arabis alpina* (rock cress) grows eight to 12 inches high. It is used for edging and in rock gardens. Plant seed in well-drained soil anytime from spring to September. It grows best in light shade. Shade summer plantings. Space plants about 12 inches apart. Seed germinates in about five days.

Armeria. *Armeria alpina* (sea pink, thrift) grows 18 to 24 inches high. It is used in rock gardens, edging, and borders. The dwarf tufted plants are also used as cut flowers. Plant seed in dry, sandy soil anytime between spring and September. Space plants 12 inches apart in a sunny part of the garden. Shade the seed bed until plants are sturdy. Seed germinates in about ten days.

Artemisia. *Artemisia stelleriana* (wormwood, dusty miller) grows about two feet high. It is used in beds, borders, and rock gardens. Plant seed in full sun from late spring to late September. It grows even in poor and dry soils. Space plants nine to 12 inches apart.

Asters. Fall-blooming asters grow from one to five feet high. They are used in rock gardens, borders, and for cut flowers, as one of our most popular late-blooming perennials. Plant seed in early spring in a sunny spot. Space plants about three feet apart. Seed germinates in 14 to 21 days.

Astilbe. *Astilbe japonica* (florists' spirea) grows one to three feet high. It is used in borders. Plant seed in early spring in rich, loamy soil. Space plants 24 inches apart. Seed germinates in 14 to 21 days. Likes a partly shady spot.

Aubrietia. *Aubrietia deltoidea graeca* (rainbow rock cress) grows about six inches high. It is grown in borders and rock gardens and along dry walls. Aubrietia is a dwarf, spreading plant. Sow seed anytime from spring to September in light shade. Space plants about 12 inches apart. Seed will germinate in about 20 days. Shade plants in summer. To propagate, divide mature plants in late summer.

Baby's breath. *Gypsophila paniculata* grows two to four feet high. It is used for borders and as a source of cut flowers and flowers for drying.

It does best in a deeply prepared soil that is high in lime content. Plant seeds anytime from early spring to September in a sunny spot. Space plants about four feet apart. Seed germinates in about ten days.

Bleeding heart. *Dicentra spectabilis* grows two to four feet high. A smaller variety, *D. cucullaria* (Dutchman's-breeches) grows one foot tall. They are used for borders, in front of shrubbery, and as pot plants. Plant seed in late autumn. Space plants 12 to 18 inches apart. Seed will germinate in the following spring.

Cerastium. *Cerastium tomentosum* (snow-in-summer) grows about six inches high. It is used in rock gardens and for ground cover. Plants form a creeping mat. Cerastium does well in dry and sunny spots. Plant seed in early spring. Space plants about 18 inches apart. Seed germinates in 14 to 28 days. Cerastium is a hard, tough plant and a rampant grower. Do not allow it to crowd other plants.

Chrysanthemums. Mums are popular all over Wisconsin because of their profusion of fall bloom and their great variety. The major types include the singles, pompons (the kind associated with football corsages), anemones, spoons, and spiders, depending on the form of their blossoms. Plant mums in a rich and well-drained soil, in a sunny location. You can buy field-grown clumps in spring (which generally must be divided before planting) or you can start cuttings. Gift plants which you receive can be planted, too. Let the gift plants finish blooming indoors, then cut them back to two to three inches above the pot rim. Plant them outside in spring, after danger of frost has passed. Chrysanthemums winter-kill quite easily, and so a heavy mulch is necessary. Do not choose the late-blooming varieties, which might have trouble reaching the blooming stage in Wisconsin's short growing season.

Columbine. Columbine hybrids (*Aquilegia*) grow 30 to 36 inches high. They are used for borders and for cut flowers. Columbine needs fairly rich, well-drained soil. Plant seed anytime from spring to September in sun or partial shade. Space plants 12 to 18 inches apart. Seed germinates in about 30 days, but germination is irregular. It is often grown as a biennial to avoid leaf miner and crown rotting.

Coralbells. *Heuchera sanguinea* grows up to two feet high. It is used for rock gardens, borders, and cut flowers. It grows best in a limed soil. Plant seed in early spring or late fall in partial shade. Space plants about 18 inches apart. Seed germinates in about ten days. Propagate by division.

Coreopsis. *Coreopsis grandiflora* grows two to three feet high. It is used in borders. Plant seed in a light loam in early spring or late fall. Choose a sunny spot in the garden. Space plants about 30 inches apart. Seed takes about five days to germinate. Coreopsis is drought resistant.

Coreopsis

Day lily. *Hemerocallis* grows one to four feet high. To have day lily flowers throughout the growing season, plant various species of this perennial. Day lily is used in borders and among shrubbery. Plant seed in late fall or early spring in full sunlight or partial shade. Space plants 24 to 30 inches apart. Seed germinates in 15 days.

Delphinium. *Delphinium elatum* grows four to five feet high. It is used for borders. background, and cut flowers. Plant seed anytime from spring to September in a well-drained and sunny spot. Plants tend to rot in wet, heavy soils. Space plants 24 inches apart. Seed germinates in about 20 days. Shade summer plantings. Foliage tends to mildew. Early staking is recommended.

Dianthus. *Dianthus deltoides* and *D. plumarius* (pinks) grow about a foot high. They are used for borders, rock gardens, edging, and cut flowers. Plant seed anytime from spring to September in a sunny spot. Space plants 12 inches apart. Seed germinates in five days. Dianthus is best when grown as a biennial. It is winter-killed in wet locations and is very susceptible to rotting at the soil line.

Gaillardia. *Gaillardia grandiflora* grows 12 to 30 inches high. It is used in borders and for cut flowers. Gaillardia is easily grown from seed, which you can plant in early spring or late summer. Choose a sunny spot in your garden. Space plants 24 inches apart. Seed germinates in about 12 days.

Geum. *Geum chiloense* grows six to 24 inches high. It is used in borders and rock gardens and for cut flowers. Geum will grow in many different locations. You can plant seed in spring or summer in a sunny spot. Space plants about 18 inches apart. Seed germinates in 25 days.

Lupine. *Lupine polyphyllus* grows to about three feet high. It is used in borders and for cut flowers. Plant seed in early spring or late fall in a sunny spot that has perfect drainage. Soak seeds before planting. and inoculate them with the same bacterial agent used for peas. Plant seed where lupine is to flower, since it does not transplant well. Space plants about 36 inches apart. Seed germinates in about 20 days.

Lythrum. Lythrum (blackblood) grows four to six feet high. Use it scattered in gardens and yards or among trees and shrubs. Plant seed in late fall or early spring in a moist, lightly shaded area. Space plants 18 to 24 inches apart. Seed germinates in 15 days. (Note: It is illegal to plant *Lythrum salicaria* and *L. virgatum* (purple loosestrife) in Wisconsin, where it is an agressive and invasive plant in wild areas.)

Oriental poppy. *Papaver orientale* grows about three feet high. It is used in borders and for cut flowers. Plant seed in early spring in a permanent location because it does not transplant well. Choose a sunny spot. Space plants two feet apart. Seed germinates in about ten days.

Penstemon. *Penstemon murrayanus grandiflorus* (beardlip, pagoda flower, beardtongue) grows 18 to 24 inches high. It is used in borders and for cut flowers. It grows best in well-drained soil and does well in rather dry soil. Plant seed in early spring or late fall in a sunny spot that is sheltered in winter. Space plants 18 inches apart. Seed germinates in about ten days.

Peony. Peony is an old-time Wisconsin favorite, a fixture in all flower gardens early in this century, and still one of our most popular perennials. It grows two to four feet tall and is used in borders and for cut flowers. It is difficult to grow from seed. Plant tubers in late fall at least three feet apart and two to three inches deep.

Phlox, summer. *Phlox paniculata* grows to about three feet high. It is used in borders and for cut flowers. Plant seed in late fall or early winter in a sunny spot. Keep seed in refrigerator one month before seeding. Space plants about two feet apart. Keep soil moist. Germination takes about 24 days and is very irregular. Plants grown from seed are especially variable in color and form.

Phlox, moss. *Phlox subulata* grows four to five inches high and is used in borders. It is normally grown from stolons (shoots). Plant in a sunny spot. Space plants about eight inches apart. Moss phlox is drought resistant.

Platycodon. *Platycodon grandiflorum* (balloonflower) grows about two feet high. It is used for borders and cut flowers. Plant seed anytime between spring and September in a sunny spot. Space plants about 12 inches apart. Seed germinates in ten days. In the fall, dig roots and store in moist sand in a cool (but frost-free) cold frame. Replant in early spring.

Primrose. *Primula polyantha* grows six to nine inches high; *P. veris* grows six inches high. Primrose is used in rock gardens. Early in the year, sow seed on soil surface in pots; water with mist; cover with glass; place outside to freeze; bring inside to germinate. Seed also can be planted outside in spring if it is first frozen in ice cubes. Usually seed is planted in late autumn or early winter. Choose a spot in partial shade. Space plants about a foot apart. Seed germinates in about 25 days but is very irregular.

Shasta daisy. *Chrysanthemum maximum* grows 24 to 30 inches high. It is used for borders and for cut flowers. Plant seed anytime from early spring to September in a sunny spot. Space plants about 30 inches apart. Seed germinates in about ten days. Shasta daisy is best grown as a biennial. Winter protection in any case is essential in Wisconsin.

Sweet William. *Dianthus barbatus* grows 12 to 18 inches high. A dwarf form also is available. It is used for borders, edging, and cut flowers. It is very hardy but grows best in well-drained soil. Plant seed anytime from spring to September in a sunny spot. Space plants about a foot apart. Seed germinates in five days.

Trollius. *Trollius ledebouri* (globeflower) grows about 20 inches high. It is used in borders. Trollius requires extra moisture. Plant seed in late fall in order to allow it to overwinter before germination in the spring. If you want to plant seed in early spring soak it in hot water for 30 minutes before sowing. Space plants about a foot apart.

Tufted pansy. *Viola cornuta* grows about six inches high. It is used for bedding edging and window boxes. It is easily grown from seed and is very hardy. Plant seed anytime from spring to September in partial shade. Space plants about 12 inches apart. Seed germinates in ten days.

Veronica. *Veronica spicata* (speedwell) grows about 18 inches high. It is used in borders and rock gardens and for cut flowers. It is easily grown. Plant seed anytime from spring to September in a sunny spot. Space plants 18 inches apart. Seed germinates in about 15 days.

Ornamental Plantings for Shady Yards

What some gardeners see as a curse, others see as a challenge—or even as blessed relief.

There are those with shady yards who lament their inability to raise blooming plants. Others take up the challenge with either cheerful pluck or grim determination, and they often create beautiful gardens through wise plant selection and hard work.

Still others—and perhaps they are the smartest—simply explain that their large trees will stand absolutely no competition from lesser plants, and so it is useless to try. They usually explain their unfortunate situation while lying in a hammock, sipping ice tea, as their shadeless friends are staking dahlias in 85-degree heat. My heart is with those in the hammock.

Nevertheless, there are flowering plants that will grow in shady yards, and most of them can be grown without much work. Ferns and many woodland plants, for instance, do beautifully in shade but would quickly perish in full sun.

The problems with shady yards are usually two. First, the shade is most often caused by large trees, and the roots of these trees are voracious competitors for soil moisture and minerals. Second, the shade itself impedes photosynthesis in plants. Some—notably those whose forebears lived in woody areas—are not bothered by this lack of sun; indeed, many require it. Other plants, however, especially those from prairie backgrounds, cannot survive without at least eight hours of sun a day. The lesson: Choose your plants very carefully.

Because of the competition from tree roots (maples are among the worst offenders), the soil in these areas is likely to be deficient in organic matter and air. Soon, small plantings will lack moisture, too, as the trees drink at will. Before planting anything in shady areas, then, you should make a special effort to improve the soil there. Cultivate it, add plenty of compost or rotted manure, and, after you have planted, top-dress plantings with the same materials at least once a month during the growing season. The increased organic content will improve the soil's water and air-retention capacities.

Some perennials that do well in shade, or in partial shade, are bluebead lily, lily of the valley, lady's slipper, bleeding heart, trailing arbutus, day lily, Virginia bluebell, Jacob's ladder, primrose, trillium, and violet.

Ferns are ideal background plants, even for dank and dark spots where it seems nothing else will grow. The ferns, once established, will come back each year.

Woodland wild flowers are also good choices, since they have been growing under large trees for centuries. Among the more popular are bloodroot, Dutchman's-breeches, hepatica, jack-in-the-pulpit, mayapple, showy orchis, Solomon's seal, trillium, and wild geranium, in addition to wild forms of some of the perennials listed previously.

The list of annuals is shorter, since most are field and meadow plants. Try browallia, coleus, impatiens, salvia (the pastel-colored varieties only), and wax begonia. (Note: When choosing blossom colors, remember that, in shade areas, white blossoms do best.)

Some gardeners prefer to cover shady areas with an attractive ground cover, one that will need no further care after it has become established. Investigate cowberry, creeping thyme (also called mother-of-thyme), winter-creeper, Japanese spurge, ajuga, crested iris (spectacular blossoms in May), and hosta (plantain lily). All are perennials, and most are evergreen. A few varieties of ivy (notably Baltic or Bulgarian ivy) can withstand the Wisconsin winters, but most will die back during deep freezes.

Many attractive shrubs will do well in the shade, including bayberry, bush honeysuckle, false spirea, five-leaf aralia, forsythia, black chokeberry (valuable as bird food), snowberry, and witch hazel. Some varieties of both rhododendron and azalea can be grown in Southern Wisconsin, in light to medium shade, if given good winter protection. Check your nursery person for good suggestions for your area.

Among climbing plants, bittersweet, Dutchman's-pipe, honeysuckle, and Virginia creeper are all recommended for covering walls and trellises.

Then, there are the bulb plants, many of which will remain cheerful in the shade. Try achimenes, caladium, scilla, crocus, daffodil, glory-of-the-snow, grape hyacinth, hyacinth, snowdrop, and tulip.

When you survey all the options (and these recommendations are not comprehensive), it becomes apparent that we can have our hammock, our ice tea, and our beautiful shady garden as well. For those who want to go more deeply into the subject, several good books are available. My favorite is Suzanne Warner Pierot's *What Can I Grow in the Shade?*

Planting in Containers and Window Boxes

With a little imagination, a modicum of research, a short trip to the garden center, and a two-hour burst of creative energy, you can have window boxes that are both delightful and unusual. There is no need to fill your boxes with the same petunias and geraniums year after year. You can also grow a wide variety of ornamental plants in pots, barrels, hanging baskets, or nearly any other containers on terraces and patios. Even apartment dwellers with no garden space—but a small balcony—can enjoy the companionship of blooming plants.

There are two broad groups of plants suited to container growing—outdoor annuals and house plants. Yes, house plants. You can either sink your present house plants—pots and all—into larger containers, or you can buy some at your favorite plant store and grow them in the containers until fall. Then you can take them indoors for the winter. In either case, the plants will make amazing progress during their summer vacation outdoors.

(Caution: If you have a really valuable or finicky house plant, do not trust it to the outdoors. And for the rest, do not put them in a place that will receive full sun for the better part of the day. A southern exposure is usually out for house plants, unless it is partially shaded by a large tree. East or west exposures are usually good—particularly the east, which will receive some gentle morning sun. A north window is usually very good.)

Let's consider outdoor annuals. (And let's forget about petunias this year.)

Lantana (not to be confused with the shrub of the same name) is perfect for window boxes. It is a colorful plant, a profuse bloomer from summer to fall, and does well under city conditions. It will do well in partial shade, but best in full sun.

Dwarf marigolds are good for window boxes because they are tough and prolific plants and will continue to bloom until the first hard frosts of autumn. Be sure to get a dwarf variety, since the standard marigolds will quickly take command of the entire box.

Geraniums, in red, white, or pink, are fine for window boxes, and they may be taken in, in fall, to be saved for another year. For new plants for the following year, you may also take leaf cuttings and grow them indoors over the winter.

Torenia is another attractive annual that is suitable for window boxes. Also a prolific bloomer, it grows 8 to 12 inches tall.

Impatiens are my personal favorite. Not only are they prolific and easy to grow, but they will bloom heartily in full shade, on the north side of the house. But impatiens have become so popular in recent years that you might wish to avoid them in favor of a more challenging plant.

Ageratum and *sweet alyssum* are two more good candidates. Both good bloomers, they are offered in varieties growing as low as six inches.

For shady boxes, in addition to impatiens, you should consider *Begonia semperflorens*, fuchsias, and lobelias. *B. semperflorens* (wax begonia) is easy to grow and comes in a variety of blossom colors. Fuchsias can be difficult. At least they are for me. They like a protected spot in shade, warm days, cool nights, and lots of humidity. If you have the right spot for them, they are absolutely beautiful, their pendent flowers cascading down over the window box or from a hanging basket. Lobelias are rewarding, too, and not difficult. Choose the low-growing edging lobelia (*L. erinus*).

For variety, a window box should have some trailing vines as well as flowering plants. Your indoor asparagus ferns will do splendidly in the boxes over the summer, but you can also bring out your ivies—English, Swedish, or grape—as well as any other trailing foliage plants you have inside. Or, you can plant any of a number of outdoor ground covers. *Vinca minor* (periwinkle) is a perfect one for window boxes and tubs. It is a trailing, hardy evergreen, with small blue or white flowers. Some other trailing house plants you can call upon for outdoor service include arrowhead, creeping fig, ivy geranium, trailing coleus, spider plant, and wandering Jew. All look good in tall containers and hanging baskets, too.

Arranging a window box will take a little thought. A good plan is to put trailing vines at both ends (and perhaps one in the middle, if the box is a long one), then put the taller flowering plants at the back of the box and the lower-growing ones along the front. Mix colors at will; nature's hues rarely clash.

To take care of any container garden, make sure first that you begin with good potting soil, one recommended for house plants. Water the containers regularly, and be sure that excess water has a place to drain out. Remember that the soil will dry out much more quickly than soil in the garden. Fertilize about once a month (fish emulsion is good) and keep the plants pinched back to encourage the good shape you want. Last, remember to remove dead blossoms if you want new blossoms to come along. Once the plant begins to produce seed, no more blossoms will be produced.

Plants for Sunny Window Boxes

Mounding

Ageratum
Alyssum
Candytuft
Dianthus
English daisy
Lobelia
Nemesia
Nemophila

Sprawling

Achimines
Lantana
Nasturtium
Petunia
Schizanthus
Torenia
Verbena

Upright

Basil
Dusty miller
Dwarf snapdragon
Geranium
Marigold
Ornamental peppers
Salvia

Trailing

Asparagus fern
English ivy
Euonymus
Pansy
Vinca

Plants for Shady Window Boxes

Sprawling

Nierembergia
Torenia
Many house plants

Trailing

English ivy
Euonymus
Strawberry begonia
Syngonium
Vinca

Mounding

Impatiens

Upright

Caladium
Coleus
Impatiens
Fibrous-rooted begonia
Tuberous begonia

Roses

The rose stands in a class by itself. It is undoubtedly the most cherished garden flower in America. And its popularity stems not from its ease in growing (it is not easy to grow), or from its resistance to insects and diseases (it is notoriously susceptible to both), or for its economy (it is one of the most expensive garden flowering plants to buy and maintain). No, its popularity can be attributed to one reason and one reason only—the sheer magnificence of its bloom. The rose is a delight to the sight and to the scent, and that is the reason why thousands of Wisconsin gardeners take up the challenge of rose growing each year.

The literature on rose growing is so extensive that the books written on this single flower would fill several library shelves. We cannot hope to do justice to rose culture here, for the subject would require an entire book of this size to give it fair treatment of any kind. The best we can hope to do is to present a bare skeleton of information, and then to recommend those rose varieties that are best for Wisconsin's climate. And that is what we will do.

Classes of roses. For all practical purposes, there are five classes of roses: bedding roses, climbing roses, creeping roses, shrub roses, and tree roses.

The bedding roses include the teas and hybrid teas, hybrid perpetuals, and floribundas.

Of these, the hybrid teas are by far the most elegant and the most prized by aficionados.

There are two general kinds of climbers—ramblers, which produce flowers in clusters, and large-flowered climbers, which produce single blossoms.

Creepers are really climbers that are suited to training along banks and walls. They are hardy and suited to the Wisconsin climate, although their flowers are not spectacular.

Shrub roses are, as their name states, shrublike in structure. They are hardy, and their blossom colors are limited to red, white, and pink. The most famous member of the family, at least to avid organic gardeners, is the *Rosa rugosa*, which provides large and vitamin C-rich rose hips after the blossoms have faded. Many organic gardeners grow *Rosa rugosa* not for its flowering beauty (it isn't that attractive) but for its fruit or hips, which are discussed in greater detail on page 179.

Tree roses are a product of the breeder's art, featuring tall and slender trunks, bushy tops, and many single blossoms of good form and large size.

Growing conditions. Roses need plenty of sun, good air circulation, deeply prepared and well-drained soil (pH 5.0-6.0), and a lot of attention. The soil should be tilled to a depth of 24 inches, and large amounts of aged manure and/or compost should be incorporated into the planting hole or trench. A season-long mulch is advised.

Moisture should be assured throughout the growing season, and the plants should be fertilized monthly, beginning in early spring and ending on August 1. A compost tea, providing that it is a rich mixture, is good for roses.

The perfect rose—in a class by itself.

Pruning. Roses are pruned very much like fruit trees. The old and dead wood should be pruned way in spring. In addition, all branches of bedding, shrub. and tree roses should be cut back to encourage bushier growth and greater blossoming. The wilder kinds of roses need be pruned little, except to remove their deadwood each year.

Winter protection. The most effective protection for hybrid teas is the "Minnesota tip," a technique developed in—where else?— Minnesota, in which the entire plant is covered with soil and mulched. It is described by Leon C. Snyder in his book *Gardening in the Upper Midwest.*

"Spray the plants with a dormant spray and tie the canes in a tight bundle, using a rot-resistant twine. Dig a trench that is the depth and width of a spade from the base of the plant. The trench must be as long as the plant is tall. With a spading fork, loosen the soil around the base of the plant. Gradually bend the canes into the trench and cover with the soil removed when digging it. . . . As cold weather arrives in November, apply a winter mulch. It should be at least 6 inches deep and should cover the entire bed, . . . In the spring remove the mulch about the first of April. As soon as the soil dries in mid-April, lift the roses, using a spading fork."

Climbers and ramblers, depending on the hardiness of the variety, might also need protection. If so, remove them from their supports, tie the long canes in a bundle on the ground, and cover them with soil for the winter.

Tree roses are most difficult to protect. The best method is to build a burlap shelter large enough for the plant, and to mound soil and add a heavy mulch to protect the trunk. The trunk can also be wrapped with the material that is used for young trees.

Insects, diseases, and other enemies. Intense breeding has deprived many modern roses of their natural resistance to insects and diseases. The battle will be a continuing one, worthwhile only to those whose love affair with roses is absolutely hopeless.

Fungus diseases that attack roses include black spot, mildew, rust, leaf spot (anthracnose), chlorosis (mosaic), and canker. These can be controlled somewhat by clean cultivation (removing diseased plant parts, removing fallen leaves promptly, removing mulches in spring, etc.) and by buying varieties that are somewhat resistant to attack—but you will probably have to resort to rose dust for really effective control.

The insect enemies of roses are legion: Aphids and rose leaf hoppers will suck the juices from the leaves. Rose sawfly and rose chafer will, together, attack and eat leaves, buds, and flowers. Rose curculio and climbing cutworm will destroy the buds. Add leaf cutters, leaf rollers, stem girdlers, and rose midge, and you will have some idea of the challenge before you. You can keep reasonable control of the situation by handpicking the insects and by clean cultivation—and by applying some of the techniques recommended in Chapter 9—but you might well have to resort to rose dusts or sprays if you are after perfect plants with perfect blossoms.

(Another consideration is that the insects and diseases that roses attract will often spread to your vegetables, fruit trees, and other flowering ornamentals.)

With all the problems entailed in rose growing, you may wonder why anybody would attempt it in the first place. And the answer is, again, that there is simply no flower in America that can match the classic and timeless grace and beauty of this magnificent flower. Thousands of Wisconsin gardeners will continue the noble struggle for rose perfection— and, each time they succeed in producing a perfect blossom, fresh with morning dew, their victory will be that much sweeter. They will have beaten the odds, overcome adversity, and been rewarded with ultimate beauty.

Roses for Wisconsin. The world-famous Boerner Botanical Gardens in Hales Corners (Milwaukee) features more than 3,000 growing rose bushes in their gardens in Whitnall Park. There are 350 varieties included in their impressive collection. Of these, the Boerner staff has named 84 as being "dependably outstanding" for growing in Wisconsin. And, of these 84, only 26 were cited for "above average hardiness." These 26, then, are the very bets for all Wisconsin gardens.

El Capitan. A medium-red grandiflora of medium height.

San Antonio. A tall orange red grandiflora that performed here as a medium red.

Tamango. A dark red floribunda of medium height.

Lucky Lady. A light pink grandiflora of medium height and a 1967 All-America winner.

Manuel Pinto de'Azevedo. A tall pink blend hybrid tea with a fruitlike fragrance.

Marie Antoinette. A medium-pink, tall hybrid tea with a fruitlike fragrance.

Nearly Wild. A medium-pink, low-growing floribunda.

Poulsen'e Bedder. A light pink, medium-height floribunda.

Show Girl. A medium-pink, medium-height hybrid tea.

Tip Toes. A pink blend, tall, hybrid tea with a fruitlike fragrance.

Vogue. A pink blend, medium-height floribunda with fruitlike fragrance—a 1952 All-America winner.

Golden Slippers. A yellow blend, low-growing floribunda.

Medallion. A tall-growing, apricot-blend hybrid tea—an All-America winner in 1973.

Golden Jubilee. A medium-yellow, medium-height floribunda.

Golden Wing. A medium-yellow, medium-height shrub rose.

Irish Gold. A low-growing, medium-yellow hybrid tea.

Lemon Spice. A medium-height, medium-yellow hybrid tea with true rose fragrance.

Soeur Therese. A tall, yellow-blend hybrid tea that grows like a grandiflora here.

Deesse. A tall-growing, multicolor pink blend hybrid tea.

Simon Bolivar. A medium-height, orange red hybrid tea.

Iceberg. A medium-height, white floribunda with a fruitlike fragrance.

Ice White. A medium-height, white floribunda.

Lily Pons. A medium-height, white hybrid tea with petals that are sometimes light yellow.

Mount Shasta. A medium-height, white grandiflora that grows like a hybrid tea.

White Prince. A medium-height, white hybrid tea.

Heirloom. A medium-height, mauve-colored hybrid tea that grows like a grandiflora and has a fruitlike fragrance.

The other roses included in Boerner's "top 84" included:

Red: Americana, Christian Dior, Chrysler Imperial, Crimson Glory, Grand Slam, Kentucky Derby, Lichterloh, Mister Lincoln, Old Smoothie (a thornless variety), Proud Land, and Scarlet Knight.

Pink: Betty Prior, Camelot. Century Two, Dainty Bess, Electron, First Prize, Garden State, Helen Traubel, Miss All-American Beauty, Permanent Wave, Pink Favorite (very glossy foliage), Pink Parfait, Portrait, Queen Elizabeth, Royal Highness, Rubaiyat, Sonoma, Swarthmore, Sweet Afton, Tiffany.

Orange: Contempo, Old-Timer.

Yellow: Eclipse, Golden Girl, Handsome, King's Ransom, Peace, Yellow Cushion.

Multicolor: Confidence, Flaming Peace, Granada, Little Darling, Redgold, Snowfire, Sunrise-Sunset.

Orange Red: Command Performance, Fragrant Cloud, Fire King, Firelight, Gypsy, Montezuma, Tropicana, Villa de Madrid.

White: Garden Party, John F. Kennedy, Pascali.

Lavender: Lady X.

Tender Bulbs, Corms, and Tubers

There are bulbous plants, such as tulips, day lilies, and daffodils, that can be left in the ground all year-round with perfect safety. These are hardy plants. Others, however, are not hardy in Wisconsin and must receive special attention.

They must be removed from the soil in the fall and brought indoors, there to be stored over the winter. In spring, they can be put back outside.

These tender bulbs, corms, and tubers do require special attention and extra care. But many Wisconsin gardeners are more than happy to give them that care because of the beauty of their bloom. The most popular plants in this category are gloxinia, gladiolus, canna, begonia, anemone, and—far above the others—the glorious and versatile dahlia.

Following is a descriptive list of ten tender bulbs, corms, and tubers, with cultural tips based on the advice of USDA horticulturists.

Anemone. This cheerful tuberous plant has many varieties, from dwarfs right up to the tall Japanese forms. Most anemones flower in May or June in Wisconsin, although the tall Japanese varieties may bloom later in the summer and right up until frost. The stems of the plant are erect and the flowers are showy, fully suitable for cutting. Anemones are used in rock gardens, beds, and borders.

A rich, well-drained, and sandy loam is best for anemones. They should be planted as early in spring as possible, since they do best in cool weather. Some varieties are at home in partial shade, although most prefer full sun. Propagation is by seed or root division.

After the blooming period has finished and before the first hard frost, the anemone tubers should be dug up and stored in sand, garden loam, or peat and held indoors until spring.

Tuberous begonia. These brightly colored and freely blossoming plants grow from one to two feet tall. The flowers are red, pink, orange, salmon, yellow, or white, and they grow up to 13 inches in diameter. Begonias are good pot plants, some varieties especially adapted for hanging pots on porches and patios. They are also perfect for tubs and window boxes, and they perform well in lightly shaded flower beds.

Plant the tubers in February or March in flats indoors. Use a mixture of equal parts of peat moss and coarse sand. Press the tubers into the mixture; make sure the "growing eyes" are upward. Space them two to three inches apart.

Keep the flats in a dark room at 65°. Water the tubers often enough to keep the sand and peat moss mixture damp. When pink shoots appear, add one-half inch of the mixture over the tubers and move them to a lighted room that is kept at a minimum of 65°.

After the plants have been in a lighted room for six weeks, transfer them to five- or six-inch pots or outdoors in the garden. Use a mixture of equal parts of garden soil, sand, and leaf mold. Grow the plants in a cool, lightly shaded area.

If you put pot plants under fluorescent lamps for 16 hours a day, they will continue to bloom throughout the winter. Keep the room temperature at a minimum of 65°.

Fertilize begonias at least every other week after you have replanted them in pots or in the garden. The USDA recommends a 20-20-20 soluble mixture, one teaspoon per gallon of water, but organic gardeners will want to substitute a liquid fish fertilizer or, outdoors, a well-made manure tea.

Water often enough to keep the soil moist. Water early in the day so that the flowers and leaves will dry quickly; they rot easily.

When the leaves turn yellow in the late summer or early fall, dig the tubers from the garden. Store the potted tubers in the pots and the dug tubers with the dirt around them in a cool and dry place away from frost. Start the growing cycle again in February or March,

Caladium. Caladium is grown for its showy and colorful leaves. The flower buds should be removed as soon as they appear, so that the leaves can develop fully.

Many varieties of caladium are available. Dwarf varieties grow up to nine inches tall. Ordinary tall varieties grow up to 18 inches, and elephant's ear grows up to six feet. Use caladium in front of shrubs, as foundation plantings, and as pot plants.

Plant the tubers close together in a flat from January to mid-May. Use a mixture of peat moss and coarse sand. Cover the planted tubers with a one-inch layer of peat moss.

Water the tubers often enough to keep the soil mixture damp. Roots grow from the tops of the tubers; they must be kept moist and covered with peat moss. Keep the room temperature no lower than 70°. Tubers often rot in cool soil.

As soon as roots develop. replant the tubers of elephant's ear outdoors or in tubs or boxes; replant the tubers of other varieties outdoors or in six-inch pots. Use a mixture of equal parts of garden soil and peat moss. Grow the plant in a lightly shaded area, never in direct sunlight. The leaves burn easily.

Try to balance the light and shade to get the most color in the leaves. When plants are grown in deep shade, the leaves will have more green coloring and less pink and red.

Water and fertilize caladium at least every other week. Do not allow the soil to become dry. Fertilize as recommended for begonias.

When the leaves turn yellow in the fall, dig the tubers from the garden and store them with the soil around them. Store potted tubers in the pots. Keep the storage area dry and at no less than 60°. Start the growing cycle again the next year.

Canna. Cannas are large and spectacular plants that will serve anywhere in the garden where bright color is needed. Many types are grown. from the dwarfs (18 to 30 inches) to the tall varieties (five to seven feet). Canna blooms for many weeks in the summer. Flowers are red. pink, orange, yellow, and cream. Use canna in the back of flower beds.

Plant rhizomes (underground stems) from March to May in flats filled with peat moss. Cover the rhizomes with one inch of peat moss and water them often enough to keep the peat moss damp.

When shoots appear, replant the rhizomes in four-inch pots. Use a mixture of equal parts of garden soil peat moss and sand. Leave the pot plants indoors until all danger of frost

has passed. Then plant them outside in full sunshine.

Dig the planting site thoroughly and mix well-rotted cow manure into the soil. Plant the rhizomes just below the soil surface. Space them 12 to 18 inches apart.

Water and fertilize the plants at two-week intervals throughout the growing season. Sidedress lightly with aged manure or compost. or use a tea solution. Stake the tall varieties; they fall over easily.

After the first light frost, cut off the stems of the plants. Then dig the rhizome clumps and let them dry. Store them with the soil around them away from frost. If your storage conditions are dry, embed the rhizomes in flats of dried peat moss for the winter. The next spring, clean the rhizomes and start the growing cycle again.

Dahlia. No other garden flower comes in a greater variety of shapes, sizes, and colors than the dahlia, a favorite of thousands of Wisconsin gardeners. By one count, there are more than 2,000 individual varieties available commercially—and more than 15,000 dahlia varieties in all! There is a dahlia for everyone.

The size of dahlia blossoms ranges from the miniature but perfectly formed pompons, as little as one-half inch in diameter, to the huge informal decorative varieties that can grow to more than 15 inches across! The plants themselves range from 18 inches to seven feet tall. There are hundreds of varieties in between these extremes, so that a dahlia can be found to fit into any garden space. Color range is equally wide, covering hundreds of shades of red, yellow, orange, white, pink, buff, lavender, bronze, and nearly infinite variations of all of these plus the many variegations that show contrasting colors within each blossom. Everyone's favorite color can be found in a dahlia.

Dahlias can be divided into six general types: formal decorative, informal decorative, cactus-type, semicactus, dwarf pompons, and dwarf single, double, and semidouble varieties. Generally, the informal decoratives produce the largest blooms, if it is size you are looking for, while the formal decoratives form blossoms not quite so large but incredibly perfect in form. The cactus varieties range greatly in size and feature petals that are numerous, long, and often curled into tubelike structures. The dwarf varieties come in many choices, far more so now than only a few years ago, since the dahlia breeders have stopped going for enormous size (a limit—at least within good taste—was reached in that area some years ago) and have begun to improve their offerings of dwarf varieties for every garden taste and purpose.

Dwarf dahlias bloom from early July on into heavy frost, while the large varieties start blooming later—usually in August—and continue until hard frosts have blackened their foliage. In the colder reaches of Wisconsin, where early frosts threaten to nip dahlias just when they have begun to bloom heavily, the season can be stretched by covering the plants with large plastic trash bags. Anchor the bags firmly on the ground, to retain ground heat. and remove them when the air warms up the following day. Quite often, the early cold snap will be followed by a week or two of Indian summer, when the plastic will not be necessary at all.

Dahlias are grown from tubers. They are planted in the spring, when danger of frost is past, and taken up in the fall, after frost has killed the tops of the plants but before the ground has frozen hard. The tubers are then packed in sand, garden loam, or peat, and are held indoors until the following spring.

Dahlias are most easily propagated by dividing the tubers. In the very early spring, when the shoots are just beginning to show, separate the clumps with a sharp knife, being sure to get at least one good bud with each clump. You can also take cuttings from the first shoots in spring, after the third set of leaves has developed. Plant the cuttings in coarse sand or vermiculite until they have developed roots—about three to four weeks—then pot them in good garden loam and keep them indoors in a shaded spot until it is time to set them outdoors.

Gladiolus. Gladiolus grows two to four feet high. It blooms in summer and fall and produces flowers of all colors. The kinds of gladiolus that are commonly grown are grandiflora, primulinus, primulinus hybrids, and colvilleii. Use gladiolus for cut flowers or in beds.

Plant gladiolus bulbs in rows 36 inches wide or in flower beds. Prepare the beds the year before you plant, incorporating plenty of manure and/or compost.

Start to plant as soon as the soil is dry enough to work in the spring. Plant the bulbs four to seven inches deep and six to eight inches apart. Continue planting every seven to ten days, until early July, in order to assure a continuous supply of flowers.

When shoots are six to ten inches tall, fertilize the plants with compost tea. Water the soil around the plants every ten days in dry weather.

Dig the bulbs every year, about six weeks after the plants have bloomed. Wash the soil off the bulbs and spread them in a shaded area to dry for several weeks. When they are dry, separate them by size and keep only those that are more than one inch in diameter. Store them in a well-ventilated area at 35° to 45°.

Gloxinia. Gloxinias are good plants for pots or window boxes. They are often grown as a winter house plant, but they will bloom outdoors in the summer, too. They produce both single and double flowers, depending on the variety, and they come in many colors.

Plant the bulbs in five- or six-inch pots in early spring. Use a mixture of equal parts of peat moss, sand, and garden loam. Keep the bulbs indoors at 65° until after the last killing frost. Grow the plants in a lightly shaded area away from direct sunlight.

Water the plants often enough to keep the soil mixture damp throughout the growing season. Fertilize every other week with compost or manure tea.

When the leaves turn yellow in the fall, gradually withhold water and allow the bulbs to dry. Store the potted bulbs in a cool and dry area at 50°. Repot the bulbs in the spring and start the growing cycle again.

Ismene. The Peruvian daffodil grows about two feet high and produces large. funnel-shaped, white flowers that have green stripes running down the funnel. Use ismene in front of shrubs, as foundation plantings around the home, and as pot plants. They will bloom during the summer.

Plant the tubers close together in a flat anytime from January to mid-May. Use a mixture of peat moss and coarse sand. Cover the planted tubers with a one-inch layer of peat moss.

Water the tubers often enough to keep the soil mixture damp. Roots grow from the tops of the tubers; they must be kept moist and covered with peat moss. Keep the room temperature no lower than 70°. Tubers often rot in cool soil.

As soon as roots develop, replant the tubers in six-inch pots or outdoors. Use a mixture of equal parts of garden soil and peat moss. Grow the plants in a lightly shaded area, never in direct sunlight.

Water and fertilize ismene at two-week intervals. Do not allow the soil to become dry. Fertilize wlth compost or manure tea, or side-dress lightly with well-aged manure.

When the leaves turn yellow in the fall, dig the tubers and store them with dirt around them. Store the potted tubers in the pots. Keep the storage area dry and at no less than 60°. Start the growing cycle again the next year.

Montbretia. Montbretia grows to about three feet in height. It blooms in August and September and produces flowers about four inches in diameter. Blossoms are orange, gold, red, or yellow. Use montbretia in borders and as cut flowers.

Plant montbretia bulbs in rows 36 inches wide. Prepare the rows the year before you plant, applying plenty of compost and/or manure, dug ten inches into the soil.

Start to plant as soon as the soil is dry enough to be worked in the spring. Plant the bulbs four to seven inches deep and six to eight inches apart. Continue to plant every seven to ten days until mid-June, to assure a continuous supply of flowers.

When the shoots are six to ten inches tall, fertilize the plants again wlth compost or manure tea, or with a light side-dressing of compost or manure. Water the soil around the plants every ten days in dry weather.

In side-dressing, or in weeding, be certain not to injure the corms that lie just below the surface of the soil. It is really best to fertilize with tea, and to remove weeds by hand.

Dig the bulbs about six to eight weeks after the plants have bloomed. Wash the soil off the bulbs and spread them in a shaded area to dry for several weeks.

When the bulbs are dry, separate them by size and keep only those that are more than one inch in diameter. Handle the bulbs carefully to avoid damaging them. Store them in a well-ventilated area at 35° to 45°.

Tigridia. The Mexican shellflower grows to about two feet in height and blooms in mid-summer. The tripetaled flowers are a mixture of white, red, yellow, and rose colors.

Plant tigridia bulbs in rows 36 inches wide or in clumps of 12 bulbs, eight to 12 inches apart. Prepare the soil well during the year before planting, incorporating plenty of compost and/or manure.

Start to plant as soon as the soil is dry enough to be worked in the spring. Plant the bulbs three inches deep and four to eight inches apart. Continue to plant every seven to ten days until mid-June, to assure continuous bloom.

Mulch the bulbs with two inches of pine bark, ground leaves, peat moss, or hay to keep the soil from drying. Remove the mulch in the fall.

When shoots are six to ten inches tall, fertilize the plants well with compost or manure tea, or with a side-dressing of compost or manure. Water the soil around the plants every ten days in dry weather.

Dig the bulbs about six to eight weeks after the plants have bloomed. Wash the soil off the bulbs and spread them in a shaded area to dry for several weeks.

When the bulbs are dry, separate them by size and keep only those that are more than one inch in diameter. Handle bulbs carefully to avoid damaging them. Store them in a well-ventilated area at 35° to 45°

Hardy Bulbs, Corms, and Tubers

This category includes more than a score of flowers that are suitable for Wisconsin's gardens. Most are the eagerly awaited spring-flowering bulbs—including crocus, tulips, and daffodils—that signal the end of winter and the renewal of outdoor gardening activity. No wonder, then, that they hold a special place in our hearts.

Here, we will treat nine hardy bulbs, corms, and tubers, eight of which can brighten your home grounds during spring, when it is still too cold to plant your tender annuals. Of the following, only the lilies bloom later in the season, but they are included here because of their unusual hardiness. All can be left in the ground year-round.

Planting and general culture. Hardy bulbs, corms, and tubers can last for as little as two years or as long as ten or more, depending on the variety. The smaller species, especially, often can naturalize in the garden, spreading in area over the years. Generally, larger bulbs should be dug up and divided every third year or so, then replanted. When your hardy bulbs begin to produce stunted flowers, it is a sign that they need dividing; they have produced little bulbs which are crowding each other.

Spring-flowering bulbs are always planted in the fall, from September up through November. It will do no good for you to plant them in early spring, since they need a winter of cold temperatures to activate their blooming in the spring.

All the following plants like a fairly light, fertile, slightly acid, and well-drained soil. Full sunlight is not essential, but certainly is preferable. (Lily of the valley will bloom in the shade.) Those bulbs planted close to the house on the south side will bloom earliest in spring.

Prepare the beds well in the fall, preparing the soil deeply (12 inches) and adding generous amounts of well-aged compost or manure, and a little bone meal. Remember, though, that these bulbs can easily be damaged by coming into contact with fresh manure. Be certain that it is fully composted before using it.

A winter mulch is not absolutely necessary for these hardy bulbs, but in the colder regions of the state it is a good safety precaution. Apply the mulch when the ground has frozen hard. If you put it down before then, mice may take up residence in the mulch and feed on your bulbs. The purpose of the mulch is not to keep the soil warm, but rather to keep it cold. An unusual warm spell during the winter can force your bulbs into premature growth; alternate freezing and thawing during winter's late days can heave the soil and crush the bulbs. In the spring, when the weather begins to moderate (March, in southern Wisconsin) the mulch can be removed.

The blossoms and stems of spring-bloomers can be cut at any time for indoor display. However, the foliage must never be cut, for it is the foliage that carries nutrients down to the bulb, where they are stored to make possible the following year's bloom. The foliage must be allowed to turn yellow and die back gradually. You can prevent this dying foliage from becoming an eyesore by planting annuals in among the bulbs after—or during—spring flowering. Petunias are particularly good for this purpose, since they spread so rapidly.

A summer mulch is also a good idea, for it will both protect the bulbs from summer heat and hold down weeds for the interplanted annuals. But do not cover the foliage of the spring-bloomers with the mulch.

Crocus. This is among the first garden blossoms to greet us in the spring. Ours usually begin to bloom in the middle of March, here in Madison, often peeking up from under a diminishing blanket of snow. The crocus is a tiny plant, as garden flowers go, and its bloom is short-lived—but it is certainly appreciated by winter-weary Wisconsin gardeners.

Plant crocus in the fall, anytime up until the ground freezes. Remember that they are small and, for best results, should be planted in mass groupings. You can plant crocus almost anywhere—even scattered here and there in the lawn, for the foliage will have matured and died back before the lawn needs its first cutting. The crocus will appreciate a winter mulch, although it should not be applied until after the ground has frozen hard. Remember also to remove it in the very early spring. Crocus needs very little, if any, dividing. Many gardeners simply add a few dozen more bulbs to the ground each year, to improve the spring showing year by year.

Crocuses (or *croci*, if you took Latin in high school) are available in many shades of blue, violet, yellow, orange, and white.

Daffodil. The daffodil (*Narcissus*), also called jonquil, is traditionally planted in October in Wisconsin, because its roots must become established before the ground freezes hard. They are planted deeply, about six inches under the soil surface, and about six to eight inches apart.

Daffodils are fast growers and they appreciate a nutrient-rich soil. Be sure to incorporate plenty of well-aged manure or compost when planting. But do be aware that they are very susceptible to injury when coming into contact with manure that has not fully decomposed.

As with crocuses, it is best to plant daffodils in very informal groupings or clumps, so that they appear to have wandered naturally into your garden. Many gardeners simply scatter the bulbs in the chosen area, and then plant them where they have fallen. In any case, do not plant them in rows, for this arrangement does not become the free spirit of the daffodil. Divide the bulbs after a few years, when they appear to be losing vigor and size.

There are many varieties to choose from, including both single-flowering and double-flowering types, in shades of yellow and white.

Grape hyacinth. These little plants, which grow only six to 12 inches tall, flower early in the spring. Most varieties are dark blue to dark violet, but there are blue-and-white, white, and pink varieties, too. They are good complements to the other spring-flowering bulbs because of their novel appearance.

A crowd of golden daffodils could welcome spring in your garden next year.

Plant grape hyacinths in October, in fertile soil and in a sunny spot. These small bulbs are set two inches deep and two to three inches apart. They can be mixed in with the crocus bulbs and planted at the same time.

Hyacinth. The hyacinth, with its many delicate and fragrant blossoms, has become our traditional Easter plant. It will bloom before the daffodils and will come along quite early if planted on the south side of the house, close to the wall, or in full sun. Varieties are available that offer various shades of blue, purple, yellow, and pink blossoms, both single-flowered and double-flowered.

Hyacinths are often planted in formal arrangements, but I still prefer to scatter them informally. They are good for planting in front of shrubs, along fences and walls, or at either side of the front steps to the house. They grow to about eight inches in height.

Hyacinths send down roots more deeply than do the other spring-bloomers, and so you must prepare the soil to a depth of two feet if you want the best results. Incorporate plenty of well-aged compost or manure, along with a handful of bone meal. Plant the bulbs five to six inches deep and six to eight inches apart. Plant an inch or two more deeply in very light soils, an inch or two less deeply in heavy soils. Late September and early October are good times to plant hyacinths.

Like other spring-blooming bulbs. hyacinths will appreciate a winter mulch, applied after the ground has frozen hard. Remove it in the early spring, to allow the plants free access to the air. After blooming has stopped, plant annuals in among the hyacinths. By the time the foliage begins to die back, the annuals will have covered them.

The bulbs of hyacinths last for a shorter time than those of any other spring-blooming bulbous plant. For best results, they should be taken up every two or three years, divided, stored in a cool and dry place for the summer, and replanted in fall. Usually you will want to replace a third to a half of them at this time, since hyacinth bulbs tend to be short-lived. When you dig up the bulbs, you will find many little bulblets attached to them. These can be separated and planted in an unused part of the garden, there to be nursed into full size—or, they can be discarded.

Iris. The iris has not taken very readily to improvement by the plant breeders, and so the varieties we grow today are very much like those grown in Europe hundreds of years ago. Fortunately, the iris is such a beautiful flower that it hardly needs improvement. It has a rich history, and is in fact named after the goddess of the rainbow. Medieval France adopted the iris (*fleur-de-lis*) as its emblem, and it has since adorned the gardens of crowned heads and peasants throughout the Western world. It is undoubtedly a regal beauty, worthy of your close attention.

Irises are offered in both rhizome-rooted varieties (which include the tall beardeds, Japanese, and Siberians) and bulbs (the Dutch, English, and Spanish). A large variety of colors and sizes tempt the iris lover. Some dwarf varieties compete with the crocuses for early blooming, while some of the giant Japanese varieties flower well into July. Blue and lavender are the traditional colors of iris, although there are many varieties in yellow, orange copper, pink, red, and white.

Planting time for the tall beardeds is in late June or July. Japanese and Siberians should be planted in September or early October. All bulb irises should be planted in September.

Select a sunny spot for your irises, prepare the soil deeply (15 inches), and incorporate plenty of well-aged compost or manure. The rhizome-rooted irises are planted shallowly—barely an inch of soil covering the top of the root clump—and about 12 inches apart. The bulb varieties are planted from three to six inches deep, depending on the particular variety.

A good winter mulch is important for the shallowly planted rhizomes. And, in fact, a mulch is a good safety precaution for all irises.

Around the end of March, sprinkle equal parts of bone meal and lime over the iris beds.

The spring rains will wash the mixture down to sweeten the soil and feed the roots.

Although irises are subject to more disease and insect attack than other spring-flowering plants, you can control these with a little individual attention. The iris borer, often a problem, can be controlled by a three-step program: (1) the cleaning up of all dead foliage in the fall; (2) the prompt removal of any torn or diseased leaves and stems during the season; and (3) the application of a paste of flour and water if the borers become numerous. They will eat the paste, bloat, and die.

Lily of the valley. Here is a little flower so eager to please that it can often become a nuisance (but never to those of us who love it). It will grow virtually anywhere, even in total shade. It never really needs dividing, although it will benefit from it, and it will spread cheerfully and rapidly where other plants will not grow. Lily of the valley prefers at least some shade during the heat of the day, and it will take well even to moderately wet soils that would drive out other flowers. You can plant lily of the valley in either fall or spring; it doesn't much care.

This said, I will also say that lily of the valley appreciates the same attention that you heap upon other spring-bloomers, and that it will respond to your extra attention with larger blossoms. (Incidentally, if you are looking for a large-flowered lily of the valley, try *fortunei.*)

Madonna lily. *Lilium candidum* grows three to four feet high and has beautiful white, classic blossoms. It is a true lily.

All the cultural suggestions given for other spring-flowering bulbs apply to the Madonna lily, as well. Prepare the soil deeply and add plenty of aged compost or manure. Plant the bulbs from one to two inches deep (or according to package directions), one foot apart. Mulch when the ground has frozen hard. The plants will bloom in June and will dazzle you with their waxy brilliance.

Snowdrop. *Galanthus* is another early-spring-bloomer, growing from five to nine inches high and producing lovely white blossoms with a green interior. They like a partly shaded location, and will respond to fertilization. Giant snowdrop (*Galanthus elwesi*) grows to 18 inches and prefers a sunny location.

Everything that has been said about other spring-blooming plants can be said about snowdrop. They look best when planted in mass, informal groupings. Plant them in early to mid-September, two or three inches deep and two to four inches apart. They will need little care after they have been established and will spread quite easily.

Tulip. No spring flower is quite so regal as the tulip, which plant breeders have improved greatly in the past few decades. Several hundred varieties are on the market today, ranging from the dwarfs to the giant hybrids, which grow to three feet in height and sport brilliant and enormous blossoms.

There are single-flowering and double-flowering tulips, Darwin tulips, cottage tulips, lily tulips, and peony-flowering tulips. There are parrot tulips and botanical tulips, and just about any kind of tulip you could want, in a

wide range of colors—golden yellow, brilliant crimson, pristine white, blushing rose, flaming orange, baby blue, and infinite varieties of these and other colors. There are many variegated varieties, as well.

Like other spring-flowering bulbs, tulips are best planted in mass groupings. Their formal structure, however, lends itself to planting in formal arrangements.

Tulips like a well-drained and light garden loam and plenty of sunlight. Plant them in the fall, from two to four weeks before the ground is expected to freeze in your area. In Wisconsin, this generally means during November. The ground should be deeply prepared, and plenty of well-aged compost or manure should be added to the soil. A winter mulch should be applied after the ground freezes and removed in early spring.

Bulbs should be planted according to specific directions given for each individual variety. Pay close attention to these directions, for too-deep planting will result in smaller blossoms, while too-shallow planting will subject the bulb to damage from heaving of the soil in late winter and early spring.

Tulips must be dug up, separated, and replanted every three or four years. They may also be stored over the summer for fall replanting, and if you do this, choose an airy, shady, and cool storage place. Some gardeners lift the bulbs each year, after the foliage has died down completely, in order to protect the prized bulbs from summer rot and rodent damage—but most gardeners will find it easier to take their chances with tulips, replacing any that are lost. Tulips do not have a very long life-span, in any case, and this temporal nature gives us a perfect opportunity to try new varieties every year or so.

Winter aconite. *Eranthis* is the very first plant to flower in the Wisconsin spring, and for that reason it holds a very special place in my heart. In my Madison garden, the little yellow blossoms of winter aconite popped up through the receding snowbank in early March, and were absolutely unaffected by subsequent winter blasts. They bloomed fully two weeks ahead of the crocuses. By June, their foliage had died back and the plant was forgotten—until the following March. Every garden should have a little patch of winter aconite to bid an early goodbye to Old Man Winter. It grows well in the shade under trees, and it seeds freely.

Why Bulbs Don't Bloom

Generally, hardy bulbs are almost guaranteed to bloom the first year, and for at least several years after that, depending on the care you give them. But here are some reasons why bulbs fail to bloom, or bloom poorly.

Improper planting. If you do not pack soil firmly around the bulb when planting, air pockets might form and prevent the bulb from getting proper nourishment and water.

Planted at wrong time. Bulbs that are not planted at the recommended time might not bloom at all. Hardy spring-fowering bulbs, for instance, must be planted In the fall in order to receive at least 12 weeks of cold treatment underground, else they will not bloom in spring.

Inferior bulbs. Good bulbs may be purchased at your local garden center or from a bulb catalog. But sometimes the "bargain" bulbs you see advertised in large-circulation periodicals turn out to be not such a bargain, after all. They are sometimes undersized and otherwise inferior, incapable of blooming well or at all.

Improper storage. If you held your bulbs for a long time before planting them, they might have been damaged in the process. They should be stored at 40° to 50° in a well-ventilated place. If they are sealed in an air-tight container, they may be forced into premature sprouting.

Bulbs planted upside down. You wouldn't do this, would you? With small bulbs, this is usually forgiven by the plant. But large bulbs may not be able to right themselves. The top of the bulb is often pointed, while the bottom often shows vestiges of roots. Look carefully.

Wrong depth. Too deep or too shallow planting can cause bulbs to produce poorly. Read the directions that come with each group of bulbs you buy. In general, the bulb is planted to three times its diameter.

Squirrel food. This is the most likely cause of failure. Your bulbs may have been eaten or destroyed by mice, rabbits, chipmunks, and moles. Squirrels like to dig up your newly planted and bulbs and rebury them, like nuts. (It's their way.). You can reduce damage by laying wire mesh over the bulbs, an inch below the soil surface, to deter squirrels. The mesh should be fine enough to deter squirrels, large enough to allow the flower stalk to pass through.

Foliage removed too soon. Bulbs store food in the bulb from the energy gathered in by the green foliage. If you cut back the foliage last season, when it was still green, the bulb might not have had a chance to store enough energy to bloom this season.

Frost damage. Hardy bulbs need cold underground, but alternate freezing and thawing of the earth causes heaving of soil and damage to bulbs and perennial plants. To eliminate the danger, put down a heavy mulch after the ground has frozen hard in late fall, and don't remove it until the crocuses have bloomed in spring.

Bad soil. Heavy clay soil may hold too much water, exclude air, and rot the bulbs before they have had a chance to bloom. A soil with poor drainage may have the same unfortunate effect. Choose a friable, well-drained soil for bulbs.

Bulbs might need dividing. After a few years, many bulblets are produced from the mother bulb, eventually creating a dense mass and fierce competition for space, water, and nutrients. Dig up and divide, every few years, the larger bulbs such as tulips, hyacinths, and daffodils. Remove small bulbs and plant them in a nursery, at the back of the yard, until they are large enough to blossom on their own.

Wild Flowers for Wisconsin

The beauty of wild flowers is a special one. Gardeners who encourage and cultivate Wisconsin's native flora are not likely to be impressed by the sight of a flaming red dahlia the size of a dinner plate—but they will go into quiet ecstasy upon spotting the blushing pink blossoms of a wild-growing bleeding heart (*Dicentra eximia*).

Wild flowers are precious to many of us because they have the independence of other wild creatures, and we respect that independence. We feel more fortunate to catch a glimpse of a bald eagle high above a Mississippi bluff than to see a lion in a zoo. And we feel a similar thrill when a family of trillium consents to live with us—even though we may love our hybrid tea roses for entirely different reasons.

The growing of wild flowers is often difficult, requiring patience, devotion, study, and careful planning. Many wild flowers have very particular needs, and we can grow them only by studying those needs and meeting them in our own gardens. Sometimes, we can adjust the conditions in our gardens to provide a suitable environment for wild flowers. Sometimes, conditions in parts of our gardens will be just right for certain wild flowers, with no further adjustment. And other times, nothing we can do will create the right environment. When it comes to wild flowers, our attitude is important. We cannot simply "buy 'em and grow 'em," but we must invite them, make them feel at home, and then hope for the best. If they like it in our gardens, they will flourish forever, with no further help from us.

If you have a burning desire to invite wild flowers to your garden, there are three essential books you should have: Norman Fassett's *Spring Flora of Wisconsin* (University of Wisconsin Press, 4th ed., 1976), which will aid you in identifying wild flowers in the woods and fields and give you their time of blooming and their distribution within the state; Marie Sperka's *Growing Wildflowers* (Harper & Row, 1973); and *Roadside Plants and Flowers*, by Marian S. Edsall (University of Wisconsin Press, 1985).

While Fassett's book is primarily for hikers with a nodding acquaintance with botany, Sperka's is for the home gardener. It is a beautiful book, now in paperback, and it tells you how to create the conditions for growing more than 200 wild flowers, including all our favorites—black-eyed Susan, bleeding heart, bloodroot, salvia, wild columbine, cat-tail, downy skullcap, Dutchman's-breeches, rock geranium, jack-in-the-pulpit, lady's slipper, pasqueflower, trillium, Solomon's seal, star-of-Bethlehem, violet, and many more. *Roadside Plants and Flowers* is a guide to more than a hundred common plants (color photos included) you might meet in your travels through the Wisconsin countryside.

Conditions for wild flowers. It is vitally important, in encouraging wild flowers, that you re-create, to the best of your ability, the conditions in which each species thrives naturally. Highly bred garden flowers, such as marigolds and dahlias, can grow in a fairly broad range of garden conditions. No so, wild flowers—or, at least, not most of them. They thrive under very narrow conditions, and they will not survive at all unless these conditions are met.

Soil and sun are the two most important considerations for wild flowers. You must remember that most woodland wild flowers grow in the shade—or partial shade—of trees, and that their soil is rich, dark, humusy, and very likely acid. The flora native to Wisconsin's northern regions will likely demand an acid soil, whereas in the south, where sugar maples and basswoods flourish, the soil will be less acid and its native wild flowers will demand a higher level on the pH scale. Sunlight is an equally important consideration. Some wild flowers, such as those native to Wisconsin's natural prairie and meadow areas, need full sun and hot days, whereas others demand cool, moist, and largely shaded conditions. Know the native habitats of the wild flowers you are considering, and be sure that you can do a good job in simulating those conditions in your own garden.

In the limited space available to us, we cannot list the conditions necessary to the cultivation of Wisconsin's several hundred wild flowers. Again, I suggest Marie Sperka's fine book for those seeking to introduce wild flowers into the home grounds, and Norman Fassett's *Spring Flora of Wisconsin* as an infallible identification guide. The Sperka book lists plants for 19 different garden environments, so that—whatever the conditions in your garden—you will be able to find those wild flowers best suited to them.

Getting wild flowers. It is a great temptation to roam the woods, fields, marshes, and

Location is important for wild flowers. Bloodroot needs shelter from the heat of summer, which overhanging tree branches can provide. It blooms in the early spring, when the leafless branches allow the sun to filter through.

streams of Wisconsin to gather wild flowers for later transplanting at home. Resist this temptation. First, your chances for success in growing these plants are not very great, considering the exacting growing conditions that most wild flowers demand. Many will not survive the trip home. Second, with civilization's continuing encroachment upon nature's wild preserves, some wild flower species are endangered—and, in fact, it is against the law even to pick some species, and certainly illegal to dig up plants in any state park or on private property. Third, every time you pick a wild flower, you deprive someone else of the experience of seeing its beauty. Last, there are wild flower nurseries that will be happy to supply you with seeds and plants of those species that have the greatest chances of flourishing in your garden. (Two good ones are Prairie Ridge Nursery, in Mt. Horeb, and Prairie Nursery, in Westfield. See appendix for addresses.)

One way in which you can pick or dig wild flowers with impunity is in saving them from destruction by bulldozers. If you are certain that an area is about to be leveled for building construction, ask for permission to remove wild flowers before the bulldozers come. Generally, you will have no problem in obtaining such permission, and you will be providing a real service, even if only a small percentage of the plants survive transplanting

Growing a Prairie Garden

A large part of Wisconsin, in particular the southwestern section, was once a natural prairie area. Here, before the time of European settlement, were millions of acres of tall grasses, interspersed with more than 300 species of flowering plants, many of them spectacularly beautiful.

There are three kinds of prairie communities—dry, mesic, and wet. Because the soils of the mesic prairies were deep and rich, and made excellent farmland, it was not long before they were subdued, virtually to the point of extinction. Only a few scattered original prairie areas remain, although the University of Wisconsin Arboretum, in Madison, has two beautiful restorations—the Curtis and the Green prairies—which are open to visitors.

Today, there is a spirited new interest in prairies and prairie plants, not just as areas to be visited and admired, but as an integral part of the home landscaping plan. Whether it occupies five acres in the country, or a small corner of the urban lot, a home prairie seems to be an idea whose time has come.

Often, a prairie lawn is seen as a practical and beautiful alternative to the traditional manicured bluegrass lawn. After it is established, the prairie lawn will save approximately 86 percent on maintenance costs each year, according to estimates made by J. Robert Smith and Beatrice S. Smith in their book, *The Prairie Garden* (University of Wisconsin Press, 1980). The Smiths are the owners of Prairie Nursery, in Westfield, Wisconsin, and have been experimenting in growing prairie plants for several decades. Their book is a perfect introduction to the subject and is beautifully illustrated with both color photos and line drawings of 70 native prairie plants.

Instead of the usual low-cut bluegrass lawn outside the living-room window, prairie gardeners see silky asters, prairie blazing star, queen of the prairie, Turk's-cap, graceful native grasses, and other prairie plants that greeted our forebears a century and a half ago. The natural lawn will change from hour to hour, day to day, season to season, to provide a never-ending source of entertainment.

Further, the prairie lawn will serve as a wildlife refuge, bringing a host of bird and mammal life to join the squirrels and English sparrows that formerly scurried through the bluegrass lawn, looking for shelter. Moles will no longer be cursed, or even noticed. And by combining the prairie lawn with some well-placed native trees, the natural-lawn gardener will gain added privacy and cut down on noise from the street. As one prairie-lawn gardener said, "Sitting by this window is more entertaining than watching TV. Every day it's a different show with new characters."

The prairie lawn also makes sense from an ecological point. In the United States, we currently support more than five million acres of lawn, which annually requires three million tons of lawn fertilizer to keep it growing, and countless millions of gallons of fuel to run the power mowers to cut what we have grown. Prairie lawns need no fertilizer, no watering, no aerating, no weeding, no thatching. Once a year, they need mowing or—in large country areas—burning off. That's it.

If you feel that you couldn't possibly part with your neat, green lawn (especially after all the blood, sweat, and tears—not to mention money—you've put into it), then you could begin on a small scale. You can replace just a part of your lawn with prairie grasses and flowering native plants; if you are pleased with the results after a few years (it does take at least three years to establish a good prairie area), then you can gradually expand the area. And you can always save enough bluegrass lawn for a barbecue or a fast game of badminton.

Once you decide to try a prairie garden, the first thing to do is to find a good site for it. Prairie plants do not demand a rich soil, but they must have full—or near full—sun. Any soil that supports weed growth will support prairie plants. They do best on a loose, sandy soil that is not rich in nutrients. Prairie plants are slow growing and deep rooted, but in rich soil they receive too much competition from quick-growing and shallow-rooted weeds.

Deciding which plants to grow will take some research. The Smiths' book recommends 70 good ones, and your library can supply other books, particularly on wild flowers. which will be valuable in making selections. Consider the height of the plants, blossom color, time of blooming, and soil requirements of any plants you choose. Concentrate on those wild plants growing in your area, for these will be dependable. (Along the railroad tracks is a good place to look, and to collect seeds.) Gar-

deners in the Madison area should tour the Curtis and Greene Prairies at the University of Wisconsin Arboretum, where a wide variety of dry, mesic, and wet prairie plants are growing.

A prairie should be from 50 to 85 percent grass, the rest wild flowers. And the grasses should be native ones, not bluegrass. The Smiths recommend eight different grasses, but you may have your own favorites.

Nearly all seeds require some special treatment, which may include scarification (nicking the seed coat), stratification (the cold treatment, moist or dry), and—in the case of legumes—inoculation. Remember that these are native plants, not finely bred for farm or garden use. This is not like sowing leaf lettuce in the garden, or alfalfa in the field, where success is virtually assured. The germination rate of collected seeds may be as low as ten percent, but commercial seed should do much better than that. Some plantings may take two years to take hold, and some will fail completely. But once plantings are established, they are perennial and virtually indestructible.

Planting the prairie is a matter of clearing the area of as much of its present vegetation as you possibly can, including bluegrass, which dedicated prairie gardeners consider a weed. (They also refer to manicured bluegrass lawns as "denuded areas.") It is best to dig up the area, perhaps in August or September, removing all plant growth. Till it frequently through the autumn, to destroy as many weed seeds as you can, and resume the periodic tillings the next spring. Around June 1, it will be time to sow the prairie grasses and some flowering plants, as well. From that point, you can watch the prairie plants grow, keep after weeds, and—in October or November—introduce as many dormant wild flower transplants as you wish.

Weeding during the first few years is important. It may be done on small plots by hand digging or by mowing, setting the rotary mower to a height of five to eight inches, so that the slow-growing prairie plants are not disturbed. Frequent mowing during the early spring will prevent annual weeds from forming seed heads, lessening their chances of returning the following year. On large plots, use farm machinery to mow, or—after the third or fourth year—burn off the plot in April to destroy early weeds and stimulate prairie plants. No mowing is done after April.

The prairie garden will take some careful watching for the first three years. New seeds and seedlings can be introduced as needed, and a constant effort to keep out weeds is necessary. But by the fourth year the prairie should be firmly established and able to care for itself. By then, the strong, deep roots of the prairie species will enable them to fight off most com-petition from undesirable weeds. All that will be required is an annual mowing or burning off, every April. Throughout the season, there will be a profusion of bloom, and in fall the prairie grasses will change with the autumn leaves into the most breathtaking of colors.

By then, you will have your own piece of prairie, as close to the real thing as you can get in this day and age. And, at sunset on a quiet October evening, you can sit on your porch and look out over your prairie. If you look for a very long time, you can sometimes see the covered wagons slowly rolling westward, or the curling smoke from a Chippewa campfire.

Lawns, Trees, and Ornamental Plantings

Go, little book, and wish to all
Flowers in the garden, meat in the hall
A bin of wine, a spice of wit,
A house with lawns enclosing it,
A living river by the door,
A nightingale in the sycamore!
　　　　　　　　—Robert Louis Stevenson
　　　　　　　　Underwoods (1887)

8 A well-landscaped home, enclosed by healthy and flourishing groundcovers, shrubs, lawn, and shade trees, is both a balm for the soul and a shrewd economic investment. The trick is to maintain your landscape plants with a minimum of care, so that you will have more time to devote to your flowers and vegetables—and the pursuit of this goal will dictate the direction of this chapter.

If you live in an older home, your landscaping is probably pretty well set, and your lawn is established. True, there are changes you would like to make in the landscaping arrangement—shrubs you would like to replace, bare areas you would like to fill in—and you might even want to replace part of the lawn with more interesting groundcover—but you are still many years ahead of those who must start from scratch in a newly built home.

If your home is newly built, your problems are entirely different. You have a major landscaping job on your hands, which probably calls for the advice of a professional. Whether or not you do the job with professional counsel, you will want to get hold of several good books on landscaping, at either your local library or your bookstore. You will also depend heavily on the advice of your local nursery person, who can tell you exactly which plants are suitable for your soil and climate. We cannot possibly do justice to the topic in the small space allotted in this general gardening book.

Living Lawns

My personal ardor for lawns has waned greatly in recent years, to the point where I see a lawn as only one part of a landscaping plan—and possibly a minor part, at that. Certainly the traditional lawn still has an important place in the landscapes of most Wisconsin homes, but the trend is actually away from lawns and toward carefree groundcovers that need no mowing and little fertilizing, toward native plantings, and toward greater variety in planting the grounds surrounding your home.

Still, the lawn must be given its just due, paid its proper respect. As I said in the last chapter, a soft and manicured lawn is still valuable for a recreation area, and you might as well create a lawn to be proud of, even if it is a small one.

Many homeowners approach the lawn as if it were some sort of animated carpet, one that has to be trimmed weekly, watered, fed with chemicals, and sprinkled with herbicide granules in order to keep it at the proper thickness and shade of green. Plant food manufacturers have nurtured this notion by flooding the market with "miracle-working" fertilizer/herbicide products that, according to the ads, will virtually solve all your lawn problems. Many homeowners pay a service company to do nothing but keep the lawn looking like the pictures in the company's own ads.

In truth, a lawn is a collection of thousands of tiny plants, some 50 to the square foot. On a 50-by-50-foot lawn, 125,000 such plants will be growing. Important, however, is that each of these is an individual plant and, like any other plant in your garden, each reacts to the particular conditions of soil, sun, and climate of its immediate location. Pay attention to the needs of these plants as you would those of any other garden perennial, and your chances for lawn success will be improved considerably.

Grasses for Wisconsin lawns. Of the many kinds of lawn grasses in America, three are most suited for growing in Wisconsin's climate: *Kentucky bluegrass, red fescue*, and *bentgrass*. The chances are that your lawn is made up mostly of bluegrass, although other kinds are doubtless mixed in with it.

Kentucky bluegrass, which comes in a number of varieties, is popular in the North because it is a vigorous and attractive grass, well suited to cool and humid conditions. During dry spells, bluegrass turns brown and wiry, but with the return of rain or artificial watering, it comes back bright and green. Bluegrasses are slow to become established, and therefore any lawn-seeding mixture also contains a certain percentage of "nurse" grasses, whose purpose it is to grow quickly, crowd out weeds, look attractive, and give the permanent bluegrass a chance to become established. (These nurse grasses, which include redtop and ryegrass, are not permanent, or are not vigorous and attractive after the first year—but they do serve a valuable purpose in getting a new lawn established.) Kentucky bluegrass reacts best to a slightly alkaline soil—pH around 7.5. Since many Wisconsin soils tend to be on the acid side, it is vitally important that you test your lawn soil regularly and, if indicated, add limestone during the spring or early fall until the condition is corrected. Bluegrass does not do well in heavy shade or on dry soil. It should never be cut lower than two inches (ideally, two

and one-half to three inches), especially during hot and dry weather. It needs fertilization in midspring and early fall, and very thorough soakings (six inches deep) during dry weather.

The fescues—especially the red fescues—are far better than bluegrass in shady areas and on poorer soils. Most lawn seed mixtures contain a percentage of red fescue. However, if your lawn area is under large shade trees, you should ask your dealer for a mixture containing a far higher percentage of this grass. A good lawn seed for a shady area might contain only 20 percent bluegrass, 60 percent fescue (often, of several kinds), and 20 percent of nurse grasses. Or, the percentage of red fescue might run as high as 75 percent. A sunny-area mixture, however, might contain 50 to 75 percent bluegrass. When buying lawn seed, go to a garden center or nursery—not to a supermarket or discount house—and take advantage of the expert advice of your nursery person. Explain your needs and get a mixture made especially for those needs.

Bentgrass will produce the most beautiful lawn of all. Unfortunately, it demands such close attention that it is rarely used for home lawns. Although Kentucky bluegrass and red fescue can be mixed freely, bentgrass is not compatible with either. If you want the perfection of a bentgrass lawn, you must plant straight bentgrass, and you must be prepared to spend a major part of your total gardening time in looking after it. Bentgrass costs much more than other common lawn grasses. It will not stand heavy foot traffic. It can be injured easily by adverse climatic conditions, and it is prone to diseases more than other grasses are. During the summer months, bentgrass must be watered daily, or at least every other day, for its shallow roots must not be allowed to dry out. If you go on vacation, be prepared to hire a babysitter for your bentgrass lawn. More likely, however, you will avoid bentgrass completely.

Establishing a new lawn. Late summer to early fall is the best time to seed a new lawn. The idea is to give the new grass plants a chance to become established before winter sets in, while avoiding the peak period for weed germination. If you cannot seed at this time, satisfactory results may be achieved by spring seeding—although, in this case, you will have to give the new lawn more attention during the hot days of summer, and spend more time in contending with weed seedlings. In any case, avoid the hot summer months as a time for seeding a new lawn.

The contour and slope of a lawn will be determined primarily by fixed installations such as the house foundation, driveway, walks, and streets. The lawn grade should slope away from the house at least six inches in 100 feet. Rocks and building debris should be removed before the soil is turned over. Cultivate to a depth of three to four inches. Periodic soaking and drying will enable the soil to settle naturally. At this time, level the lawn by scraping soil from high spots and filling in holes and depressions.

Prior to seeding, the soil should receive a shallow cultivation. The seed bed should be firm, but not packed. The ideal seed bed should consist of moderately coarse particles from a pea to golf ball in size. These particles prevent washing, reduce crusting, and provide crevices in which the seeds can lodge.

While mulching is not essential for lawn establishment, a thin, uniform, weed-free covering can be beneficial in establishing grass, particularly on sloped areas. Benefits derived from mulching include conservation of moisture and reductlon of seed loss due to washing, wind, and birds. Clean straw, salt hay, shredded bark, burlap bags, wood shavings, and peat are some mulching materials that can be used with success. Apply the material evenly and lightly so soil can easily be seen.

Germination depends upon a continuous presence of light, moisture, and warmth. Without water, seeds cannot germinate even when other conditions are ideal. Apply water as a gentle spray. Keep soil moist, but not flooded. Try to set sprinklers so that there is a minimum of walking over the wet surface. Once the seedlings have sprouted, a continuous supply of moisture is essential. This will involve frequent, light waterings, especially during the hot period of each day. An example of a watering schedule would be ten o'clock, two o'clock, and four o'clock. On days when there are drying winds or high temperatures, additional waterings are advisable. As seedlings develop, watering frequencies should be reduced until the total water, including rainfall and irrigation, equals approximately one to 1½ inches per week.

Start mowing as soon as growth of any kind is tall enough to cut. Try to do so when the soil surface is fairly dry, otherwise muddy mower wheels may pull out some seedlings. Set your mower to cut at 1½ to 2 inches. Mow frequently to reduce weed competition. For best results, catch or sweep up the clippings.

Maintenance of established lawns. The three most important considerations in caring for an established lawn are feeding, mowing, and watering.

A lawn can be fertilized regularly by either chemical or organic methods. There is little doubt that chemical preparations will get the nutrients to the roots and help the grass plants to vigorous growth—but there are several disadvantages to consider in chemical fertilization. First, these preparations are expensive, as most homeowners know. Second, they are quick-releasing and short-lived. You must keep on spoon-feeding your lawn to maintain it, your wallet growing thinner while your lawn grows thicker. Third, chemical fertilizers do absolutely nothing to improve the quality of your soil—and it is the soil that eventually will determine the condition of your lawn. Constant use of chemicals brings diminishing returns because it does not improve the texture of the soil.

Organic fertilizers, on the other hand, are slow acting and long lasting, and they are apt to be less expensive. They will not produce instant results, but they do build up the soil's natural fertility, providing a storehouse of nutrients that grass plants can call upon as their need dictates. They work constantly to improve the texture of the soil, making it spongy and humus-rich, eventually forming a soil environment that can support a rich, green, and healthy lawn.

Which organic fertilizers? You can work toward the best interests of your lawn by slowly weaning it from chemical fertilizers while changing over to organic methods. You can do this gradually, over two or three years, eventually depending entirely on organic fertilizers and soil conditioners.

Which organic fertilizers? Some good ones are cottonseed meal (for its high nitrogen content), tobacco stems (potash), bone meal (phosphorus and nitrogen), castor pomace (balanced formula), cattle manure, and sheep manure. Good garden compost is an excellent all-around lawn fertilizer. It is not as high in nitrogen as the chemical preparations, but all this means is that your lawn will grow more slowly and need less frequent mowing. It will be just as healthy, or more so.

How to apply organic fertilizers. If you are establishing a new lawn, it is important to incorporate a good supply of organic material into the topsoil before sowing the lawn seed. Be sure, however, that all manures are fully composted and that all materials are finely screened. If your lawn is an older one, you may simply top-dress with organic matter in spring or fall, or you may go over the lawn with a spiked roller and then spread the organic materials so that they will work themselves into the spike holes. A thorough soaking after application of materials will help to wash the nutrients down into the soil. Remember, also, that every time you add organic materials you are slowly building up a layer of humus. Eventually, the entire soil foundation of your lawn will be transformed into an ideal one.

Mowing. The most common mistake homeowners make in mowing is in setting the mower blades too close to the ground. Although grass grows from the crown of the plant and not from the top of the leaf or blade, the plant still must manufacture its own food from its blades. If you

reduce the length of the blades by more than one third at any one time, their ability to manufacture food will be impaired, disease will be invited, and the plant will suffer. Kentucky bluegrass should not be cut lower than two and one-half inches during the summer, or two inches in the fall.

It doesn't matter much whether you use a reel or rotary type mower, although a reel type will give you a neater cut and a better looking lawn. A rotary mower, on the other hand, can be used for other garden purposes, such as cutting down tall weeds, shredding leaves and plant wastes for mulching or composting, and "sheet-mulching" your autumn leaves on your lawn. It's your choice.

Watering. A lawn based on a deep, rich, and humusy soil will withstand dry conditions with relative ease, because the grass roots in such a soil will penetrate deeply to bring up moisture. If the soil is lacking in good texture, tending to become hard and baked at the first sign of drought, the roots will likely be shallow and will demand frequent artificial watering. Again, the secret lies in establishing a good soil under that lawn. All efforts should be made to upgrade the soil quality by the carrying out of a year-round organic feeding program.

If you must water, be sure to soak the soil thoroughly, four to six inches deep. You will get far better use from each gallon of water by these infrequent-but-thorough soakings than by sprinkling the lawn frequently. The water from sprinklings will be taken up by the air in short order, by evaporation, and the roots of the grass plant will be forced to grow laterally and shallowly, where they will bake out as soon as dry conditions reappear.

Weed control. Weeds in the lawn drive some homeowners crazy. They see each dandelion as a criminal trespasser, each plantain as a sinister intruder seeking to mock their weed control programs. Other gardeners, doubtless more content with their lives, see dandelions as a nice spring salad plant, and plantain as good and cheap rabbit food. Weeds, obviously, are in the eye of the beholder, and part of the answer to the "weed problem" rests in the homeowner's attitude.

Nevertheless, weeds do crowd out the lawn grasses you are attempting to cultivate, and you should make some attempt to keep them within reasonable numbers. (If your goal is to eliminate lawn weeds entirely, on the other hand, prepare yourself for a life of frustration and misery.)

When it comes to lawn weeds, the best defense is a good offense. Build your soil organically, seed the lawn well, feed your lawn grass, and it will drive out most weeds by its own aggressiveness. If your lawn is not too large, dig weeds by hand. The job will not take more than a good afternoon of work, and it is a great job for the kids, too. Keep your mower blades set high, also, for weeds are encouraged by close cropping of the lawn. Regular mowing is equally important, because it will trim most weeds before their seed has had a chance to set.

Use herbicides if you absolutely cannot stand the sight of weeds. But first, try this: Simply mow the lawn carefully, then stand back and ask yourself, "Are the weeds really that horrible looking?" If the answer is yes. then stand back a little farther. Eventually, you will get far enough away to be unable to distinguish the weeds from the grass. And that, after all, is how most people see your lawn.

Patching bare spots. This job is not difficult. Define the exact area you wish to renew, then dig up the soil in that area to a depth of six inches. Add screened compost and bone meal to the soil, rake it smooth, top it with a thin layer of potting soil or fine garden loam, and sow the seed. Water the area regularly with a fine spray, so that the soil is kept moist but not saturated, and then treat it just as you would a new lawn. The lawn seed you choose should, of course, be dictated by the location of the lawn area.

Twenty Ground Covers for Wisconsin

Lawn grass is actually a kind of ground cover—obviously, the most popular of ground covers. But there are others, many of which can find a welcome place in your landscaping program. The beauty of these other ground covers is that they are easy to maintain (no mowing every Saturday), they add interest to many outdoor areas with their variety of heights, colors, and form, and they grow in places where lawn grasses will fail or are impractical—on difficult slopes, in irregular places difficult to mow, in total shade, under taller shrubs, etc.

Here are 20 ground covers, growing from two inches to three feet tall, one or more of which will certainly solve a problem on your home grounds.

For Sunny Areas

Bearberry (*Arctostaphylos uva-ursi*). Evergreen, growing 6 to 12 inches high. Pinkish flowers, red fruits. For dry sites and acid soil.

Crown vetch (*Coronilla varia*). Herbaceous plant, growing 12 to 24 inches high. Pinkish pealike flowers; widespreading. For dry bank plantings.

Cranberry cotoneaster (*Cotoneaster apiculata*). Deciduous plant, growing 12 to 18 inches high. Large red fruits and wine-red autumn foliage. The hardiest of the low-growing cotoneasters.

Creeping juniper cultivars *J. Horizontalis* 'Bar Harbor,' 'Douglasi,' 'Plumosa,' and 'Wiltoni.' Evergreen plants, growing from 8 to 12 inches high. Most cultivars turn purple in winter. They tolerate dry and poor soil.

Japgarden juniper (*J. procumbens*). Evergreen, growing 8 to 12 inches high. Tufted needles on trailing stems, bluish-green year-round.

Canby pachistima (*Pachistima canbyi*). Evergreen, growing 8 to 12 inches high. Tiny hollylike leaves turn bronze in fall. Plant spreads by underground shoots.

Moss phlox (*Phlox subulata*). Herbaceous plant, growing to about 6 inches in height. Forms needlelike carpet with white, pink, or red flowers.

Reynoutria fleeceflower (*Polygonum reynoutria*). Herbaceous plant, growing 4 to 6 inches high. Pink flowers in late summer, red fall color. A very aggressive plant.

Wineleaf cinquefoil (*Potentilla tridentata*). Evergreen, growing 2 to 12 inches high. White flowers in spring, purple autumn foliage. For dry areas.

Stonecrops (*Sedum species*). A herbaceous evergreen, growing from 2 to 6 inches high. Summer bloom, fleshy leaves that may turn red or purple in winter.

For Shaded Areas

Silveredge bishop's groutweed (*Aegopodium podograria*, 'Variegatum'). Herbaceous plant, growing from 6 to 14 inches high. Leaves with white margin and white flowers. Aggressive on any soil.

Hosta. There are many species and varieties of this popular ground cover (also called plantain lily), which grow from 10 to 36 inches in height. They have large ribbed leaves and produce blue or white flowers, although they are grown for their attractive foliage. Hosta makes a fine edging plant. Once established, it will last for generations.

Carpet bugle (*Ajuga reptans*). A herbaceous evergreen, growing from 4 to 12 inches high. Blue flowers, evergreen foliage when protected from winter sun, purple and variegated leaf form are available.

The beauty of ground covers is in their versatility. Here, a low-growing and shade-loving cover is used as a graceful border for a wooded path.

Wild ginger (*Asarum canadense*). A herbaceous plant, growing to 8 inches in height. Large heart-shaped leaves. Needs ample moisture.

Lily of the valley (*Convallaria majalis*). A herbaceous plant, growing to 8 inches in height. Fragrant white flowers. Foliage may be unattractive in late summer.

Purpleleaf wintercreeper (*Euonymus fortunei* 'Colorata'). Evergreen, growing 6 to 12 inches tall. Shiny, dark green leaves which turn purple in winter.

Bulgarian ivy (*Hedera helix* 'Bulgaria'). Evergreen, growing 6 to 8 inches tall. Hardiest of the English ivies; best in rich, moist, organic soil.

Canby pachistima. (See description under Sunny Areas.)

Pachysandra (*Pachysandra terminalis*). A herbaceous evergreen, growing up to 8 inches in height. Sparse white flowers. Prefers a moist, organic soil.

Periwinkle (*Vinca minor*). A herbaceous evergreen, growing up to 6 inches in height. Blue flowers; white and purple flowered varieties available.

Violets (*Viola species*). Herbaceous plants, growing to 6 inches in height. Violet, white, pink, or yellow flowers. Some remain evergreen.

Shrubs for Beauty and Practicality

An intelligently planned collection of shrubs can serve many purposes on the home grounds. Shrubs can break up the harsh vertical and horizontal lines of a house, softening and enhancing its appearance. They can filter the sunlight that enters certain rooms, thus reducing summer heat and improving the view from both inside and outside those rooms. They can provide backyard privacy for family barbecues, or simply for sitting and relaxing. They can provide nesting, refuge, and food for birds. And they can—well, just make a house look warmer and more inviting.

Shrubs are woody plants that grow from several stems instead of one. It is this characteristic, plus their generally smaller size at maturity, that distinguishes shrubs from trees. Shrubs rarely grow taller than ten feet, and they can grow as low as two feet. When choosing shrubs, be certain that you know how tall each is expected to grow, so that you can choose each to fit your particular needs. Tall-growing shrubs should not be forced down to an unnatural size by pruning, for they will lose their natural grace and beauty of form.

Shrubs, like trees, are either evergreen or deciduous, and for the most interesting effect every home should feature some of each. Some deciduous varieties flower beautifully in the spring, and others produce brilliant autumn foliage, while the evergreens add color to the home grounds all winter long.

Choosing shrubs. In addition to the above considerations, there are four factors to consider when choosing shrubs:

1. **Foliage**. What is its shade of green? What is its texture? How large are its leaves? Will it produce autumn color? Choose shrubs that have foliage to your liking.

2. **Flowering**. Will this shrub flower in the spring? At what time? Will the blossom color complement your house color?

3. **Fruiting**. Is food for birds important to you? If so, choose at least several shrubs good for this purpose. (Recommended trees and shrubs for birds are listed later in this chapter.)

4. **Soil, sun, and climate requirements**. Will this shrub be absolutely hardy in your area? Is it particularly sensitive to drainage conditions—and does the particular location you have in mind offer suitable drainage? Does this shrub need full sun? Remember that shrubs are comparatively expensive plantings, and you hope that they will become permanent residents. Know their needs and be certain that you can provide them.

The best way to survey the world of Wisconsin shrubs is to see them growing, live and up close. Pay a visit to a nursery that has a large assortment of shrubs. Tour a public garden or arboretum at various times of the year. Send for and browse through mail-order nursery catalogs, and look at color picture books at your public library. Then ask for professional advice about the specific varieties that interest you. Learn all you can before investing in shrubs, since you hope to be planting for many decades ahead.

Planting shrubs. Shrubs can be planted either in spring or fall in Wisconsin. In the harsher regions of the state, the less hardy shrubs are better planted in spring, so that they will have an entire summer to become established before facing the rigors of their first winter. On the other hand, fall-planted shrubs are less likely to face insect and disease problems for the first seven or eight months of their establishment. Your nursery person can tell you whether it is better to plant any particular variety in spring or fall.

Shrubs should be planted with the same care as you would give in planting a tree. The hole should be dug very generously, so that the roots can be spread out with no cramping at all. A moderate amount of well-aged compost may be mixed with garden loam and a few good handfuls of bone meal and wood ashes. (Skip the wood ashes if the shrub requires a very acid soil.) Line the hole with several inches of this mixture, and then spread the roots out naturally in the bottom of the hole. Fill in the hole with the planting mixture, packing it carefully around the roots in order to leave no air spaces. Water the hole thoroughly several times during the planting operation, so that no air spaces remain. When the hole is filled, make a small basinlike depression around the plant, with the walls of the basin extending beyond the reaches of the roots, in order to catch rainwater and direct it down to the roots.

Pruning. The pruning of shrubs is not a difficult task, nor need it be done very often. Deadwood should be pruned regularly, of course, and those branches that get out of hand may be trimmed back, preferably when the plant is dormant, either in early spring or late fall. Branches that decide to grow in a manner contrary to the general form you are trying to encourage may be pruned away, as well. In general, the rules that apply to the pruning of trees apply to shrubs, also. Spring-blooming shrubs (lilac, dogwood, mock orange, honeysuckle, etc.) should not be pruned in fall, but just after the blooming period in spring, else many of the latent flower buds will be trimmed off. Summer—and fall-blooming shrubs may be pruned before spring growth begins.

Fertilization. Shrubs do not need much fertilization, since their roots drive vigorously into the ground to bring up minerals from deep within the subsoil. They will, however, respond favorably to fertilization, especially in the first few years when their root systems are becoming established. An annual topdressing of compost, spread out to the drip line, will be sufficient for all shrubs, while a year-round mulch will slowly increase the organic matter content of the soil. Once established, shrubs need very little care at all.

Winter protection for shrubs. Heavy, wet snow can wreak heavy damage on shrubs. Compounding the problem is that many shrubs are placed under roof lines, and when snows are particularly heavy, the homeowner's first concern is to protect the roof by shoveling the snow off of it—right onto the shrubs below. In the following spring thaw, the damage becomes evident.

It certainly is discouraging to invest a considerable number of dollars to have a nice arborvitum or yew planted, nurse it along for several years, then see half of it destroyed by snow. If you want to protect your shrubs and small trees, the time to act is in the fall, after the fruits and vegetables have been harvested but before the first snows. With some scrap or second-grade lumber, and very little skill in carpentry, you can build some inexpensive and simple structures that will protect prize plantings over the winter. In spring, they may be removed, collapsed, and stored easily. And they will serve for many, many years.

There are two goals to keep in mind when designing and building any of these structures.

The first is to keep large amounts of snow off the plants. The second is to support the plant so that snow accumulation cannot bend and break branches.

Low-growing boxwoods and evergreens may be protected by driving in four thick stakes at the corners of the plant, close in to the plant, then wrapping thick cord around the stakes, in spiral fashion, bottom to top, to support the branches. This structure won't keep snow off the plants, but will prevent snow from breaking their branches. For more delicate specimens, you may, in addition to the wrapping, add a lath roof to the four stakes, which will keep most snow off the plants.

Tall evergreens such as arborvitae are particularly susceptible to damage. A good protective structure here includes the basic four stakes, tall enough to come to within two feet of the top of the plant, augmented with horizontal supports (one-by-four-inch stakes are good) running around the vertical stakes. One horizontal stake every three feet should do the trick. If you paint the stakes dark green, and fasten them with bolts and wing nuts, the structure should disassemble easily, look attractive, and last for many years.

Simple lath structures may be constructed in pyramld shape. Hinged at the top, they may be collapsed and stored flat in the spring. These are particularly effective, since their A-frame shape does not allow snow to accumulate.

The use of burlap with small evergreens is also recommended. Much browning out of evergreens is the result of winter freezing and sun scald—two problems that a burlap shield will help to prevent. The burlap may be wrapped around the plant and tied snugly with heavy cord. In this case, four stakes should be driven in around the plant. Or, the burlap may be wrapped around the four stakes, a method that will give the plant more sun and air, while still offering protection from bitter winds and strong sun.

During the winter, remember to brush the snow from shrubs and small trees. If you want to take a few pictures of your home grounds as a picture postcard "winter wonderland," fine. But do not let heavy, wet snow turn to ice on your prize plantings, or you might well lose your "summer wonderland."

Forty-seven shrubs for Wisconsin

Hardinesss, as we have said, is a vitally important factor in choosing any shrub. You want your shrub plantings to be permanent garden residents, and the only way you can assure this is to select varieties that will make it through every Wisconsin winter with ease.

The following list of 47 shrubs was drawn up by University of Wisconsin landscaping expert George Ziegler. Of these 47, there are four which are of doubtful hardiness in the colder sections of Wisconsin, and these are so indicated. The others, however, will withstand our typical winters with scarcely a whimper.

Tall Shrubs—Eight to Ten Feet

(Plant Five to Six Feet Apart)

Siberian pea shrub (*Caragana arborescens*). Very hardy, good on sandy soil.

Gray dogwood (*Cornus racemosa*). White flowers, white berries. Good for areas with harsh winters. Native to Wisconsin.

Redosier dogwood (*Cornus stolonifera*). Hardy red twigs, white flowers. A good northern selection.

Winged euonymus (*Euonymus alatus*). Excellent accent shrub.

Peegee hydrangea (*Hydrangea p.g.*). Large white to pink flowers.

Tartarian honeysuckle (*Lonicera tatarica*). Fast growing.

Sweet mock orange (*Philadelphus coronarius*). Single, fragrant flowers.

Common ninebark (*Physocarpus opulifolius*). White flowers, red seeds. Native to northern areas. Native to Wisconsin.

Double flowering plum (*Prunus triloba plena*). Pink flower.

Chinese lilac (*Syringa chinensis*). Lavender flowers.

Bridal wreath (*Spiraea vanhouttei*). White flowers. An old-fashioned favorite.

Double bridal wreath (*Prunifolium*). Double white flowers. Check for hardiness in your area.

Weigela (*Weigela* in varieties). Pink and red flowers. Check for hardiness in your area.

Common lilac (*Syringa vulgaris*). Lavender or white flowers.

Hybrid lilac (*Syringa* in varieties). Many colors.

Arrowwood (*Viburnum dentatum*). Good fall colors. Plant in sun or shade. Native to Wisconsin.

American cranberry bush (*Viburnum trilobum*). White flowers, red fruit.

Wayfaring tree (*Viburnum lantana*). White flowers, red fruit.

Nannyberry (*Viburnum lentago*). White flowers, colored berries. Native to Wisconsin.

Medium Shrubs—Five To Eight Feet

(Plant Three to Four Feet Apart)

Peking cotoneaster (*Cotoneaster acutifolia*). Good for hot, dry spots.

Many flowered cotoneaster (*Cotoneaster multiflora*). Pink bloom and red berries.

Dwarf winged euonymus (*Euonymus alatus compacta*). Excellent accent shrub.

Forsythia (*Forsythia* in varieties). Very popular shrub. Early yellow flowers. Check for hardiness in your area. May blossom irregularly.

Morrow honeysuckle (*Lonicera morrowi*). Fast growing, white blossoms.

Zabel honeysuckle (*Lonicera zabeli*). Red flowers.

Double mock orange (*Philadelphus* in varieties). Many kinds are available. Check for hardiness in your area.

Golden currant (*Ribes aureum*). Yellow flowers, very hardy.

Father Hugo rose (*Rosa hugonis*). Yellow flowers, hardy.

Rugosa rose (*Rosa rugosa*). Different colors, hardy.

Low Shrubs—Two to Five Feet

(Plant Three Feet Apart)

Potentilla (*Potentilla* in varieties). Yellow flowers.

Snowhill hydrangea (*Hydrangea arborescens*). White flowers. Likes shade.

Dwarf ninebark (*Physocarpus op. nana*). White flowers. Native to Wisconsin.

Fragrant sumac (*Rhus aromatica*). Good fall color. Native to Wisconsin.

Avalanche mock orange (*Philadelphus lemoinei*). White flowers, fragrant.

Alpine currant (*Ribes alpinum*). Very hardy. Good in shade.

Froebel Spirea (*Spiraea frobeli*). Red flowers, hardy.

Common snowberry (*Symphoricarpos albus*). White berries in winter.

Coralberry (*Symphoricarpos orbiculatus*). Red berries. Native to Wisconsin.

Clavey dwarf honeysuckle (*Lonicera claveyi*). Good in almost all situations.

Evergreens—Medium Height

Pfitzer juniper and varieties (*Juniperus phitzeriana*). Spreading habit. Needs sun.

Olfield common juniper (*Juniperus communis depressa*). Use in sun. Native to Wisconsin.

Savin juniper (*Juniperus sabina*). Semi-upright in growth.

Mugho pine (*Pinus mughus*). Semiball shaped. Needs sun.

Spreading yew (*Taxus cuspidata nana*). Thrives in shade.

Dwarf yew (*Taxus cuspidata nana*). Thrives in shade.

Globe arborvitae (*Thuja occidentalis globosa*). Good at house entrances.

Evergreens—Low

Andorra juniper (*Juniperus h. plumosa*). Purple in fall. Needs sun.

Other varieties of creeping types of juniper.

(Note: These are some of the more popular species, but there are many other suitable shrubs for Wisconsin gardens.)

Shade Trees—a Gift to Future Generations

Shade trees play an important part in our lives. They provide protection from the hot sun in the summer and they shelter us from the wind in the winter, making our homes more comfortable throughout the year (while saving heating and cooling costs). They, along with other plants, produce all the oxygen that we need for survival. They are an important part of our water cycle, bringing water from deep within the earth and releasing it into the atmosphere, where it later returns as welcome rain. Trees trap and filter dust, and they reduce noise pollution from the street. Most of all, trees fill that deep need within all of us to be among living and growing things, and therefore they are beautiful. We need trees for our happiness.

There are important considerations in choosing shade trees for your home grounds. Here are ten to think about:

Hardiness. A tree is planted not only for your lifetime, but for future generations. It is your gift to those who will come after you, just as our giant oaks of today are gifts to us from those who lived several generations ago. The shade trees you plant, therefore, should be absolutely hardy in your climate zone. The accompanying table, which lists 31 street trees for Wisconsin, will be a dependable hardiness guide in your selection process—but it will always be worth your while to check with your nursery person or Extension agent to see which trees are most dependable in your particular area.

Mature size. Survey the location for your proposed tree, and then choose one that—after it has reached maturity—will fit nicely into that area. Allow at least half the diameter of the tree as the space between that tree and any other tree. If you are planting a tree by the street curb, check the city regulations that govern such plantings, and consider overhanging utility lines that might be injured or broken by the tree's growth in a few years. In any case, do not plant trees closer than 25 feet from the corner of an intersection, for reasons of auto safety.

Shade patterns. Know the route of the sun in both the summer and winter skies, and calculate the shade patterns that the tree will cast at maturity. Will it shade the only good garden location on your lot? If so, perhaps you should choose a lower-growing variety or change the proposed location. You will also want to choose a location wherein the tree will offer cooling shade to the house during summer. It has been estimated that one mature shade tree has the cooling power of ten room-size air conditioners running 20 hours a day. It would be nice of you to offer this cooling power to your neighbor's house, but perhaps you would rather plan the location so that your own house receives the benefit.

Tolerance to pollutants. If you live in the country or in a sparsely settled suburb, you will not worry very much about this factor. City dwellers, however, must pay attention to it. Norway maples, for instance, are very adaptable to all city conditions, but sugar maples are

Table 14. Street Trees for Wisconsin

Botanical and Common Name	Height	Spread	Growth Rate	Remarks
Acer platanoides Norway maple	50'	50'	Medium	Greenish yellow flowers before leaves. Avoid using in areas where turf is to be maintained; withstands adverse city conditions.
var. "Columnare" or "Erectum" Columnar Norway maples	40'	10-15'		Columnar forms of the species.
var. "Emerald Queen" Norway maple	50-60'	30'	Fast	Oval form of the species with crisp, dark green, glossy foliage.
var. "Globosum" Globe Norway maple	20'	20'	Slow	Low-crowned globe form of the species.
Acer rubrum Red maple	50-60'	30-40'	Fast	Prefers moist, acid soil; bright red flowers before leaves; brilliant autumn foliage; smooth gray bark. New varieties are available with superior autumn color.
var. "Armstrong" or "Columnare" Columnar red maples	40'	10-20'		Columnar forms of the species.
var. "Bowhall" red maple	50-60'	30'		Oval form of the species with orange autumn foliage.
Acer saccharum Sugar maple	60'	50'	Slow	Avoid using in congested city areas or on sandy soils; excellent fall foliage. Intolerant of salt.
var. "Newton Sentry" or "Temple's Upright" Columnar sugar maples	45'	15-20'		Columnar forms of the species.

Table 14. Street Trees for Wisconsin (continued)

Botanical and Common Name	Height	Spread	Growth Rate	Remarks
Aesculus hippocastanum "Baumanni" Baumann horse chestnut	30-60'	30'	Medium	Bears double white sterile flowers. Casts dense shade.
Celtis occidentalis Common hackberry	30-50'	40'	Medium	Interesting pebbled bark; hard black fruits; "Witches-broom" may be a problem; similar in habit to the elm. Tolerant of both dry and wet soils.
Crataegus phaenopyrum Washington hawthorn	20-30'	15-20'	Medium	Bears thorns; white flowers, tiny orange fruits, and red to orange autumn foliage. Tolerant of adverse city conditions.
Fraxinus americana White ash	50-80'	50'	Medium	Broad-headed tree with diamond-shaped fissures in bark and yellow to purple autumn foliage.
var. "Autumn Purple" white ash	50'	50'		Seedless form of the species with orange to purple autumn foliage.
Fraxinums pennsylvanica subintegerrima "Marshall Seedless" green ash	50-60'	30-40'	Fast	Dark green, glossy foliage turning yellow in autumn; uniformly pyramidal in habit. Tolerant of salt and both dry and wet soils.
Ginkgo biloba Ginko	60'	30-40'	Slow	Picturesque growth habit; fan-shaped leaves turn yellow in autumn; tolerant of city conditions. Adapted only to southern and eastern Wisconsin.
var. "Fastiglata" Sentry ginko	60'	10-15'		Narrow columnar form of the species. Adapted only to southern and eastern Wisconsin.
Gleditsia triacanthos inermis varieties: "Imperial" honey locust and "Skyline" honey locust	60'	40'	Fast	Podless and thornless varieties; fine-textured foliage that casts a Light shade. Tolerant of salt, adverse city conditions, and both dry and wet soils.

Table 14. Street Trees for Wisconsin (continued)

Botanical and Common Name	Height	Spread	Growth Rate	Remarks
Gymnocladus dioica Kentucky coffee tree	60'	40'	Medium	A picturesque tree with unusual, deep-furrowed, twigless branches.
Malus varieties: Flowering crab apples: Chinese pearleaf (*rinki*), columnar siberian, strathmore, Van Eseltine	20-30'	to 15'	Medium	Use only where fruits up to ¾" in diameter can be tolerated. Flowers are white, purplish red, or pink; fruits are yellow, red, or purple, depending on variety.
Ostrya virginiana Hop hornbeam or ironwood	25'	20'	Slow	Similar in appearance to American elm, but much more refined; interesting fruits. Tolerant of dry soil and shade.
Phellodendron amurense Amur cork tree	45'	30'	Fast	A sturdy tree with ashlike leaves, yellow autumn color, and a thick corky bark. Tolerant of dry soils.
Platanus occidentalis Sycamore or American plane tree	60'	50'	Fast	Mottled gray green exfoliating bark; pendulous ball-like fruits; tolerant of city conditions; use only on moist soils. Adapted only to southern and eastern Wisconsin.
Quercus palustris Pin oak	40-50'	30-40'	Medium	Symmetrical in form; fine autumn color; avoid using on alkaline soils. Tolerant of wet soils.
Quercus rubra Red oak	60'	40-50'	Medium	Dark red autumn foliage. Intolerant of heavy or poorly drained soils.
Tilia cordata Littleleaf linden var. "Chancellor" or "Greenspire" Pyramidal littleleaf lindens	40'	30'	Medium	Oval to pyramidal in form; tolerates adverse city conditions. Uniformly pyramidal in form.
Tilia euchlora "Redmond" linden	50'	40-50'	Medium	Pyramidal form; coarse and lustrous foliage.

SOURCE: University of Wisconsin-Extension

intolerant to salt; if the city habitually salts your street during winter, a sugar maple is not the wisest choice. Other city trees that are especially tough are the Washington hawthorn, ginko, honey locust, sycamore, and littleleaf linden.

Soil conditions. Although trees send theilr roots deeply into the subsoil to bring up moisture and nutrients, you should pay attention to basic soil conditions if you wish your tree to make it to maturity. Consider soil fertility, moisture, and pH. You can get good clues to the suitability of any variety by checking to see whether others of its kind are growing nearby. Your nursery person or county Extension agent also will be willing to advise you in this area.

Resistance to insect and disease damage. One can never tell when a plague might spread among any tree species. Years ago, our American chestnuts were virtually wiped out by blight. Later, many midwestern cities were stripped of their elm populations because of Dutch elm disease. Oak wilt has become a serious problem in many areas, striking especially red and black oaks. One never knows what might come next, but we can lessen the chances of heavy tree loss in the future by planting a broad variety of different trees, and by avoiding those that do not show good resistance to diseases currently active. Certain trees attract harmful insects, also, and these insects can harm not only the host tree but others as well. Chief among these is the boxelder tree, which brings the boxelder bug (which in turn may harm your maple and ash tree foliage, as well as invading your house as it seeks a fall hibernating spot), and the black locust, which is subject to borers.

Tolerance to light, heat, and wind conditions. Certain trees will be harmed by sweeping winter winds in an unprotected location. Others cannot withstand intense heat, and therefore can be harmed if planted against a highly reflective white house. Check with your nursery person or Extension agent for advice.

Potential refuse. All deciduous trees shed their leaves in fall, of course, but others deposit inedible fruits, nuts, pods, flowers, or twigs, as well. The chief offenders in this area are the catalpa, poplar, willow, maple, mulberry, cottonwood, and many nut trees (especially black walnut) and ornamental fruit trees. Many people are not bothered by these natural tree products, but others prefer arboreal tidiness.

Natural strength. Some trees, including the boxelder, poplar, cottonwood, Siberian elm, tree of heaven (*Ailanthus altissima*), silver maple, and willow, lack the natural wood strength to see them easily through to maturity. It will be best to avoid these, unless one of them happens to be your very favorite.

Root behavior. The roots of some trees cause inordinate trouble on city lots. The roots of the poplar and willow, for instance, are known to block sewers more than those of other varieties, while silver maple roots tend to heave pavements. Avoid these along sidewalks.

Using these ten broad considerations and the accompanying table as your general guide, study your likes, your needs, and the restrictions of your location, narrowing your choices down to a few likely candidates. Then go to your nursery and try to discover more about these finalists. Talk to the nursery person, look at saplings, and try to find out where mature varieties might be growing nearby. Eventually you will find the right tree for the right place—one that you can plant with every good hope for the future.

How to Buy a Good Tree

The American Association of Nurserymen offers the following tips on selecting a good tree:

"The first way to determine the health of the tree is to examine its roots. In container-grown plants, the root system should be well-developed, and the root and soil mass should retain its shape when removed from the container.

"In a rootbound plant, the roots coil around one another and fill the container tightly. Large roots may coil around the trunk, or each other, causing girdling. Avoid container-grown trees in which you can see roots circling on the surface or coming out of the drain holes.

"When purchasing bare-root trees, choose those with a large percentage of fibrous roots. Avoid those whose major roots are crushed or broken. Do not buy a tree whose roots have dried out. To help keep bare-root trees moist, you can store them in moist sawdust, compost, or wet paper until they are set into the planting hole.

"Just as it is important to check out the root systems of plants before you buy, you should also check out the form and shape of any tree. Most trees have a natural shape. There should not be major bare spots caused by missing or broken limbs. Most shade trees, if properly pruned in the nursery, will have only one central leader and an appropriate spacing of branches.

"If shrubs are overcrowded, they may become misshapen. The lower and side branches will die and plants will be unnaturally tall for their width. In healthy, well-formed plants, the trunks should be straight in the container or the ball, depending upon which type of root system you have selected, and the tree should not have slanted, twisted, or deformed stems.

"Last, when examining plants for form and shape, be sure to keep an eye out for damage caused by exposure to insects or disease."

Planting trees. Shade trees are planted in either spring or fall in Wisconsin. Tree planting advice is given freely in Capter 5, on fruit and nut trees. The same advice applies to the planting of shade trees, for the needs of both are the same at this stage of the game. I will repeat only one piece of advice, because I think it is so important: "It is better to plant a one-dollar tree in a five-dollar hole, than to plant a five-dollar tree in a one-dollar hole." Do it right.

Pruning shade trees. Any tree should come from the nursery properly pruned for planting. If the top growth seems particularly large and the root system very small, you might have to cut back the top after planting. Do not cut back the main leader, but trim the side branches by as much as one third. For the first several years, prune away only deadwood, crossing branches, and suckers that appear on the main leader. Although shade trees do not require the care in pruning that fruit trees do, you might check Chapter 5 for a rundown of pruning principles.

Fertilizing. Your shade tree will appreciate an annual application of compost or well-rotted manure, at least for the first several years when it is becoming established. You can most easily apply this as a topdressing, simply spreading it around the tree out to the drip line of the branches, and then shallowly raking it into the soil. If you cannot rake in compost because of a lawn, then it will be better to give the tree several applications of compost or manure tea. This will be washed down into the soil, reaching and stimulating the roots. After the tree is several years old, it will need no more fertilization, since its top growth and root system will then be large enough for the tree to manufacture ample food for itself.

Problems. Shade tree problems are seldom the most serious on a gardener's list. When a prized tree does show signs of injury or disease, however, it is best to determine the cause immediately, since early treatment may be critical to the tree's recovery.

Insects—both day feeders and night feeders (such as June bugs)—may chew ragged holes in leaves. The damage may appear to be severe, but generally the tree will recover nicely after the insects have moved on. A late frost can also injure leaf buds, causing ragged holes that are mistaken for insect damage.

Spots and bumps on the leaves may be caused by attacks of insects, fungi, or bacteria, or by chemical damage. Usually, the damage is not permanent.

When leaf margins turn brown, you may suspect a condition called scorch, which often occurs after a hot, dry spell. The condition is usually temporary, but can be intensified by road salt that has washed into the soil, or by sucking insects.

A lack of healthy, green color in the leaves usually suggests a nutrient lack, often of iron or manganese. Deep fertilization and heavy watering are the answers.

Sudden leaf drop may be caused by any number of factors, including drought, squirrel feeding, and insect and disease damage. In oaks, however, it might signify oak wilt; in elms, Dutch elm disease. Both are serious and require the services of an expert arborist.

Twisted or malformed leaves are often caused by herbicide drift, by aphid attack, or by drought.

If leaves come into fall coloration prematurely, the tree's feeding system may not be operating properly. The roots might be under attack, or the vascular system beneath the outer bark may have been damaged in some way. Call in an expert.

Winter injury may affect a tree's performance, especially after a late spring cold snap. Some branches may die, and some young trees may be killed entirely. Sunscald can injure the bark on the south or west sides of young trees; use tree wrap for young specimens. Cold winter weather may also cause frost cracks, inviting fungus and bacterial attack during the following season.

For the Birds

A well-landscaped home will attract many songbirds in both summer and winter. But there are certain plants that offer special enticements to our feathered friends, and you will want to include some of these in your landscaping plan, if you enjoy watching a variety of birds from the kitchen window.

Birds that like dense landscape plantings include the blue jay, flicker, rose-breasted grosbeak, white-breasted nuthatch, and scarlet tanager. Shrubs are important refuges for the robin, house wren, mourning dove, catbird, cardinal, and goldfinch. Robins appreciate a nest platform, and both house wrens and flickers like nesting boxes.

Large trees that offer good food supplies for birds include yellow birch, common hackberry, black cherry, Canada hemlock, and oak. Among medium-size and smaller trees, choose pin cherry, serviceberry, pagoda dogwood, cockspur hawthorn, spike hawthorn, Washington hawthorn, dotted hawthorn, eastern redcedar, common chokecherry, American mountainash, and European mountainash.

Shrubs that are excellent sources of bird food include silky dogwood, gray dogwood, redosier dogwood, American elder, silver buffaloberry, rugosa rose, Allegany blackberry, red raspberry, and blackcap raspberry.

There are also some vines that provide food for birds: trumpetvine, virginia creeper, fox grape, riverbank grape, and frost grape.

If roaming neighborhood cats are a problem, include hawthorns or thornapples in your landscaping plan. These small trees provide excellent nesting cover for many songbirds, and because of their thorny stems they keep out cats. Cockspur hawthorn and Washington hawthorn retain their fruits all winter long.

Yellow warblers and goldfinches are especially attracted to American elder and common elderberry shrubs.

Mulberry is very attractive to birds, but less so to homeowners because of the messy ripe fruits that are tracked underfoot into the house, and the intense purple bird droppings that stain automobiles, sidewalks, and nearly anything else outdoors.

For a winter food supply for birds, the American cranberrybush viburnum and the nannyberry viburnum are especially recommended. The bright red berries of American cranberrybush are attractive to grosbeaks and cedar waxwings, and both shrubs attract cardinals. Don't plant European cranberrybush, because birds will not eat those berries.

Insects, Pests, Diseases—Control Without Poison

Along with the possibility of the extinction of mankind by nuclear war, the central problem of our age has therefore become the contamination of man's total environment with such substances of incredible potential for harm—substances that accumulate in the tissues of plants and animals and even penetrate the germ cells to shatter or alter the very material of heredity upon which the shape of the future depends.
—Rachel Carson,
Silent Spring (1962)

9 When I was a young editor at *Organic Gardening*, back in the 1950s, we organic gardeners and farmers were largely dismissed variously as nuts, alarmists, fringe-living wackos, or possibly subversives marching to a pinko tune. When Rachel Carson's book *Silent Spring* alerted the nation to the dangers of hydrocarbon and organic phosphate poisons, in 1962, we organic people gained a measure of respect. And by the time of the first Earth Day, in 1970, organic people were ready to take their place at the head of the parade.

Today, organic gardeners are in a position they never expected to be, back in the 1950s—squarely in the mainstream. Most gardeners today are organic—or at least mostly organic—or at least as organic as they can be without losing a crop. Even the major agricultural colleges, which for years have lived off grants from the chemical companies, are adopting a "least is best" policy when it comes to chemical controls.

In 1975, when I wrote the first edition of the *Wisconsin Garden Guide*, I began this chapter with an impassioned polemic against chemical fertilizers and pesticides. Such a plea, happily, is no longer needed (which is a shame, actually, since polemical writing is so much fun). Instead, I will argue for a "*very* least is best" policy. When

the cucumber beetle attacks, I suggest that, instead of reaching for the insecticide bottle, you learn the ways of the cucumber beetle.

The agribusiness corporate farm with a thousand acres of tomatoes is likely to have much more trouble with tomato-attacking insects than the home gardener who has two rows of tomatoes interspersed with a dozen other vegetable crops. In most cases, the home gardener can take care of insect and disease problems without resorting to poisons at all. And if stern measures are necessary, today there are products available—rotenone, pyrethrum, diatomaceous earth, insect-killing soaps, sticky traps, etc.—that are non-toxic to all warm-blooded animals. It is much easier to be an organic gardener than it used to be.

Insects, Good and Bad

Scientists have, thus far, identified more than 1,000,000 different insect species on this earth, and they are identifying more than 10,000 new ones each year. But don't let these figures overwhelm you. In North America north of Mexico, there are not many more than 100,000 identified species, and many of these don't come as far north as Wisconsin. Of those that do, probably fewer than 100 are likely to be garden pests. And so—lesson number one—*there are far more harmless insects than harmful insects.* Wholesale chemical warfare makes little sense, even if it were not for the potential dangers to humans, so long as safe alternatives are available to us.

Lesson number two is that many insects perform valuable services for mankind. Chief among these is the pollination of the flowers of literally thousands of plant species, many of which we depend upon for food. Honeybees are most noted for this service, perhaps because they have gained our affections through the production of honey, but actually many other flying insects perform pollination services—either by accident or design—therefore permitting the survival of valuable plant species.

Insects are also soil builders. Those that live in the soil help to break down raw organic matter into plant-supporting humus. Insects that burrow into the earth create spaces for life-giving air, and they bring nutrients to the upper soil layers where hungry plant roots can feed. Still other insects prey on some of the insects that give our gardens the most trouble. These insect allies—including lady beetles, dragonflies, praying mantids, aphis lions, wasps, and spiders—must be given the chance to establish their places in the natural order of the garden. They cannot do so under continual chemical bombardment.

Resistant Varieties For Disease Prevention

Disease in plants is very similar to disease in humans. Diseases affect the health of the plant in one way or another, and they are carried by minute organisms—fungi, viruses, bacteria, slime molds, and other low forms, including nematodes. There are hundreds of different plant diseases that might affect Wisconsin home gardens. Some of the more familiar are scab, rust diseases, mildew, anthracnose, fusarium and bacterial wilts, mosaic, and—in seedlings—damping-off.

By far, the most effective way of fighting plant diseases is to choose disease-resistant varieties to begin with. I have, insofar as possible, indicated those resistant varieties in the various chapters of this book dealing with individual plants and plant species. But you can get further clues by studying seed and nursery catalogs, government and university bulletins, and by consulting with your nursery person or county Extension agent whenever in doubt. Good strides have been made in recent years in developing disease-resistant varieties—more are being introduced every year—and the home gardener should take full advantage of these efforts.

Preventing Disease in the Garden

The key to disease control is in providing a garden environment where the trouble-causing organisms cannot live. Choosing resistant varieties is one way of effecting this control, since these varieties act as poor hosts for the fungi, bacteria, and other organisms that carry the diseases. But there are other methods to be used, the combination of which can keep disease damage to a minimum in your garden.

Removal of diseased tissue. Diseased tissue is a breeding ground for diseased organisms. Remove all diseased plants or plant parts promptly. Either burn them or bury them deeply in the hot part of the compost pile, where the organisms will be destroyed. This action alone will reduce the number of organisms, and the incidence of disease, tremendously in your garden.

Clean cultivation. Various weeds act as hosts for disease organisms. In some cases, a disease could not exist if it were not for its host weed, and yet gardeners unknowingly tolerate such weeds. Tomato and cucumber mosaic, for instance, is encouraged by the overwintering of the virus in the roots of milkweed, ground-cherry, pokeweed, and catnip. Keep your garden cleared of weeds, to reduce the number of possible disease hosts.

Crop rotation. This may be difficult for small-space gardeners, but essential for those with larger plots. Rotate crops annually. If any crop is bothered by a disease one year, move that crop as far away as possible next year and fill the diseased area with a crop that is totally resistant to the particular disease. Having no plants to live on, the disease organisms will die out.

Air and moisture control. Many diseases thrive when the weather is wet and the air is still. You cannot control the weather, but you can follow spacing directions carefully so that every plant will have optimum air movement around it, and you can work for good soil drainage so that your soil will not become waterlogged for long periods. In the case of some diseases—tomato blossom-end rot, for instance —the trouble is caused by uneven soil moisture. The addition of copious amounts of compost will correct this problem within a few years, since it will build a soil texture capable of holding moisture adequately.

Companion planting. This is an area just beginning to be understood, and more is said about it in Chapter 4. There are, however, a few suggestions worth heeding in companion planting for disease prevention. The first is that members of the same family—cabbage and broccoli, for instance, or tomatoes and potatoes, or any other two crops that are in the same family and subject to the same diseases— should not be planted next to each other. If this rule is followed, a disease that strikes one crop will not easily spread to another.

You may also plant rows of tall crops in between shorter, disease-prone crops, in the hope of reducing the spread of airborne diseases. This method might well be more effective than it appears to be, on the surface. Some gardeners have gone so far as to erect sheets of cheesecloth on all sides of plantings that are particularly susceptible to an airborne disease, in order to reduce the number of organisms entering the area. A great deal more research is needed in this area, and it seems to be the duty of the gardener/scientist, or at least the gardener with an active interest in scientific exploration, to conduct most of this research for us.

Companion planting for insect control is important, also, since insects are among the major carriers of disease organisms. More is said about companion planting for insect control later in this chapter.

Safe Insect Control

There are two approaches to safe insect control. One is to create conditions in your garden that will keep the number of insects within reasonable bounds. These are general controls, aimed at no particular insect, and they should be worked into your regular gardening schedule just as mulching, fertilizing, or any other necessary activity. The other is to put into effect controls for particular insects when they present serious problems. If you are conscientious in carrying out a program of general control, however, the times you will have to use specific controls should be fairly few.

General Insect Control Methods

Soil Fertility. For many years, the late J.I. Rodale expressed the belief that insects and diseases prefer to attack sick plants, being repelled by healthy plants. He observed this phenomenon in his own experience at his farm in Emmaus, Pennsylvania, and he received confirmation from other gardeners and farmers. The theory seemed to fit well into the evolutionary concept (survival of the fittest, etc.), but, with little scientific evidence to back up his belief, scientists dismissed the concept. As with so many of Rodale's concepts, however, science is now catching up to observations that seemed obvious to Rodale 50 years ago.

This scientific confirmation is well exemplified by Dr. Selman A. Waksman, discoverer of streptomycin, who wrote: "Plant deficiency diseases are usually less severe in soils well supplied with organic matter not only because of the increased vigor of the plants but because of antagonistic effects of the various soil microorganisms which become more active in the presence of an abundance of organic matter."

Other plant scientists have reported, also, that sick plants seem to draw more than an average number of attacking insects and diseases, while healthy plants are bothered less. Again, we do not know all the reasons, but we must heed the observations.

If you build your soil to a peak of health, by the incorporation of organic matter and natural mineral substances, you will raise healthy plants that will show greater resistance to the attacks of both insects and diseases. I believe this.

Clean cultivation. The prompt removal of weeds, plant debris, and other garden clutter—including boards, old seed packages, pieces of clay pots, etc.—will remove many of the harboring and breeding places of insects and will aid in reducing their populations. Fall plowing or tilling is also important, since the turning of the soil just before the ground freezes will overturn many insect eggs, exposing them to the cold air and destroying them. Another tilling in the spring, as soon as the ground can be worked, will accomplish more of the same purpose.

Encouragement of birds. It is difficult to overestimate the importance of birds in the natural order of the garden. They should be encouraged by the building of houses, birdbaths, feeders, shelters, and nesting places. When selecting trees and shrubs, choose some that will offer shelter and food for the birds.

In building birdhouses, you might concentrate on attracting the house wren. It is a common summer resident throughout Wisconsin, in the first place, and it is one of the birds that will consent to live in a birdhouse. Most important, the house wren is a voracious consumer of insects. Other Wisconsin birds that prefer insects over seeds and berries are barn swallows, swifts, gnatcatchers, purple martins, flycatchers, brown creepers, and some warblers. Generally, it is birds that migrate out of Wisconsin during the winter that depend on insects for food. It is unfortunate that the ubiquitous English sparrow does not like insects.

Our friend, the toad. Toads, admittedly more rare than birds, are also hungry pursuers of insects, particularly cutworms, grubs, and slugs. You should encourage neighborhood children to bring a few toads into your garden. If you pen them up for a few days, they might adapt themselves to the area and decide to stay. To encourage their staying, you should provide brush cover for them, some water, and perhaps a toad house (described in Chapter 5). Toads toil while we sleep, gathering up insects that carry out night raids on our garden plants.

Our friend the bat. If ever a flying mammal received an undeserved bad reputation, it's the common North American brown bat. Bats are not blind, will not get caught in your hair, and will not suck your blood. It's *mosquitoes* that suck your blood, and a single brown bat can eat more than 600 mosquitoes in an hour. That's why many gardeners are building bat houses today, or at least are doing nothing to discourage bats from becoming part of the local ecosystem.

Insect allies. Do all you can to encourage the presence of the predator insects—those that feast on other insects, many of which are harmful. The two most important of these allies are prayng mantids and lady beetles, both of which can be purchased commercially. The others can be encouraged simply by the avoidance of poisonous sprays.

Praying mantids, fearsome-looking creatures, attack and eat a variety of destructive insects, including the large ones that no other insect will dare to attack. Mantid egg cases can be purchased during the dormant season—late fall to midspring—and should be tied to trees or other plants where you want them to hatch. They will withstand subzero temperatures without harm, and each case will produce from 50 to 400 young mantids. So great is the appetite of the female mantid that she habitually devours her own mate after fertilization has taken place, and she often eats her own young. We overlook these excesses, however, since the

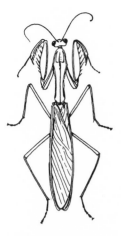

(feed on the immature forms of many insects), *ground beetles* (eat caterpillars and other insects), *minute pirate bugs* (eat mites and other small insects, and the larvae of larger insects), *spiders and mites* (eat many harmful insects), *syrphid flies* (the larvae eat insects, including aphids), and *wasps*. Trichogramma, tiny parasitic wasps, lay eggs in the bodies of insects, and the developing larvae then kill the insects; large wasps feed on young caterpillars; Trichogramma wasp eggs are available commercially. Learn to recognize all these insects and do not kill them when you see them.

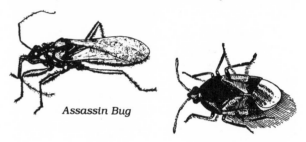

Assassin Bug

Minute Pirate Bug

rest of her diet is so beneficial to the growth of our garden plants.

Lady beetles are perennial favorites of small children, who delight in the examination of tiny things. The lady beetle is easy to spot in the garden because of its bright red wing covers with black polka dots. It should not, however, be confused with the harmful Mexican bean beetle, which is slightly larger than the lady

beetle, copper colored, and has 16 black spots on its wing covers. Lady beetles, which have fewer spots, feed on soft-bodied insects, particularly aphids, spider mites, scales, and mealybugs. You may buy lady beetles by mail order, but you do take a chance, since, when released, the beetles might decide to take up residence in some other garden.

Other helpful insects include *aphis lions* (which eat aphids, mealybugs, scales, thrips, and mites, and are available commercially), *damsel bugs* (eat aphids, fleahoppers, and small larvae of other insects), *assassin bugs*

Companion planting. Any kind of companion planting will reduce your insect problems significantly. Why any kind? Because the very fact of mixing different plants together in the garden seems to make it more difficult for insects to locate their favorite plants. Experiments at Cornell University comparing insect populations between interplanting and monoplanting demonstrated this principle without much doubt. "The amount of total plant-eating insects turned out to be significantly higher in the monoculture," said Richard B. Root, a Cornell entomologist. By monoculture, of course, he means the large-area planting of a single crop.

Entomologists still do not understand very well the sensory apparatus of insects. The key might or might not be in the odor that each plant releases. But we do know that strong-smelling plants such as onions, garlic, marigolds, and many herbs and spices seem to repel or at least confuse many harmful insects.

Table 15. Insects and Their Plant Repellents

Ants	Tansy
Aphids, bean beetles	Nasturtiums
Cabbageworm	Tomatoes, sage, catnip
Cucumber beetle	Radishes, marigolds, nasturtiums
Cutworms	Onions
Spider mites	Coriander, anise
Verticillium wilt in potatoes	French marigolds
Many harmful bacteria	Garlic
Many harmful insects	*Artemisia* family, asters, chrysanthemums, marigolds, other members of the aster family.

When planting your garden, therefore, do not plant large areas of a single crop, but work for diversity. Some gardeners mix their crops freely, spreading tomato plants or cabbages among other plants throughout the garden, for instance, instead of grouping them all together. By all means, ring your garden with marigolds, which are easy to grow and which have perhaps the most effective insect repellent qualities of any plant—and intersperse your vegetable garden with other plants that have shown repellent qualities.

Table 15 lists some common garden pests and some of the plants that have been reported to repel them. I cannot vouch for the effectiveness of each companionship, but there certainly can be no harm in trying these in your own garden and noting the results. (See also the table on companion planting in Chapter 4.)

Specific Insect Controls

Safe insecticides. Some insecticides are of such low toxicity, and of such short-lasting effect, that they are considered safe to use even by avid organic gardeners. Chief among these are dormant oil sprays, ryania, rotenone, pyrethrum, and microbial preparations.

Dormant oil sprays are used mainly on fruit trees, although sometimes on other trees, shrubs, and evergreens, too. The oil, applied in early spring before leaf growth begins, spreads a film over the eggs of hibernating insects, suf-focating them. The leaves, blossoms, and fruit which later emerge are in no way affected by the oil. More is said about dormant oil sprays in Chapter 5.

Ryania, a plant-derived insecticide made from the South American *Ryania speciosa*, is effective against corn borers, cranberry fruit-worms, codling moths, Oriental fruit moths, and some other insects. Ryania does not always kill the insects on contact, but it often makes them too sick to eat and they eventually starve to death.

Rotenone is another plant-derived insecticide, this one made from one or more of several tropical plants, including derris, cube barbasco, and timbo. It is effective against asparagus beetles, twelve-spotted beetles, flea beetles, thrips, cabbageworms, cucumber beetles, tomato fruitworms (corn earworms), pea weevils, and European corn borers. Its toxicity to warm-blooded animals is very low. Fish are very susceptible to rotenone. Keep it away from ponds.

Pyrethrum, made from the flower heads of *Chrysanthemum coccineum*, a popular summer-blooming perennial, is effective against a number of soft-bodied insects. You can grow your own pyrethrum insecticide by drying the flower heads and grinding them as finely as possible. Pyrethrum is often mixed with rotenone—but, like rotenone, it is sometimes also mixed with toxic chemical insecticides. Always read the label of any product carrying the names pyrethrum or rotenone, to see whether it is the pure product. If you cannot find the pure product, go to a pet store or veterinarian and ask for it.

Microbial insecticides contain millions of microorganisms that are lethal to one or more harmful insects. Biotrol, Bio-Guard, and Thuricide are the brand names of some of the more popular of these preparations, which are effective against gypsy moths, oakmoth larvae, cankerworms, tent caterpillars, cabbage loopers, imported cabbageworms, tomato hornworms, and grape leaf folders. The active ingredient in these products is the *Bacillus thuringiensis*, which paralyzes the digestive tract of the insect, causing it to stop eating and starve to death over a period of several days.

Last, there are many homemade insecticides or repellents that can be made from plants growing right in the garden. Many of these are listed in a book called *The Encyclopedia of Natural Insect & Disease Control*, published by Rodale Press. But you can experiment with your own recipes, starting with the plants recommended previously as repellents and going on to the strong-smelling parts of other plants, including garlic, onions, chili peppers, etc. One good way to begin is to use a plant that is absolutely unaffected by the insect you wish to repel. Grind up parts of that plant, mix with water, and wash the affected plants with it. If the harmful insect is not airborne, then sprinkle the mixture liberally around the plants on the ground. Note the results carefully. Constant experimentation by thousands of gardeners in this area will build a mountain of data, which can then gradually be refined into genuine body of gardening knowledge. You can be a leader in insect control, instead of a follower!

Traps. Traps have been used for centuries in controlling insects both on farms and in gardens. It has been just since the introduction of chemical pesticides that we have lost much of our knowledge in this area, but now most of that knowledge is being recaptured, and much is being added by modern technological methods.

Simple traps include the laying down of a board or an inverted cabbage leaf, under which snails and slugs will hide during the day to escape the heat of the sun. Simply remove the board or leaf and shovel up the insects into a jar of kerosene.

A shallow pan of kerosene set under a shaded light, outdoors, will kill many night-flying moths and other insects. They will dive into the pan and be killed in short order.

Various products of sticky material are available commercially. Wrapped around the trunks of trees, or hung from branches, they trap insects that crawl up the trunks to lay eggs in the bark. There are traps for apple maggots, cabbage loopers, corn earworms, fruit flies, codling moths, leafrollers, leafminers, and other harmful insects. One of the major sources of organic insect control products is Four Winds Farm Supply (Rt. 1, Box 206, River Falls, WI 54022) which offers a free catalog.

Specific Control Methods for 20 Common Garden Insects

The following 20 insects are among the most common pests in Wisconsin gardens. The general control principles presented earlier will go far in eliminating any serious trouble from these garden attackers. However, if any of them should become uncommonly numerous and destructive, you might wish to use one or more of the following specific control methods.

Aphids (plant lice)
Description. There are many species of aphids, but all are tiny, green to black, and soft bodied. They cluster on the undersides of leaves or on stems or roots.

Damage. Aphid damage results in curled and distorted leaves and stunted plants. Aphids attack turnips, melons, cucumbers, peas, beans, tomatoes, potatoes, celery, peppers, spinach, and cabbage. Aphids transmit certain virus diseases of vegetables.

Control. Aphids are repelled by soil that is high in organic matter. They are repelled also by chives, garlic, nasturtiums, and tobacco. Many tobacco-containing preparations are used in repelling or killing aphids. Lady beetles, available commercially, are the aphid's natural enemy. Aphids are attracted to the color yellow; a shallow, yellow pan, filled with water and a thin film of detergent, will destroy thousands of them when the pan is set on the ground near the plants. An Idaho gardener found that aphids are attracted to the yellow blossoms of sunflowers, and that they stick to the undersides of the blossoms like flies to flypaper. Aphids can easily be washed off plants with a forceful stream from the garden hose. On woody perennials, a dormant oil spray will control them.

Asparagus Beetles

Description. The adult is a metallic blue to black, with orange to yellow markings, one-fourth inch long. The larvae are olive green to dark gray, one-third inch long. The eggs, which are laid on spears by female beetles, look like shiny black specks.

Damage. Both adults and larvae eat the foliage of the asparagus. The shoots are disfigured.

Control. Fall plowing or tilling will upset the beetles' winter environment, seriously reducing their population. Country gardeners can turn a few chickens loose in the asparagus patch for effective control. Tomatoes and/or marigolds planted next to asparagus are said to repel the beetles. Garden cleanliness is also vitally important in control of the asparagus beetle. Rotenone dust will provide effective control if the infestation is serious.

Cabbageworms (imported cabbageworm)

Description. This worm is velvety green, up to one and one-fourth inches long. It is often difficult to spot because its body blends in so well with the foliage. It is the larva of the white cabbage butterfly.

Damage. The cabbageworm feeds on the undersides of leaves, producing ragged holes in cabbage, broccoli, and related plants.

Control. The butterfly is repelled by tomatoes, sage, tansy, rosemary, sage, nasturtiums, catnip, mint, hemp, and hyssop. Any or several of these plants grown around the cabbages will help to reduce the incidence of egg laying. Yellow jacket hornets kill cabbage-worms, and so does trichogramma, a commercially available parasite. Several homemade preparations repel the cabbage-worm and its parent butterfly: sour milk spooned into the center of the plant; a mixture of two parts flour and one part salt sprinkled on the heads while dew is present; plain salt sprinkled on the heads; and rye flour sprinkled on the heads, also when dew is present. The worms are large enough to be picked off by hand and dropped into a jar of kerosene. Covering the plants with cheesecloth will keep the butterfly from laying eggs. Rotenone, pyrethrum, and *Bacillus thuringiensis* are effective and safe insecticides.

Corn Borers (European corn borers)

Description. This caterpillar is pale pink or brown, with a dark brown head, growing to one inch in length. It is the larva of a night-flying moth.

Damage. The corn borer feeds in the stalks and ears of corn, entering at the base, side, or tip. It is also a serious attacker of pepper, lettuce, potatoes, and other garden vegetables, as well as ornamentals and even some fruiting trees and plants.

Control. Traps with daylight blue lamps have been found to be effective in reducing the night moth population. More important, however, is the removal of plant debris—especially cornstalks—in fall. The borer over-winters in the corn stubble and emerges in early May as a moth. Fall removal of debris will destroy many of the caterpillars. *Bacillus thuringiensis* is effective against the caterpillars, as well as Ryania, rotenone, and pyrethrum.

Corn Earworms (See Fruitworms.)

**Cucumber Beetles
(Striped cucumber beetles)**
Description. The adult is yellow to black, with three black stripes down the back. It is approximately one-fifth inch long. The larva is white, slender, brownish at the ends, and up to one-third inch long.

Damage. The adults feed on leaves, stems, and fruit, and they also spread bacterial wilt. The larvae bore into roots and stems below the soil line. The cucumber beetle usually attacks young plants, causing them to wilt and sometimes die. Plants most commonly attacked are

cucumbers, muskmelons, squash, and watermelons.

Control. Try a mixture of three parts colloidal phosphate and one part wood ashes. Sprinkle the young plants generously with the mixture. (It is a good fertilizer, as well as a cucumber beetle repellent.) A Mississippi gardener reported success by interplanting radishes among his melons. Nasturtiums, marigolds, tansy, and castor beans are also reported repellents. Rotenone is an effective, safe insecticide. Perhaps the best method is to wait until the first horde of beetles has swept through the area and left. They will seldom return to bother your late-planted crop, and there will be plenty of time left for good yields. (The cucumber beetle usually appears in late May or early June.) If your first planting is decimated by the beetles, replant after three or four days, and you will likely have better luck with the second planting.

Cutworms
Description. There are many species. The worms are dull gray, brown, or black, and may be striped or spotted. They are stout, soft bodied, and smooth, up to one and one-fourth inches long. They curl up tightly when disturbed.

Damage. Cutworms are among the worst threats to very young plants. They cut off the stems above, at, or just below the soil surface. Some cutworms feed on leaves, buds, or fruits, while others feed on the underground portions of plants. Those plants most often attacked are peppers, tomatoes, members of the cabbage family, peas, and beans.

Control. Fall tilling will do much to disturb the overwintering places of the cutworm. When setting out plants in spring, cardboard collars placed around the young stems, pushed one inch into the ground, will bar the cutworm's entrance. A neat trick is to take a one-inch plastic soda pop straw, slit it lengthwise, and slip it around the stem of the seedling, pushing it into the ground for about a third of its length (being careful not to injure roots). The straw will prevent cutworm damage and will not impede plant growth. A ring of wet ashes around each plant is also said to be effective. Toads are especially fond of cutworms. A pie pan, filled with stale beer and sunk into the ground to the brim, will trap and kill cutworms during the night (although my father said it merely makes them drunk and happy). *Bacillus thuringiensis* bacterial spray is effective.

Flea Beetles
Description. There are many species, black, brown, or striped. These are beetles with great jumping ability, about one-sixteenth inch long.

Damage. Flea beetles attack potatoes, tomatoes, eggplants, peppers, beets, spinach, turnips, radishes, and members of the cabbage family. Young plants, especially transplants, are severely damaged, looking as if they had been shot full of holes.

Control. Rotenone dust is effective, although its use should be discontinued before the plants begin to blossom. More important is clean cultivation. Remove all weeds and plant debris in which the tiny beetles hide. Because the flea beetle is also repelled by shade, susceptible crops should be interplanted among shade-giving ones. Catnip is said to be a repellent.

Fruitworms (tomato fruitworms)
Description. The tomato fruitworm is green, brown, or pink, with light strips along the sides and on the back. It grows up to one and three-fourths inches long. When the same insect appears on corn, it is called the corn earworm.

Damage. The fruitworm eats holes in both the fruits and buds of tomatoes. On corn it feeds on the central shoot early in the season, later burrowing through the silk and feeding on kernels near the tip of the ear. On beans the fruitworm eats holes in pods, attacking usually in the fall. It will also attack okra.

Control. Fruitworms are easily picked by hand from tomatoes, beans, and okra. On sweet corn, a few drops of mineral oil dropped into the top of the ear will eradicate the worm. (Do it when the ears are small, and repeat every two weeks.) Asparagus, marigolds, and borage are said to be repellents. Dill lures them away from tomatoes. Rotenone is an effective and safe insecticide.

Grasshoppers
Description. There are many species of grasshoppers, one of the most easily recognized of Wisconsin insects. They are brown, gray, black, or yellow, up to two inches long, with strong hind legs. Most grasshoppers are strong flyers.

Damage. Grasshoppers are voracious eaters of vegetation, and they are not particular about their diet. When abundant, they may destroy complete plantings of such crops as lettuce and potatoes.

Control. Frequent cultivation is important, since grasshoppers lay their eggs in the top three inches of soil. Fall tillage will expose many eggs and kill them. Deep cultivation in spring will kill further numbers. Birds are especially fond of the meaty grasshopper, and this insect is very easy prey for the birds, too. A good homemade trap for grasshoppers consists of a high backboard (about four feet) attached to a ground-level trough, any length you wish. The trough is filled with water and covered wth a good film of kerosene. Put the trap at one end of the garden. Then gather together the neighborhood children, and perhaps your dog, and begin a shoulder-to-shoulder march through the garden, preferably banging on pots and pans. The grasshoppers will be stampeded toward the trap, crashing into the backboard, falling into the trough, and dying in the kerosene. (If this doesn't work, it will at least delight the kids and amaze your neighbors.)

Grubs (white grubs)

Description. There are several species of white grubs. They are white or light yellow, with hard brown heads. They are curved in structure, one-half to one and one-half inches long. White grubs, which are the larvae of May beetles, live in the soil and require three years to mature.

Damage. The larvae feed on roots and underground parts of potato and many other plants. Adults feed on tree foliage.

Control. Grubs will likely be a serious problem on lands that have grown heavy crops of weeds or grasses during the previous season. Try to avoid planting vegetables in newly plowed grasslands. If grubs are a real problem, till the soil repeatedly in both spring and fall, uprooting as many grubs as you can for the birds to eat. Let the land lie fallow for a year, if it has been in grass for a long time. This will reduce the grubs food supply and thus reduce the population. Grubs are also a favorite food of toads, when the toads can find them.

Hornworms (tomato hornworms)

Description. There are two species of hornworms. Both are green, with diagonal lines on the sides and a prominent horn on the rear end. They grow up to four inches in length.

Damage. Hornworms eat the foliage and fruit of the eggplant, pepper, and tomato. They are large worms with hearty appetites, and they work quickly.

Control. Since hornworms are so large, they may easily be picked off plants and destroyed. *Bacillus thuringiensis* is an effective and safe insecticide.

Leafhoppers

Description. There are several species of leafhoppers. The adults are green, wedge shaped, and up to one-eighth inch long. They fly quickly when disturbed. Nymphs resemble the adults, but are smaller. They crawl sidewise like crabs.

Damage. Adults and nymphs attack beans, whose leaves curl, or roll downward, crinkle, and tend to become yellow or bronze. Some plants are dwarfed and may die. The six-spotted leafhopper spreads the virus of aster yellows to lettuce, carrots, and asters. Leafhoppers also attack potatoes and cause hopperburn. Tips and sides of potato leaves curl upward, turn yellow to brown, and become brittle.

Control. Plants, or parts of plants, should be removed immediately upon discovery of infestation. Pyrethrum is an effective and safe insecticide.

Leaf Miners

Description. The larva is yellow, about one-eighth inch long, and lives in leaves. The adult is a tiny fly, black and yellow in color. Several generations of this insect develop in a summer.

Damage. The larvae make long, slender, winding, white tunnels in the leaves of tomato, pepper, and spinach plants.

Control. It is not difficult to spot the infected leaves, for they have a distinct blotchy appearance. Remove these leaves as soon as you spot them, and bury them deeply in the compost heap where the miners will be destroyed. Clean cultivation is also important in control of the leaf miner, since weeds harbor them. Sabadilla dust is also effective against leaf miners. It is a natural insecticide, made from the seeds of a South American plant of the lily family. It seems to become more powerful during storage, and is effective against a number of other chewing insects as well.

Loopers (cabbage loopers)

Description. This caterpillar, an inch-worm or measuring worm, is pale green with light stripes going down its back, growing to one and one-half inches in length. It doubles up, or loops, when it crawls.

Damage. Loopers feed on the undersides of leaves, producing ragged holes. Large loopers burrow into the heads of cabbage. They also attack collards, Brussels sprouts, broccoli, and kale.

Control. Repellent plants include sage, rosemary, mint, leeks, and hyssop. Trichogramma, a commercially available Lepidoptera egg parasite, is very effective in controlling the looper, as is *Bacillus thuringiensis*.

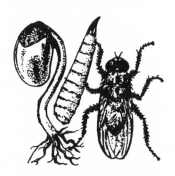

Maggots

Description. A maggot is the larva of a fly, and there are many species to cause trouble in the garden, including root maggot, onion maggot, seed-corn maggot, and pepper maggot. All are white or yellowish white, legless, and one-fourth to one-third inch long.

Damage. The seed-corn maggot bores into sprouting seed and prevents the development of plants. Root maggots attack the very young plants and transplants of cabbage, peas, and radishes, tunneling into roots and stems and causing rot. The onion maggot burrows into the young bulbs, causing them to rot.

Control. Eggs are laid on the soil surface near the stems of the plants. If the eggs can be found and destroyed, damage can be avoided. Tar paper collars will reduce the incidence of egg laying around plants. Wood ashes sprinkled around the young plants is also said to discourage egg laying. If onion maggots are a recurring problem, scatter the onion sets throughout the garden instead of planting them in rows. Damage will be reduced greatly. Rotation of crops is also important, as it is for the protection of any crop against underground insect attackers. Pepper maggots are the larvae of the barred-wing fly. Some gardeners have reported success by sprinkling a little talc right on the growing fruits of the pepper plant. This should be done during the egg-laying season, in July and August. Radishes are said to lure some maggots away from sprouting corn and cabbage. Fall cultivation will also help to disturb winter hibernating places.

Slugs and Snails

Description. There are many species of slugs and snails, which are grayish insects, legless, with wormlike bodies. Snails differ from slugs in that they have a protective shell.

Damage. Slugs and snails attack a wide variety of garden vegetables and flowing ornamentals, doing their dirty work at night.

Control. Slugs and snails are easily trapped under boards. They must find a cool and moist place to rest during the day, and old boards placed on the ground offer this refuge. Simply lift the boards daily and dispose of the insects. They are repelled by sharp sand (which irritates their soft bodies), and also by slaked lime and wood ashes. Sprinkle one or more of these around any area you wish to protect. Toads are also nocturnal enemies of snails and slugs, and will dispose of hundreds of them in your garden. A good trap is an old pie pan filled with a mixture of vinegar and sugar. Set the pan into the ground, so that the slugs can fall into it easily.

Squash Bugs

Description. The adult is brownish, flat-backed, about five-eights inch long, and is otherwise known as the stink bug (a name you will appreciate, if you will crush one). The nymph varies from bright green with a red head and legs, to a dark greenish gray with black head and legs, and grows up to three-eights inch long. The egg clusters, found on leaves, are shiny brick red.

Damage. Both adults and nymphs feed in colonies, sucking sap from the leaves and stems of many plants, particularly squash and pumpkins. Often, the plants wilt and die.

Control. Radishes, nasturtiums, tansy, and strong-smelling marigolds will repel the squash bug. Handpicking is also effective. Boards placed on the ground can also trap the squash bug, since it finds refuge in cool, dark, and moist places.

Thrips (onion thrips)

Description. The adult is yellow or brownish, winged and active, about one-twenty-fifth inch long. The larva is white and wingless, looking like a smaller version of the adult, but is almost too small to be seen with the naked eye.

Damage. Both the adult and larvae suck out juices from onion plants, as well as from beans, cabbages, and many other garden plants. White blotches appear on the leaves, and the tips of the leaves wither and turn brown.

Control. Some onion varieties, including Spanish onions, show resistance to damage by thrips. Both larvae and adults overwinter on onions and other plants, including weeds. Eliminate their overwintering places by clean cultivation and by the prompt removal of weeds during the growing season. If thrips are a major menace to any particular crop during one year, try to eliminate that crop the next year, and plant a nonsusceptible crop in its place. This, plus clean cultivation, can starve out the population. Fall tillage is also very important. Do not let rotted onions remain in the soil over the winter. Rotenone is an effective and safe insecticide.

Vine Borers (squash vine borers)

Description. This larva is wormlike, white, up to one inch long.

Damage. The larvae bore into vines, eating holes in stems near the base of the runner. The runner wilts and either dies or is unproductive.

Control. A thick hay mulch will keep vines off the ground and prevent some infestation. If injury has occurred, locate points of injury. Split one side of stem with razor blade or sharp knife and puncture worm. Put a mound of moist dirt around each cut stem to prevent drying and to induce root growth beyond point of injury. The eggs are laid in July, and the sprinkling of black pepper around the plants before this time may reduce egg laying. Butternut varieties of squash have shown some resistance.

Wireworms

Description. There are many species of this slender, rather hard-shelled worm. It is colored yellow to white, with a dark head and tail, growing one-half to one and one-half inches long.

Damage. Wireworms puncture and tunnel into stems, roots, and tubers of many garden plants, including beans, carrots, beets, celery, lettuce, onions, potatoes, and turnips.

Control. Wireworms are particularly troublesome in soil that had been planted to sod the previous year. Four to six plowings or tillings of the soil in fall, at one-week intervals, will reduce populations and disturb winter hibernating. Poor soil drainage will also encourage wireworms, and so additional organic matter should be incorporated into the soil, in order to open it up and improve drainage. One trap involves the placing of a piece of potato slightly underground, a stick running through it and poking up out of the ground. In a few days, the potato is removed by gently pulling the stick. As many as 20 wireworms have been found adhering to the potato.

Outwitting Rabbits, Coons, and Other Varmints

There is no easy answer to the problem of rabbits, gophers, raccoons, moles, groundhogs, squirrels, deer, and related critters.

Wholesale poisoning isn't the answer, unless you want to decimate the region's population of household pets (and remember, it's the cat who kills the rat).

Some sharp-eyed shooting is the method preferred by some, but it does take a lot of time and is only partially effective, and then only with gophers, groundhogs, raccoons, and a few other species. And besides, many of us hate violence.

Trapping will get rid of a few, but again this method takes a lot of time.

The best general approach, it seems, is to try to understand the animal's habits, then to outwit it. In this way, also, we sometimes prove that we are smarter than the beasts of wood and field. Other times not.

Squirrels. Squirrels are, along with raccoons, the most clever, ingenious, and determined of pests. Short of a full cage over your plants, no method is foolproof. Fortunately, their tastes lead them more readily to seeds than to plants, although they certainly do not always pass up the latter. They will readily dig into squash hills (and this applies especially to ground squirrels).

You can cut down your squash seed losses by presprouting your seeds before planting them, thus making them less attractive to squirrels, who prefer dry nuts and seeds. Then, put a couple of layers of plastic bird netting over the hill, loosely, and anchor it down with earth around the edges. The squirrels get their feet tangled up in the netting, find it foreign and uncomfortable, and turn to easier pickings. Remove the netting when the seedlings are several inches high.

Some gardeners claim that some red pepper sprinkled over the planted seeds will discourage squirrels.

Rabbits. Unlike squirrels, rabbits forego dry seeds for tender young greens. They can wipe out 100 feet of bean seedlings in a remarkably short time.

Rabbits cannot climb, and so a chicken wire fence only three feet high should keep them out. Sink the fence at least six inches into the ground. Although the rabbits can certainly dig under it, the chances are that, before doing so, they will turn to easier pickings.

Other reported rabbit deterrents include (1) sprinkling dried blood around plants—an

effective but short-lived technique; (2) tying aluminum "scare plates" with strings to poles; (3) scattering mothballs around the garden; (4) sinking open-ended coffee cans around young plants; and (5) sprinkling either limestone or red pepper on plants when they are wet. One interesting method calls for placing quart jars, half-filled with water, around the garden. The wind whistling across the tops of the jars is supposed to suggest the hoot of an owl. Some gardeners empty their cat litter box near the garden. Others plant a ring of leaf lettuce around the outer ring of the garden, hoping to buy off the rabbit with a blatant offering.

To prevent rabbit damage to your fruit trees in winter, be sure to wrap their trunks with rabbit-proof material.

Deer. A deer can undo hundreds of hours of garden work in a single morning's feeding. The deer problem is not unheard of in the suburbs, and is often common in the country.

Says *Organic Gardening* magazine, "One Oregon gardener has found success with a four-foot-high mesh chicken wire fence and, about three feet outside of that, a single, parallel strand of wire 2½ feet above the ground. The deer evidently have trouble leaping high enough to clear the mesh fence with the single strand wire in the way."

Deer are also wary of human scent, a trait taken advantage of by a Pennsylvania gardener. He collected hair clippings from the local barber shop and sprinkled them around the edges of the garden, reporting success with the method.

Raccoons. The major damage created by raccoons is in August, when they gingerly strip and eat your ripe ears of corn. The infuriating thing is that they don't eat the entire ear—just enough to ruin it before moving on to the next ear.

Gardeners have placed transistor radios in the corn patch, set up kerosene lanterns, spread dog manure, sprinkled red pepper on the corn tassels (or black pepper, sprinkled on the leaves about 30 inches off the ground), grown pumpkins among the corn which is supposed to confuse the coons), and erected a five-foot chicken wire fence that is unsupported at the top 18 inches, so that the fence curls down on the coon as it climbs. Both raccoons and opossums can be trapped easily with honey-soaked bread, marshmallows, or other sweets.

An Iowa gardener found that his own B.O. is the best raccoon repellent. He throws in some old, sweaty clothes among the corn rows, and has not been bothered by coons since. (I suppose you shouldn't shower before working in the garden, to make this method most effective.)

An electrified fence is also effective. String one wire six inches off the ground, and another six inches above the first. Use steel or fiberglass posts, since raccoons are smart enough to climb up and over wooden posts to avoid the wires.

Moles. I dislike moles not because they raise ridges in the lawn but because their main food source is earthworms, and I work too hard to encourage my earthworm population. A foolproof way to discourage moles is to dump some good, strong, used cat box litter down their holes. Moles are terrified of cats and will soon find new homes far away.

Gophers and groundhogs. These two are less often a problem, but, when they are present, the problem can be major. The best answer for both is to trap or shoot them. For the tender-hearted, I recommend one of the "live" traps, with which you can transport the offender to a distant woodlot, give it a new name, and encourage it to begin a whole new life free of crime.

Finally, depend on a good dog to keep down populations of all these pests, and to keep deer away. After all you've done for Fido, the least he can do in return is perform a little police duty around the garden.

Indoor Gardening

I hold it for a most pleasing and delicate thing, to have a fair Gallery, great Chamber or other lodging, that openeth fully upon the East or West Sun, to be inwardly garnished with Sweet Herbs.

—Sir Hugh Platt
1552-1611

10 Indoor gardening, which includes the growing of those plants usually seen outdoors as well as traditional "house plants," is especially important to Wisconsin gardeners. In a section of the country where the outdoor season lasts for as few as six months, indoor plants form a green and valuable bridge from season to season, helping us to glide through each succeeding winter surrounded by living and growing things.

Recent strides in indoor gardening—especially the introduction of new, superior plant varieties and the use of fluorescent lighting—have opened up new worlds to the gardener. Where, just a generation ago, most indoor gardeners were content to raise a few African violets, philodendron, and a dozen or so other standards, today's gardener is likely to be raising tomatoes on a solar-heated sun porch and miniature orchids in a terrarium, along with the standard favorites.

Further, the increased use of tub plantings on terraces and patios has begun to erase the formerly sharp lines between indoor and outdoor gardening. While we cannot duplicate the California style in indoor-outdoor living, our changing architecture and gardening procedures have, even in Wisconsin, helped to bring

This chapter is based largely upon materials found in *No Time for House Plants: A Busy Person's Guide to Indoor Gardening,* by Jerry Minnich, University of Oklahoma Press, 1979. Sections are reprinted here with the permission of the publisher.

the outdoors inside, enhancing the quality of all our lives.

Understanding Indoor Plants

Every plant has its own preferences and requirements for soil type, light, temperature, ventilation, humidity, and several other factors that are within our power to control or at least to mitigate. It will be well worth your while to gain some understanding of these factors, because this basic knowledge will enable you to avoid much work later on while achieving routine success in growing plants.

In addition to understanding these basic needs, you will want to know something about pots and other containers, repotting plants, propagation, and a few other matters that, while not vital to routine success, will help you to gain further enjoyment in raising better plants.

The Basic House Plant

The major difference between a house plant and an outdoor plant is that of location. All house plants could live and flourish outdoors in the proper climate. All are derived from forebears that lived, reproduced, and died outdoors, whether it was on a forest floor in central Europe or in the bough of a tree in a South American rain forest. Over many centuries of adaptation and evolution each plant species embraced those characteristics that enabled it to survive; even today every house plant carries within its genetic structure the characteristics of its distant progenitors. Thus the

Maranta might lose some of its leaves each autumn, even though autumn's weather does not come to the top of the bookshelf where the plant rests. And a cactus, no matter how long we have been feeding and watering it with unfailing regularity, will continue to hoard food and water within its swollen stems. In plants old habits might recede, but they are never forgotten.

At no time are these innate plant characteristics more noticeable than during the autumn and winter, when many plants—particularly those from temperate regions—enter a period of rest or dormancy. Then new growth ceases and the plant takes on a listless and washed-out appearance. Other plants, including many of tropical origin, will maintain their bright appearance but will stop growing completely for several months each year, emulating the natural rest periods of their forebears.

Of course, indoor plants will respond to reduced light conditions of the winter months, and it is difficult to separate this environmental factor from a plant's genetic tendencies. In any case, however, you will do well to watch for these signs of dormancy and respond to each plant's needs at that time. When any plant enters a dormant or rest period, water should be reduced and fertilizer withheld completely, until new growth once again begins, usually in the late winter or early spring. At that time water the plant freely and resume its normal doses of fertilizer in order to encourage new growth. By your proper treatment of the plant at this time you will emulate the advent of spring, working with the plant in carrying out its rhythmic cycles.

With some plants, especially those of tropical origin, you can escape any natural rest period by providing the plant with artificial light and good humidity over the winter months. Whether this forcing of a plant to maximum growth is harmful or not is a matter of debate. In any case it is best done in a terrarium, where conditions can be maintained easily at any time of the year.

Some plants also are naturally short-lived and will last no more than a year or two in your home despite your careful attention, because their genetic structure dictates a finite life span. Garden annuals, for instance, will germinate, grow to maturity, flower, produce seeds, and die, all in as little as six months. For this reason very few annuals are selected as house plants. Although a few short-lived plants are cultivated indoors for their unusual characteristics, such as the sensitive plant, which is easily grown from seed, the house plants that we have cultivated over the generations are most often those that will give years of pleasure. Some house plants, in fact, live to be literally hundreds of years old.

Still other house plants are attractive when young but grow ungainly or otherwise unattractive when they approach maturity. The only plants of this kind I have chosen for inclusion in this book are those that are very easy to propagate from cuttings, so that the parent plant may be discarded after a year or two and replaced by its children.

From the thousands of plant species in the world, those traditionally cultivated as house plants are the relatively few that have shown a wide tolerance to conditions of heat, light, moisture, humidity, and ventilation—in other words, those that can withstand a human environment. They are both attractive to the eye and tough. Still, we should spend some time to learn the characteristics of each plant, recognizing its individual needs and fulfilling them to the best of our abilities.

Soil and Potting Mixtures

Every house plant will, assuming hoped-for longevity, someday need repotting, and you will want to provide it with a potting mixture that will serve its special needs. You might even wish to propagate some of your favorite house plants to share with friends and to give as gifts. In any case a basic knowledge of potting mixtures and soils is essential to a complete understanding of all your plants.

Two simple definitions are in order here to

avoid any confusion later. *Soil,* when mentioned here, refers to garden loam, that combination of mineral matter, organic matter, air, and water commonly found in your garden or under your lawn. A *potting mixture* is soil with the addition of other materials, such as sand, compost, peat moss, limestone, and bone meal, that together form an ideal environment for the roots of your house plants.

The easiest way to assure your plants of a perfect loam is to buy prepackaged, sterile potting soil from your garden center or flower shop. This soil will have not only the proper texture, but it will also be free of disease organisms, insects (some too small to be seen), and weed seeds. To this loam you will add the other ingredients, which together will form an ideal potting mixture. You may also buy packaged potting mixture—but if you do, read the package carefully to ascertain the ingredients, making sure that the mixture is right for your plants.

It is, of course, far less expensive to make your own potting mixture from your own garden loam (free), sand (free or next to free), and small amounts of purchased ingredients. If you choose this route, then it is important that you be able to make at least a cursory analysis of the garden loam that will form the basis of the potting mixture. Texture is important. A heavy clay soil will hold water for too long, encouraging disease and root rot, and it will bake cement-hard when dry. On the other hand, a course sand will not hold water well nor will it hold nutrients long enough for the plant's roots to absorb them. Strive, then, for a happy medium—a good loam, containing both clay and sand, that will hold both water and nutrients, yet offer adequate drainage. Be sure, also, to sterilize the soil by spreading it in a shallow pan and placing it in an oven (medium heat) for one hour.

To this basic loam we usually add one or more other materials—peat moss to increase water-holding capacity and to add organic matter, compost for organic matter and nu-trients, sand to open the soil to air, and some form of supplemental mineral fertilizer, usually bone meal and lime.

Acidity/alkalinity

A discussion of soil acidity/alkalinity, as expressed by the pH scale, begins on page 18. Most house plants, as outdoor garden plants, do best in a slightly acid soil (6.0 to 6.9). Most Wisconsin garden soils are within this range, and gardeners need not worry unduly about the pH of ordinary garden loam. If you are concerned about your soil's pH, have the soil tested. (Commercial potting mixtures are, of course, controlled by the manufacturer to fall within the ideal range for most house plants.)

Potting Mixture Recipes

There are as many different basic potting mixtures as there are plant experts—maybe more. Perhaps the most common one, however (and one that can be trusted), calls for two parts loam, one part finely screened compost (or a mixture of peat moss and compost), and one part builder's sand (not sea sand). To this is added a small amount of bone meal (about one teaspoon for a five-inch pot) and a pinch of ground limestone. Other recommendations call for more of one ingredient and less of another. Do a little experimenting of your own. After a while you may find your favorite mixture, which you can recommend to others.

And now that you have the basic mixture formula well in mind, we will consider the exceptions:

1. Acid-loving plants, such as azaleas, camelias, gardenias, and heathers, should be given no lime. In fact, they should have some form of acid organic matter—acid peat moss or oak leafmold.

2. Foliage plants need somewhat more compost in the mixture, although half of it should be comprised of peat moss (which is low in nutrients and will not overstimulate the plant).

3. Fast-growing and hungry plants need

more bone meal and lime, since they use them up quickly.

4. Some plants, such as cacti, succulents, and orchids, have very special soil requirements; these are mentioned later in the discussions of individual plants.

Nutrient Maintenance

The mineral nutrients contained in any fresh potting soil or mixture, whether it is homemade or a sterilized commercial brand, should be sufficient for your plant's needs for the first four to six months. After that you should begin to replenish those nutrients on a regular and carefully measured basis.

Organic fertilizers may be purchased commercially in balanced formulas (fish emulsion, made from fish wastes, is a popular one for house plant use) or may be made at home from a combination of ingredients. Blood meal is a good choice for supplying substantial amounts of nitrogen (its NPK formula is 15.00-1.30-0.70), while bone meal (4.00-21.00-0.20) is good for phosphate and wood ashes (0.00-1.50-7.00) are high in potash content. A combination of one part blood meal, one part bone meal, and two parts wood ashes will make a 5—6—4 formula, which is a good one for house plants.

How often should plants be fertilized? The answer is unclear, because experts disagree sharply on the subject. But one thing is very clear: Do not fertilize as often, or as much, as recommended by the manufacturer of a commercial plant food. Manufacturers understandably overestimate the need for their products. Most gardeners, furthermore, are looking not for wild and rank growth among house plants but for controlled growth and healthy plants. To achieve this goal go very easy on fertilizer of any kind. My personal policy is to apply half as much as the manufacturer recommends and only half as often, meaning that my plants get only one fourth of the recommended feeding. Many more plants have been killed or injured by the overapplication of fertilizer than by mineral starvation.

If a plant shows a spurt of active growth in late winter or early spring, increase the dosage to the manufacturer's recommendation for a short while. During a dormant or rest period, withhold fertilizer entirely. If you are using a homemade organic fertilizer, such as the one suggested above, use it sparingly at first. A level teaspoon of the blood meal/bone meal/wood ash formula, applied monthly, should be plenty for a plant in five-inch pot. You may also put some of the mixture in a bottle, fill the bottle with water, and use this "tea" to water your house plants. A mild tea solution, applied weekly, will give all your plants a continuing and gentle supply of the essential nutrients.

Containers

Nearly any container that offers adequate drainage and doesn't leak is suitable for house plants. After checking a container for leakage, consider drainage carefully. If the container has a hole in its bottom, there is no problem. If not, then you should put coarse gravel or broken crockery in the bottom of the container to fill one fifth its depth. In this way you will avoid the likelihood of waterlogging your plants and encouraging root rot.

The traditional terra-cotta clay pot offers definite advantages. It is inexpensive, easily replaced, and—most important—allows air to be exchanged through its porous walls. This same porosity, however, allows water to evaporate fairly quickly, necessitating frequent watering. If a plant's location makes it awkward for you to water, you will save yourself some effort by choosing a glazed or otherwise impervious container.

Some metal containers, notably copper, might produce adverse chemical reactions with soil and fertilizer elements, injuring plants therein. Copper planters, however, are usually lacquered to prevent such reactions.

Wooden tubs and boxes are ideal for very large house plants. You can make any wooden container watertight by lining it with several sheets of heavy-gauge plastic or, for permanent results, sheet metal.

Finally, if you want the best advantages of both a terra-cotta pot and a decorative container, place the former inside the latter, leaving one-fourth inch or more of space for air circulation around the walls of the inner pot. Sometimes sphagnum moss is inserted here to help conserve moisture. A base of gravel in the decorative pot can provide good drainage while lifting the inner pot to the level of the outer container.

Watering

More house plants are killed by overwatering than by any other cause. This killing with kindness can be avoided, if you learn to understand just when your plants need water and when they should be left alone.

The best rule of thumb is that a plant should be watered when the soil surface is dry to the touch. Then water thoroughly, either by adding water to the soil surface or by immersing the pot (up to but not over the lip) in a larger container of water.

With certain plants, such as African violets and other woodsy varieties, there are many conditions that call for more or less water, as indicated in Table 15.

Immersion is the best method of watering, because it is the surest. The soil in any pot might tend to form water channels, which, upon receiving water from the surface, will rush it to the bottom of the pot and out the drainage hole, leaving large parts of the soil bone-dry. Then some potting soil mixtures will shrink when drying, leaving many spaces along the wall of the pot where water can run past. Immersion is the one sure way to soak the soil thoroughly (provided that the pot is porous). You can do it in any large container, a sink, or a bathtub. Set the potted plants in the water, but do not let the water flow over the lips of the pots. After the surface of the potting soil has become moist—10 to 30 minutes—remove the potted plant, drain off any excess

water, and put it back in its place. Never go out for the afternoon, leaving your plants standing in water.

When you water from the top, remember to remove any excess water from the saucer. Plants should never be allowed to stand in water for fear of root rot. In time, you should learn to give each plant just enough water to soak it thoroughly, with very little excess drainage. (And speaking of saucers, get glazed ones—not unglazed terra cotta—if you want to protect your furniture.)

Some other watering tips:

1. Do not let water rest in the crown of any plant (the plant section at the soil surface), for this will encourage decay.

2. Never use very cold water, especially for tropical plants. Keep an open jar of water at room temperature for your house plants. Not only will the proper temperature be assured, but—if you use tap water—some of the chemicals will have dissipated by the time it is given to plants. This method takes no more time than others. It is simply a matter of filling the jars for the next watering *after* you have watered rather than before.

3. Water that is artificially softened may be detrimental to plant growth. There is also some evidence showing that fluorine is not good for some house plants. If you can, use rainwater or water that has not been softened.

4. If your water is especially hard, lime salts might cause trouble with such acid-loving plants as orchids, *Primula, Rhododendron,* Azaleas, and others whose natural soil is woodsy (indicating a high organic content) and acid. Either choose plants that prefer a more neutral range in the pH scale, or plan to collect rainwater for your calcifuges (lime haters).

Humidity

Much of our trouble with house plants, especially in winter, can be traced to insufficient moisture in the air. Except for cacti and other succulents, nearly all house plants

Table 16. Watering Needs of Plants Under Various Conditions

Plants will need more water when . . .	Plants will need less water when . . .
. . . they are in a period of active growth.	. . . they are in a period of rest (usually during winter).
. . . they are in bright light.	. . . they are in dim light or under artificial light.
. . . room humidity is low.	. . . room humidity is high.
. . . room temperature is high.	. . . room temperature is under 70°.
. . . they are contained in small pots.	. . . they are in large pots.
. . . they are in clay pots.	. . . they are in nonporous pots.
. . . they are fast-growing varieties.	. . . they are slow-growing varieties.
. . . they are planted in sandy-soil.	. . . they are planted in heavy soil.
. . . they are in flower or about to go into flower.	

thrive best in a relative humidity of between 40 and 60 percent, while that of most homes in winter is under 40 percent—often considerably under 40 percent. House plants will virtually cry for moisture under these conditions, and it is incumbent upon you to answer that cry.

There are several ways to add moisture to the air in your home. The more expensive include the adding of a humidifying device to your furnace, if you live in a house, or installing an electric humidifier. This step will benefit not only the plants but everyone living in the house, too. But there are less expensive ways to bring moist smiles to the faces of your plants:

The Pebble Tray. Line the bottom of a waterproof tray with decorative pebbles and arrange your plants, in pots, on top of the pebbles. Keep the tray filled with water, being sure only to avoid blocking the pots' drainage holes. Sprinkle a little charcoal among the pebbles to keep the water fresh. It takes no work to maintain the pebble tray, after it has been set up, since you simply keep the water level up as you water your plants.

Decorative Containers. If you keep a clay pot inside a decorative container (which is called double potting), keep a pool of water in the bottom of the larger vessel. Again, provide some means of support for the clay pot so that

it is not resting in water at any time. Or fill the space between the walls of the two pots with wet sphagnum moss and keep it wet, in which case you will not have to maintain a pool of water.

Standing Water Devices. Water left standing in a room will gradually evaporate, meaning that the lost moisture is added to the room atmosphere. If your house or apartment is particularly dry during cold weather, take the trouble to place pans of water on tops of radiators or over heat vents; grow ivy, *Philodendron*, or wandering Jew in containers of water; maintain an aquarium; do anything, short of making a major project of it, to add water to the home atmosphere—even to the point of keeping a little water in the bathtub.

Plant Bathing and Showering. When the air is dry, most house plants will appreciate a brief misting every day or two or at least as often as you can manage to provide the treat. Little brass-plated atomizers are ubiquitous in mail-order catalogs and at house plant centers, but more dependable (albeit less decorative) are plastic sprayers available at house plant centers and art supply stores. These hold a pint or a quart of water and feature an adjustable shower head, affording an entire range of water action from a sharp jet capable of carrying 20 feet (the kids love this one) all the way to a fine mist. Your plants, of course, will like the fine mist. Remember to fill the container after every use, so that the following day's spray will be at room temperature. Remember also to avoid spraying plants that have been subjected to very cool temperatures (perhaps spending the autumn on a cold sun porch).

Rubber plants and others with large leaves should be cleaned thoroughly and gently with a damp cloth every week or so. Commercially sold leaf polish is permissible, if you want really stunning looking, large-leafed plants, but never use any other kind of oil, since it can block the leaf's pores and impede respiration. Ivies and other rugged small-leafed plants can be held under the gentle stream of a faucet for their weekly bath.

Grouping. Plants will maintain moist surrounding air with greater facility if they are grouped together (leaves not touching) rather than separated. During the coldest part of winter, you might want to group most plants on a pebble tray under a light window to take advantage both of maximum light and greatest humidity.

Ventilation

Plants, like people, benefit from fresh air. Like people, also, they react badly to drastic changes in air movement and temperature. Provide adequate ventilation for your house plants, but do not subject them to sharp winds, winter drafts, or heat rising directly from radiators or vents. Think of your own comfort in this respect, and you will know what will please your plants. If in autumn you bring your plants in from a summer outdoors, help them adjust to indoor conditions gradually by placing them by an open window for the first several days. Gradually lower the window day by day, keeping a watchful eye on night temperatures.

Temperature

The temperature requirements of house plants vary widely, according to the natural habitat of their forebears and also according to other conditions. Many cool-weather plants prefer a range of 50° to 60° and cannot tolerate temperatures above 70°, while tropicals may thrive in a moist 70° to 75°. Know the temperature preferences of any house plant before you adopt it, and then place it in the best possible temperature location in your home. You might find, for instance, that a cool-loving *Aspidistra* will do best in a back bedroom, while tropical plants thrive happily next to (but not above) a living room heat vent. A *Coleus* may perish where an African violet thrives and vice versa.

The temperature requirements or tolerances of plants are included in their descriptions throughout this chapter. Heed them well, make liberal use of an indoor thermometer, and do not be afraid to experiment by placing different plants in different locations for up to a month at a time. You might notice in your plants distinct preferences for particular locations throughout the house, and their preferences will not always corroborate expert advice.

Air Conditioning

Some people have the mistaken idea that air conditioning is bad for plants. On the contrary, most house plants thrive in the constant, moderate temperatures that air conditioning provides. The only caution is that no plant be placed directly in the path of a cold stream of air.

Light

Light and temperature needs are closely related. In their native environments, many tropical plants can thrive at high temperatures, because they receive long hours of sunlight. In the home and especially during winter's short days, they cannot receive enough light to enable them to stand high indoor temperatures.

Except for most cacti and succulents, house plants should not be placed in windowsills where they will receive long periods of direct sunlight. Simply place a thermometer in this position; you will soon see that your plants can literally be cooked to death even in the dead of winter. Strive instead for a bright spot that receives filtered sunlight, at least for most plants.

Individual varieties differ in their light needs, of course, and these needs are specified in the descriptions of individual plants in these pages. Again, do not be afraid to experiment with different locations for different plants.

Pruning

Most plants should be pruned and pinched back occasionally, in order to encourage bushy and stocky growth. Pinching back takes little time; it can be done in a few seconds simply by pinching off, between thumb and forefinger, much of the new growth of a plant. This pinching back, done in odd moments, will save much work, since you will never have to deal with rank and ungainly growth of any of your plants.

Many people hesitate to prune at all, feeling somehow that they will hurt the plant or interfere with its natural development. Actually plants will respond to judicious pruning with new and bushier growth and vigorous health. Plants like geraniums, *Coleus,* and begonias should be pinched back routinely in order to encourage lateral growth. If you find that a plant is growing too tall, when you would prefer that it remain shorter and bushy, simply pinch back the growing tips at the top of the plant; or, if the growing tips are too thick, use a sharp knife. However you do it, the plant will respond by sending out side shoots below the central tip, and the main stem of the plant will then become thicker and sturdier. If this is done several times a year or even more often with quick-growing species, each plant should eventually attain the vigorous and well-rounded form you desire. Without any pruning or pinching back, a plant might grow "leggy" with a weak main stem, requiring some kind of support. Many older plants as well will benefit from occasional pinching back or shearing of outside growth.

There are a few house plants that should never be pruned or pinched back. They include Norfolk Island pines, African violets, gloxinias, flowering bulbs, succulents, ferns, and cyclamens.

Plant Supports

Vines and trailing plants often need some kind of support, unless you prune them severely or prefer to let them cascade from a hanging basket. Nevertheless, you may decide that the attractive appearance of a climbing plant warrants your time in giving it something to climb on. The usual practice is to sink a slab of cork or tree bark into a pot and then train the vines of the plant to grow around and up the support, eventually concealing it.

Another effective device is the sphagnum moss cylinder. Pack thoroughly wet moss fairly tightly around a stake and secure it in a cylinder of the proper diameter from the pot. The cylinder can be made easily from either wire mesh or green plastic material made for this purpose and available at house plant centers. If you wish, sink a small clay pot into the top of the cylinder, so that you can add water regularly to keep the moss damp. (Otherwise the moss will require regular spraying.) Tie the vines gently to the cylinder as they grow; eventually, *Philodendron*, ivy, and similar plants will anchor themselves to the moss, making other support unnecessary.

Repotting

A plant needs repotting only when it has become pot-bound—when the roots have filled the entire container and are creeping from the drainage hole. If you find that a plant really needs repotting, then choose a new pot only one size larger than the old, for a house plant will not do well in a pot that is too large. If the larger pot has been used before, scrub it thoroughly to remove any possibility of disease. Soak new clay pots for a few hours until they become saturated. Then, with ample moist potting soil, gravel, and a tongue depressor or similar wood tool, set to work.

To remove the plant from its old pot, slide your hand over the top of the pot, index and second fingers cradling the plant stem. Turn the pot upside-down, thus supported, and tap the lip of the pot sharply on the edge of a bench or table. After a few taps the entire soil ball, ringed with plant roots, should come out easily, in one neat piece. Set it aside. Take the larger pot and line the bottom with a layer of coarse gravel or broken crockery to provide good drainage. Then add potting soil on top of the gravel, placing the plant and soil ball on top of the new soil several times to ensure that it reaches the proper depth. (The top of the soil should be about one-half inch below the lip of the new pot in a four-inch pot, and one inch below the lip in an eight-inch pot, to leave room for watering.) When enough soil has been added to raise the plant to its proper height, center it well; using the tongue depressor, begin to pack soil around the sides of the soil ball. Take your time in doing this, for it is the most crucial part of the entire operation. It is important to pack the soil firmly so that no air spaces are left. Roots cannot draw nutrients in air spaces, and many of them will thus be injured or die, affecting the health of the entire plant. When the new soil is finally brought to a level even with the top of the soil ball, the job is finished. You might want to add a little more soil over the top of the root ball, especially if roots have been forced up to the soil surface. But don't add any more than you must, for you do not want to change the planting depth of the plant. Repotting is shock enough for many plants without altering the planting depth. Water the plant thoroughly and return it to its usual location.

How often should you repot? Obviously, only as each plant indicates a need. For slow growers, this might be once every two or three years; a mature slow grower may go for many years without repotting, if new growth is cut back. For fast-growing and very young plants, repotting might be needed once or twice a year for the first several years. Plants that do not need repotting after one year should have the top one-half to one inch of soil replaced annually to keep their soil fresh.

Propagation

A time may come when you want to start your own house plants—to increase your own plant population, to use as personal gifts for friends and family, or to replace a short-lived plant or one that has become ungainly with age. Propagation of most house plants is not difficult, and it is most rewarding.

There are two general methods of doing the job: by the collecting and planting of seeds and by the cutting and rooting of plant parts—stems, leaves, or underground structures. The first way (sexual reproduction) is usually less satisfactory than the second. Propagation from seed is ideal for garden annuals but not for most house plants. The seeds from hybrid plants are likely to produce plants vastly inferior to the parent plant. (A hybrid, incidentally, is any plant produced by cross-pollinating two plants of different varieties, species, or genera.) Last, many house plants do not flower and produce seeds under home conditions, requiring the house plant gardener to purchase seeds from specialty houses. The one advantage of growing house plants from seed is that you can create new hybrids by the cross-pollination of plants. The excitement of this activity creates a fascinating hobby for some house plant enthusiasts but is unlikely to appeal to those who cannot devote significant amounts of spare time to the activity.

Far more simple, and yielding far more reliable results, is the propagation of plants by the cutting and rooting of plant parts. Less care is required, and the offspring will look just like the parent, even when the parent is a hybrid.

Plants can be propagated at any time of year, though it is best to avoid tackling the job when the plant is going into a dormant period. Early spring, just before active growth begins, is perhaps the ideal time.

Cuttings. The most common method of propagating is by the taking of stem cuttings, which are then rooted in either water or some sterile rooting medium such as perlite, vermiculite, or sand. If you have never rooted a cutting before, then begin with African violets, *Coleus, Dracaena, Fuchsia, Gardenia, Impatiens,* ivy, *Philodendron,* wandering Jew, or wax begonia. These are the easiest, because all can be rooted in water. Simply take a cutting, containing four to six leaves, from an actively growing tip of the plant, severing the stem cleanly just below a joint with a clean razor blade. Place the cutting (you may take several at a time from the same plant, if you wish) so that the bottom portion is submerged in water—a colored or clear bottle is fine—remembering only to keep the leaves above water. (Cut off the bottom leaf or two, if necessary, to get more of the stem into the water; about one third of the entire length should be in water.) Place the container in diffused light—not direct sun—and wait until vigorous roots appear. When they have, the little plant may be removed from the water and potted in a small pot, using the potting mixture recommended earlier. Be sure to pack the potting mixture firmly around the roots of the plant to avoid any air spaces, and water thoroughly afterwards.

Stem cuttings that cannot be rooted in water are rooted in perlite, vermiculite (both available wherever house plant supplies are sold), or builder's sand. Be sure that at least one node is below the surface of the potting medium. The process is basically the same as for rooting in water. The cuttings are inserted in the moist medium, which may be contained in a small clay pot or, for larger numbers of cuttings, a shallow plastic tray. The planted container is then placed in a plastic bag, which is tied shut (the self-sealing kind, used for food storage, is convenient, effective, and reusable) and placed in diffused light at a temperature of 65° to 70°. You can tell whether the cuttings have developed roots by testing them weekly. Open the bag and pull gently on a plant. If it moves easily, then the roots have not yet

formed; if it resists your gentle tug, however, then the roots probably are mature enough to stand repotting. The process can take as little as two weeks, or as long as several months, depending on the variety of the plant and the size of the cutting. When the roots are strong and vigorous, pot the plant in a small pot, and treat it as you would any other plant.

Some plants that produce canes (hollow or pithy stems), including Chinese evergreen, *Dracaena,* and *Dieffenbachia,* can be propagated by taking cuttings of the canes, which have discernible "eyes." Press each cane section (containing one eye) into moist sphagnum moss, secure it with wooden clothespins at each end so that it does not pop up, seal it in a plastic bag, and put it in a cool place out of direct sun. In six to eight weeks move it into a warm place (70° to 90°), still out of direct sun. Soon a shoot will grow from the eye. When the shoot has attained a respectable size, the cane may be cut close to the shoot on both sides, and the new plant may be lifted from the moss and potted.

Plants that have fleshy leaves are best propagated by taking leaf or leaf-petiole cuttings. (A petiole is a leaf stalk, or stem.) Leaf cuttings work well when large and mature leaves are available. Cut the leaf close to the stem of the parent plant, using a razor blade for a clean cut. The leaf may then be cut horizontally into smaller sections, so the main vein runs from top to bottom along the center of the leaf section. (Long-leafed plants like *Sansevieria* and *Streptocarpus* may be cut into as many as ten sections, each of which will produce an individual plant.) Each leaf section is then sunk halfway into the rooting medium, after which the process is the same as that described for stem cuttings. Patience is required here, for this method is often very slow to produce results.

Smaller leaves may be rooted by taking leaf-petiole cuttings. Cut one leaf stem close to the main stalk and sink the stem into the rooting medium; the leaf should almost (but not actually) touch the medium. African violets, begonias, snake plant, piggyback plant, and *Peperomia* respond well to leaf-petiole cuttings.

Underground Division. Older plants that have thick main roots can be propagated by taking root cuttings. This is usually done when the plant is being repotted. Cut about one inch of the main root, making sure that it has at least one eye. Cover this with one-half inch of rooting medium, and treat it as you would any other cutting.

Thick-rooted perennials may be propagated simply by root division, in which the root mass is forced apart into two or more clumps, each of which is then repotted.

Plants that produce rhizomes may be propagated by dividing the rhizome so that one leaf bud is contained on each piece and planting the section under one-half inch of rooting medium. Plants that produce potatolike tubers can be propagated by cutting the tubers apart with a sharp knife, keeping one eye to each section, and planting the sections in the rooting medium just as you would plant potatoes in the open field.

Some plants produce "suckers," small plants that grow up from an underground stem or root. These may be separated from the parent plant and potted in soil immediately.

Anyone who has seen strawberries grow outdoors knows what runners are—the baby plants that grow from a long stem coming from the base of the parent plant. Among house plants, Boston fern, strawberry geranium, and spider plant produce runners, which can be started in a rooting medium and, only after they have rooted, severed from the parent plant.

Other methods of underground division include the separation and replanting of baby bulbs or corms, which are produced by the mother bulb or corm.

Air Layering. A fairly simple (and most impressive) way of propagating larger or woody-stemmed plants is by air layering. Here a sharp cut is made into the stem, perhaps a third of the way in, into which a toothpick is placed, horizontally, to keep the cut open. That stem section is then wrapped with moist sphagnum moss and covered with clear plastic and tied above and below so that moisture cannot escape. Roots will develop at the incision and will soon show through the plastic. When a fair number of them have appeared, cut the stem below the plastic wrap, remove both plastic and moss, and pot the new plant immediately in potting soil.

As you might imagine, the propagation of plants can often be integrated with the cutting back, pruning, and shaping of older plants. It seems a shame to throw away plant parts when they can be used to produce more plants. But precisely this attitude of thrift, if not controlled, can lead to frightening multiplication of house plants. The answer, of course, is to share plants with friends, thus encouraging still more enthusiasts and still more house plants.

Can Your Plants Survive Your Vacation?

What will you do with your plants while you are gone for a long weekend, for a week, or for a month?

The best solution is to have someone come in to water them for you. Be sure to give the volunteer specific instructions, however, since anyone unfamiliar with the needs of house plants might easily kill them with kindness by overwatering them.

A long weekend should present no problem whatsoever, except perhaps for vegetables and a few others that need daily watering. Simply soak your plants thoroughly by immersion and drain them; they should easily last for four days. If you will be gone for a week, enclose each pot in a plastic bag, and tie it snugly around the base of the plant stem. This device will cut surface evaporation greatly. Smaller plants can be enclosed completely in plastic bags, as long as some support is provided so that the plastic does not touch the foliage. Thus covered, most plants can remain in good health for at least a month. When uncovering them after your vacation, expose them to the outside air very gradually. They probably will have luxuriated in the greenhouselike atmosphere of the plastic bag and can drop their leaves from shock if the bag is removed quickly.

Water wicks will keep a plant happy for weeks at a time. Wicks and pots are sold as units, usually called self-watering pots, but you can easily make your own at far less expense. Buy several yards of broad lamp wick. Cut off a six- to ten-inch section for each potted plant, depending on the pot size. Invert an empty pot in a larger container of water, until the water level comes to just below the top (the bottom, actually) of the inverted pot. Knock out the soil ball of the potted plant, insert the wick into the drainage hole, and flare out the end of the wick so that it covers as much of the bottom of the pot as possible (the wick should spread out above the drainage gravel just under the soil ball). Replace the soil ball and plant. Thread the loose end of the wick through the drainage hole of the inverted bottom pot and into the water, and set the potted plant on the inverted pot. Water the plant once, from above, and the action should be continuous from then on. Test this method on several plants while you are still at home, in order to determine just how well it works for you and how long you can afford to be away from home without worry. It is a most effective method.

The ABCs of Artificial Light

Fluorescent lighting opens up opportunities for you to expand your range of indoor gardening. Now you can grow lush, green plants in areas where they would never grow before. A windowless bathroom, which might offer ideal humidity and temperature conditions, can now be made into an ideal plant-growing environment. Plants growing on a drab northern windowsill can now receive supplemental light during winter's short, dark days. Dim corners of any room can be transformed into green showplaces. Under artificial light, cuttings and seedlings can now make faster and surer progress than ever, and we can even grow vegetables in the dead of winter in the bedroom or kitchen. Artificial lighting is not essential for house plant success, but it certainly does broaden our horizons, reduce work and worry, and increase chances for maximum rewards.

The old incandescent bulb does offer some help to growing plants, although the heat it produces makes it impossible to offer plants the amounts of light they need without drying or burning the plants. Also, incandescent bulbs offer a very short spectrum of light wavelengths, falling far short of simulating the beneficial rays of the sun. Ordinary daylight or fluorescent lights are far better for growing plants, because they not only have a wider and more effective light wavelength, but they also produce light with three times as much efficiency as incandescent bulbs, thus reducing heat by nearly two thirds. Lights designed especially for plant growing have become popular during the past decade. Independent tests show, however, that plants do not grow significantly better under these lights than under ordinary fluorescent tubes, which are considerably less expensive.

Fluorescent tubes can solve virtually any light problem for the indoor gardener. By attaching them to a 24-hour timer you can control light exposure perfectly, even for such tricky operations as forcing plants to bloom out of season.

The best way to begin with artificial light is the most simple way. Purchase two 40-watt fluorescent tubes—one warm, one cool—with the proper fixture, and hang it over a table where you will conduct your experiments. Be sure you have some method of raising and lowering the fixture, for you will want to adjust the lighting intensity to meet different plant requirements. Ferns and snake plants, for instance, have low light requirements, so the tubes should be placed 12 to 18 inches above them; succulents, ivy, most flowering plants, and all vegetables have high light requirements, requiring the lowering of the tubes to eight inches or less above the plants. The closest you can bring the tubes and still avoid injury from heat is two inches above the plants. Guidebooks available from tube manufacturers give the exact light requirements of most common plants. In many cases excellent books on artificial-light gardening can be found in your public library.

If you enjoy artificial-light gardening and the gratifying results it brings, you will have no problem in expanding your activities in this area. Manufacturers have introduced a wide variety of special plant-growing stands, some with several tiers capable of holding dozens of plants, others decorative enough to enhance the beauty of any room. Your choices are limited only by your imagination and your checkbook balance.

Should You Send Your Plants to Summer Camp?

Nearly all house plants will enjoy a summer outdoors, and many will make considerable growing progress under the ideal light conditions of the outdoors. Many gardeners, however, would never send indoor plants outdoors, thinking of the possibilities of insect and weather damage. Also, they do not want their plants to grow rankly, preferring to keep them in a controlled and pleasing shape. There is no doubt that plants are better controlled indoors. The choice is yours.

Some dangers are involved in sending your plants outdoors at any time. Shock, resulting from either sharp light or temperature changes, is the main danger. Gardeners can avoid these by placing plants outdoors only when the night temperatures will go no lower than the minimum recommended for each plant. It might be best to put

them on a sheltered porch or breezeway for the first few days, until they have become accustomed to the outdoors, or to put them out for only a few hours in the morning, bringing them in again before the heat of the day sets in. After a week or so they may be placed outside for the summer. Choose a spot shaded totally away from the sun. After a week of shade, those plants that can take some direct sun can be moved into diffused sunlight, perhaps under the protection of a large tree. Many house plants will be severely injured or killed by long exposure to a hot summer sun.

Keep the plants in their pots, and do not sink them directly into the ground because of soil insects and grubs. You may sink them, if you line the bottom of the hole with two inches of gravel, or they may be kept above ground, in which case you will have to watch soil moisture very carefully.

Check the plants every week for signs of insect infestation. If any appears, wash the plant thoroughly and bring it inside. Isolate it from other house plants, until all signs of the insects are gone.

Well before the first frost prepare to bring the plants indoors for winter. Again, inspect each for insect infestation. Wash each with a sharp spray of water. Knock out the soil ball, and inspect it carefully for insects or larva. Repot the plant at this time, if it is pot-bound. Prune back any excess growth that might have misshaped the plant; then bring it indoors. Keep it near an open, screened window for a week or two, in order to reintroduce it gradually to its indoor habitat, and then treat it normally. Your house plants should enjoy their summer at camp, even if they do act like sheltered children away from home for the first time. They should reward you with increased health and vigor that will last through the winter.

Foliage Plants

In this section, we will survey many of the house plants grown primarily for their foliage.

Some of them, under favorable conditions, will flower from time to time, although few should be selected for their flowering abilities. Nearly all of these plants are fairly easy to grow and maintain, providing a wide variety of plants from which to choose.

The plants are listed in alphabetical order according to their common or popular names. If there is no popular name for a plant, or if there is more than one, none dominant, the plant is listed by its scientific or Latin name.

The symbols next to each plant name will provide a quick and convenient guide to that plant's requirements. Remember, however, that these are guides and not sharp demands. Many of these plants are tolerant by nature and will take to an east window as well as an indicated west window; many can tolerate some direct sunlight even if none is recommended. Most crucial, perhaps, are the guides to humidity and moisture, since overwatering is one thing that few plants will tolerate.

The following symbols are used throughout to indicate the temperature preference, light needs, soil moisture and humidity needs, and best window locations for each plant described:

Temperature Preference

  warm, 60°-80°

  moderate, 50°-70°

  cool, 45°-60°

Light Needs

  full sun

  tolerates some direct sun

  bright spot with no direct sun

  tolerates continuous shade

Soil Moisture and Humidity Needs

  higher than room humidity, constantly moist soil

  moderate humidity and soil moisture

  tolerates dry conditions

Best Window Location

  north

  south or west

  east

Aralia *(Fatsia japonica)*

Sometimes sold as *Aralia sieboldii*, this cheerful plant boasts beautiful, bright green, leathery, maplelike leaves. In appearance it is similar to the castor-oil plant and in fact is sometimes called false castor-oil plant. It thrives in a cool spot. Aralia can easily grow leggy, and so it should be pruned annually or even more often in order to encourage bushy growth. It will attain a height of four feet at maturity.

A striking hybrid, *Fatshedra lizei* (a cross between *F. japonica* and ivy or *Hedera*), forms a climbing plant with maple-shaped leaves; it is quite tolerant of adverse conditions. False aralia *(Dizygotheca elegantissima)* has graceful and feathery foliage. It bears no resemblance to the true aralia and is difficult to grow.

Asparagus

Two common kinds of *Asparagus* are suitable for growing as house plants: fern asparagus *(A. plumosus)*, with slender, needlelike, dark green leaves and a feathery appearance, and emerald feather *(A. sprengeri)*, which has thicker yellow green leaves and drooping stems. The latter makes a good plant for hanging baskets, and the older plants of this species produce red berries around Christmas. Both like some sun in the summer and full sun in the winter, and both can grow to a height of about two feet.

A. *meyeri*, less common but equally attractive, has tiny fernlike leaves that arch out on long stems from the center of the plant.

Australian Laurel
(Pittosporum tobira)

Here is a tolerant and slow-growing plant whose glossy and leathery leaves resemble those of *Rhododendron*. Australian laurel will grow vigorously bushy and does not ask much attention. Florists often use the leaves in floral arrangements.

An interesting variegated form is *P. tobira variegata*, which grows quite large.

Australian Umbrella Tree
(Schefflera actinophylla)

This very attractive and vigorous-growing treelike plant has rich and glossy leaves that radiate umbrellalike from the ends of several leaf stalks. It is a tough and rewarding plant, growing to six feet, which can be propagated by air layering.

Australian umbrella tree is also sold as *Brassaia actinophylla*. A dwarf variety, *B. actinophylla compacta*, is also available.

Baby's Tears
(Helxine soleirolii)

This low creeper is also called Irish moss. It likes a constantly moist (but not soggy) soil and higher than average humidity. It makes a good ground cover for terrariums but will also grow in a pot if adequate humidity is provided. Baby's tears may appear to die in colder months, but after an adequate rest period it

will spring back to life. It is very sensitive to fertilizer burn and salt accumulation.

Boxwood *(Buxus)*

The same plant that grows the most prized hedges outdoors can make a very attractive house plant. Boxwood, with its glossy, bright green leaves, is slow growing and dependable, a good subject for bonsai, the ancient oriental art of growing dwarf trees and shrubs. Japanese boxwood *(B. microphylla japonica* and *B. sempervirens)* are the two most popular species.

Bromeliads

There are more than eighteen hundred varieties of this popular group, many of which are suitable for growing as house plants. Some of them produce attractive flowers, but most are grown for their striking and variegated leaf patterns. One distinctive feature of a bromeliad is the rosette of leaves that forms a small water cup, which the plant uses to hold reserve supplies of water in its natural habitat. Since the plant lives in the crotches of trees in Central and South America, the water cup is an evolutionary survival characteristic. In the home keep the cup filled with water, changing it weekly to keep it fresh.

Common bromeliads include *Aechmea*, pineapple *(Ananas)*, *Billbergia*, *Cryptanthus*, *Dyckia*, Spanish moss *(Tillandsia)*, and *Vriesia*.

Caladium

Caladium, with its spectacularly colored and variegated leaves, is equally at home in the outdoor garden and on the windowsill. It is an ideal addition to plant groupings on porch or patio in the summer and early autumn. Give it bright light but not long periods of direct sun in summer, if you want the brightest leaf colors. It will not last more than a season and should be treated as an annual.

Caladium is grown from a tuber, which can be divided easily to produce new plants. Start the tubers in regular potting soil at a very warm temperature—80° to 90°—and move the young plant to a cooler spot when it has appeared. It will attain a height of about one foot.

Cast-Iron Plant
(Aspidistra eliator)

This is perhaps the easiest plant in the world to grow, as its name suggests. It is virtually impossible to neglect it to death. It is also called saloon plant, since it was one of the few that could survive in Victorian taverns. And it was made immortal by George Orwell in his novel *Keep the Aspidistra Flying.* If you cannot grow *Aspidistra,* you may safely conclude that you have a hopeless case of purple thumb and had best invest in plastic plants.

Cast-iron plant, which grows about two feet tall, seems to thrive even better when kept slightly pot-bound, and it will appreciate having its leaves washed occasionally. An attractive white-striped species is A. variegata.

Chinese Evergreen
(Aglaonema)

Here is an attractive plant that is very easy to grow. It will stand abuse nearly as well as the cast-iron plant.

There are at least 10 common species of *Aglaonema,* the most popular of which, *A. modestum,* has interestingly mottlvd leaves. Perhaps the prettiest, however, is *A. pseudobracteatum* which is often difficult to find in shops and garden centers.

Cissus

Cissus is a tiny genus that offers a number of interesting and attractive species. Most are vigorous climbers, suitable for training on a trellis or for adding to hanging baskets.

Among the more popular species are grape ivy *(C. rhombifolia),* which is one of the most popular and easy to grow of all house plants; kangaroo vine *(C. antarctica),* which prefers a small pot; miniature kangaroo vine *(C. antarctica minima); C. rotundifolia;* and begonia ivy *(C. discolor),* which is perhaps the most spectacular of the genus, although it is difficult to grow.

Coleus

This old favorite has leaves (some velvety) sporting bright splashes of reds, pinks, purples, and yellows. There is a seemingly endless number of varieties of *Coleus,* nearly all of them interesting, most growing 12 to 18 inches in height.

Coleus is equally happy outdoors, grown as an annual in the North, or in the window garden. It can be grown easily from seed, and stem tip cuttings can be taken from established indoor plants nearly any time of the year. If you grow *Coleus* outdoors in summer, take some cuttings before the first autumn freeze, and root them for growing as house plants.

The soil for *Coleus* should be kept damp but not soggy. Pinch back plants often to encourage bushy growth.

Dieffenbachia

There are many species of this popular plant, often called dumbcane. It is prized for its large leaves with interesting markings, usually variations of cream and white on dark green. *Dieffenbachia* is a fairly tough plant and is not too difficult to grow. Most varieties attain a height of 18 to 24 inches, although growth is slow.

D. arvida 'Exotica' is very popular, because it is even more durable than other members of the family. Other well-known species include *D. picta, D. amoena, D. sequina,* and *D. bowmannii.*

There are no special cultural requirements, although *Dieffenbachia* does like a warm spot and will appreciate having its foliage cleaned regularly. The plant may be propagated by taking stem cuttings and rooting them in moist and warm peat.

Caution: Eating or nibbling on the leaves of *Dieffenbachia* can cause severe swelling of the tongue and mouth tissues, hence its popular name, dumbcane. It is *not* a plant to grow in a home with toddlers.

Dracaena

The many species of *Dracaena* vary so greatly in appearance that some appear to be unrelated. Most grow tall—five feet or more—on sturdy stalks. They are very tough plants, tolerant of a surprising amount of neglect. All in all they are one of our most dependable house plants.

Some varieties to investigate are *D. deremensis* "Warnecki," *D. fragrans* (which has cornlike leaves), *D. fragrans massangeana* (whose leaves feature yellow stripes), *D. marginata* (a truly exciting plant, with grasslike, cream-colored foliage, edged in red—sometimes sold as *D. marginata tricolor*), *D. sanderiana* (with white-banded leaves), *D. godseffiana* "Florida Beauty," *D. draco* (the dragon tree of the Canary Islands), and many others, some of which will doubtless be offered by any good supplier. These mentioned, however, are some of the most attractive and also some of the easiest to grow.

Fatshedra
See Aralia.

Fatsia Japonica
See Aralia.

Ferns

Ferns are the oldest plants—on the evolutionary scale—that you are likely to cultivate. They are predated only by algae and mosses.

Everyone knows and admires ferns for their graceful, feathery fronds. They are among the few house plants that reproduce themselves by spores rather than by seeds. Some ferns grow regally upright, while others trail with modesty and grace. There are many sizes of ferns, from miniature plants suitable for the windowsill all the way to the seven-foot tub plants that can add a touch of class to entryways, patios, and conservatories.

The secret to the successful raising of ferns is in offering them an environment matching, as nearly as possible, that of their natural habitat. They need warmth, a decent degree of room humidity (not under 30 percent), and a moist and humusy soil (at least 50 percent organic matter). They appreciate bright light but will be affected adversely if allowed to stand for long periods of time in direct sun.

There are a great many ferns from which to choose. Among the smaller ones are these:

The maidenhair fern *(Adiantum)* is available in several varieties. It sends forth fragile-looking fronds in sprays and needs good light and high humidity. It is a rather difficult plant.

Asparagus fern *(Asparagus plumosus),* the most popular of the small "ferns," is really not a fern at all but a member of the lily family and reproduces by seeds rather than spores. It is treasured for its delicate, hairlike leaves.

Other smaller "ferns" of the *Asparagus* group include simlax *(A. medeoloides),* a trailer; emerald feather *(A. sprengeri),* a climber; break fern *(Pteris multifida);* chain fern *(Woodwardia orientalis),* hare's-foot fern *(Polypodium aureum);* and many others of a similar nature.

Among the larger true ferns are these:

Holly fern *(Cyrtomium falcatum)* has holly-shaped fronds. Bird's-nest fern *(Asplenium nidus)* has broad lance-shaped fronds. *Nephrolepis exaltata* has long, sword-shaped fronds and is often called sword fern. *N. exaltata* "Bostoniensis," is the everpopular

Boston fern. Staghorn fern *(Platycerium bifurcatum)* has fronds which are usually attached to a piece of bark or other support. They can become parched quite easily in a dry atmosphere.

The world of ferns is a large one, full of interest, and extremely rewarding. No house plant collection should be without at least one or two representatives of these proud families. If you have never grown ferns before, start out with the asparagus fern or the break fern, which are probably the easiest to grow.

Ficus

This large group of indoor plants, whose best-known member is the rubber plant, offers species ranging from large, treelike plants to small-leafed trailers. Although they are not difficult plants to grow, the large species are especially sensitive to both overwatering and sudden temperature changes and will react to either by dropping their leaves.

There has been much improvement in the rubber plant *(F. elastica)* since World War II. The best now is perhaps *F. elastica* "Robusta," which is remarkably trouble free. There are many decorative varieties, as well, including *F. elastica* "Doescheri," which has light and dark green patched leaves and cream-colored leaf margins, and *F. elastica* "Schryveriana," another mottled-leafed variety. *F. elastica* "Decora," from which "Robusta" was developed, is still a popular slow-growing variety. Most rubber plants will grow as tall as any room but may be cut back to encourage bushiness.

Chinese banyan *(F. retusa)*, another treelike *Ficus*, showers forth a profusion of small, leathery leaves. Indian laurel *(F. retusa nitida)* resembles mountain laurel.

The fiddleleaf fig *(F. lyrata)* is a tough and attractive treelike species with large, dark green, fiddle-shaped leaves. It needs warmer conditions than other *Ficus*. Weeping fig *(F. benjamina)* is another *Ficus* tree that has

small, densely growing foliage; it is especially sensitive to low humidity and is likely to be worrisome. Mistletoe fig *(F. diversifolia)* is an easy-to-grow species that features yellowish berries in profusion.

The genus also contains many small plants. Most popular perhaps is creeping fig *(F. pumila)*, a small-leafed creeper that has been developed to include several variations—*F. pumila minima*, slower growing and smaller, and *F. pumila variegata*, a variegated variety. All will adhere to rough surfaces, sending out aerial roots similar to those of ivy, and all are easily trained.

The tree-type *Ficus* are propagated by air layering, while the small-leafed climbers and trailers may be reproduced easily by simple division or cuttings.

Ivy *(Hedera)*

Ivy is surely one of the most popular of house plant species, both easy to grow and cheerful and attractive in appearance. The great number of varieties is continually enhanced with new improvements.

English ivy *(Hedera helix)* is the most popular of the true ivies and is available in more than 50 varieties to suit nearly any taste. There are varieties with large leaves and small, fast or slow growing habits, plain green or variegated colors. The best way to choose an English ivy to your liking is to visit flower shops and greenhouses or to beg a few cuttings from a friend who has a plant that appeals to you.

Propagation of ivy is easy, and in fact the plant does half of the job for you. Small rootlets will form on the stem of the plant, just below the leaves, which the ivy uses to attach itself to rough surfaces, helping it to climb. Make cuttings just below the rootlets, and plant these cuttings directly in potting soil or a sterile rooting medium.

It would be fruitless to attempt to recommend all the good varieties of English ivy. For starters, however, you might investigate Japanese ivy *(H. helix conglomerata),* an upright-growing plant with small, densely growing leaves; "Curlilocks" and "Ivalace" with curled leaf margins; "Green Ripples," "Maple Queen," "Merion Beauty,""Needle-point," "Pittsburgh," "Pixie," "Rochester," *H. helix scutifolia,* and "Shamrock," the last of which likes more than average moisture and which is good for terrariums.

Among the variegated English ivies, try "Golddust," " Glacier," and "Goldheart," the last of which has dark green leaves with sharply contrasting bright yellow centers.

Canary Islands ivy *(Hedera canariensis)* is another easy-to-grow ivy, which has larger leaves than English ivy. It is often trained around a piece of bark, much like a *Philodendron,* to form a striking plant with a very bushy appearance. You may also let it trail from a hanging basket. More popular than the basic green-leafed variety is the variant *H.*

Maranta

canariensis variegata, also known as "Glorie de Marengo," whose leaves are slate green to cream in color.

Maranta

Here is a genus of plants that has striking foliage. It is not very difficult to grow and will reach a height of about eight inches.

Prayer plant *(M. leuconeura kerchoveana)* is perhaps the most popular *Maranta* and is so named because its leaves fold up at night, as if in prayer. The leaves are large and oval, and the plant requires a fairly humid atmosphere. In the autumn some leaves may begin to die. If so, do not be alarmed. Cut off the affected leaves, and reduce watering until late winter, when new growth begins; then water normally.

A red-veined variety, even more striking, is *M. erythroneura.* Another with red veins is jungle plant *(M. leuconeura erythrophylla),* which has olive green leaves. Still another handsome variation is offered by *M. leuconeura massangeana.*

Most house plant growers will want to include at least one *Maranta* among their collections. The key to success with this plant is in giving it lots of bright light but no direct sun at all.

Miniature Holly
(Malpighia coccigera)

This is not a true holly but is a bushy evergreen shrub with dense hollylike foliage. The leaves are shiny and dark green, and have spiny teeth. Miniature holly does produce small flowers, but it is grown primarily as a foliage plant. It is propagated easily from cuttings.

Norfolk Island Pine
(Araucaria excelsa)

This popular evergreen, graceful and symmetrical, is seen with increasing frequency. It will hold up well under adverse conditions, although its branches will droop in dim light. Give it a damp (but not soggy) soil, for it is very susceptible to overwatering. It does well when kept slightly pot-bound.

Norfolk Island pine is a slow grower and should never be pruned. It will grow gracefully to a height of about six feet, after which it tends to become ungainly.

Palms

In Victorian times and through the 1930s and 1940s, the potted palm was a symbol of exotic elegance, bringing a bit of the tropics to shivering northerners. The elegant palms lost much of their allure after World War II, but now they are making an impressive comeback.

You can achieve success with palms by giving them bright light (even though they will endure shade), relatively little water, and no plant food during winter. Palms actually seem to thrive on inattention, doing well when slightly pot-bound. They are slow growing in any case.

The palms are a plant family—*Palmae* is the scientific name—that comprises many genera and far more species. Few, however, are both attractive and manageable as house plants. Here are some palms you might wish to investigate:

European fan palm *(Chamaerops)* has fan-shaped leaves on long stalks and will become quite large at maturity.

A coconut palm species *(Howeia)* is among the most popular of all indoor large palms. *H. belmoreana,* thought by many to be the most stunning species, can eventually grow to 10 feet or more in height, given many years and sufficient room.

Neanthe is an agreeable and easy-to-grow dwarf that can tolerate a dry room.

The date palm *(Phoenix)* can be grown easily from the stone of a fresh date. Plant the stone in potting soil, and keep it warm (70° to 80°); it should germinate in about a month. It is slow growing during the first year or so, but within 10 or 15 years it will become as tall as any room.

Pellionia

This colorful, slow-growing, creeping plant is fine for hanging baskets and is a good filler plant for groupings. It has small, oval leaves with interesting variegated patterns. Two popular varieties are *P. daveauana* and the more compact *P. pulchra.*

Pellionia is not difficult to propagate. As it creeps along the soil, it sends down roots from the stems. Just cut the stems into sections, and root them in potting soil.

Peperomia

There are many species and varieties of this popular and cheerful little plant (eight inches or less in height), most of which are low and upward growing, some with deeply ridged leaves. They are tough plants, tolerant of most conditions, although they will rot at the groundline if the top of the soil is not allowed to dry out between waterings. *Peperomia* like bright light but not much direct sun in the summer.

Among the more popular varieties are the following:

Emerald ripple peperomia *(P. caperata)* has deeply ridged heart-shaped leaves; the tops of the ridges are green and the valleys are brown, giving an appealing effect.

P. rotundifolia is a low grower with light green, thick leaves.

Oval-leaf peperomia *(P. obtusifolia)* has solid green leaves, while *P. obtusifolia variegata* is the variegated form of the same species.

Watermelon peperomia *(P. sandersii)* is identified by its red petioles and silver-striped leaves.

P. grieseo-argentea hederaefolia has ridged, glossy, silver-hued leaves and purple olive veins.

There are many other varieties of the *Peperomia,* some of which may be seen at your local flower shop or greenhouse.

Philodendron

These plants constitute what is probably the most popular group of house plants in America today. There are many, many species and varieties, with leaves ranging from small to very large, in an assortment of shapes offered by no other house plants. Most are climbers and will appreciate a support that can be kept moist, such as that described on page 260.

Philodendron are not difficult plants to grow, unless you disregard the rules. Growth will be stunted by poor light, and the leaves can turn yellow and drop from lack of water, too small a pot, low temperatures, or poor drainage. They will appreciate a monthly washing with a mild soap (not detergent) solution. Cut back the growing tips if you wish to encourage bushy growth, and use the tip cuttings to form new plants.

You may wish to try one of these popular varieties:

Sweetheart vine *(P. scandens)* is a very popular climber that can withstand the dry air of a typical apartment. *P. oxycardium,* the most commonly grown form, has heart-shaped leaves very similar to *P. scandens.* It is often grown in water or wet moss. Cut-leaf philodendron *(P. dubium)* is a slow grower with star-shaped leaves. Fiddleleaf philodendron *(P. panduraeforme)* has irregularly shaped, olive green leaves. *P. pertusum* has irregularly shaped perforated leaves. The adult form, known as *Monstera deliciosa,* has broad, thick leaves with many perforations.

Anchorleaf philodendron *(P. squamiferum)* has leaves and petioles that are covered with red hairs. The leaves are shaped like daggers. Twice-cut philodendron *(P. bipinnatifidum)* is a large-leafed variety; the leaves resemble the smaller *P. dubium* in shape but are more deeply notched. *P. selloum* is another cut-leaf variety, with the cuts becoming more pronounced as the plant reaches maturity. This species will tolerate temperatures down to freezing with no apparent harm. *P. wendlandii* is another large-leafed species and is very tolerant of a wide range of temperature and humidity. Its leaves are long and narrow.

Piggyback Plant
(Tolmiea menziesii)

Its name is derived from its unusual habit of bearing young plantlets from the junction of the leaf and the petiole. These can be rooted easily to grow new plants. The leaves are toothed, lobed, and covered in down. It is an easy plant to grow.

Pilea

There are at least four cultivated house plants in this interesting group, none of which grows more than a foot in height. All like moist soil, warm temperatures, and full sun in the winter. The plants become less attractive as they grow older, but cuttings are easily made so that older plants may be discarded when desired. Fertilize *Pilea* liberally when growth is active.

Aluminum plant *(P. cadierei)* has dark green leaves with striking aluminum-colored markings. A dwarf variety, *P. cadierei minima,* is preferred by many, as *P. cadierei nana,* a compact variety. Artillery plant *(P. microphylla)* is fine in texture with bright green, fernlike leaves. When its flowers are dry, pollen literally explodes from the blossoms, hence its common name.

South American friendship plant *(P. involucrata)* is bushy in growth and has coppery leaves. It can be made to be even more bushy, if several cuttings are taken and then rooted in the same pot, to the sides of the parent plant. *P.* "Silver Tree" has bronze-hued leaves with silver markings.

Pothos *(Scindapsus)*

Pothos is very similar in appearance and growth habits to the heartleaf *Philodendron scandens,* but it needs less water and warmer temperatures—not below 65°. It likes bright light but cannot stand direct sun. Pothos is a natural trailer, although it can be trained upward along a support, again like *Philodendron.* The leaves are heart-shaped and green with pale yellow markings.

The most popular species is *S. aureus,* which offers several variegated varieties, some of which require even warmer temperatures.

Screw Pine *(Pandanus)*

This old favorite will withstand most adverse conditions. It is recognized by its long, arching swordlike leaves, which have sawtoothed edges.

P. veitchii has green and white striped leaves. Often preferred, however, is *P. veitchii compactus,* a dwarf variety with clearly variegated leaves. *P. baptgstii* has no marginal spines, as do the other species. All screw pines like moist soil but never soggy soil. They can take some direct sun except in the heat of summer, although they do best in a bright location out of direct sun altogether.

Sensitive Plant
(Mimosa pudica)

This is a fascinating plant for both adults and children, because its delicate and feathery leaves and petioles droop and fold up instantly (and temporarily) whenever it is touched or even if a lighted match is held close to it. Plants may be grown easily from seeds, which are often available in stores. It becomes leggy and rank after about a year, but it is not difficult to grow more plants at any time. It is very sensitive to mealybugs.

Silk Oak *(Grevillea robusta)*

This is a pleasant plant with graceful and feathery foliage similar to that of the false aralia. It will grow to three feet in height. Silk oak likes cool and moist conditions and can spend the summer outdoors with benefit. It does tend to become leggy if unchecked, so the growing tips should be cut back regularly. Silk oak will do poorly if its soil becomes dry.

Snake Plant *(Sansevieria)*

The snake plant is actually a succulent, but few of us think of it as such, and so we include it among the foliage plants. It has long been very popular probably because of its great tolerance to adverse conditions. It is also called mother-in-law tongue and bowstring. Like the cast-iron plant, *Sansevieria* can grow perfectly well in hot, dry, and dim locations (including, it seems, most old hotel lobbies in the country). It is slow growing and tough.

Sansevieria's thick, sword-shaped, usually upright leaves grow to 18 inches or more in height, but in some varieties hug the ground. It is propagated easily by division of the rootstock or by taking a leaf cutting. (Be careful not to turn the leaf cutting upside-down when setting it in the rooting medium, for roots grow only from the downward portion of the cutting.)

Many varieties of snake plant are available:

Variegated snake plant *(S. trifasciata laurenti)* has handsome yellow bands along its leaf margins. *S. trifasciata* is similar in form but without the yellow bands. Dwarf Congo snake plant *(S. trifasciata laurenti "compacta")* has shorter leaves and yellow margins. Hahn's dwarf snake plant *(S. trifasciata "hahni")* has light and dark green bands along the leaves.

There are many other interesting variegated varieties of this old standby.

Spider Plant
(Chlorophytum comosum)

Spider plant is one of the most popular house plants. Its grassy leaves, variegated cream and green in color, arch gracefully from either pot or hanging basket. Mature plants produce perfectly formed baby plants on the ends of long runners that resemble spiders hanging from a thread. Propagation is simply a matter of rooting one of the "baby spiders" in a rooting medium. The spider plant can store water in its tubers and can take dry soil for a fairly long time because of this characteristic. It is easy to care for and can take a fair amount of inattention.

Strawberry Geranium
(Saxifraga sarmentosa)

This trailing plant, also called strawberry begonia and mother of thousands, is good for both hanging baskets and terrariums. All it really asks is a woodsy soil, containing plenty of organic matter, and a cool location. Leaves of the strawberry geranium resemble those of the true geranium, and it sends out runners just as strawberry plants do. The leaves of the standard variety are deep olive in color with silver gray markings. An interesting variant, *S. sarmentosa* "tricolor," has dark green leaves marked with white and pink and is considerably more difficult to grow. Strawberry geranium can easily be harmed by overfertilization.

Ti Plant
(Cordyline terminalis)

C. terminalis is only one of many species of *Cordyline*, but it is certainly the most popular. Also called firebrand, it will last for only one to three years and grow to two feet in height before dying out, but its spectacular young life is certainly worth your placing this plant on the list of house plant candidates. It has long, upward-reaching leaves of cerise, purple, and green, which grow from a cane trunk. Another popular species is *C. australis,* which features long and slender leaves. The ti plant is very popular in Hawaii, where its colorful leaves are used in making grass skirts. It is sold there in tourist shops as ''ti log.'' In recent years breeders have developed variations of the original plant, including a dwarf and a variegated variety, which are sold under various names.

Umbrella Sedge
(Cyperus alternifolius)

This popular exotic plant has narrow, pointed, grasslike leaves that grow in clusters. It will grow up to two feet tall in a pot. Constant moisture is essential, and propagation is a simple matter of root division.

Related species include *C. papyrus,* similar in appearance and requirements but which grows to seven feet in height over the years, and a dwarf variety, *C. alternifolius gracilis.*

Velvet Plant *(Gynura)*

This is a vigorous-growing plant with dark red, velvety leaves. It will offer a fine contrast to your green plants. It is best to train velvet plant to some support, to keep it in bounds. The plants tend to become spindly and leggy with age and should not be counted on for the long run.

There are two common varieties—*G. aurantiaca,* which is upright in growth habit, and *G. sarmentosa,* a smaller and loosely twining plant. The flowers of both have a disagreeable scent and should be removed immediately after they bloom. The plant also tends to harbor mealybugs.

Wandering Jew *(Tradescantia)*

Tradescantia and *Zebrina* both claim the common name of wandering Jew, and the two genera are so similar that they are commonly interchanged. They are easy to grow, tolerant, and vigorous trailers, which make them perfect for hanging baskets. Feed them regularly for good growth, less often for controlled growth. Propagation is simplicity itself. Take cuttings of growing tips and root them in water.

There are very many interesting species of this plant. *T. fluminensis,* the original wandering Jew, has silver markings, but there are many variants of different markings and colors available today. *T. albiflora* has bluish green leaves with white stripes. *Z. pendula* is an excellent house plant whose leaves have purple undersides. Again, there are several interesting variegated varieties.

Flowering House Plants

The flowering house plants, of which there are thousands, comprise many families and have a very wide range of cultural requirements. Those native to warm regions will grow readily under home conditions, and those from temperate regions demand cool temperatures, especially at night. Some are spring- and summer-flowering plants that we will force into bloom in midwinter. And still others have such attractive foliage that they are grown for this beauty alone; their flowers are an added bonus.

The plants and plant groups selected for individual attention in the following pages are those that are both attractive and easy, or fairly easy, to grow. Many of the most beautiful plants seen in greenhouses, including some that fairly blaze with hundreds of colorful blossoms, will soon wilt and die in your care, simply because no average home can possibly match the special conditions offered by a greenhouse. Further, the florist has learned the subtle art of manipulation of both light and special chemicals to force plants to flower at certain times of the year. Such plants are not included in this chapter.

Two requirements of flowering house

plants deserve your special consideration. First, in order to flower these plants need plenty of light, especially in the winter and during the period of flower formation. Second, most of them require very cool night temperatures—as low as 50° and certainly not over 60°. If you cannot meet these requirements, then you must choose your flowering plants with great care, or learn to be happy with foliage plants, cacti, and succulents.

Achimenes

This plant, grown from a rhizome planted in March, April, or May, produces petunialike blossoms of red or blue, which appear in the summer. Its rambling nature makes it perfect for hanging baskets, and it will be happy on porch or patio as well as indoors. Give *Achimenes* a sunny window but some protection from the sun during the scorching days of summer. After its flowering period has

finished, allow the entire plant to dry, and then store the rhizome in its pot, or in sand, at 50° to 60°, watering only if the rhizome begins to wither. The foliage of this plant is handsome, also, providing an extra bonus.

African Violet

The African violet, a low-growing member of the gesneriad (gloxinia) family, is certainly the most popular flowering house plant and is possibly the most popular of all house plants. Its virtues are both simple and irresistible: It is easy to grow, and its blossoms are both attractive and profuse.

This plant does have special requirements that, although not difficult to provide, are essential to success. It likes a warm temperature—68° to 75°—which happens to be the range of many warmer homes (and which also might explain why the African violet seems to be the favorite plant of everybody's elderly aunt). It likes good light (but no

The ever-popular African Violet is one of the very few houseplants that will bloom freely in constantly warm temperatures and limited light.

long periods of direct sun), moderate to high humidity, and a constantly moist (but not soggy) soil. Its soil should be humusy, with a high percentage of peat or other organic matter. (Most suppliers, even supermarkets, offer potting soil for African violets.) In watering, be sure not to splash the foliage without drying it thoroughly afterward (since standing water droplets on leaves causes spotting). The leaves should, however, be washed regularly in a mild soap solution, after which they should be rinsed thoroughly and allowed to dry in the shade. Last, avoid chilling the plant, either with air or water. Temperatures should never go below 60°, and cold water should never be used. Follow these rules and your chances with an African violet should be good indeed.

There are so many varieties of this plant that we will not attempt to select any for inclusion here. There are both single- and double-flowered varieties in various shades of red, pink, blue, lavender, purple, and white. There are also some handsome bicolored varieties.

African violets rarely need repotting—certainly not more than once every two years and then only to a pot one size larger. Some can go for much longer periods without repotting. Supplemental light during the evening hours does help the plants to attain greater vigor, especially during the short days of autumn and winter. Be advised, also, that unglazed clay pots are not the best choice for African violets, since the bottom leaves, resting on the lips of moist pots, can easily rot. Use plastic or glazed ceramic pots, or dip the rims of unglazed pots in paraffin before using them.

Propagation of African violets is simple with leaf cuttings. Root your favorite varieties, and in a year or so you will have some dandy Christmas presents for family and friends.

Amaryllis

Here is a bulb plant that is perfect for indoor growing. In the dead of winter, it produces spectacular trumpet-shaped blossoms, borne in a cluster on top of a 12- to 18-inch stalk. The blossoms are of very good size and are available in a variety of colors—white, red, pink, or orange.

It is difficult to fail with amaryllis. Many bulbs are sold prepotted, so judicious watering is your only responsibility. If you buy unpotted bulbs, however, be sure to select a very small pot, with a diameter no larger than three inches greater than the bulb itself. Use humusy soil, setting the bulb firmly so that from one half to two thirds of it is *above* the soil line (or plant according to the grower's directions). October to March is the usual potting time. The plant should be placed in maximum sunlight, and the soil should be kept moist but not soggy. The stalk should grow vigorously and produce blossoms within two months.

After the blossoms have faded, cut the flower stalk, but do not disturb the leaves (which must produce food that the plant will use for next year's blossoming). When the danger of spring frost has passed, sink the pot in soil outdoors. Bring it back in before the first autumn frost and let it dry out in a cool basement until after New Year's Day. Then repot the bulb in fresh soil, and resume watering for new blossoms. For blooming around Christmas, bring the plant indoors about the first of August, remove the bulb from its pot and let it dry for eight to ten weeks. Then repot it, move it to a sunny spot, and resume watering.

Begonia

There are more than six thousand varieties of this popular plant, many of which produce both showy and colorful leaves and beautiful blossoms. So loved are these plants that some growers deal in them exclusively, and many home enthusiasts find time for no other indoor plants. Begonias may be temperamental in their requirements, although your chances of success will be improved greatly, if you choose the right varieties to begin with. They will, depending on the variety, grow from six to 18 inches in height.

Tuberous begonias are good for porches and terraces but not as house plants. Rex begonias have spectacular foliage and, again, are fine outdoors but not indoors.

Wax begonias will do well either indoors or outdoors and are not difficult to raise in either place. They like full sun in the winter and partial shade during the heat of summer. Give them a constantly moist soil and warmer-than-average temperatures. (But do remember that they might not flower if autumn and winter night temperatures are over 70°.

Fibrous-rooted begonias are the largest group of all and are by far the best house plants of this far-flung family. Scores of varieties are commonly available, including many that flower constantly and profusely. Many tumble freely from hanging baskets. Their culture is similar to that recommended for wax begonias. Most florists and greenhouses can show you a variety of fibrous-rooted begonias, among which you can select a favorite for experimentation in your home.

Geranium *(Pelargonium)*

These are common and popular plants for patio and window box production, and they can be successful indoors, too, if the rules are followed. Critical to vigorous growth and profuse blossoming are full sun and cool temperatures. The ideal night temperatures for geraniums range from 55° to 60°, while warmer night conditions can inhibit flowering. Since the geranium's foliage is susceptible to rot, do not let water stand on the leaves.

There are several large groups of geraniums. The best for indoor production, however, are the varieties of *Pelargonium hortorum,* sometimes called the "house group" or zonal geraniums, of which there are hundreds.

You may start either by buying potted specimens from your plant dealer or by begging cuttings from friends. The cuttings are rooted quite easily in a sterile rooting medium and may soon be potted. If you want flowers in winter, take cuttings in May and start them immediately. Pot the plants as soon as vigorous roots have formed, and pinch off all flower buds until mid-autumn in order to encourage foliage growth. If, however, you want flowers in the spring and summer—perhaps with the idea of moving the plants to porch or patio—then begin the same process in October.

Gloxinia *(Sinningia speciosa)*

After the African violet, the gloxinia is certainly the most popular member of the gesneriad family. It is low growing, no more than 10 inches in height, with large velvety leaves and large bell-shaped flowers in shades of violet, red, pink, and white, including many bicolored and double-blossomed varieties. It is a good plant for either outdoor or indoor culture.

Gloxinia likes warm temperatures, moist soil, and especially good air circulation for good health. It grows from tubers, which are generally started in midwinter. After the plant has finished flowering (about four months after planting), dry out the plant thoroughly, then store the tuber in its pot or in sand, in cool temperatures (around 55°). Water the tuber only enough to keep it from withering. In February or March repot the tuber in fresh soil and resume watering and warm temperatures. In four months another round of spectacular blooming should take place. Gloxinia is more susceptible than most plants to a number of insect pests.

Goldfish Plant *(Columnea)*

The goldfish plant is so-called because its tubular flowers, in bright shades of red, pink, orange, or yellow, resemble the fantail goldfish. Some varieties are vinelike in growth and are perfect for hanging baskets. Others have very pretty variegated foliage. The cultural requirements are the same as those for African violets. Propagation from stem cuttings is simple.

Shrimp Plant
(Beloperone guttata)

The flower of this unusual plant does, indeed, resemble the shape of a shrimp. It tends to become leggy in growth, and so it should be pinched back often in order to encourage bushy growth and a height of about 12 inches. The shrimp plant will appreciate a summer outdoors, but it should be pruned back severely beforehand. It is more difficult to grow than most plants included here, although some people appear to have no trouble at all with it.

Wax Plant *(Hoya carnosa)*

Here is an old favorite and a vigorous grower. It has waxy leaves, variegated in some varieties, and alluring flowers in yellow, pink, or white, all of which have a very nice scent. *H. carnosa variegata* has white leaf margins but is only representative of the many variegated varieties that have interesting markings in white, green, pink, cream, yellow, or silver. The wax plant is another that is grown as much (and sometimes more) for its foliage as for its flowers. Good dwarf varieties include *H. bella, H. minima,* and *H. lacunosa.* Rope hoya *(H. carnosa compacta)* has an unusual leaf shape.

Wax plants are suitable for either pots (although some will need support) or hanging baskets. Keep them on the dry side, especially during their autumn rest period. They seem to

bloom better when slightly pot-bound. Take care not to injure the long shoots produced each season. Pruning these will cost a season of flowers.

Forcing Spring Bulbs

A most pleasant way to enjoy a touch of spring in the dead of winter is to force spring-flowering bulbs for indoor bloom. Tulips, hyacinths, daffodils and other *narcissi,* crocus, grape hyacinths, lily of the valley, scilla—all can be coaxed into fragrant and colorful bloom during the gray days of January, February, and March.

The prerequisites for bulb forcing include special bulb pans (which are nothing more than shallow clay pots, available at any garden center), a suitable soil mixture, a proper place for cool and dark storage of the potted bulbs, and a little special attention.

Selecting Bulbs. Hyacinths are the easiest of all bulbs to force, while tulips are the most difficult. The rest should present no great problems if you bear in mind the rules. If you are attempting the process for the first time, however, start with hyacinths. Table 16 will suggest the varieties of each plant most suited to indoor forcing, although you should also depend on the advice of a nursery person whom you trust. In general choose the largest and most perfectly formed bulbs. Since you will not be buying a large quantity for indoor use, you might as well pay a little extra for top quality. See that the paper-thin skin is intact and that the bottom of the bulb, from which the roots will grow, has not been injured. If you are buying a large number of bulbs for planting outdoors, save some of the best for your indoor project.

Storage Before Potting. If you will not be potting the bulbs immediately, store them at 55° to 63° in a location with good ventilation. If they begin to shrivel from dryness, moisten them daily with a plant mister. The actual potting process should take place no earlier than October 1 and no later than December 1. Earlier potting, of course, means earlier bloom.

Potting. The potting soil for bulbs should be low in nutrients and high in drainage capacity. A good mixture is three parts garden loam, two parts peat moss, and one part builder's sand. Do not add compost or manure, since nothing will be gained in doing so (the bulbs already hold all the nutrients the plant will need), and rotting can become a problem.

To help both drainage and ventilation of the root system, put some broken crockery in the bottom of the bulb pan, being certain to place one piece directly over the drainage hole—not to seal it but to prevent soil from being washed out of the pot. Then fill the pan partially with the potting mixture, set the bulbs firmly but gently on top, and work more potting mixture around the bulbs until only the tips show. In the end, the soil should come to one-fourth inch to one inch from the top of the pan, depending on its size. At least one inch of soil should be used; a great amount more is not needed.

Bulbs may be spaced as closely together as you wish, as long as they do not touch each other. Tulip bulbs have a flat side that should be pressed against the side of the pan. Working around the pan in this manner, you can plant six to nine bulbs in a six-inch pan, including one in the middle.

Water the potting mixture thoroughly after planting, and label each pot with the specific name of the bulbs and the planting date. Your bulbs are now ready for the most

---

Table 17. Recommended Bulbs for Indoor Forcing

Tulips (to bloom in January and February)
    Red: Bing Crosby, Cassini, Cellini, Charles, Christmas Marvel, Olaf, Paul Richter, Prominence, Topscore, Trance
    Yellow: Bellona, Levant
    White: Pax, Snow Star
    Salmon: Apricot Beauty
    Variegated: Kees Nelis, Madame Spoor, Merry Widow, Roland
    Pink: Blenda, Preludium

Tulips (to bloom in March and April)
    Red: Albury, Cardinal, Couleur, Danton, Robinea
    Yellow: Makassar, Ornament, Yellow Present
    White: Blizzard
    Orange: Orange Sun
    Variegated: Carl M. Bellman, Denbola, Edith Eddy, Golden Eddy, Paris
    Pink: Palestrina, Peerles Pink, Pink Supreme, Rose Beauty, Virtuoso

Hyacinths (to bloom in January and February)
    Red: Amsterdam, Jan Bos
    Pink: Anna Marie, Delight, Eros, Lady Derby, Princess Irene
    Blue: Bismark, Delft Blue, Ostara
    White: Edelweiss, L'Innocense, Madame Kruger

Hyacinths (to bloom in March and April)
    Red: Amsterdam
    Pink: Eros, Lady Derby, Marconi, Pink Pearl, Princess Irene
    Blue: Blue Giant, Blue Jacket, Marie, Ostara
    White: Carnegie, Colesseum

Daffodils (to bloom in January and February)
    Carleton, Golden Harvest, King Alfred

Daffodils (to bloom in March and April)
    Cheerfulness, Geranium, Gold Medal, Rembrandt, Van Sion

Crocuses (to bloom from January through April
    Grand Maitre, Joan of Arc, Peter Pan, Pickwick, Remembrance

Richard E. Widmer, *Care of House Plants,* Agricultural Extension Service, University of Minnesota, Extension Bulletin 274, rev. 1970, p. 24. Based on studies conducted at Michigan State University.

important step—the winter sleep.

Winter Sleep. Outdoors in your yard, spring-flowering bulbs spend the winter in cold, dark storage. They are not inactive in their outdoor sleep, however; they are sending out vigorous white roots, while the snow flies above, in preparation for their great spring fling. Indoors you must recreate this winter sleep to give the bulbs a chance to develop roots. If you provide temperatures that are too warm, the bulbs will be triggered into premature and stunted growth.

The winter sleeping location will depend on the climate in your area and any supplemental refrigeration you can provide. The temperature should be no lower than 35° and no higher than 50°. Hyacinths can take a higher temperature—up to 55°—with no apparent harm. Wisconsin gardeners might start by storing the potted bulbs on a back porch, moving them later to an unheated garage and, when the temperatures dip below freezing, to a cool part of a basement. Record the temperatures in several locations around the house and move the plants accordingly. If the weather does not cooperate, you can store them in a refrigerator, which should provide the proper temperature constantly. In any case, keep the bulbs out of strong light and keep the soil moist. Total darkness is fine, and the occasional light from a refrigerator bulb will do no harm. On a porch or another open location protection from light can be provided in many different ways. An inverted pot placed on top of the bulb pan will do the trick. Or the pots may be set in a box and covered with sand. A closed box is fine. Soil moisture may be retained if you seal off air from the potted bulbs. Enclosing them in a dark green plastic trash bag is an effective and simple method. Or they may be covered with sand, which should be kept just slightly moist. In a refrigerator they can be watered occasionally. However you choose to provide these conditions, it is essential that the potted bulbs receive relative darkness, cool temperatures, and adequate soil moisture.

In about six weeks the bulbs should begin to send out roots. In a minimum of 12 weeks from the time of potting, or as long as 20, they should be ready to emerge from the bulb pan.

Active Growth. When the root system is well developed, and a white growing tip is evident, the bulb is ready to be brought out into the open for active growth. As a test, knock out the soil ball from one pan and examine the roots. If they are strong and vigorous, covering the bottom of the soil ball in a thick mat, you may be sure the plant is ready.

At this time place the plant in an open location, out of direct sun, at a temperature of 50° to 60°. Be especially careful to keep hyacinths in a very dim location for the first few days to encourage the flower stalk to make rapid upward growth. The need for cool temperatures during this stage will again dictate a storage place. You might find that an unheated sun porch or a north window of a basement is ideal.

After the growing tip has changed from white to green, the plant may be moved into a sunny location and given a slightly warmer temperature—up to 65° during the day and 5° to 10° cooler at night. Many people simply transfer the pots from the north to the south basement windows. Be sure to keep the soil well watered during this entire period.

After the buds are nearly ready to open, the pans may be brought to the place where you want them to bloom. Keep them well watered until the plants have finished their colorful performance.

The only drawback to the entire process of forcing bulbs is that the bulbs often cannot be reused. Some people do let the plants turn yellow, then dry the bulbs, and plant them outdoors in the fall. But these bulbs rarely produce well again, because we have tampered with their biological time clocks. But since any bulb has a life-span of only a few years anyway, most of us feel that one brilliant indoor performance is enough for any bulb to provide.

Care of Gift Plants

Most commercially produced flowering gift plants should be regarded as nothing more than long-lasting cut flowers. After the plant has stopped flowering, it should be thrown away. Most of these, including *Chrysanthemum*, azaleas, cyclamen, and primroses, are suitable only for outdoor culture. Some can be planted outdoors after they have bloomed, provided that they are varieties hardy in your area. Others, including azaleas and poinsettias, make good indoor-outdoor plants that can provide pleasure year after year, given proper care. Here is a rundown of some of the more popular flowering gift plants:

Azalea. You may keep a potted azalea blooming for two months or more if you give it cool temperatures, diffused sunlight, and plenty of water. After it has stopped blooming, continue to water the plant frequently and keep it in a bright location. In spring after all danger of frost has passed, transplant the azalea into the open garden, giving it an acid soil. Prune it moderately around June 1. Before the first autumn frost, repot the plant, again giving it acid soil, and keep it in a very cool and light location for at least a month. An unheated sun porch or a cold frame is usually ideal for this purpose. During November bring the plant indoors. With cool temperatures and diffused sunlight the plant should bloom again in six to 10 weeks.

Chrysanthemum. Most potted *Chrysanthemum* that come from florists cannot be replanted outdoors in Wisconsin, because they are varieties suited to the South; killing frosts will arrive in autumn before the plants have had a chance to bloom. As house plants, however, they are long lasting and most beautiful. Keep them in your sunniest window at a temperature of 60° to 70°, and give them plenty of water. If you do receive a hardy variety (your florist might be able to advise you), give it a dormant period after it has bloomed. Then cut it back severely, and replant it outdoors in spring. You will have no guarantee of

success, but it might be worth a try.

Cyclamen. There is no practical way to preserve this plant after it has finished flowering indoors. However, the flowering period can be prolonged greatly if room temperatures are held between 50° and 55°. Admittedly at temperatures such as these your cyclamen's pleasure will be your personal discomfort. Perhaps, though, you have an unheated sun porch with a window opening into the living room, where the plant can be displayed effectively. At warmer temperatures the blossoms will last probably for no more than two weeks. In any case keep the plant in a bright spot, and do not let water stand in the crown of the plant because of the probability of rot.

Easter lily. This hardy plant can be transplanted outdoors after it has bloomed but with no guarantee of success. After you receive the plant, keep it in bright light, water liberally every day, and try to keep the night temperatures down to 55° to 60°. Although most people simply discard the plant after it has finished blooming, you may try to return it to natural conditions. Keep watering the plant after it has bloomed, until the leaves have turned yellow. After the danger of spring frost has passed, plant the bulb in the garden under six to eight inches of soil. New growth should appear by summer, and the plant might even bloom again by autumn. More likely, however, the next flowers will appear during the following summer, which is the normal blooming time for the Easter lily.

Poinsettia. A newly arrived poinsettia, like most other gift plants, should be given plenty of water, a cool room, and full sun. The colored bracts (they are not actually flowers) should last for three weeks at 70°, up to two months at 55° to 60°.

Since the leaves of the poinsettia are attractive, many people simply keep them as foliage plants, making no attempt to induce flowering the following year. They will do perfectly well as such, given ample water and diffused sunlight. If you want flowers to be produced the next year, however, there is a special procedure to follow:

After the bracts of the gift plant have fallen, move the plant to a cool basement or sun porch, where it will get plenty of light. Withhold water, giving it just enough to prevent complete dryness, and the plant will enter its dormant period. Around May 1, cut the plant back to within six inches of the soil line, and repot it in fresh soil. Resume watering at this time. If night temperatures will not go below 60°, you may place the pot outdoors for the summer, protecting the plant from very strong sunlight. When night temperatures again drop below 60°, move the plant indoors to a sunny, well-ventilated location.

If you want the poinsettia to bloom for Christmas, begin special treatment on October 1. At that time be sure that the plant receives a night temperature of 60° and a day temperature of 68° to 70°. Give the plant exactly 14 hours of darkness every day from October 1 until the Christmas blooming period. Providing the extra light is simple with a 24-hour timer attached to an artificial light source. Adjust it every few days. Admittedly this is a bothersome procedure, especially when it is so much easier to buy a blooming plant from a florist, but some enthusiasts take up the challenge each year as a matter of pride.

Primrose *(Primula).* A primrose may become a part of your permanent outdoor garden, after it has served indoors. When the blossoms have faded, move the plant to a cool basement and withhold water until spring, when the plant may be cut back severely, watered, and planted outside. Only *P. obconica* may be carried over to a second year indoors. After *P. obconica* has finished flowering, move it to a cool place and withhold water, forcing it to enter a dormant state. Water only enough to keep the soil from drying out completely. Then in autumn it may be repotted, placed in full sunlight, and watered freely. All primroses do best in full sunlight and cool night temperatures.

Cacti and Other Succulents

The succulents (and cacti are but one group of succulents) are remarkably colorful and interesting subjects, easy to care for, and responsive to special attention. Further, they require less attention than other plants. Most succulents ask little more than a sunny window, occasional water, and very occasional fertilizing. There is no pruning, no tying up, no staking, no repotting. They are slow growing and thoroughly dependable.

There are literally thousands of species in this plant category, including more than 2,000 cacti alone. Of these, several hundred, both attractive and suitable for indoor culture, are bred and sold as house plants.

Although cacti are succulent plants, the two are treated as separate groups in common practice, and in these pages we will follow that practice. Botanists classify cacti according to their flower characteristics, although most of us recognize them because of the unusual physical properties they have developed in surviving the demanding climates of their native habitats. The leaves of desert cacti (xerophytes) have evolved into sharp and hard spines that grow from small tufts of hair called areoles. Their stems have become enormously swollen and enlarged, which enables the plant to hold stores of water. Quite a different cactus group are the forest cacti (epiphytes), which come to us from the mountains of Brazil, where they live in the crotches of trees. They have no spines, but their inaccessibility to ground water has forced them to develop elongated stems. The Christmas cactus *(Zygocactus)* is the best known of the epiphytes.

The succulents are similar to the cacti in many basic characteristics, but they have no areoles. By far the best known of the succulents is the ubiquitous snake plant *(Sansevieria),* which is commonly considered as one of the foliage plants and is discussed on page 275. Among the hundreds of other house plant succulents are an amazing array of shapes, sizes, colors, and flowering characteristics, including some of the most unusual plants to be found in domestication. Here we find the fascinating *Lithops*, which looks for all the world like stones. Growing no more than two inches high, it produces beautiful yellow and white flowers that are larger than the plants themselves. *Euphorbias obesa*, on the other hand, grows into the form of a rust and green ball with perfectly regular markings. (If you don't like *E. obesa*, there are more than 2,000 other *Euphorbias* to consider.) Elk's horn *(Rhombophyllum nelii)* bears a close resemblance to its common namesake and then leaps out of character by producing the most exquisite, daisylike flowers. Certainly every house plant grower can find among the succulents' dazzling array of plant form and color one that will bring beauty to the home and pleasure to the grower.

Care of Cacti and Succulents

The secrets to success in raising cacti and succulents might very well be in exploding several myths that, if believed and acted upon, will retard the plants' development.

Myth number one says that cacti should rarely be watered. Believing this, many house plant growers virtually starve these poor plants into a state of retardation and total listlessness. In truth cacti should be watered nearly as liberally during their growing season as other plants. Only during autumn and winter, during the cacti's inactive period, should water be cut back severely. A good general rule is to soak the plants thoroughly and briefly once a week during spring, summer, and early autumn, being sure to provide for fast and thorough drainage. Near the middle of fall, water not more than once every two weeks—less frequently, if you are working to produce blossoms the following summer—and continue this reduced amount until the latter part of March, when watering may be increased gradually until, by the middle of April, the weekly schedule has been resumed.

Myth number two states that cacti rarely, if ever, need fertilization. In truth they will respond well to normal applications of plant food but only during their active growing period. (Some people, acting upon myths one and two, never realize that cacti *have* a growing period.)

The last myth says that cacti, since they are desert plants, require a hot and dry environment. Not true. While it is true that constantly damp and cool conditions will hurt these plants, cacti respond most favorably to a very cool atmosphere during the winter rest period (temperatures as low as 40°), and in summer they really don't care what the temperature is. You must remember that, in their native desert climates, daily temperatures in summer can have a spread of 50 degrees or more. Most experts recommend, for cacti's best health, winter resting temperatures of 45° to 50°, suggesting that a cool sun porch might make a fine wintering place for your cacti. During summer forget about temperature. More important are good ventilation and lots of sunshine. Cacti are among those plants that will do very well outdoors in the summer. (But do not expose them to long periods of direct sun immediately after their winter rest period in a shaded spot.)

Succulents require much the same conditions as cacti, but they do appreciate some protection from strong sunlight, if they are to show their true colors; and they require a little more water during the winter. Like the cacti, they appreciate a winter rest in cooler temperatures, as low as 50° and preferably not over 60°.

Potting Soil for Cacti

Although cacti and succulents should not be grown in pure sand, they do need a soil that will offer very good drainage. There are several good recipes, one calling for equal parts of commercial potting soil, builder's sand, and peat (with a moderate amount of bone meal) and another that substitutes compost for peat. Whichever you use, be sure to provide more sand than is called for in other potting soils, and don't neglect to provide pebbles or broken crockery in the bottom of the pot for good drainage. They do best in clay pots, where moisture can escape through the pot walls.

Introducing the Cacti

There are so many individual cactus species, and so much grafting of one species onto another, that we will here limit our survey to the larger groups of cacti. If you should become totally enamored of these plants, a trip to your public library will reveal at least several good books devoted exclusively to the group.

The prickly pears (Opuntia) are a large group, most of which have broad and flat joints. The best known of the group is bunny-ear cactus *(Opuntia microdasys)*, which does indeed resemble a series of bunny ears set one atop the other at odd angles.

The Cereeae constitute the largest of the cactus tribes incorporating hundreds of individual species. Best known among the Cereeae are the picturesque "candelabras," which were a stock item in every Hollywood western film of the 1930s. Another interesting member is the old-man cactus, which sports long white "hair." Actually several different species share this common name.

The Hylocereanae are climbers and crawlers that sometimes send out aerial roots like ivy. They produce the most beautiful flowers of all cacti and often bloom at night. The stems of the Hylocereanae are often weak and easy to break.

Another large group is the hedgehog cacti (Echinocereanae). They are prized by house plant growers, because they flower more readily, and at a younger age, than other cacti. One of the most popular is *Echinocereus fitchii*, found wherever cacti are sold, which produces beautiful pink flowers on plants as young as two years. *Rebutia* is very popular, too, and very numerous. It flowers easily, producing blossoms around the base of the plant.

The Echinocactanae are also called hedgehog cacti. They resemble the Echinocereanae, but the Echinocactanae send their blossoms forth from the tops of the growing tips rather than from the base of the plant. Depend on these two families for easy-flowering cacti.

The Coryphanthanae are distinguished from all other cacti in that they have large, protruding tubercles (wartlike knobs) over the entire surface of their stems. The largest genus in the Coryphanthanae family is *Mammillaria*, which exudes a watery or milky sap when pierced.

The forest cacti, including the prized Christmas cactus *(Zygocactus truncatus)*, live in tree crotches in the wild. They take to grafting quite readily and in fact are often grafted onto terrestrial rootstock in order to increase their vigor. Nevertheless, most Christmas cacti are not so grafted and will thus appreciate a loose-textured potting mixture that contains a large percentage of sphagnum moss or peat.

The Unusual Succulents

In many ways succulents are even more interesting than cacti. For one thing most have a most pleasant leaf and/or stem texture that the spines of a cactus cannot match. Many succulents are beautiful to feel (somewhat like a very smooth stone) as well as to look at. Here again the variety of color, form, and texture is nearly mind-boggling. There is certainly room for a few succulents in every house plant collection, the more so because they are easy to grow.

Aloe is very easy to grow and is distinguished by sharply pointed leaves that end in needlelike spines, almost like a cactus that has not finished its evolutionary process. Best known is *A. variegata*, a modest and rewarding plant.

Agave is another popular succulent group, many of whose members produce spectacular flowers. Best known in this group is century plant *(A. americana)*, a tolerant and attractive low-growing species.

The genus *Echeveria* forms a very large group of pleasant, if not spectacular, plants. Most have fleshy leaves that are very tidy in arrangement, and some flower quite freely. *Echeveria* are easy to grow and easy to propagate. Many varieties require no more for this purpose than cutting off a leaf and placing it on top of moist sand. Roots and plants soon will form.

Hawarthia is a small plant that comes in a wide variety of forms and textures. It is ideal for dish gardens.

Sempervivum comprises a most attractive group. Its tight rosettes form low mats of gorgeous color, indoors or out. Where the winters are not too severe, *Sempervivum* may be grown on the patio, if some protection can be offered when frost threatens. It needs much more light than most succulents, and so some artificial illumination might be necessary. But it is very rewarding if its special requirements can be met. Some varieties are hardy in the north.

Crassula forms another large family, offering plants in a wide variety of both colors and forms. Start with jade plant *(C. argentea)*, a popular species that is very attractive and easy to grow. On a thick, treelike stalk, it sets forth dark, thick, jade green leaves. Princess pine *(C. pseudolycopodioides)* is a freely growing plant with small, closely spaced, thick leaves. Like most *Crassula*, it is tidy in form and not difficult to grow. *C. perfossa* (necklace vine) has thick, triangular leaves growing on vinelike stems. It is a carefree and rambling plant.

Kalanchoes are both attractive in appearance and easy to grow, although many are short lived, lasting no more than a year. Like most short-lived house plants, however, they are remarkably easy to propagate, so you should have no trouble in keeping your favorite varieties in constant supply. The best-known of the *Kalanchoes* is *K. blossfeldiana*, of which there are many varieties. They are often seen in stores at Christmas time going under many popular names, including vulcan plant. *K. blossfeldiana* produces a profusion of small red blossoms. These, contrasted with its dark green and leathery leaves, explain its Yuletide popularity. Also try mother of thousands *(K. diagremontiana)* and *K. tubiflora*, both of which produce young plants freely along the edges of their leaves. Propagation of these two plants involves no more than your placing a leaf on moist sand and weighting it down with several pebbles. The young plantlets can soon be separated and nursed along in flats or separate pots. There are several other good *Kalanchoes* available and also other varieties and subvarieties of the species mentioned above. For quick and sometimes spectacular results they are good succulents for any home.

The genus *Sedum* (stonecrop) includes more than three hundred fifty varieties. Many of these are low and slow growing (although some grow quite vigorously), making them perfect for dish gardens. One of the more interesting members of the family is *S. stahlii* (coral beads), which has small, beadlike leaves. These drop off regularly and can be rooted with little trouble.

These are perhaps the most popular groups of succulents. There are, of course, many more, including some to suit any taste and most growing conditions. Some of the more popular of these are crown of thorns *(Euphorbia splendens)*, hen and chickens *(Sempervivum tectorum)*, rosary vine *(Ceropegia woodii)*, deer's tongue *(Gasteria verrucosa)*, cushion aloe *(Hawarthia)*, and elephant bush *(Portulacaria afra)*. None is very difficult to grow.

Special Indoor Gardens

Much of the fun of house plant growing revolves around special and unusual projects through which we can give full play to our imaginations and experimental natures. We can create a temporary miniature woodland scene in a terrarium or a colorful cactus garden in a soup bowl. We can grow beautiful house plants from kitchen scraps or plant lettuce on top of the refrigerator. By exercising our options more completely, by trying things we have never tried before, we gain a new sense of achievement. And with the aid of fluorescent lights, few of these special projects are beyond the capabilities of any house or apartment dweller.

Dish Gardens and Planters

Attractive displays of several different plants may be created by arranging them in a dish garden or a planter. A dish garden should be used for low- and slow-growing plants, while larger ones may be grouped in a larger planter of nearly any size or shape.

Any shallow container may be used for a dish garden—a soup bowl, a baking dish, or an attractive ceramic planter designed for this purpose. It need not have a drainage hole, but it must be watertight and rustproof. First place a layer of gravel to hold excess water in the bottom of the container. Charcoal is even better for this purpose, since it will keep the water fresh. Then place a layer of potting mixture on top, leaving one-half to three-fourths inch of room for watering. If you wish, you may add a thin layer of sand or colorful pebbles to enhance the final appearance of the dish garden. The trick is to choose low- and slow-growing plants—so that no one quickly dwarfs the others—and also plants that have similar cultural requirements. Good plants for dish gardens include boxwood, the smaller *Dracaena*, Irish moss (baby's tears), ivy, mother of thousands, *Pellionia*, *Peperomia*, *Pilea*, *Podocarpos*, wax plant, cacti, and smaller succulents. (Cacti and succulents, of course, should not be combined with plants that require higher soil moisture.)

Planters can be used for larger-growing plants of nearly any variety, as long as they, too, have similar cultural requirements. Some modern homes have built-in planters, often under picture windows, but you may construct one to fit anywhere in your home. It is best to keep plants in porous clay pots when adding them to a large planter, since most house plants react badly when they are given too much growing room. A good plan is to line the bottom of the planter with at least one inch of gravel, set the potted plants in the desired positions, and then fill in around them with sphagnum moss or peat moss. Smaller pots may be raised to the proper height with the aid of bricks or inverted pots. The plants may then be given the proper amount of moisture by adding water to the peat, letting the water soak through the clay pots. Plants may easily be added and removed, also, if they are kept in their individual pots. Plans for constructing planters are given in many larger indoor gardening books and in monthly magazines for home beautification. Make a thorough search of your local library's resources if you are interested in building a planter.

Bottle Gardens and Terrariums

Our fascination with bottle gardens and terrariums is both universal and understandable. Here we can create a self-enclosed plant world in miniature, completely landscaped to our liking, with rocks, pebbles, perhaps an attractive piece of driftwood, and plants of varied color, texture, and form, all artfully and perfectly placed. In the humid atmosphere of the glass garden, we can easily grow plants that would not survive on our windowsills. We can grow not only tropical plants but also native woodland varieties that would never tolerate the dry, artificial heat of the average home. The fascination of glass-enclosed gardens extends down to the youngest child, making this an enjoyable project for everyone in the family.

A further bonus is that glass gardens, once established, need less care than any other house plant environment. A terrarium establishes in itself a nearly perfect environment for the growing of tropical plants. They will need less water and less attention of all kinds.

Any clear glass enclosure (colored glass will not do) will make a fine bottle garden or terrarium, as long as it has a removable top. Your options include ordinary bottles, aquariums, brandy snifters, apothecary jars, and old fish bowls. Bottles with narrow necks can present quite a challenge, not incomparable with that of building a ship in a bottle, but special tools can be purchased or devised at home to solve most problems of arranging plants in these close quarters.

The plants you choose to include in a glass garden should be low and slow growing and should have similar cultural requirements, since they will share the same environment. The three general groups of glass-garden plants are tropical plants, native woodland plants, and cacti and succulents. The members of any one group should never be mixed with the others. Of the three the

A terrarium

woodland plants require a temperature of under 70°, while the other two should be maintained at 75° to 78° for best results. Cacti and succulents should have no cover, since they appreciate low humidity and good ventilation; they are not good subjects for bottle gardens but are ideal for terrariums.

Any glass garden should first have a bottom layer of gravel or charcoal to provide good drainage. After that, prepare a mixture of equal parts of potting soil, sand, and peat moss. (Cacti and succulents can take half again as much sand.) For a nice touch you may line the sides of the glass enclosure with moss, which you have dug from the woods, or sheet moss, which is available from most florists. Place the green side of the moss against the glass, and it will remain green as long as adequate moisture is given. Provide at least one and one-half inches of potting mixture but not so much that the open area of the enclosure is reduced to a point of aesthetic imbalance or that there will be inadequate room for top growth. To create extra interest form slopes and terraces with the soil, perhaps using flat stones for the special terracing effect. Arrange the plants with thoughtful care to create the balanced effect you desire. In bottles long tweezers or photographer's tongs can be used for planting, and a cork attached to a slender stick is fine for tamping the soil.

After the plants have been arranged, there probably will be soil adhering to the sides of the glass. Wash this down with a plant sprayer; then water the entire garden, and put the top in place.

The glass garden should be kept in a bright spot but never in direct sunlight. Not only will the strong rays of the sun create temperatures far too high for any plant to stand (the so-called greenhouse effect), but in some cases a magnifying-glass effect can be created, bending the sun's rays in such a way to burn a plant instantly. The top of the glass garden should be kept on at all times, unless the glass becomes excessively fogged. Then the top should be removed until the fog disappears. Ideally the glass garden should be watered just enough so that excess fogging does not occur. The moisture that the plants release should enter the miniatmosphere and be recirculated by the plants, making frequent watering unnecessary.

Frequent pruning in the glass garden is a necessity, especially since the lush and tropical microenvironment will encourage many plants to grow wildly. Do not be afraid to cut back any terrarium plant at will. The only result will be a bushier and healthier plant. Again, in bottle gardens this chore will require a special pair of scissors, which can be found at some specialty houses and, if unavailable elsewhere, at medical supply houses. (The latter will be very expensive.)

Tropical plants for glass gardens include African violet, begonias, Chinese evergreen, *Coleus*, creeping fig, small *Dracaena*, *Fittonia*, grape ivy, Irish moss (ideal for ground cover), Joseph's coat, strawberry geranium, *Peperomia*, small *Philodendron*, snake plant, pothos, wandering Jew.

Native woodland plants for glass gardens include bloodroot, dogtooth violet, Dutchman's breeches, evergreen seedlings, smaller ferns, ground pine, jack-in-the-pulpit, juniper seedlings, maidenhair fern, money wort, moss (for ground cover), *Pipsissewa*, rattlesnake plantain, partridge berry, pitcher plant, violet, wild strawberry, wintergreen, other low-growing and attractive plants found growing in shaded areas.

Warning: Be sure of state regulations before picking any wild plants.

House Plants From Kitchen Scraps

Turning kitchen wastes into house plants is an enjoyable family project and a most instructive one for children. The seeds, pips, stones, or tops of nearly all fruits and vegetables will germinate and grow under proper conditions. And even though few of them will make good permanent house plants, you can keep enough projects going around the kitchen to provide a continuing show.

The best seeds and pips for easy germination are those from tropical fruits, including oranges, lemons, grapefruits, limes, and pomegranates. In nature these germinate and grow in constantly warm temperatures similar to those found in your home. Seeds and pips of hardy plants, such as apples and pears, and the stones of cherries and apricots may not germinate until they have undergone a period of alternate freezing and thawing, such as they find in their natural environments. To satisfy this need you must carry out a process called stratification, in which the seeds are buried in a tray of moist sand and then placed in the refrigerator for four months, moving the tray back and forth between the freezing compartment and the vegetable storage area every week or so. After that, they should be potted in a regular mixture, about one-half inch deep, and kept in cool temperatures until they have germinated. When green sprouts have shown, move the pots to a warmer place in full sunshine.

Vegetable tops. The tops of carrots, beets, turnips, and parsnips may be planted in moist potting soil or merely set in a saucer of water to produce interesting and attractive, albeit short-lived, house plants. Simply cut off the top inch of the vegetable, trim off any greens, pot it, and put it in a warm and sunny spot. New growth should begin within a week or two and should make quick progress after that.

A sweet potato can quickly produce a lush and vigorous vine that may be trained around a kitchen window. Simply place the narrowed end of a whole sweet potato (one that has several eyes on the upper portion) in a jar just wide enough to support the potato. Keep the water level of the jar high enough to cover only the bottom of the sweet potato. If you keep it in a warm and sunny spot, roots will soon grow into the water, and shoots will emerge from each of the eyes on top. The vine's progress will be quite rapid after that. The sweet potato has enough stored energy to keep the plant going for a long while without supplemental fer-

tilizer. (The same thing can be done with other potatoes, although most of them prefer a cool, dark place for germination, after which they should be moved to a warmer and brighter spot.)

Some kitchen scraps may be turned into permanent and very attractive house plants. The most popular example is the avocado, which grows into a handsome tree indoors and can become very large over the years. Some others include the date palm, the pineapple, and the coffee tree.

Avocado. Wash the avocado stone in warm water, removing all the brown skin. Suspend the stone in a jar of water, using galvanized nails (which serve better than toothpicks) if necessary for support and keeping the water level just high enough to cover the bottom of the stone. Place the jar in a warm, dim spot, watch the water level carefully, and change the water weekly to keep it fresh. The stone should split in from four to eight weeks, sending out roots below and a growing tip above. Move it to a brighter spot, now, still maintaining warm temperatures. After strong roots have formed and the first leaves have begun to show, pot the young plant in a mixture containing plenty of sand and keep it in a warm, sunny spot. Water the avocado only when the soil becomes dry.

Date palm. A date stone can be planted to produce a very attractive potted palm which can grow eventually to an impressive size. Begin with a good-sized stone from a fresh date. Plant it one-half inch deep in a regular potting mixture with plenty of sand. Keep the pot in a temperature range of 70° to 80° in a dim spot; it should germinate in about a month. After the first green shoots have appeared, move the pot to a bright location. Normal room temperatures should be good for the date palm, which will grow slowly but steadily for years to come. Repot only when really necessary.

Pineapple. Here is a very attractive bromeliad that can serve in the house plant ranks for years. Cut off the top inch of the pineapple, keeping the leaves, and allow it to dry for 48 hours. Then plant it in a potting mixture containing plenty of sand. Maintain normal room temperatures—from 65° to 75°. Active growth will begin after an adequate root system has developed. Since the pineapple is a bromeliad, and since bromeliads take in water and nutrients through their leaves, take care to spray the plant regularly and keep its water cup (at the base of the leaves, in the center) filled with fresh water. After the plant has become well established, spray it occasionally with a fish emulsion solution to provide nutrients for vigorous growth.

Coffee tree. Plant a few fresh (unroasted) coffee beans in ordinary potting soil, about one-half inch deep, and give them warm temperatures. After they have germinated, select the best one or two seedlings and transplant each into a small pot. If you keep them in a shaded location in moderate temperatures, they should grow nicely. The coffee tree will flower at an early age, producing attractive white blossoms followed by red berries, which, of course, become coffee beans. One day you might be lucky enough to drink a cup of coffee brewed with beans from your own tree.

An Indoor Vegetable Garden

Annual vegetables require moderate temperatures, good humidity, constant soil moisture, heavy fertilization, and long hours of intense light. We have long been able to provide the first four requirements, only to be stymied by the last. Even in the sunniest south window, the amount of light received during winter's short days is inadequate for the heavy demands of annual vegetables, which must find sufficient energy to germinate, establish strong foliage, flower, then set fruit, and bring it to maturity—all in 120 days or less.

Now with fluorescent lights we can do much better than ever before, if not as well as we can outdoors during summer. Look at indoor vegetable gardening as a bold adventure

with no guarantee of success. Do your best to simulate outdoor conditions, and learn by your experience. You will find some vegetables that do well, and you will grow these again and again, slowly building up your list of annual crops until you have perhaps a dozen different vegetables growing around the house at any time during the winter.

The vegetables recommended here for indoor growing need 16 hours of light a day. You can provide this best by setting up your pots and flats in a sunny south window and supplementing the window's light with a fixture holding two 40-watt tubes attached to an automatic 24-hour timer. Keep the tubes two to four inches above the tops of the growing plants in order to provide the strong light intensity needed. Give the plants moderately high humidity—not a steamy hothouse atmosphere but more than is found in a dry apartment. Provide good drainage, and water the plants every day, so the soil is soaked thoroughly but never allowed to puddle. Fertilize with a complete formula weekly. Spray the plants with water once a day and preferably twice. Keep the temperature at moderate levels—75° during the day, 60° at night. The exceptions will be noted below.

Almost any vegetable can be grown indoors, as long as its root requirements are not inordinately heavy or its top growth not exceptionally large. Sweet corn, broccoli, asparagus, melons, squash, okra, and similar spreading vegetables are obviously out, unless you are blessed with a greenhouse. Quick-growing salad greens and radishes are relatively easy. And many other plants with requirements in between these two groups can be grown with moderate success if sufficient care is exercised. Here are some of the likely candidates for indoor vegetable growing:

Carrots. Choose short and dwarf varieties. Thin young seedlings to one inch apart. Use the plucked seedlings in salads.

Radishes. These are easy to grow. Thin to one inch apart. Most globe-shaped varieties are ideal for indoor growing.

Beets. Thin plants to three inches apart after they have become established. Fertilize heavily for quick growth and tender roots.

Chinese cabbage. One plant will fit an eight-inch pot. Harvest three months after planting.

Peppers. These are slow to grow—four months to harvest—but the foliage of the plant is so attractive that we are happy to wait. Peppers like warm temperatures and good humidity. When flowers appear, pollinate by transferring pollen from one flower to another, using an artist's soft brush, or no fruit will form.

Lettuce. Leaf lettuce is the best bet. It likes cooler temperatures than other vegetables on this list and can be grown well under a cool basement window with supplemental light. Fertilize heavily for fast and succulent growth.

Tomatoes. These are a challenge, but they are fun to try. Choose dwarf varieties or cherry tomatoes, with one plant per 12-inch pot. Give tomatoes the brightest window in the house, and add supplemental light for fully 16 hours. Fertilize twice a week. The foliage will feed heavily, perhaps to the detriment of flowering and fruiting. Prune back foliage beyond the point of flowering for larger fruit. Pollinate as for peppers.

Mushrooms. These are ideal for dim and cool basements, but they require high humidity and good ventilation. Buy specially prepared mushroom-growing kits, which contain spawn preplanted in compost, and follow the producer's directions.

Cress. The quickest salad green known, cress is ready to harvest in two weeks. Fertilize heavily and give ample soil moisture. Plant every week for a continuous supply over the winter.

Chard. Chard is a rewarding green and is easier to grow than lettuce. It doesn't seem to mind low humidity as much as other greens.

Corn salad. Another quick producer, this is also easy to grow.

Shallots. For the gourmet in you, plant shallots in sandy soil, and give ample moisture and fertilizer.

Seed sprouts. The seeds of many plants may be sprouted in a few days and then used in salads, stews, and many recipes. Buy untreated seeds from a health food store. Soak them overnight, drain, and spread out in a shallow container. Cover with a double layer of cheesecloth, and put in a warm place. Rinse and drain the seeds three times a day; they will be ready to eat in three to five days, when they have sprouted. Almost any seeds can be sprouted, although the best include barley, alfalfa, soybeans, lentils, mung beans, rye, millet, and wheat.

Growing Herbs Indoors

A wide variety of herbs may be grown indoors, some in sunny windows with no supplemental light (although, for serious growing, you should provide supplemental fluorescent lighting to assure 16 hours a day). Most herbs have attractive foliage and so make good decorative plants as well. Many are suitable for hanging baskets, and can serve to decorate a kitchen window.

Some of the larger-growing herbs (including dill and fennel) will develop indoors in miniature form, and should be replanted every month for a continuing supply. Others will grow as house plants, continuing to grow bushier as you snip growing tips for kitchen use.

There are many potting soil formulae recommended for herbs. Indoor herb aficionados, in fact, employ as many as six different mixtures, depending on the herb being planted. Most herbs, however, will do well in two parts ordinary potting soil, one part vermiculite, and one part perlite.

Keep indoor temperatures between 55° and 67° for best growth. A south window is best, although the plants will do well under a fluorescent tube (perhaps an under-cabinet light in the kitchen) where they receive 14 to 16 hours of light a day. A kitchen location will also offer good humidity, especially if soups are often simmering on the range; herbs need a relative humidity of about 50 percent for best growth.

Keep the potting mixture moist, but not soggy, and fertilize no more than once a month, since herbs do best with only moderate supplies of nutrients.

Here are 10 popular herbs, all of which are candidates for the kitchen garden:

Chives. Buy a pot of chives in the supermarket, or dig from the garden in early autumn. Repot the clump (the supermarket potting mixture is usually inadequate). For quicker growth, break the plant apart and repot in several individual pots. Cut back the tips often for good growth.

Dill. You can't repot this one from the garden, but you can grow it from seed. The plants won't become as large as they will outdoors, but you will be rewarded. Use an average-to-rich potting mix. Keep the soil barely moist, feed it monthly with a high-nitrogen formula (blood meal is good), and expect plants to remain viable for no more than six months. Periodic reseeding is necessary for a continuous supply.

Fennel. Another herb to grow from seed, which will germinate in about two weeks. Water and fertilize moderately.

Marjoram. Add just a little bone meal to the potting mixture, keep the mixture moist, feed it moderately, and give it all the light you can.

Lemon balm. This mint will grow from seed, germinating slowly (three to four weeks) but growing strongly after that. Use a rich mix without lime, keep the soil moist at all times, and give it plenty of light.

Basil. Use a rich mix with added bone meal, and keep the potting mixture moist at all times. Fertilize it every three weeks with a balanced formula.

Oregano. Treat the same as marjoram. Try to get a true Italian variety. Many American "oregano" plants are actually marjoram.

Parsley. Grown easily from seed, although it is slow to germinate. It forms a taproot, so use a deep pot (four to five inches). Use a rich mix, keep it fully moist, fertilize moderately once a month, and keep the plant in a cool spot.

Rosemary. An attractive plant that grows easily indoors. Use an average mix with bone meal, keep the mix fully moist at all times, and fertilize it heavily once a month. Cuttings root easily, even from woody stock.

Thyme. Use a lean mix with bone meal, let the soil dry on top before watering, and give it full sun and adequate supplemental lighting.

(Note: In the foregoing recommendations, a "rich mix" indicates more potting soil and less vermiculite and perlite. A "lean mix" indicates less potting soil and more of the nonorganic ingredients.)

Plant Troubles and Cures

Your indoor plants stand a far better chance of avoiding insect and disease attack than those plants that live outdoors. For one thing, the leaf surfaces of house plants are most often dry, meaning that a host of harmful fungi and viruses—which commonly attack outdoor plants—will never bother your indoor green guests. Then, unless you do not use window screens, the chances of insects entering your home to nest in house plants are reasonably slim. Your house plants, merely by being indoors, are offered a high degree of protection.

Still, occasional problems present themselves, interfering with the health and good appearance of plants. The troubles may be divided into three broad areas—insects, diseases, and improper handling. We will approach the last of these first, since improper handling and care are likely to be the cause of many common troubles.

Improper Handling and Care

Overwatering is by far the most common cause of plant problems. Too much water impedes air exchange in the soil, excluding the oxygen that is vital to plant health. If your plants' leaves begin to lose color and drop (usually starting at the base and proceeding upward along the stalk), look first to your watering habits. Overwatering also can cause leaves to spot, and continual overwatering can cause root rot and the eventual loss of the offended plant.

Underwatering, on the other hand, can cause wilt and stunted growth. If you have neglected watering to the point of your plant's wilting, submerge the pot immediately in water of room temperature, until the soil is thoroughly moistened, and spray the foliage thoroughly. The plant should be revived by the following day.

Shock can also cause drastic changes in a plant's health. Leaves can change color and fall if the plant meets a sudden and severe temperature change or a sudden change in daily light received. Cold drafts will result in a browning of the tips of leaves, although this

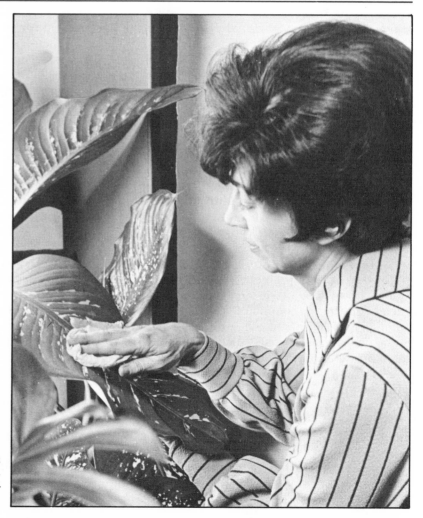

Large-leafed plants will appreciate an occasional bath. Use a mild soap solution and rinse thoroughly with clear water — both at room temperature.

condition can also be caused by overfertilizing, insect attack, or improper watering. The shock of transplanting is usually overcome within several days and can be meliorated by your following the rules carefully.

A lack of fertilizer can gradually lead to a loss of normal leaf color and a generally unhealthy appearance of the plant. Again, though, it is better to underfertilize than to overfertilize.

Spots on the leaves may also result from the spraying of a plant while it is standing in direct sunlight. The little droplets on the leaves act as magnifying lenses, causing burn spots. Spots may also be caused by spraying leaves with overconcentrated pesticides or by insect attack.

Insect Foes

Many house plant growers can go along for years with nary an insect problem. The atmosphere of a normal home is, first, often unconducive to insect breeding, so any insects that do enter the home quickly die out. Second, most of us insulate our homes carefully against winged, crawling, and creeping intruders, and our indoor plants should rest assured in our protection.

Yet there are times when insects do attack—and in some instances, the infestation of one plant can rapidly spread to all household plants, creating a problem of massive proportions. It will be wise for you to learn to recognize the symptoms of insect attack and to guard against them.

One common-sense rule is to isolate all newcomers for at least one week and preferably two. If you bring plants indoors after a summer vacation outdoors, inspect them carefully with the aid of a hand lens, and then place them in a separate room of the house, keeping the door closed. Inspect the plants several times during the isolation period for signs of attack. If none appears after two weeks, you may be fairly certain that no harmful insects are being harbored nor

diseases spread. Only then should you return the plants to the greater community.

Spider Mites. Spider mites, or red spiders, are among the most virulent attackers of house plants. They thrive in the warm, dry atmosphere of your home and will readily take up residence among your prize plants. Spider mites are almost too small to be seen with the naked eye. Small white spots on plant leaves may be evidence of spider mite activity, the result of the mites having sucked juices from the leaf surface. If the infestation is sizable, leaves will gradually take on a fine webbed appearance, have a vaguely fuzzy feeling on their undersides, and eventually feel crumbly. The attack if unchecked can prove fatal.

Since spider mites thrive on warmth and dryness, control rests on making them cold and wet. At least in the early stages they can be eliminated by washing the plant with a mild soap (not detergent) solution and then spraying the entire plant vigorously with cold water, being sure to hit the undersides of leaves where the mites are usually harbored. Repeat this process weekly until the infestation has ceased. In the meantime spray plants daily with a fine mist, preferably in the morning, again being sure to reach the undersides of leaves. If the infestation is truly severe, a solution of rotenone and/or pyrethrum may be used. Both are of low toxicity to warm-blooded creatures, including children, dogs, and cats, although rotenone is very toxic to fish.

Mealybugs. Mealybugs concentrate on the undersides of leaves, at stem joints, and along leaf veins to cause the stunting of plants by sucking their juices. They can be detected easily, since the adult is about one-fourth inch long, and the young are contained in small cottony cases. The egg cases may be destroyed by wiping them off with a cotton swab dipped in rubbing alcohol. Try to avoid alcohol contact with the plant, however, and rinse the plant thoroughly afterward. Adult mealybugs may be combatted with the same methods as recommended for the control of spider mites.

Mealybugs sometimes infest the roots of plants, also, causing stunting and general ill health of foliage. In cases of heavy root infestation, it is best to take a few cuttings, inspect them carefully for infestation, start new plants, and discard the old plant, taking care to scald the pot and scrub it thoroughly before putting it back into service. Discard the old soil.

Cyclamen Mites. Cyclamen mites are most often a danger to African violets, begonias, *Cissus,* cyclamen, English ivy, *Episcia,* geraniums, and gloxinias. These minute creatures can cause leaves to darken and curl and can stunt the plant. They prefer to attack soft and growing shoots and buds, causing the latter to drop or be deformed. Cyclamen mites are devilish to combat, because they congregate in plant parts that are difficult to reach. Furthermore, they can be transmitted from one plant to another with alarming ease, simply by your touching one plant and then another. For control, again use the methods recommended for spider mite control. House plant expert Raymond P. Poincelot recommends, as a last resort, immersing the entire plant for 15 minutes in water heated to 110°.

Springtails. Springtails, or *Collembola,* range in size from microscopic to one-fifth inch in length. They live on or near the soil surface and can readily be seen jumping about when the plant is watered from the top. They often feed on the tender parts of plants. Rotenone and/or pyrethrum will control springtails easily.

Whiteflies. Whiteflies are treacherous, largely because they can fly from plant to plant. The infestation of one plant, therefore, can result very quickly in the attack upon all. The adults are, as their name implies, white in color, about one-sixteenth inch long. They usually can be seen when the plant is disturbed, for they will dart about in the air, together resembling a snow flurry. Like most insect pests, they suck the juices from the leaves, causing them to shrivel, to turn yellow, and eventually to drop. The first measure to adopt is complete isolation of the infested plant in order to protect others in the green community. Wash the plant immediately in a mild soap solution; then rinse it thoroughly, allow the foliage to dry, and finally dust with rotenone and/or pyrethrum.

Aphids. Aphids *(aphis,* or plant lice) are tiny insects, ranging in color from green to black, that cluster on the undersides of leaves, on stems, or on roots. They suck the sap of the plant, causing distorted leaves and eventually stunted plants. Aphids can be washed off plants with a strong stream of water. Tobacco sprinkled on top of the potting mixture seems to repel them.

Scale. Like aphids, scale insects are tiny creatures that cluster on leaves and stems, suck the sap from the plant, and eventually cause its parts to become distorted and stunted. Scale can be removed easily by a strong stream of water, by wiping the plants with a cotton swab dipped in alcohol or by washing with a strong soap solution.

Diseases

Diseases—caused either by fungi, bacteria, or viruses—are unlikely to cause serious problems for your house plants. Many fungi and bacteria need cool and constantly damp surfaces in order to become established, and these conditions simply will not be offered by the normal home environment.

Still there always exists the possibility of disease, and you should be aware of that possibility and be prepared to meet the problem. The diseases most likely to affect house plants are *Botrytis,* crown and root rot, damping-off, leaf spot, powdery mildew, rusts, and various viral infections. The symptoms vary, although all will cause a general lack of vigor, a dull appearance, and stunted growth of the plant. *Botrytis* causes a fuzzy gray mold, while powdery mildew leaves a gray-white powdery mold on leaves and stems. Rusts leave red or brown spots on leaves. Not all of these are serious, except those that attack roots and crowns of plants and the virus diseases for which there are no cures.

Against disease organisms the best offense is a good defense. Create the conditions for your house plants that will lessen the chances of disease attack. These include all the advice on proper handling and care that has been offered in preceding pages. Especially avoid continuing cool and damp conditions, overcrowding, overwatering, and lack of ventilation.

Damping-off is a particularly pernicious disease that can wipe out hundreds—or thousands—of young seedlings overnight. The disease attacks plants at the soil line and simply mows them down dead. It can be prevented by using a sterile rooting medium.

Many growers spread about one-fourth inch of sterile sand on top of the regular starting medium; damping-off cannot exist on sterile sand. Other prevention methods include moderate and proper watering of seedlings, proper ventilation, and a prompt thinning.

Sanitation is crucially important in disease prevention. Since organisms are spread easily through air movement, by the transfer of soil, and by your hands, take extra precautions whenever you suspect the presence of a plant disease. Wash your hands thoroughly after handling a diseased plant or any newcomer. Sterilize garden soil before using it for house plants (an hour, spread out on a tray, in a medium oven will do the trick), and boil for 15 minutes any pot that has contained a diseased plant. Last, never reuse soil that has supported a diseased plant.

Plants for Cool Temperatures
(50°-60° at Night)

Aloe	*Fuchsia*
Aspidistra	Geranium
Australian laurel	German ivy
Azalea	Honeysuckle
Baby's tears	Hyacinth
Black pepper	*Jasmine*
Boxwood	Jerusalem cherry
Bromeliads	*Kalanchoe*
Cacti	Kangaroo vine
Calceolaria	Lily of the valley
Camellia	*Lithops*
Cape ivy	Miniature holly
Christmas begonia	Mother of thousands
Chrysanthemum	*Narcissus*
Cineraria	*Oxalis*
Citrus	Primrose
Creeping fig	Sensitive plant
Cyclamen	Silk oak
Easter lily	Snake plant
English ivy	Spindletree
Fatshedra	Tulip
Fiddleleaf fig	*Vinca*
Flowering maple	Wandering Jew
Freesia	White calla lily

Plants for Medium Temperatures
(60°-65° at Night)

Achimenes	Grape ivy
Aechmea	*Hibiscus*
Amaryllis	*Hydrangea*
Ardisia	*Maranta*
Asparagus fern	Norfolk Island pine
Aspidistra	Palms
Avocado	*Peperomia*
Begonia	*Philodendron*
Bird's-nest fern	*scandens*
Browallia	*Pilea*
Chenille plant	Poinsettia
Christmas cactus	Rubber plant
Chrysanthemum	Shrimp plant
Citrus	Silk oak
Coleus	Snake plant
Copper leaf	Staghorn fern
Crown of thorns	Ti plant
Cryptanthus	Tuberous begonia
Dracaena	Umbrella tree
Easter lily	Velvet plant
Echeveria	Wax begonia
English ivy	Wax plant
Gardenia	Weeping fig
	Yellow calla lily

Plants for High Temperatures
(65°-75° at Night)

African violet	Fiddleleaf fig
Aphelandra	*Gloxinia*
Arrowhead	*Gold-dust plant*
Banded maranta	*Goosefoot plant*
Cacti and succulents	*Mistletoe fig*
Caladium	*Philodendron*
Chinese evergreen	Pothos *(Scindapsus)*
Cocos palm	Seersucker plant
Croton	Snake plant
Dieffenbachia	*Spathiphyllum*
Dracaena	Umbrella tree
Episcia	Veitch screw pine
False aralia	Zebra plant

Plants for Dry and Semidry Conditions

Aloe	*Hedera* (ivy)
Aspidistra	*Kalanchoe*
Bromeliads	*Lithops*
Cacti	Norfolk Island pine
Cape ivy	Oval-leaf peperomia
Coleus	Pothos *(Scindapsus)*
Crown of thorns	Snake plant
Dracaena marginata	Spider plant
Echeveria	Wandering Jew
Fatshedra japonica	Wax flower
Fatsia lizei	

Vines and Trailing Plants for Totem Poles

Arrowhead	*Pellionia*
Black pepper	*Philodendron*
Canary Islands ivy	Pothos *(Scindapsus)*
Creeping fig	*Syngonium*
English ivy	Velvet plant
Grape ivy	Wax plant
Kangaroo vine	

Plants for Hanging Baskets

African violet	Honeysuckle
Artillery plant	Italian bellflower
Asparagus fern	Ivy geranium
Baby's tears	*Peperomia* (some
Begonia (some types)	types)
Black pepper	*Philodendron* (some
Creeping fig	types)
English ivy	Pothos *(Scindapsus)*
Episcia	*Saxifraga*
Fuchsia (some types)	Spider plant
German ivy	*Syngonium*
Goldfish plant	Trailing coleus
Grape ivy	Wandering Jew
	Wax plant

Plants for Large Tubs

Dracaena	Rubber plant
False aralia	Silk oak
Fatshedra	Tuftroot
Fiddleleaf fig	Umbrella tree
Norfolk Island pine	Veitch screw pine
Palm	Weeping fig
Philodendron (some types)	

Tools and Sources

Public Gardens

National Garden
Organizations

Organic Products
for the Garden

Mail Order Nurseries
and Seed Houses

Suggested Reading

Public Gardens

The following public gardens are good places to see plants grown successfully and to get good ideas for your own garden. All-American Selections (AAS) Display Gardens show annual flowers and vegetables, and are indicated with an asterisk (*).

Arlington

University of Wisconsin
Horticultural Research Farms*
Kampen Rd.

Eau Claire

UW-Eau Claire
Phillips Science Hall Courtyard*

Madison

University of Wisconsin
Allen Centennial Gardens
1575 Linden Dr.
    Located on the University of Wisconsin campus, this is a virtual replication of the history of ornamental horticulture. In a relatively small space, the gardens feature spectacular perennials and annuals, ornamental grasses, pond plants, herb gardens, flowering fruit trees, and much more. Well worth a visit.

Olbrich Botanical Society Gardens*
3330 Atwood Ave.
    Extensive plantings of annuals, perennials, and herbs, and a conservatory featuring tropical rain forest plants. The Olbrich Gardens get bigger and better each year.

University of Wisconsin Arboretum
1207 Seminole Highway
    The arboretum, in 1,270 acres, features an impressive collection of lilacs and ornamental fruit trees, as well as a restored prairie and pine forest. Wonderful walking trails.

Milwaukee Area

ARN Garden Plots*
Vincent High School
7501 N. Granville Rd.
Milwaukee

Alfred L. Boerner Botanical Gardens
Whitnall Park
5879 S. 92nd St.
Hales Corners
    Annuals, perennials, and flower and vegetable displays are featured at these breathtaking gardens. There is also a bog walk, a daylily walk, a shrub mall, and a very popular rose festival held every June. Home gardeners will find lots of good ideas here.

Mitchell Park
Horticultural Conservatory
524 Scout Layton Blvd.
Milwaukee
    Three huge steel-and-glass domes, each 140 feet wide and 85 feet high, house a tropical rain forest, an arid garden, and, in the third dome, a frequently changing horticultural display.

UW-Extension*
9668 Watertown Plank Rd.
Milwaukee

Mineral Point

Shake Rag Alley*
18 Shake Rag St.

Randolph

Jung Seed Co.*
335 S. High St.

National Garden Organizations

The following organizations are glad to provide much information in their particular areas of interest. Many have local chapters which you can join.

African Violet Society of America
P.O. Box 3609
Beaumont, TX 77704

American Begonia Society
P.O. Box 1129
Encinitas, CA 92024

American Bonsai Society
P.O. Box 358
Keene, NH 03431

American Daffodil Society
2302 Rt. 3
Byhalia Rd.
Hernando, MS 38632

American Dahlia Society
c/o James Moore, Jr.
14408 Long Ave.
Midlothian, IL 60445

American Gloxinia and Gesneriad Society
5320 Labadie St.
St. Louis, MO 63120

American Gourd Society
Box 274
Mount Gilead, OH 43338

American Herb Assn.
P.O. Box 353
Rescue, CA 95672

American Hosta Society
c/o Peter Ruth
9448 Mayfield Rd.
Chesterland, OH 44026

American Iris Society
7414 E. 60th St.
Tulsa, OK 74145

American Peony Society
250 Interlachen Rd.
Hopkins, MN 55343

American Plant Life Society
P.O. Box 985
National City, CA 92050
    (American Amaryllis Society Group)

American Rock Garden Society
c/o Carole Wilder
221 W. 9th St.
Hastings, MN 55033
    (for growers of wild or native species of plants)

American Rose Society
P.O. Box 30000
Shreveport, LA 71130

Azalea Society of America
c/o Mrs. William Lorene
8610 Running Fox Ct.
Fairfax Station, VA 22039

Cactus & Succulent Society of America
c/o Charles Glass
Box 3010
Santa Barbara, CA 93130-3010

Herb Society of America
9019 Kirtland Chardon Rd.
Mentor, OH 44060

International Geranium Society
4610 Druid St.
Los Angeles, CA 90032

International Lilac Society
P.O. Box 315
Rumford, ME 04276

Men's Garden Clubs of America
5560 Merle Hay Rd.
P.O. Box 241
Johnston, IA 50131

National Council of State Garden Clubs
4401 Magnolia Ave.
St. Louis, MO 63110

North American Gladiolus Council
c/o James Martin
20337 Township Rd. 59
Jenera, OH 45841

North American Lily Society, Inc.
P.O. Box 476
Waukee, IA 50263

Organic Gardening Clubs

(For an up-to-date list of local Wisconsin organic gardening clubs, write to Organic Gardening magazine, Emmaus, PA 18049.)

Perennial Plant Assn.
217 Howlett Hall
2001 Fyffe Ct.
The Ohio State University
Columbus, OH 43210

Seed Savers Exchange
RR 3, Box 239
Decorah, IA 52101

Terrarium Assn.
P.O. Box 276
Newfane, VT 05345

Organic Products for the Garden

Natural fertilizers, safe pesticides, and other products for organic gardeners are not always easy to find in ordinary garden centers. Write to any of the following companies for information on these environmentally-safe products.

Beneficial Insects

Association of Applied Insect Ecologists
100 N. Winchester Blvd., #260
Santa Cruz, CA 95050

Bio-Control Co.
P.O. Box 337
57A Zink Rd.
Berry Creek, CA 95916

Bio-Resources
1210 Birch St.
P.O. Box 902
Santa Paula, CA 93060

Four Winds Farm Supply
Rt. 1, Box 206
River Falls, WI 54022

National Gardening Research Center
Hwy. 48
P.O. Box 149
Sunman, IN 47041

Necessary Trading Company
One Nature's Way
New Castle, VA 24127-0305

Rincon-Vitove Insectaries
P.O. Box 475
Rialto, CA 92376

Unique Insect Control
5504 Sperry Dr.
Citrus Heights, CA 95621

Natural Fertilizers

The Fertrell Co.
P.O. Box 265
Bainbridge, PA 17502

Francis Laboratories
1551 E. Lafayette
Detroit, MI 48207

Mellinger's
2310 W. South Range Rd.
North Lima, OH 44452-9731

Nitron Industries
4605 Johnson Rd.
P.O. Box 1447
Fayetteville, AR 72702

Super Natural American Distributing Co.
13906 Ventura Blvd.
Sherman Oaks, CA 91423

Zook & Ranck, Inc.
RD 2, Box 243
Gap, PA 17527

Diatomaceous Earth

Dyna-Prep, Inc.
2215 Broadway
Yankton, SD 57078

Necessary Trading Company
One Nature's Way
New Castle, VA 24127-0305

Perma-Guard
1701 E. Elwood St.
Phoenix, AZ 85040

Insect Control Products

Fairfax Biological Lab, Inc.
Clinton Corners, NY 12514
(Milky spore powder)

Four Winds Farm Supply
Rt. 1, Box 206
River Falls, WI 54022

Necessary Trading Company
One Nature's Way
New Castle, VA 24127-0305

Reuter Labs, Inc.
8540 Natural Way
Manassas Park, VA 22111

Safer, Inc.
60 William St.
Wellesley, MA 02181

General Organic Gardening Products

Gardener's Supply Co.
128 Intervale Rd.
Burlington, VT 05401-2804

Green Earth Organics
9422 144th St., E.
Puyallup, WA 98373-6686
(Lawn care products)

Green Pro Services
380 S. Franklin St.
Hempstead, NY 11550

Growing Naturally
P.O. Box 54
149 Pine Lane
Pineville, PA 18946

Natural Gardening Company
217 San Anselmo Ave.
San Anselmo, CA 94960

Necessary Trading Company
One Nature's Way
New Castle, VA 24127-0305

Nitgron Industries
4605 Johnson Rd.
P.O. Box 1447
Fayetteville, AR 72702

Ohio Earth Food, Inc.
13737 DuQuette Ave., N.E.
Hartville, OH 44632
   (Sea products)

Ringer Corp.
9959 Valley View Rd.
Eden Prairie, MN 55344

Smith & Hawken
2 Arbor Lane, Box 6900
Florence, KY 41022-6900
   (Fine garden hand tools, supplies, roses, clothes)

Mail Order Nurseries and Seed Houses

Catalogs are not only fun, but they are valuable in planning the garden. The catalogs of most nurseries and seed houses are available free for the asking. A few, which are particularly large and sumptuous, might cost several dollars, although the fee is applicable to any order. Spring catalogs are usually available in December and January, while fall catalogs come out in the summer. If you make a purchase from any nursery or seed house, you wlll doubtless receive a catalog automatically the following year.

Wisconsin Firms

Asgrow Seed Company
Walter Baehmann
9919 Mequon Rd.
Mequon, WI 53092

Johnson's Nursery
W180 N6275 Marcy Rd.
Menomonee Falls,WI 53051

J.W. Jung Seed Co.
335 S. High St.
Randolph, WI 53957
   (Fruit, vegetable, flower, ornamental, and landscaping plants and seeds.)

Knight Hollow Nursery
3333 Atom Rd.
Middleton, WI 53562

McKay Nursery
P.O. Box 185
Waterloo, WI 53594

Milaeger's
4838 Douglas Ave.
Racine, WI 53402
      (Great perennial catalog.
      Very large garden shop.)

Prairie Nursery
P.O. Box 306
Westfield, WI 53964
      (Prairie plant seeds; catalog $3)

Prairie Ridge Nursery
9738 Overland Rd.
Mt. Horeb, WI 53572
      (Prairie plants and other natives; catalog $3.)

Out-of-State Firms

Ahrens Strawberry Nursery
Rt. 1
Huntingburg, IN 47542

Bear Creek Nursery
P.O. Box 411
Northport, WA 99157
   (Specializing in fruit and nut trees)

Kurt Bluemel, Inc.
2740 Greene Lane
Baldwin, MD 21013
   (Ornamental grasses, perennials, ferns, etc.)

Breck's Dutch Bulbs
6523 N. Galena Rd.
Peoria, IL 61632

Burpee Seed Company
300 Park Ave.
Warminster, PA 18974

C&O Nursery
P.O. Box 116
Wenatchee, WA 98807

Farmer Seed and Nursery
818 NW 4th St.
Faribault, MN 55021

Fedco Trees
Box 340
Palermo, ME 04354

Henry Field Seed & Nursery
415 N. Burnett
Shenandoah, IA 51602
   (General seed house, perennials)

Gurney Seed & Nursery Co.
4724 Page St.
Yankton, SD 57079
   (General seed house, supplies, etc.)

Inter-State Nurseries
Catalog Division
Louisiana, MO 63353

Johnny's Selected Seeds
Albion, ME 04910
   (General seed house, supplies, books)

Kelly Nursery
1708 Morrisey Dr.
Bloomington, IL 61704

Lake County Nursery, Inc.
Rt. 84, P.O. Box 122
Perry, OH 44081-0122
   (Perennials, trees, shrubs, ground covers)

Makielski Berry Nursery
7130 Platt Rd.
Ypsilanti, MI 48197

Earl May Seed & Nursery
208 N. Elm St.
Shenandoah, IA 51603
   (Plants, bulbs, seeds, supplies)

Mellinger's, Inc.
2310 W. South Range Rd.
North Lima, OH 44452-9731

Miller Nurseries
West Lake Rd.
Canandaigua, NY 14424

Moon Mountain
P.O. Box 725
Carpinteria, CA 93014-0725
   (Wildflower specialists)

Harris Moran Seed Co.
3670 Buffalo Rd.
Rochester, NY 14624

Newark Nurseries
P.O. Box 578
Hartford, MI 49057

North Star Gardens
19060 Manning Trail North
Marine, MN 55047

Northrup King Company
P.O. Box 959
Minneapolis, MN 55440

Northwind Nursery & Orchards
7917 335th Ave., NW
Princeton, MN 55371

Nourse Farms
Box 485, RFD
South Deerfield, MA 01373

Ornamental Edibles
3622 Weedin Court
San Jose, CA 95132

George W. Park Seed Co.
Cokesbury Rd.
Greenwood, SC 29647-0001
    (Seeds, plants, bulbs, supplies)

Pinetree Garden Seeds
RR#1, Box 397
New Gloucester, ME 04260

Raintree Nursery
391 Butts Rd.
Morton, WA 98356

Rocky Meadow Orchard & Nursery
Rt. 2, Box 2104
New Salisbury, IN 47161

Ronninger's Seed Potatoes
Star Route
Moyie Springs, ID 83845
    (Many potato varieties, including heirlooms)

St. Lawrence Nurseries
R.D. 5
Potsdam, NY 13676

SeedWay, Inc.
Hall, NY 14463

Seeds of Change
P.O. Box 15700
Santa Fe, NM 87506-5700
    (Many native varieties)

R.H. Shumway
P.O. Box 777
Rockford, IL 61105
    (Seeds, green manure crops, fruits)

Spring Hill Nurseries Co.
6523 Galena Rd.
Peoria, IL 61632
    (Flowering plants & shrubs, ground covers, etc.)

Stark Brothers Nurseries
P.O. Box 10
Hwy 54
Louisiana, MO 63353
    (Fruit & ornamental trees & shrubs)

Stokes Seeds, Inc.
P.O. Box 548
Buffalo, NY 14240
    (General seed house)

Swedberg Nurseries
Box 418
Battle Lake, MN 56515

Thompson & Morgan , Inc.
P.O. box 1308
Jackson, NJ 08527-0308
    (Large variety of seeds)

Tomato Growers Supply Co.
P.O. Box 2237
Fort Myers, FL 33902
    (Everything for the tomato grower)

Tsang & Ma International
P.O. Box 294
Belmont, CA 94002
    (Specializing in Oriental vegetables)

Otis S. Twilley Seed Co.
P.O. Box 307
Feasterville, PA 19047

Vermont Wildflower Farm
Rt. 2
Charlotte, VT 05445
    (Specializing in wildflower seeds)

Wafler Farms
10662 Slaght Rd.
Wolcott, NY 14590

Wayside Gardens
P.O. Box 1, Garden Lane
Hodges, SC 29695-0001
    (Large variety of ornamental trees, shrubs,
    perennials)

White Flower Farm
Rt. 63
Litchfield, CT 06759-0050
    (Large variety of ornamental trees, shrubs,
    perennials,)

Suggested Reading

Of the hundreds of gardening books on the market today, it would be difficult or impossible to choose "the best" of the lot—and the following list is no attempt to do so. Instead, these are books known personally to the author which have been of help in answering problems. The selections are, like this book, slanted toward the organic approach to gardening. It is hoped that some of them might be helpful to the reader, and might lead to a trip to the nearest public library or bookstore where new worlds of gardening are waiting. Some of these books are available at bookstores, while others are available only in public libraries and, if you're lucky, in used bookstores. (Note: Government and university publications are not included here because, first, they are so numerous, and, second, because they are so often revised or out of stock. For current selections of these publications, pay a visit to the office of your county Extension agent.)

General Books

The Encyclopedia of Organic Gardening
Edited by Fern Marshall Bradley
and Barbara W. Ellis
Rodale Press, 1992
> This is the latest version of this enormously popular title. But if you should happen upon an old copy of one of the earlier editions, dating back to 1959, be sure to pick it up. It seems that every new edition drops some fascinating material.

10,000 Garden Questions
Edited by Marjorie J. Dietz
American Garden Guild-Doubleday. 3d ed., 1974
> The famous F.F. Rockwell book. 1,400 pages. A wealth of useful information provided in question-and-answer style, arranged by subject area.

The Wise Garden Encyclopedia
Pamela B. Art, Project Editor
HarperCollins, 1980
> Truly an encyclopedic work, a revised version of the original 1970 edition. It will answer many gardening questions

Gardening in the Upper Midwest
Leon C. Snyder
University of Minnesota Press, 1978
> Trustworthy advice for all northern gardeners.

How to Have a Green Thumb without an Aching Back
Ruth Stout
Cornerstone, 1968
> Ruth's original classic. No gardener should be without it.

Gardening without Work
Ruth Stout
Cornerstone, 1974
> Ruth's "other" book—just as entertaining and valuable as her first.

Marlyn's Garden: Seasoned Advice for Achieving
Spectacular Results in the Midwest
Marlyn Dicken Sachtjen
Chicago Review Press, 1994
> Sachtjen is an expert Wisconsin gardener who shares a lifetime of experience in this 226-page book. It is chock-full of practical advice, including hundreds of recommended varieties of perennials, trees, shrubs, prairie and meadow plants, herbs, and other plants for Wisconsin gardens.

Square Foot Gardening
Mel Bartholomew
Rodale Press, 1981
> Bartholomew's book has drawn tens of thousands of adherents to his "square-foot" method of gardening, which increases production, allows easy access to all garden plants, and conserves time, space, and resources. Great for small-space gardeners. Still in print in a paperback edition.

Vegetables, Fruits, and Herbs

Growing Fruits and Vegetables Organically
Jean M.A. Nick and Fern Marshall Bradley
Rodale Press, 1994.
> A good, general guide to cultivation techniques. Like most Rodale books, it is full of down-to-earth, practical information.

The Vegetable Encyclopedia and Gardener's Guide
Victor A. Tiedjens
Avenel Books, 1963
> A treasure trove of compacted information presented in no-nonsense fashion by a Rutgers professor. Now, sadly, out of print—but do try your public library or used bookstore.

The Herb Garden: Month by Month
Barbara Segall
David & Charles, 1994
> Of all the herb books that have come out recently, this is one of the best, combining both beauty and practicality in a single volume. If you are serious about getting your herb garden started, start with this book.

Gardening for Maximum Nutrition
Jerry Minnich
Rodale Press, 1983
> How to grow a vegetable and fruit garden with the very highest nutritional yield, through careful selection of varieties, soil treatment, and harvesting and storage techniques. Now out of print, but many libraries still have this volume.

Wild Plants

Growing Wildflowers
Marie Sperka
Harper & Row, 1973
> The best book on growing wild flowers for Midwest gardeners because it is written by a Midwestern gardener with decades of experience. Beautifully produced. Out of print for some years, it is now back in a paperback edition.

The Prairie Garden: 70 Native Plants You Can Grow in Town or Country
J. Robert Smith with Beatrice S. Smith
University of Wisconsin Press, 1980
> All you need to grow to plan, establish, and maintain your own prairie garden. Good pen-and-ink drawings and color photos of all 70 plants.

All About Weeds
Edwin Rollin Spencer
Dover, 1974
> Originally published in 1940. A classic worth keeping.

Flowers and Ornamentals

Organic Flower Gardening
Catharine Osgood Foster
Rodale Press, 1975
> A comprehensive guide to growing flowers without chemicals. Good color photos.

The Year-Round Flower Gardener
Anne Moyer Halpin
Summit Books, 1989
> Beautiful color photographs and a mountain of information on growing flowers throughout the year. Features a monthly blooming schedule for 300 flowers.

Flowers for Northern Gardens
Leon C. Snyder
University of Minnesota Press, 1983
> Includes an alphabetic guide to more than 800 species of herbaceous plants and their botanical and horticultural varieties known to be hardy in northern zones.

Landscaping

Garden Design Workbook
John Brookes
Dorling Kindersley, 1994
> This is indeed a practical workbook to help you devise your landscaping plan. Full of charts, overlays, and other helpful aids.

The Rodale Illustrated Encyclopedia of Gardening and Landscaping Techniques
By the Editors of *Organic Gardening*
Rodale Press, 1990
> Just about everything you need to know to carry out your landscape plans.

Trees and Shrubs for Northern Gardens
Leon C. Snyder
University of Minnesota Press, 1980
> The core of this book is an alphabetical listing of more than 400 species of trees, shrubs, and woody vines and their cultivars and botanical varieties.

Plant Propagation and Pruning

Plants-A-Plenty
Catharine Osgood Foster
Rodale Press, 1978
> A solid guide to propagating both indoor and outdoor plants through cuttings, root division, grafting, layering, and seeds.

The Seed-Starter's Handbook
Nancy Bubel
Rodale Press, 1978

> All you need to know about growing vegetables from seeds. If you seem to have problems in bringing indoor-started plants to the transplanting stage, you'll find the answers here.

Soil Treatment

The Rodale Book of Composting
Edited by Doborah L. Martin and Grace Gershuny
Rodale Press, 1992

> Supplants the popular 1960 *Complete Book of Composting* and the 1979 *Rodale Guide to Composting*. Reflects the new knowledge about composting, especially as it relates to the environment.

The Earthworm Book
Jerry Minnich
Rodale Press, 1977

> Everything you want to know about earthworms, including how to use these remarkable creatures to build soil and increase crop yields. Out of print, but check your public library or used bookstore.

Food Preservation

Stocking Up
Edited by Carol Hupping Stoner
Rodale Press, 1973

> How to preserve all the fruits and vegetables you have worked so hard to produce.

Keeping the Harvest
Nancy Thurber and Gretchen Mead
Garden Way, 1976

> An attractive, large-format paperpack with solid advice on all forms of food preservation and storage. Includes some good recipes.

Home Food Systems
Edited by Roger B. Yepsen, Jr.
Rodale Press, 1981

> Emphasis is on tool and procedures. Explores new way of making foods, including backyard aquaculture, solar growing, tofu making, etc. State-of-the-art technology for the home gardener.

Root Cellaring
Mike and Nancy Bubel
Rodale Press, 1980

> How to bring back the root cellar, even if you live in a suburban ranch. Good plans and diagrams.

Insects and Diseases

The Encyclopedia of Natural Insect &
Disease Control
Edited by Roger B. Yepsen, Jr.
Rodale Press, 1984

> Organic controls for insects and disease problems. 500 pages of solid advice—a valuable friend when trouble strikes. (If you can find one in a used book store, also pick up a copy of this book's predecessor, *Organic Plant Protection*, which has some good material not included in the new book.)

Bedside Reading

Onward and Upward in the Garden
Katharine S. White
Farrar Straus Giroux 1979

> First published in 1979 and reprinted numerous times since, this is a delightful collection of gardening essays that originally appeared as a series of articles in the *New Yorker* magazine from 1958 to 1970.

The Essential Earthman
Henry Mitchell
Indiana University Press, 1981

> This volume collects many of Mitchell's most memorable pieces from his long-running *Washington Post* column, full of wit, common sense, and sound advice to novice and veteran gardeners alike.

The Gardener's Year
Karel Capek
University of Wisconsin Press, 1984

> This is one of my favorite gardening books, a little volume of unforgettable essays by the Czech writer Karel Capek, who also wrote science fiction and coined the word "robot." It is a volume full of wit and humor, proof positive that gardeners share a common world view, no matter what their age or nationality. (Originally published in Prague, in Czech, in 1929.)

The Gardening Year
Thalassa Cruso
Lyons & Burford, 1973
> Many fans of the irrepressible Thalasa will love to
> follow her through the year as she expounds at will
> upon hundreds of gardening topics. A very per-
> sonal book, excellent bedside reading, and still
> available at bookstores.

Miscellaneous

The Natural Shade Garden
Ken Druse
Clarkson Potter, 1992
> How to have a flourishing and colorful garden,
> even when tall buildings and trees make it diffi-
> cult for you.

Shade Gardens
Edited by Brenda Cole
Camden House, 1993
> A comprehensive book and a "must" for anyone
> who faces major shade problems.

Build It Better Yourself
By the editors of Organic Gardening
Rodale Press, 1977
> A massive, attractive, and very practical book on
> building more than 200 structures for garden and
> farm. Hotbeds, cold frames, compost bins, solar
> greenhouses—they're all here, with plans and dia-
> grams. A dream volume for the home carpenter.

Note: Wood Violet Books, 3814 Sunhill Dr., Madison,
WI 53704 (608 837-7207) specializes in new and
used gardening books. You may write or phone them
for a catalog.

Index